子連れ狼

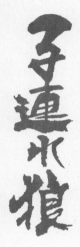

LONE
WOLF
AND
子連れ狼 CUB

story
KAZUO KOIKE

art
GOSEKI KOJIMA

DARK HORSE COMICS

translation
DANA LEWIS

lettering & retouch
DIGITAL CHAMELEON

cover illustration
MATT WAGNER

publisher
MIKE RICHARDSON

editor
TIM ERVIN-GORE

assistant editor
MIKE CARRIGLITTO

consulting editor
TOREN SMITH for **STUDIO PROTEUS**

book design
DARIN FABRICK

art director
MARK COX

Published by Dark Horse Comics, Inc., in association
with MegaHouse and Koike Shoin Publishing Company.

Dark Horse Comics, Inc.
10956 SE Main Street, Milwaukie, OR 97222
www.darkhorse.com

First edition: October 2002
ISBN: 1-56971-598-x

1 3 5 7 9 10 8 6 4 2

Printed in Canada

To find a comics shop in your area, call the
Comic Shop Locator Service toll-free at 1-888-266-4226.

STRUGGLE IN THE DARK

子連れ狼

By **KAZUO KOIKE**
& GOSEKI KOJIMA

VOLUME
26

A NOTE TO READERS

Lone Wolf and Cub is famous for its carefully researched re-creation of Edo-Period Japan. To preserve the flavor of the work, we have chosen to retain many Edo-Period terms that have no direct equivalents in English. Japanese is written in a mix of Chinese ideograms and a syllabic writing system, resulting in numerous synonyms. In the glossary, you may encounter words with multiple meanings. These are words written with Chinese ideograms that are pronounced the same but carry different meanings. A Japanese reader seeing the different ideograms would know instantly which meaning it is, but these synonyms can cause confusion when Japanese is spelled out in our alphabet. *O-yurushi o* (please forgive us)!

LONE WOLF AND CUB

TABLE OF CONTENTS

the hundred and
twenty-eighth

Tales of the Grass: Nindō Ukon

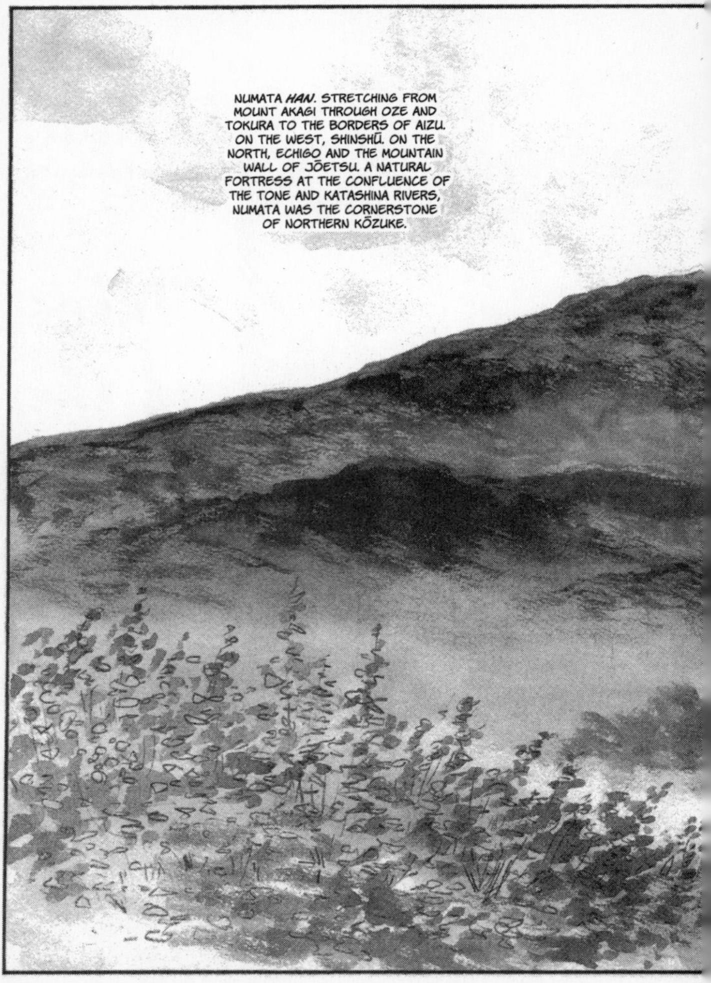
NUMATA *HAN*. STRETCHING FROM MOUNT AKAGI THROUGH OZE AND TOKURA TO THE BORDERS OF AIZU. ON THE WEST, SHINSHŪ. ON THE NORTH, ECHIGO AND THE MOUNTAIN WALL OF JŌETSU. A NATURAL FORTRESS AT THE CONFLUENCE OF THE TONE AND KATASHINA RIVERS, NUMATA WAS THE CORNERSTONE OF NORTHERN KŌZUKE.

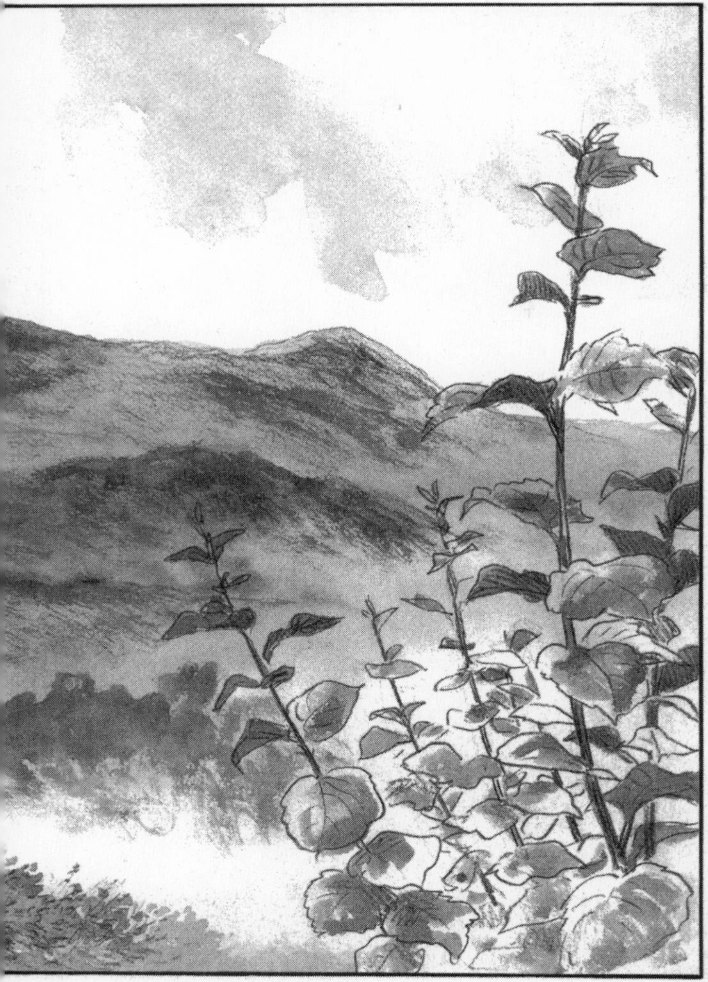

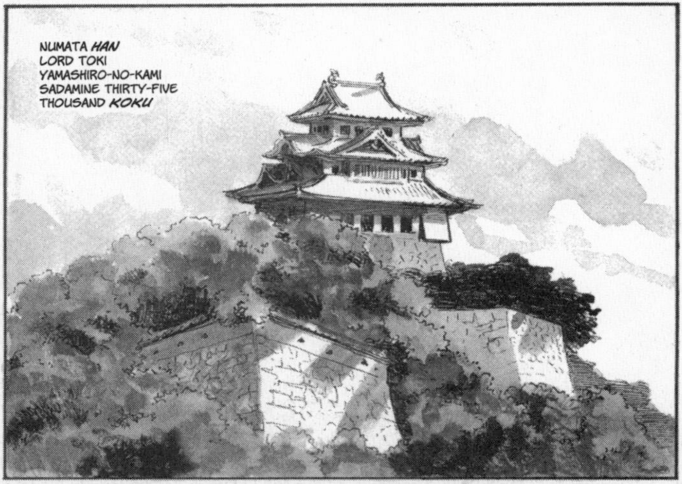
NUMATA *HAN*
LORD TOKI
YAMASHIRO-NO-KAMI
SADAMINE THIRTY-FIVE
THOUSAND *KOKU*
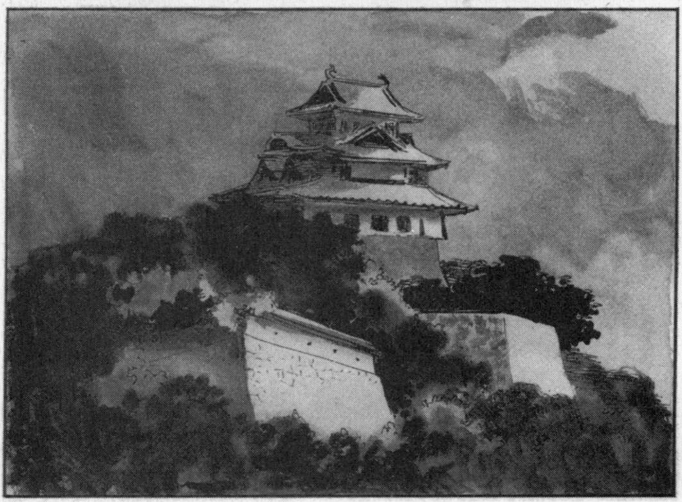

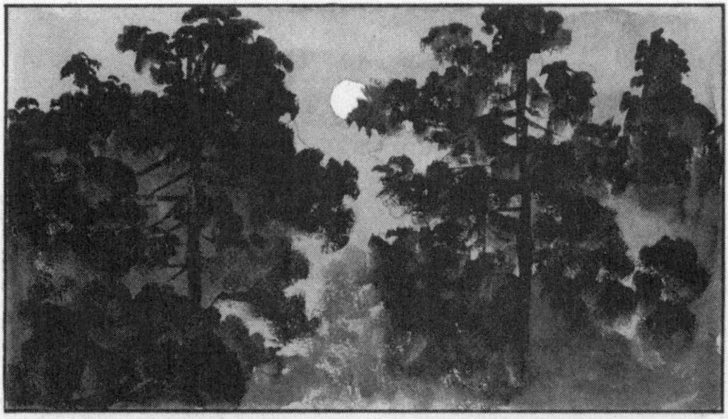
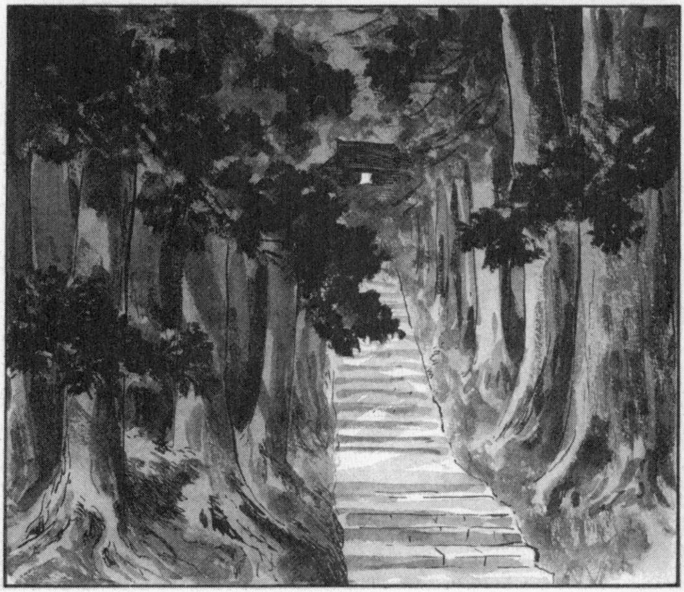

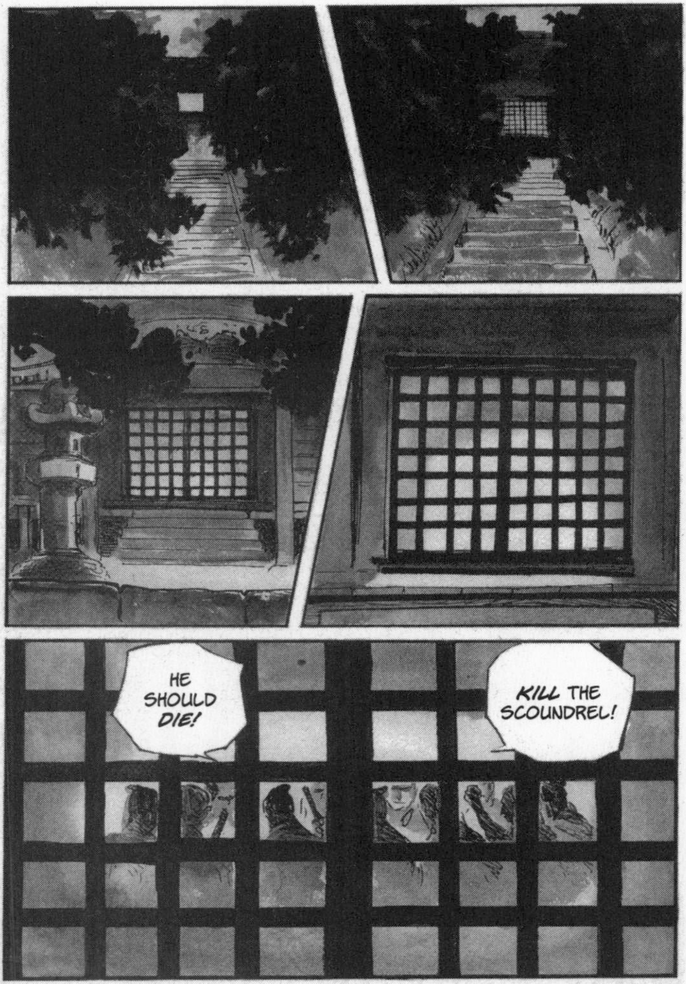
HE SHOULD DIE!
KILL THE SCOUNDREL!

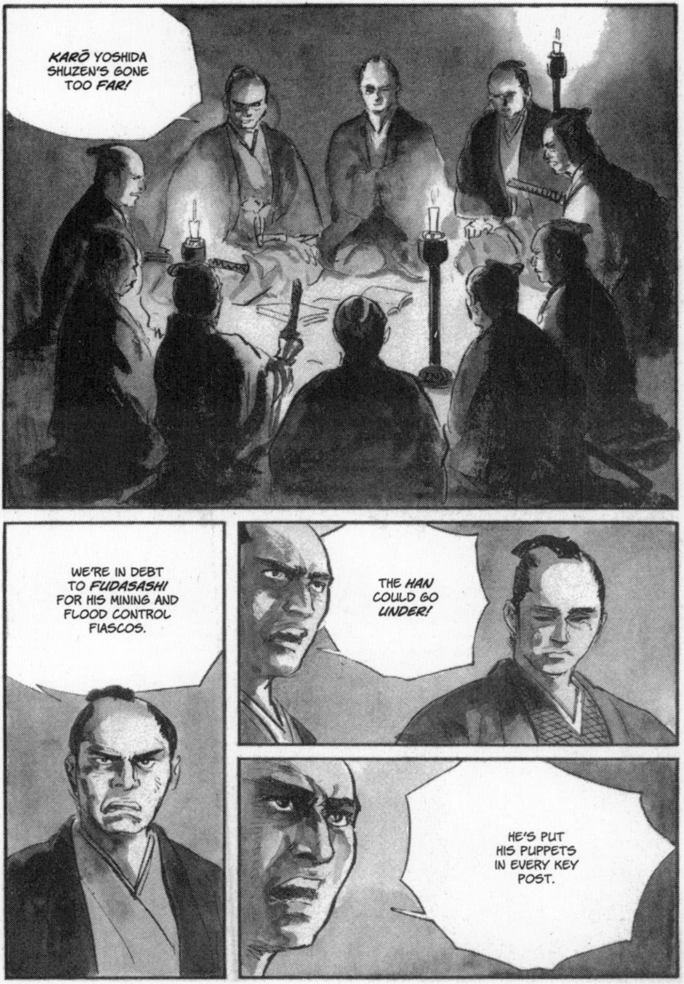
KARŌ YOSHIDA SHUZEN'S GONE TOO FAR!
WE'RE IN DEBT TO FUDASASHI FOR HIS MINING AND FLOOD CONTROL FIASCOS.
THE HAN COULD GO UNDER!
HE'S PUT HIS PUPPETS IN EVERY KEY POST.

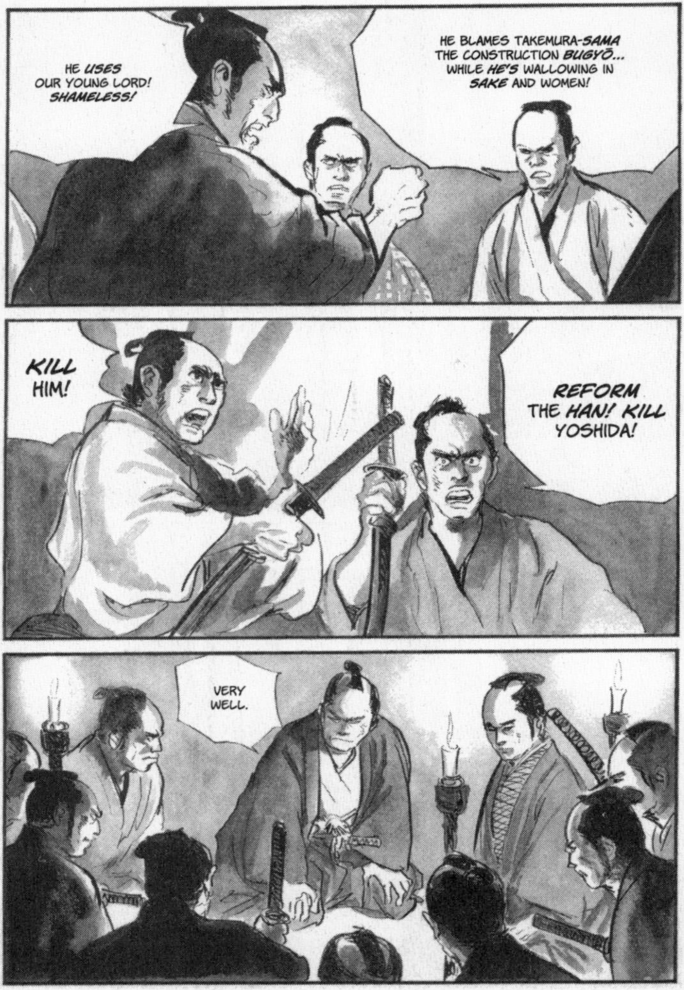
HE USES OUR YOUNG LORD! SHAMELESS!
HE BLAMES TAKEMURA-SAMA THE CONSTRUCTION BUGYŌ... WHILE HE'S WALLOWING IN SAKE AND WOMEN!
KILL HIM!
REFORM THE HAN! KILL YOSHIDA!
VERY WELL.

DOES ANYONE OBJECT?!
THEN SIGN. IN BLOOD.

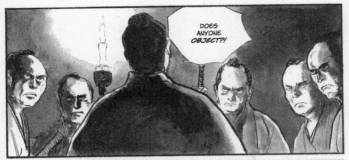

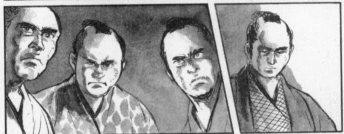

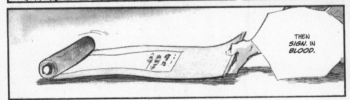

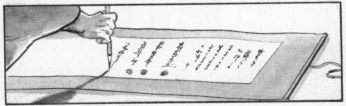

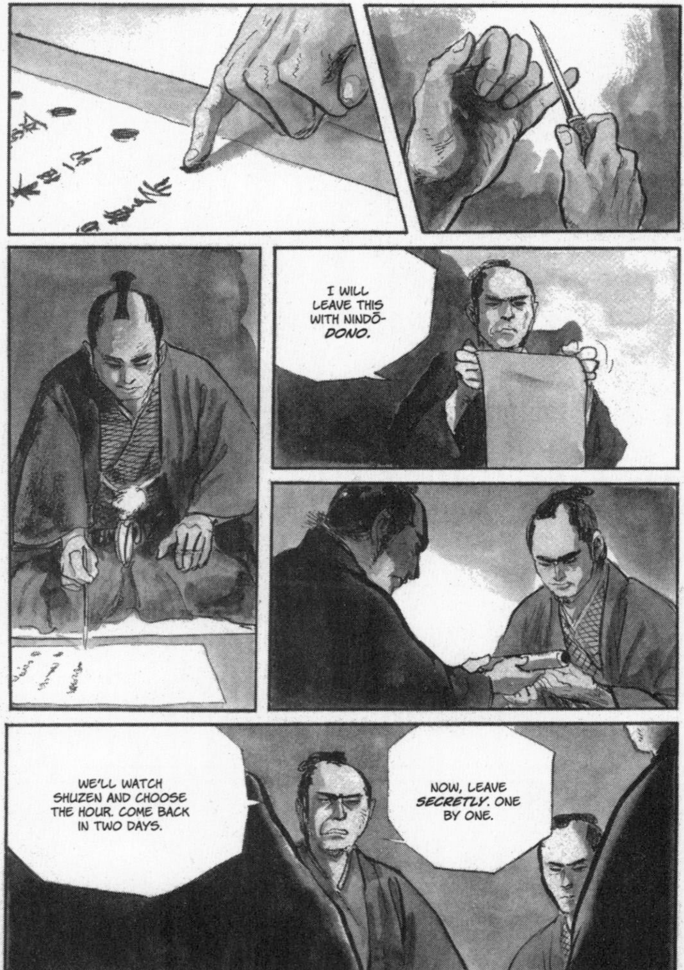
I WILL LEAVE THIS WITH NINDŌ-DONO.
WE'LL WATCH SHUZEN AND CHOOSE THE HOUR. COME BACK IN TWO DAYS.
NOW, LEAVE SECRETLY. ONE BY ONE.

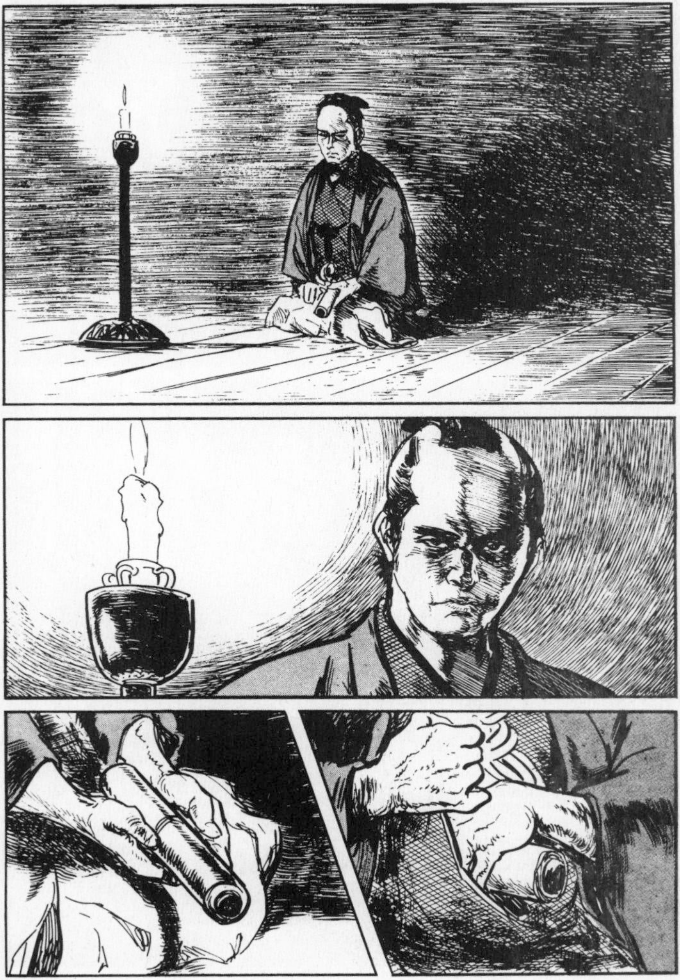

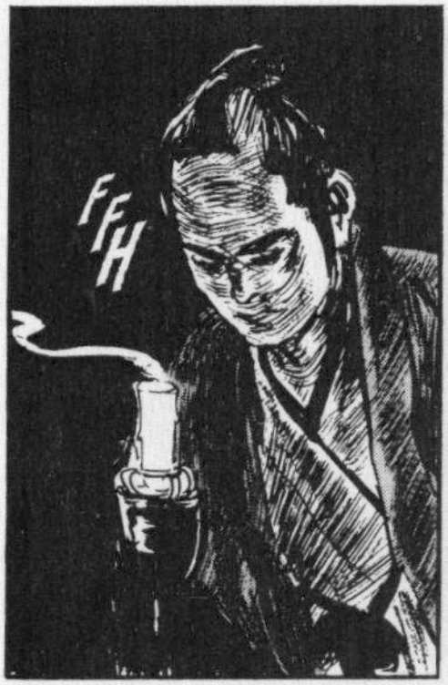
FFH

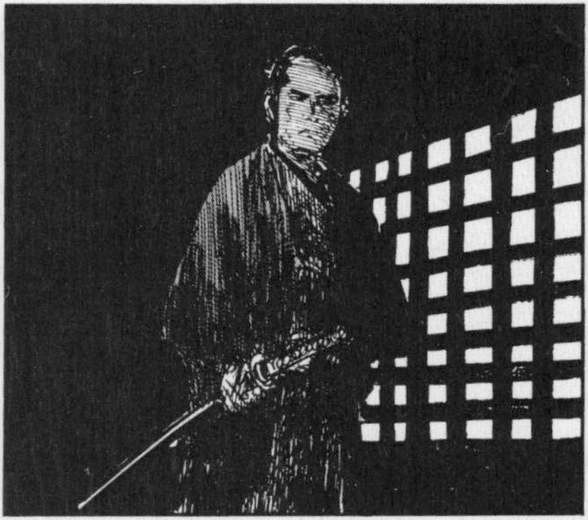

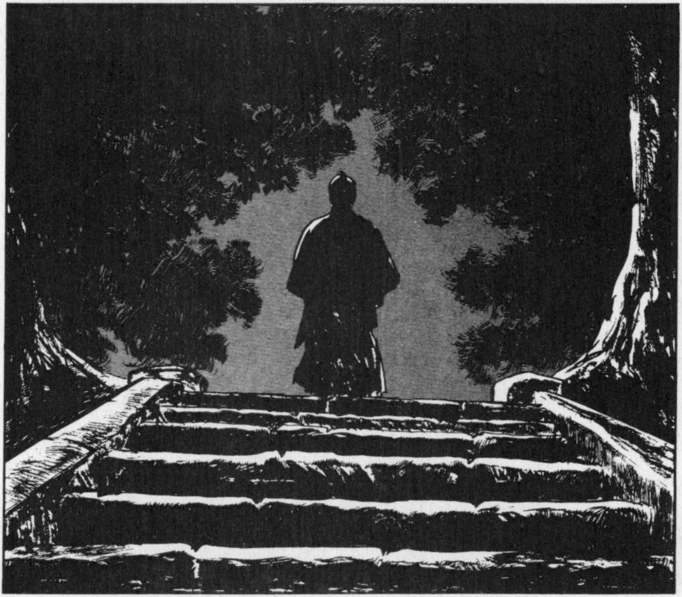

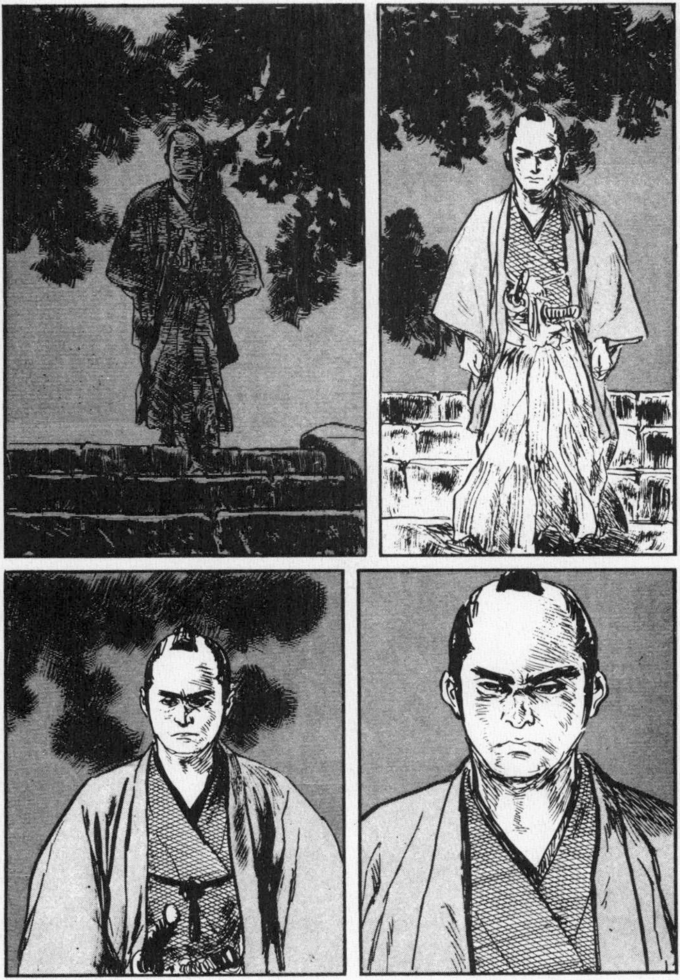

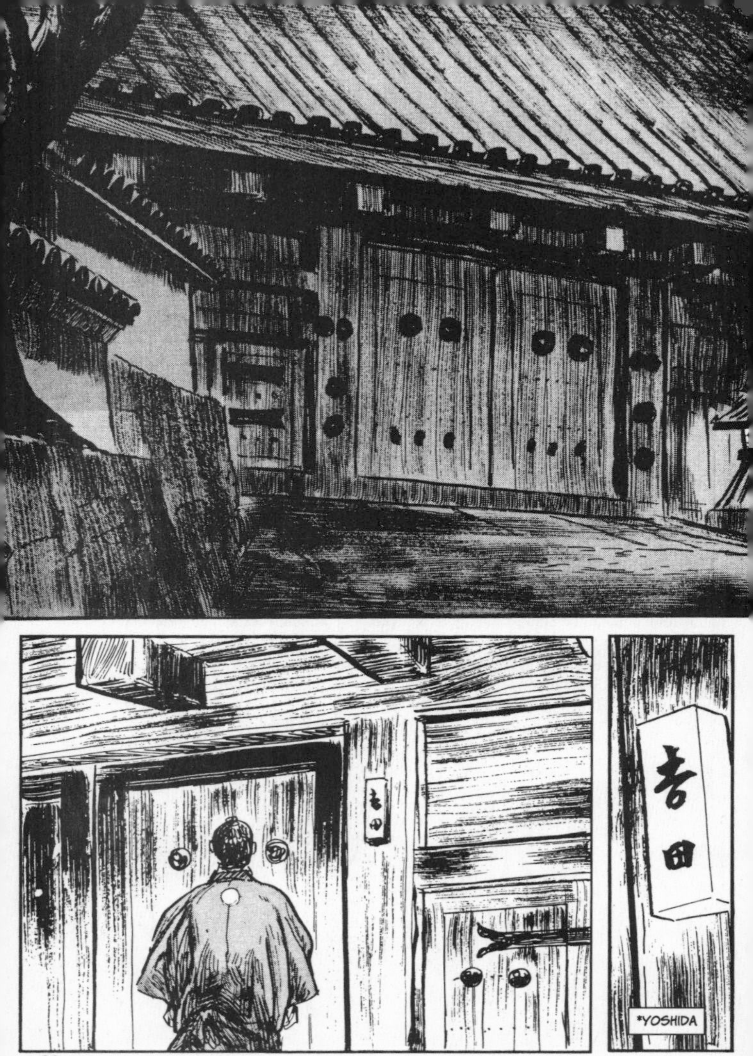
吉田
*YOSHIDA

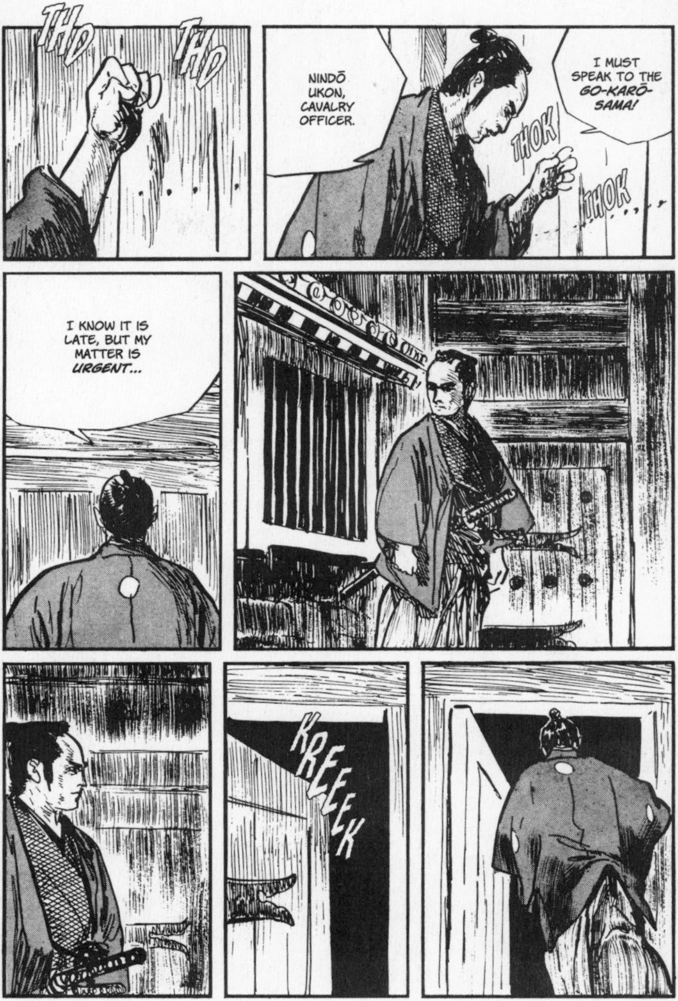
THD THD
NINDŌ UKON, CAVALRY OFFICER.
I MUST SPEAK TO THE GO-KARŌ-SAMA!
THOK THOK
I KNOW IT IS LATE, BUT MY MATTER IS URGENT...
KREEEK

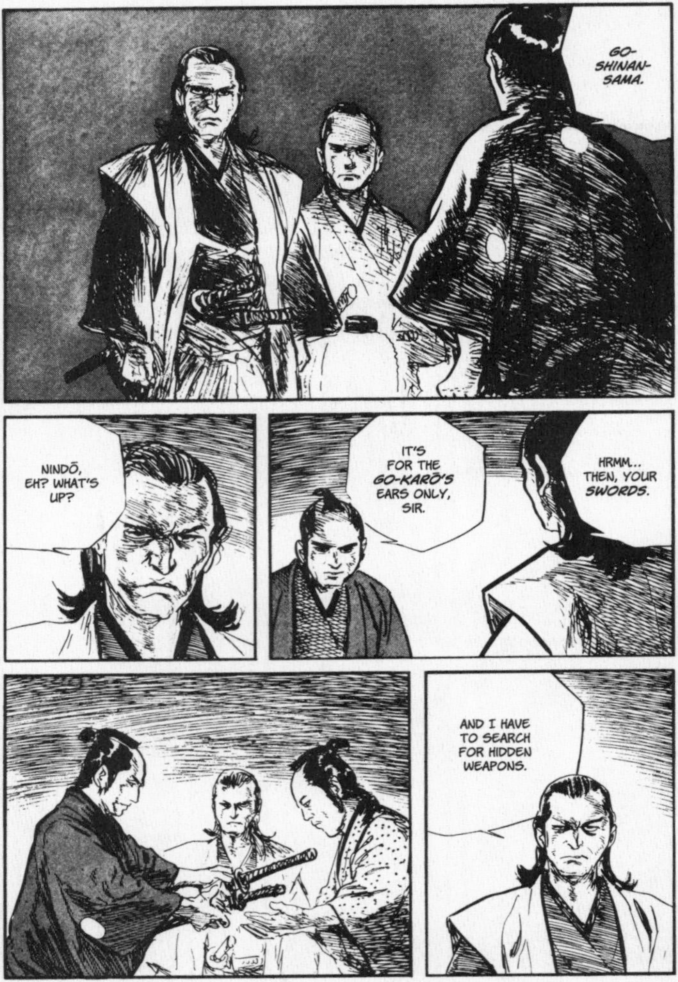
GO-SHINAN-SAMA.
NINDŌ, EH? WHAT'S UP?
IT'S FOR THE *GO-KARŌ'S* EARS ONLY, SIR.
HRMM... THEN, YOUR *SWORDS.*
AND I HAVE TO SEARCH FOR HIDDEN WEAPONS.

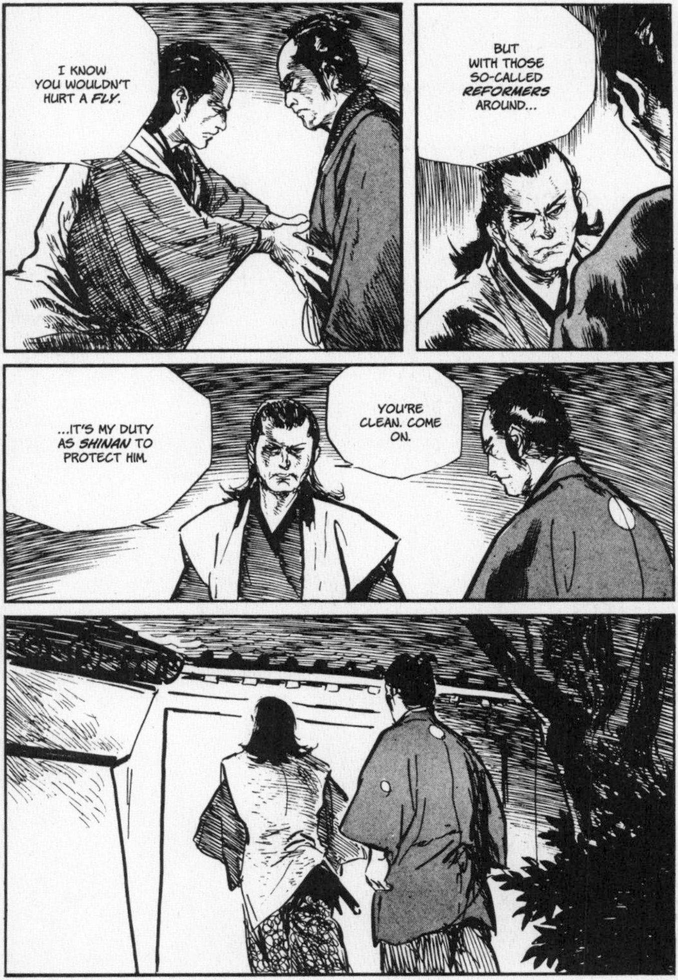
I KNOW YOU WOULDN'T HURT A *FLY*.
BUT WITH THOSE SO-CALLED *REFORMERS* AROUND...
...IT'S MY DUTY AS *SHINAN* TO PROTECT HIM.
YOU'RE CLEAN. COME ON.

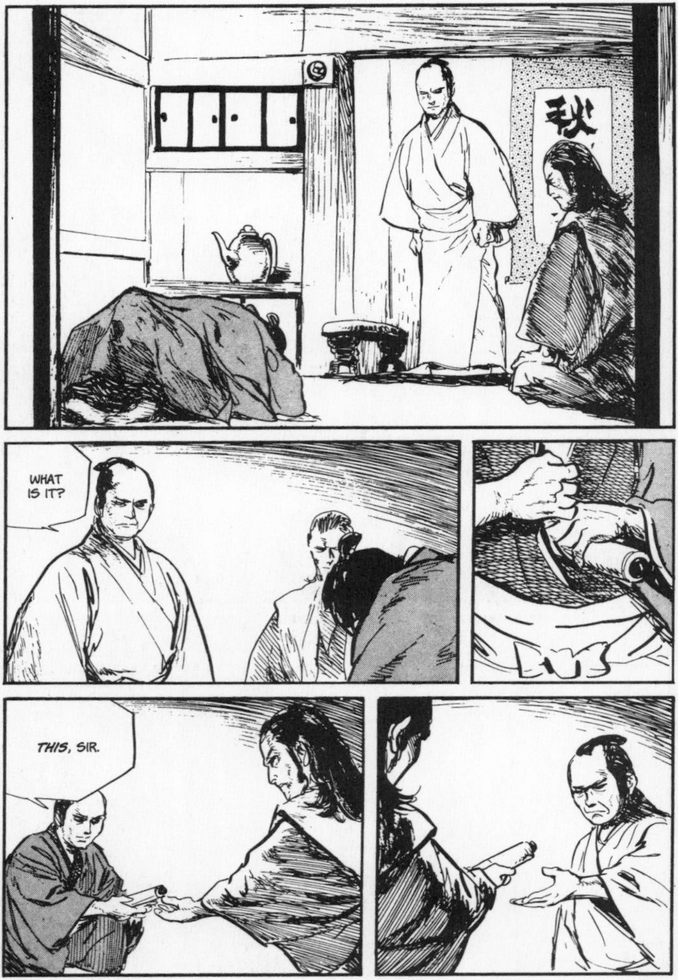
秋
WHAT IS IT?
THIS, SIR.

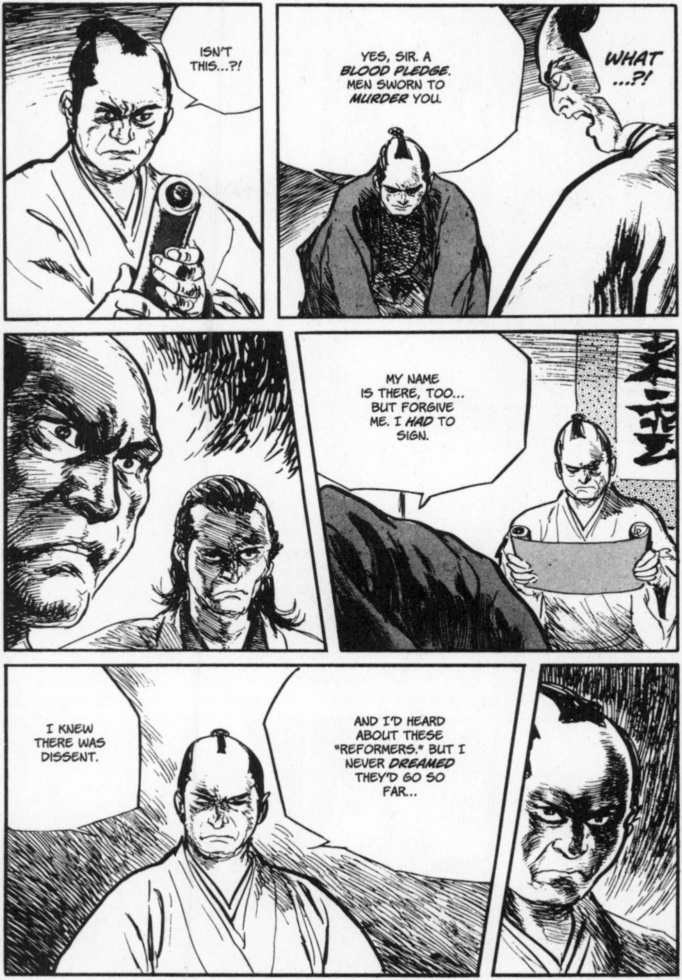

ISN'T THIS...?!
YES, SIR. A *BLOOD PLEDGE*. MEN SWORN TO *MURDER* YOU.
WHAT ...?!
MY NAME IS THERE, TOO... BUT FORGIVE ME. I *HAD* TO SIGN.
I KNEW THERE WAS DISSENT.
AND I'D HEARD ABOUT THESE "REFORMERS." BUT I NEVER *DREAMED* THEY'D GO SO FAR...

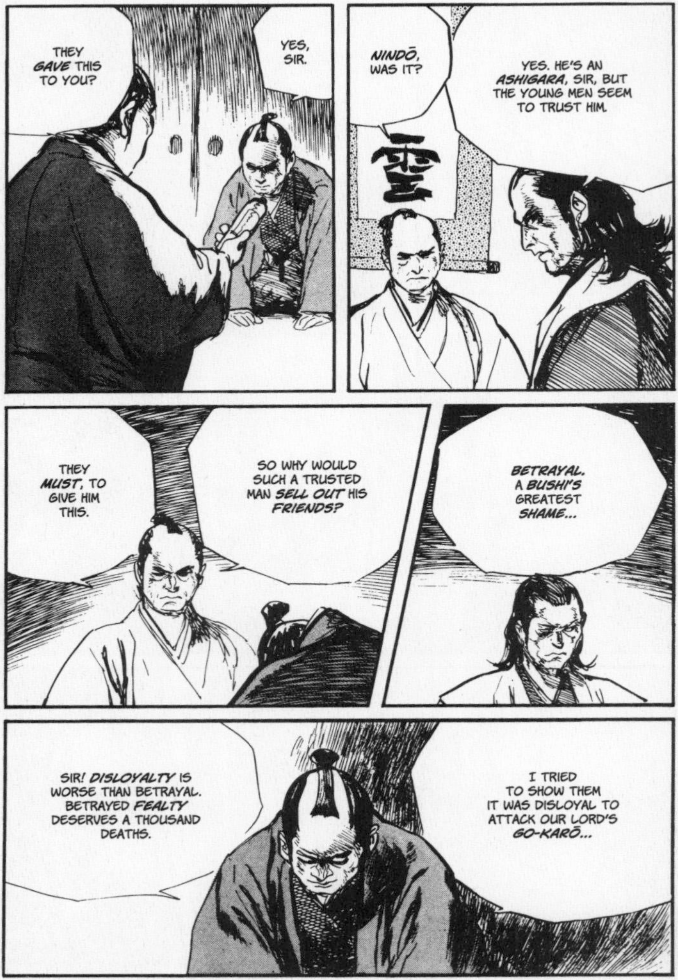
THEY GAVE THIS TO YOU?
YES, SIR.
NINDŌ, WAS IT?
YES. HE'S AN ASHIGARA, SIR, BUT THE YOUNG MEN SEEM TO TRUST HIM.
THEY MUST, TO GIVE HIM THIS.
SO WHY WOULD SUCH A TRUSTED MAN SELL OUT HIS FRIENDS?
BETRAYAL. A BUSHI'S GREATEST SHAME...
SIR! DISLOYALTY IS WORSE THAN BETRAYAL. BETRAYED FEALTY DESERVES A THOUSAND DEATHS.
I TRIED TO SHOW THEM IT WAS DISLOYAL TO ATTACK OUR LORD'S GO-KARŌ...

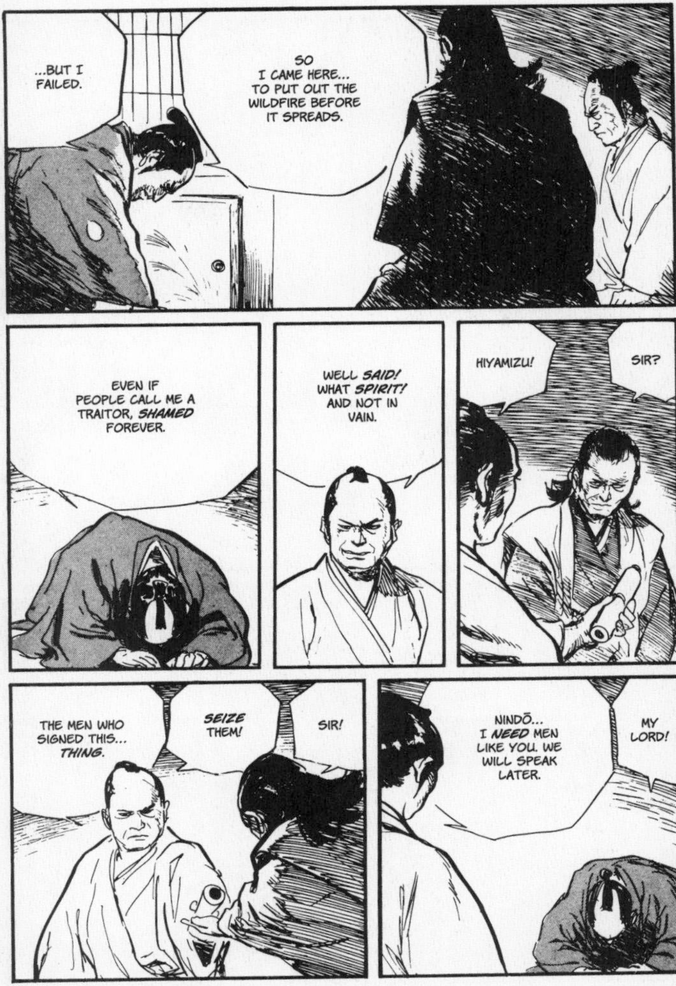
...BUT I FAILED.
SO I CAME HERE... TO PUT OUT THE WILDFIRE BEFORE IT SPREADS.
EVEN IF PEOPLE CALL ME A TRAITOR, *SHAMED* FOREVER.
WELL *SAID!* WHAT *SPIRIT!* AND NOT IN VAIN.
HIYAMIZU!
SIR?
THE MEN WHO SIGNED THIS... *THING.*
SEIZE THEM!
SIR!
NINDŌ... I *NEED* MEN LIKE YOU. WE WILL SPEAK LATER.
MY LORD!

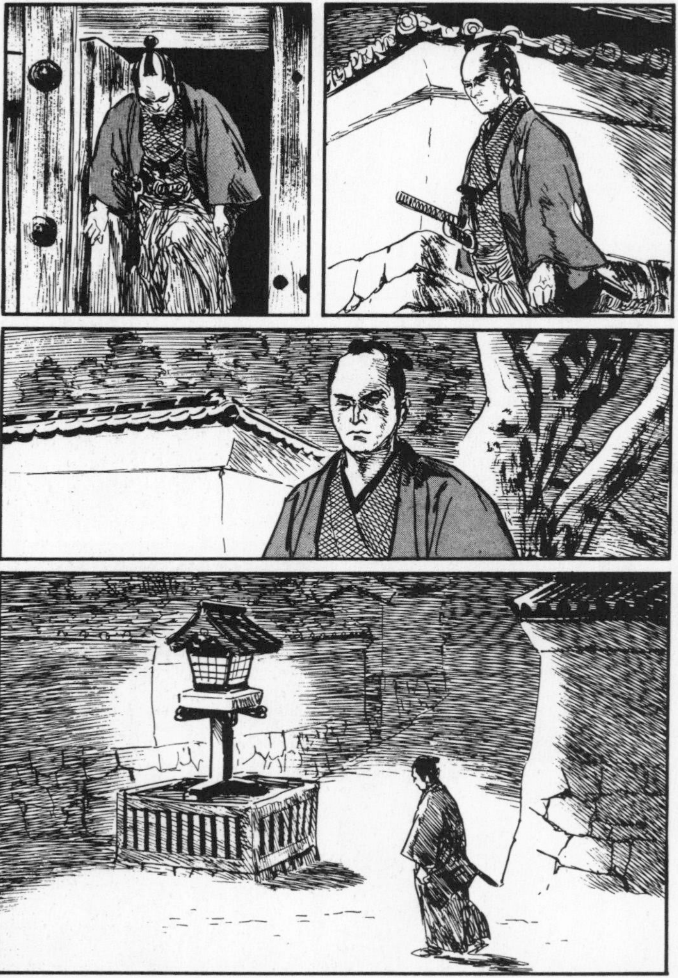

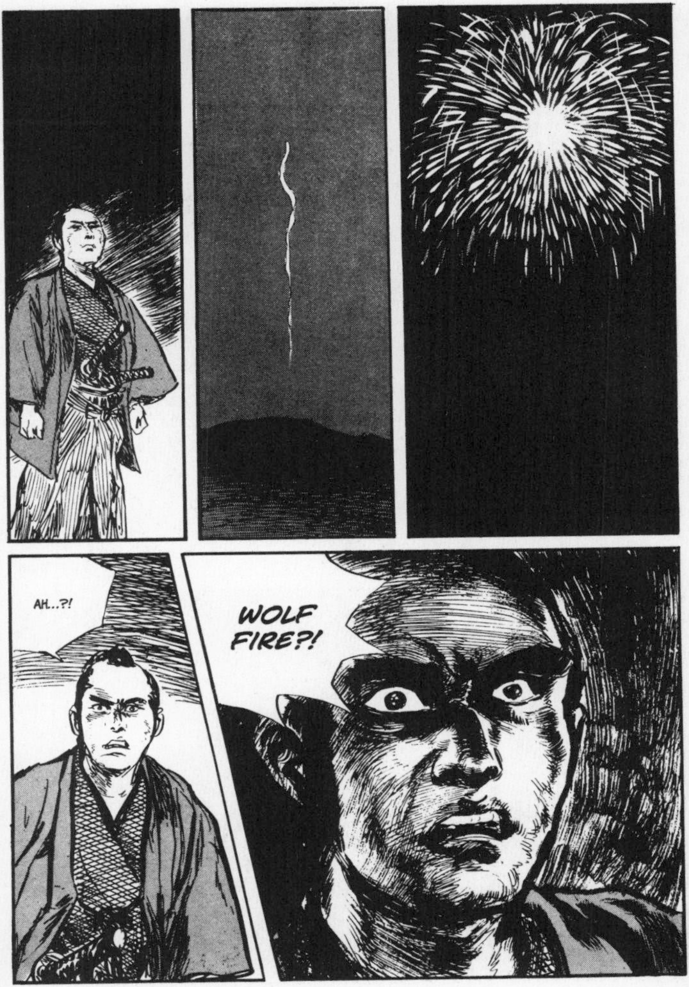
AH...?!
WOLF FIRE?!

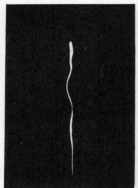

NO!!
NOT *NOW!*

THD THD THD

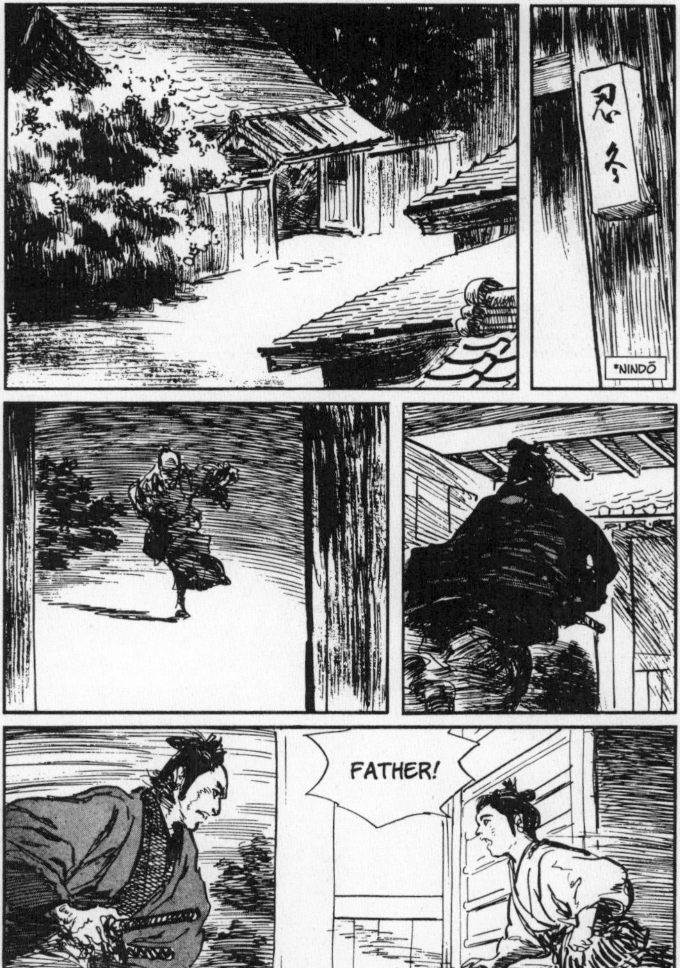
忍冬
*NINDŌ
FATHER!

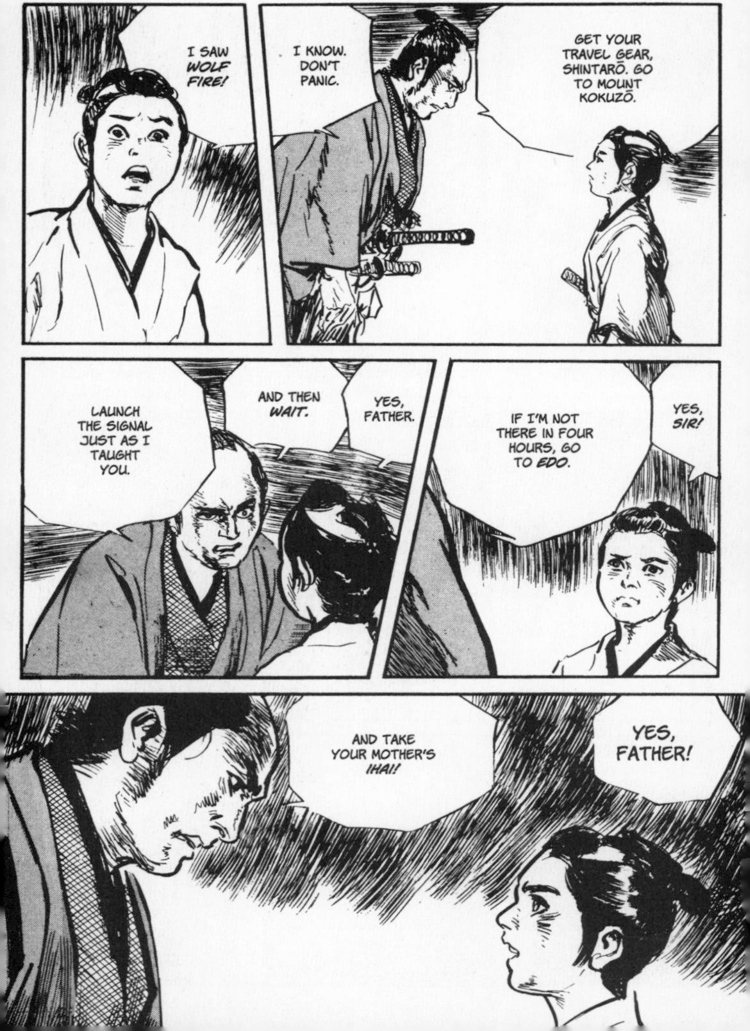

I SAW *WOLF FIRE!*
I KNOW. DON'T PANIC.
GET YOUR TRAVEL GEAR, SHINTARŌ. GO TO MOUNT KOKUZŌ.
LAUNCH THE SIGNAL JUST AS I TAUGHT YOU.
AND THEN *WAIT.*
YES, FATHER.
IF I'M NOT THERE IN FOUR HOURS, GO TO *EDO*.
YES, *SIR!*
AND TAKE YOUR MOTHER'S *IHAI!*
YES, FATHER!

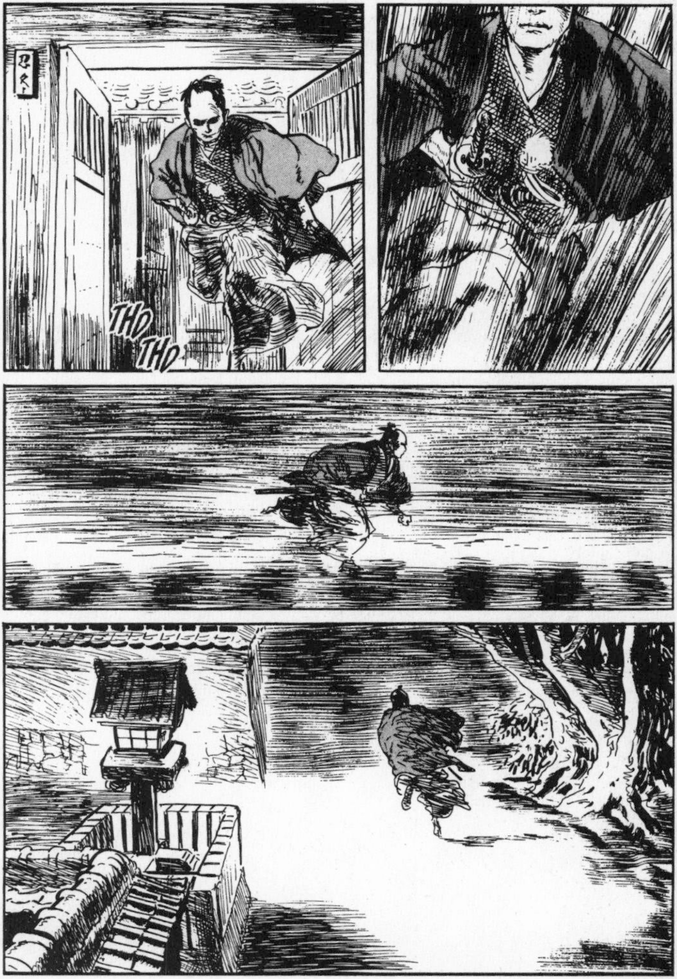
THD
THD

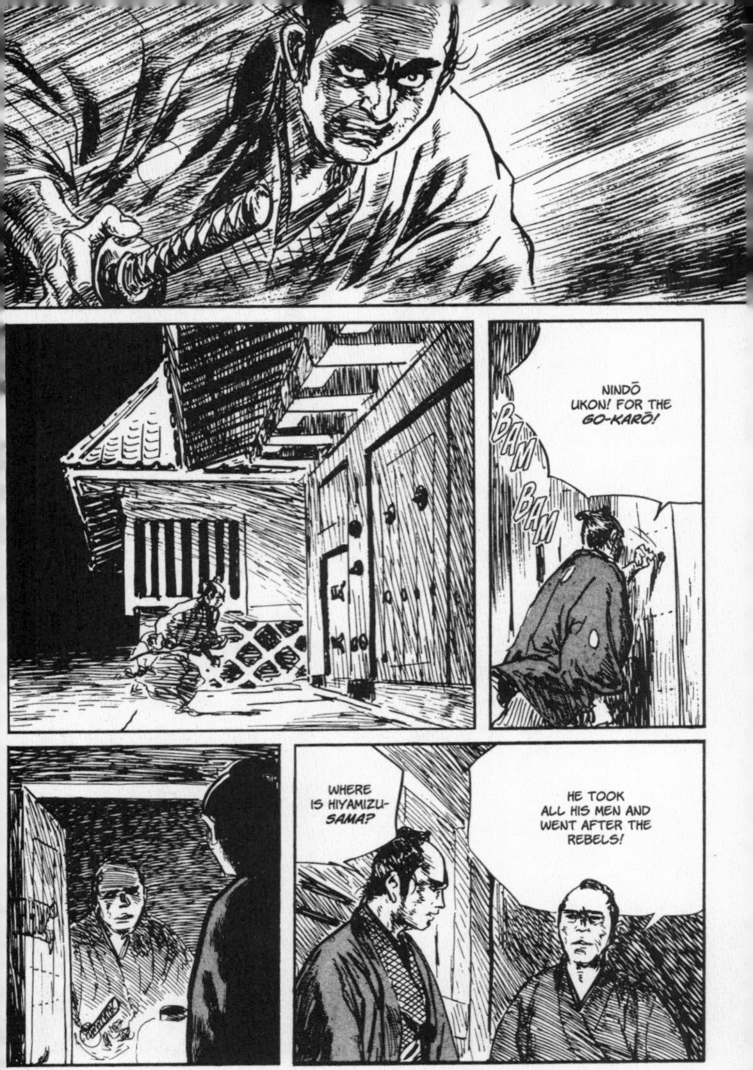
BAM
BAM
NINDŌ UKON! FOR THE *GO-KARŌ!*
WHERE IS HIYAMIZU-*SAMA?*
HE TOOK ALL HIS MEN AND WENT AFTER THE REBELS!

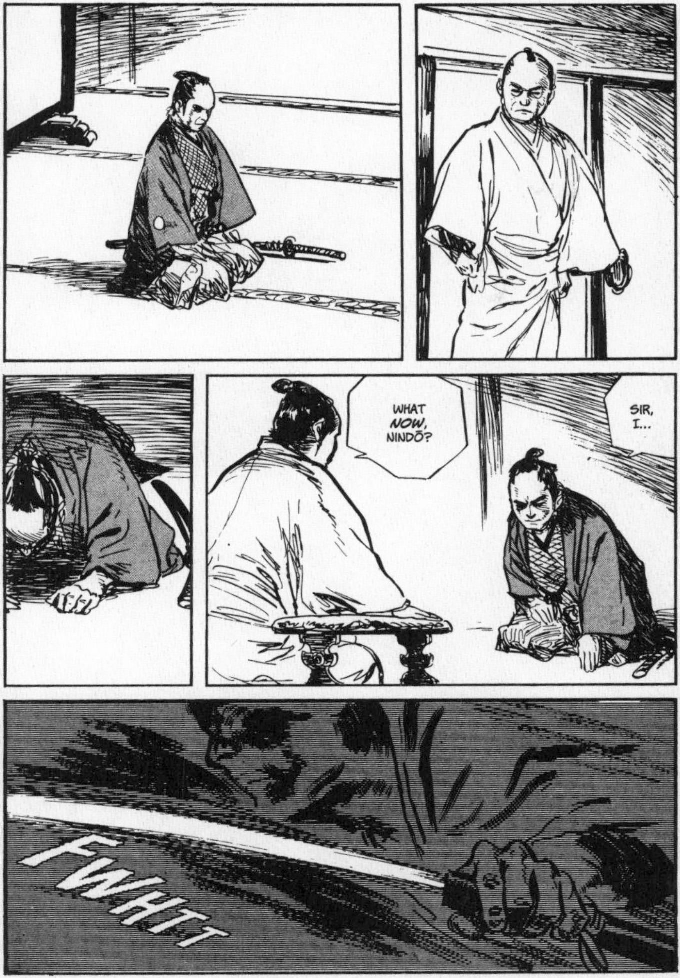
WHAT NOW, NINDŌ?
SIR, I...
FWHTT

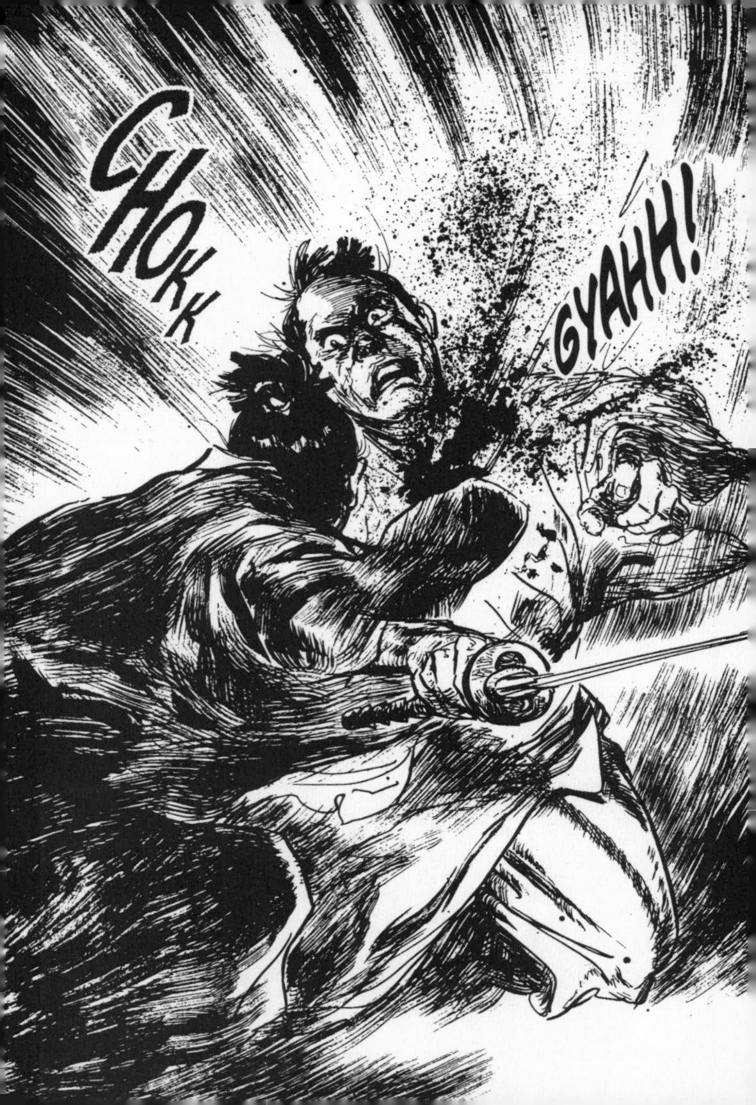
CHOKK
GYAHH!

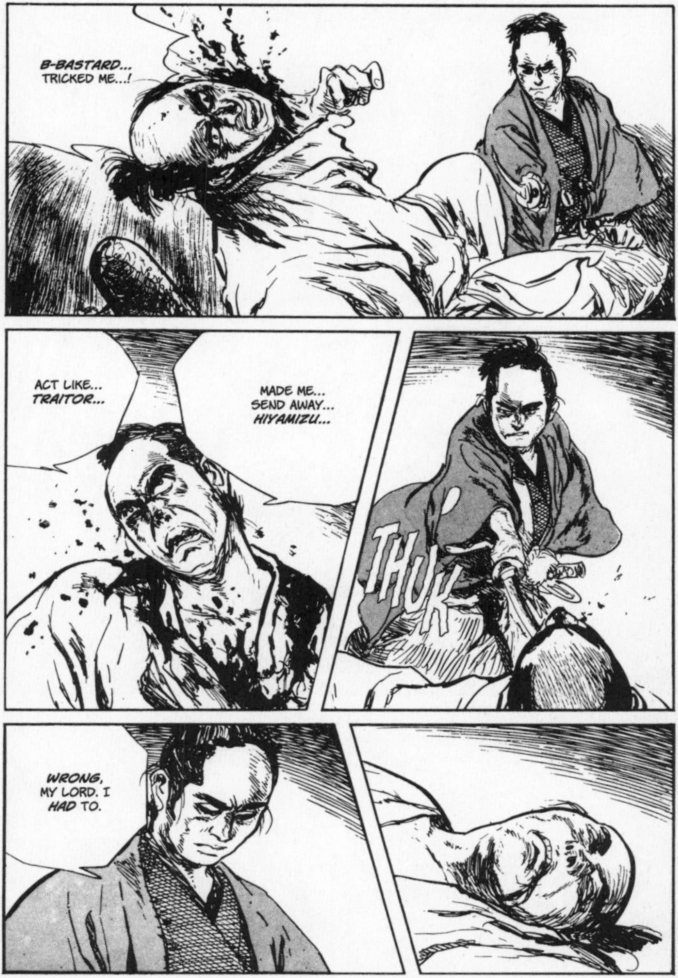
B-BASTARD... TRICKED ME...!
ACT LIKE... TRAITOR...
MADE ME... SEND AWAY... HIYAMIZU...
THUK
WRONG, MY LORD. I HAD TO.

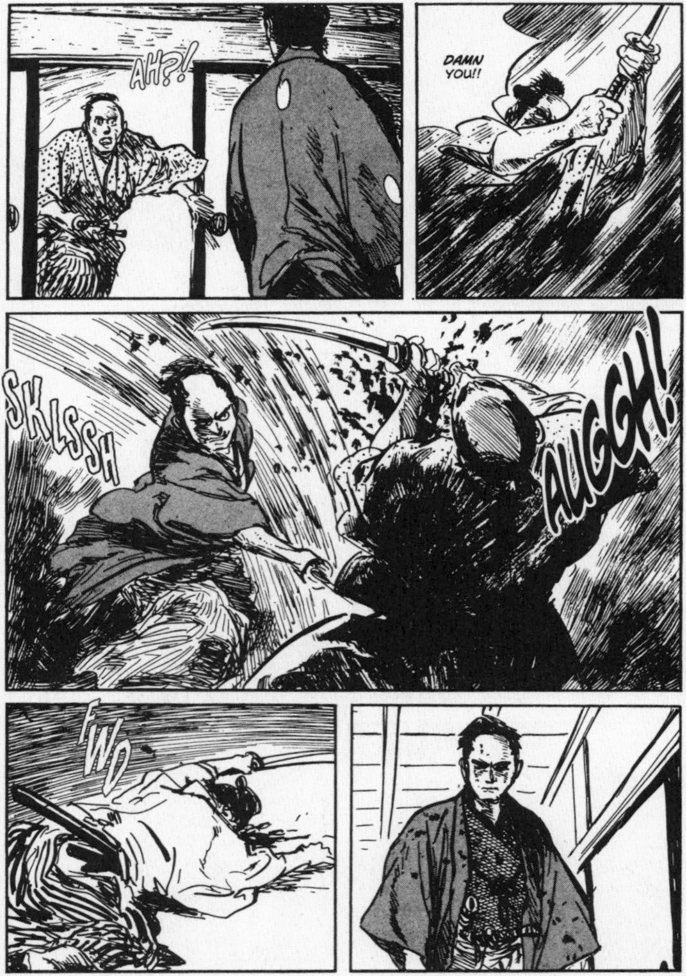
AH?!
DAMN YOU!!
SKLSSH
AUGGH!
FWD

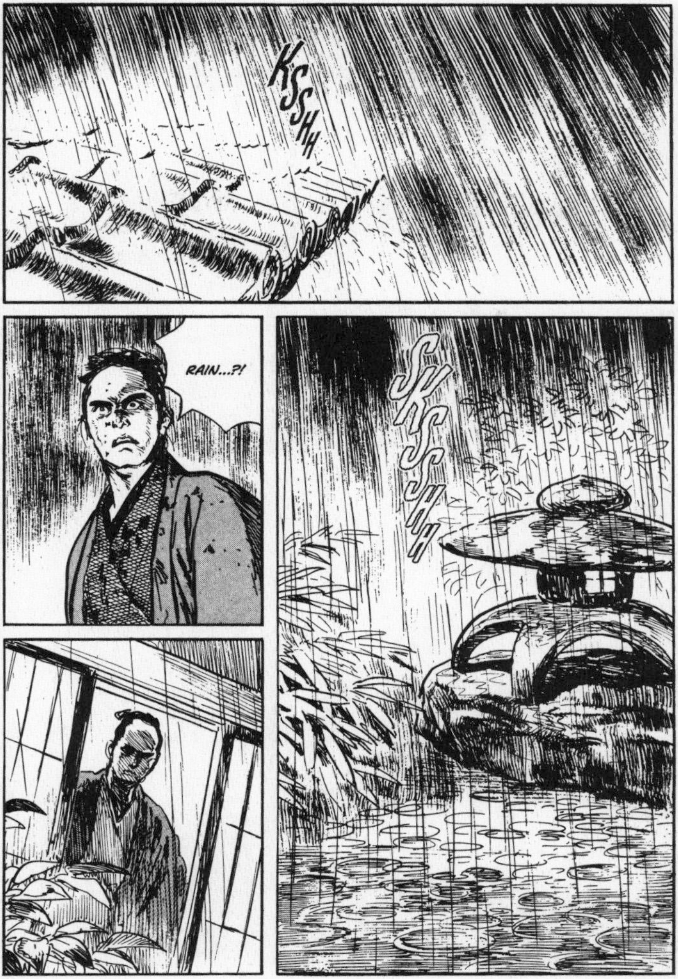
KSSHH
RAIN...?!
SKSSSHH

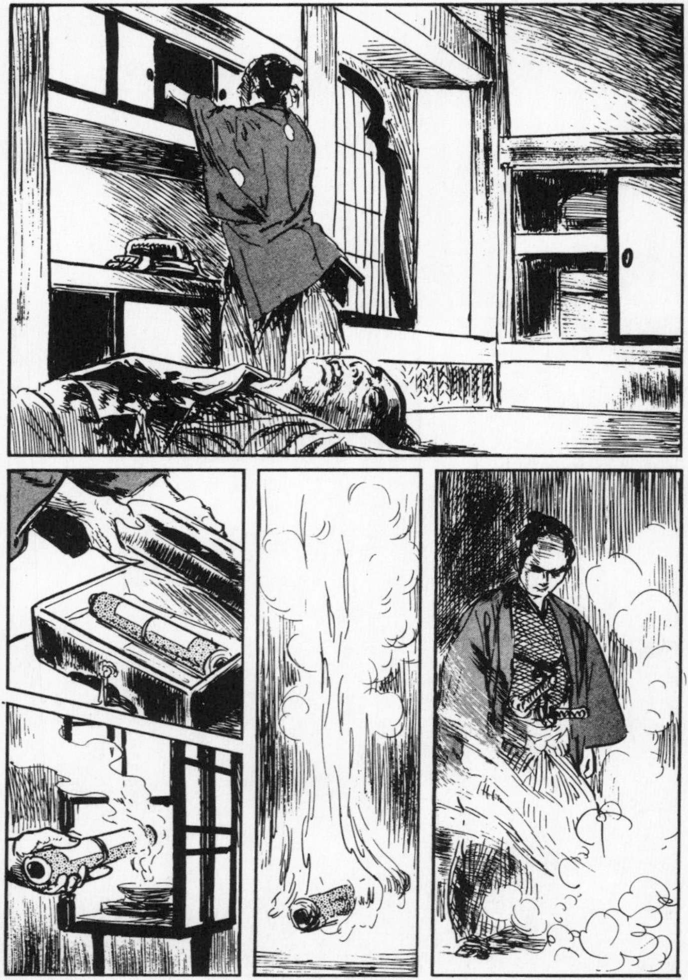

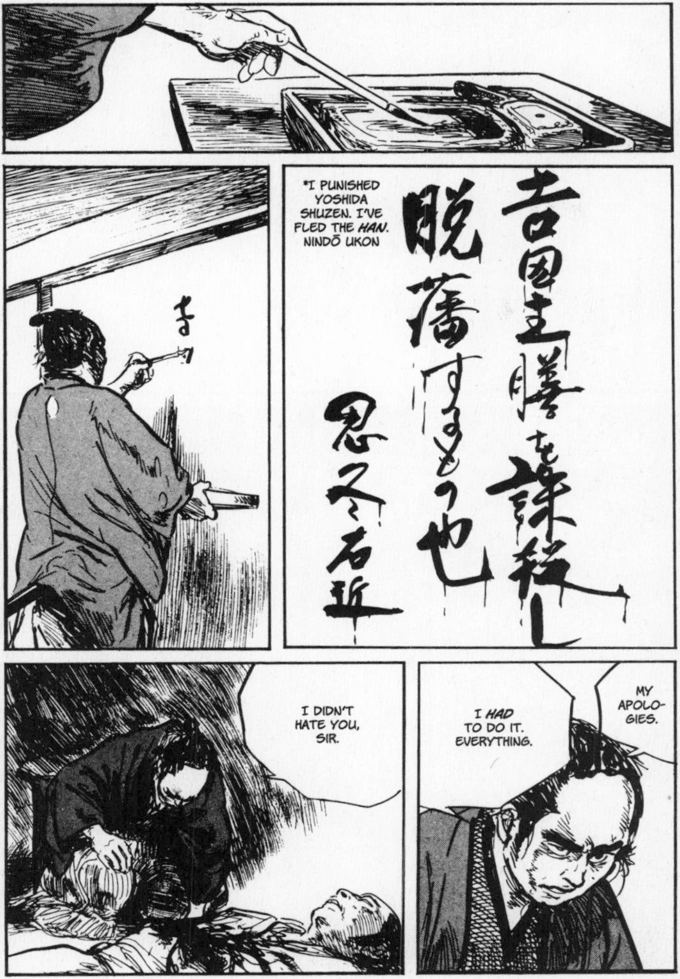
吉田主膳を誅殺し
脱藩するもの也
忍冬右近
*I PUNISHED YOSHIDA SHUZEN. I'VE FLED THE *HAN*. NINDŌ UKON
I DIDN'T HATE YOU, SIR.
I *HAD* TO DO IT. EVERYTHING.
MY APOLOGIES.

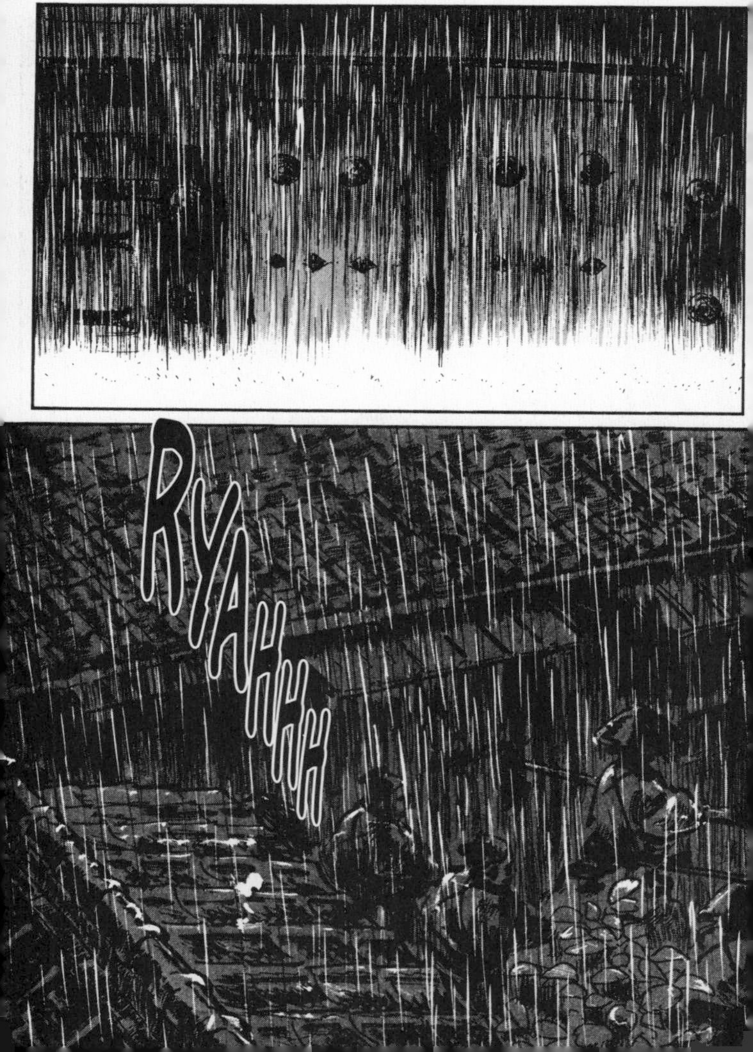
RYAHHHH

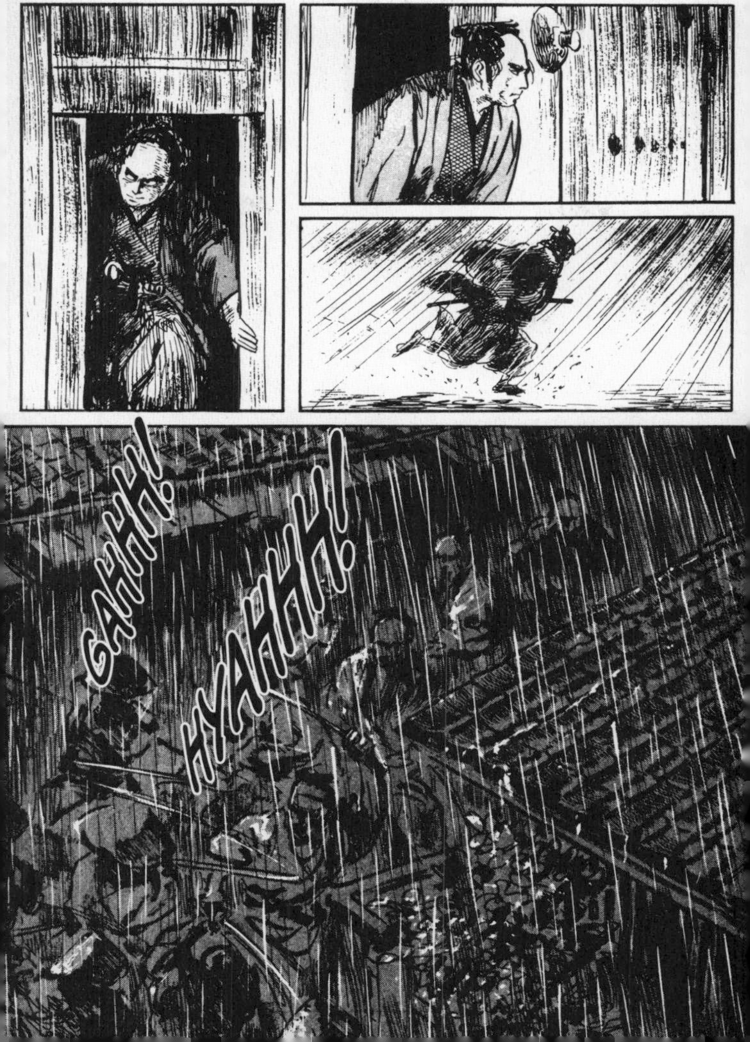
GAHHH!
HYAHHH!

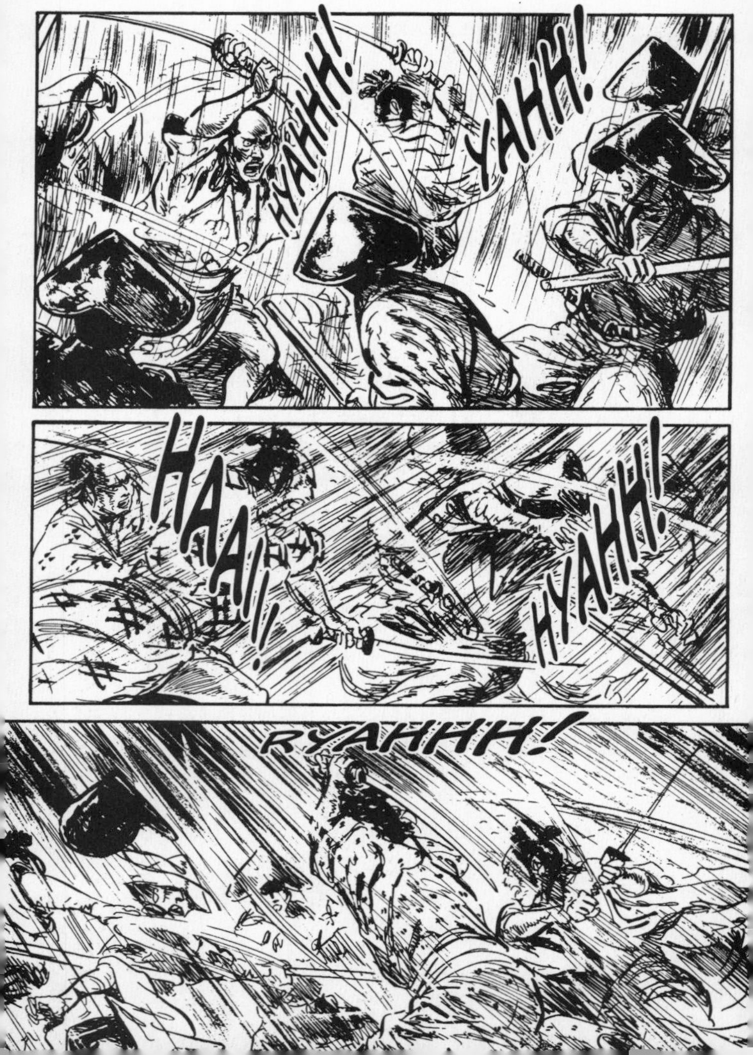
HYAHHH!
YAHH!
HAAA!!!
HYAHH!
RYAHHHH!

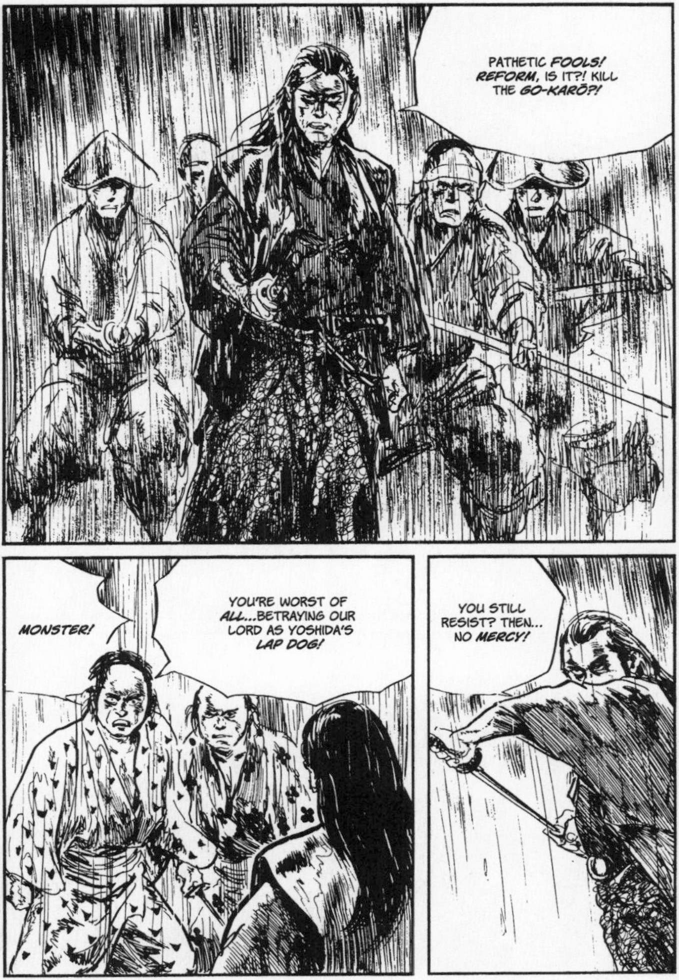
PATHETIC *FOOLS!* *REFORM*, IS IT?! KILL THE *GO-KARŌ?!*
MONSTER!
YOU'RE WORST OF *ALL*...BETRAYING OUR LORD AS YOSHIDA'S *LAP DOG!*
YOU STILL RESIST? THEN... NO *MERCY!*

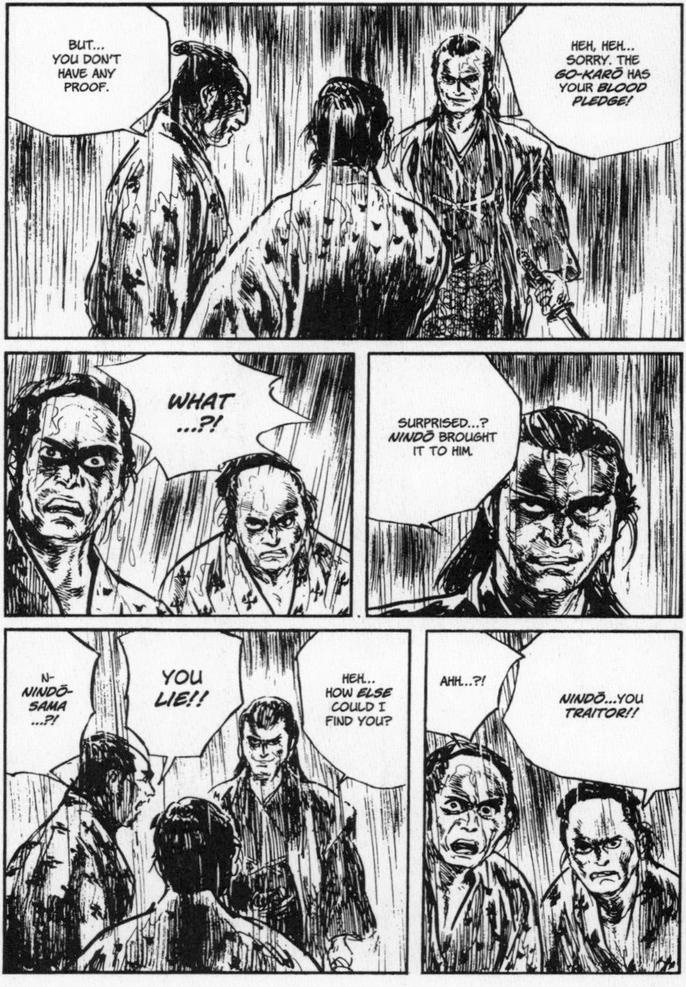
BUT... YOU DON'T HAVE ANY PROOF.
HEH, HEH... SORRY. THE GO-KARŌ HAS YOUR BLOOD PLEDGE!
WHAT ...?!
SURPRISED...? NINDŌ BROUGHT IT TO HIM.
N-NINDŌ-SAMA ...?!
YOU LIE!!
HEH... HOW ELSE COULD I FIND YOU?
AHH...?!
NINDŌ...YOU TRAITOR!!

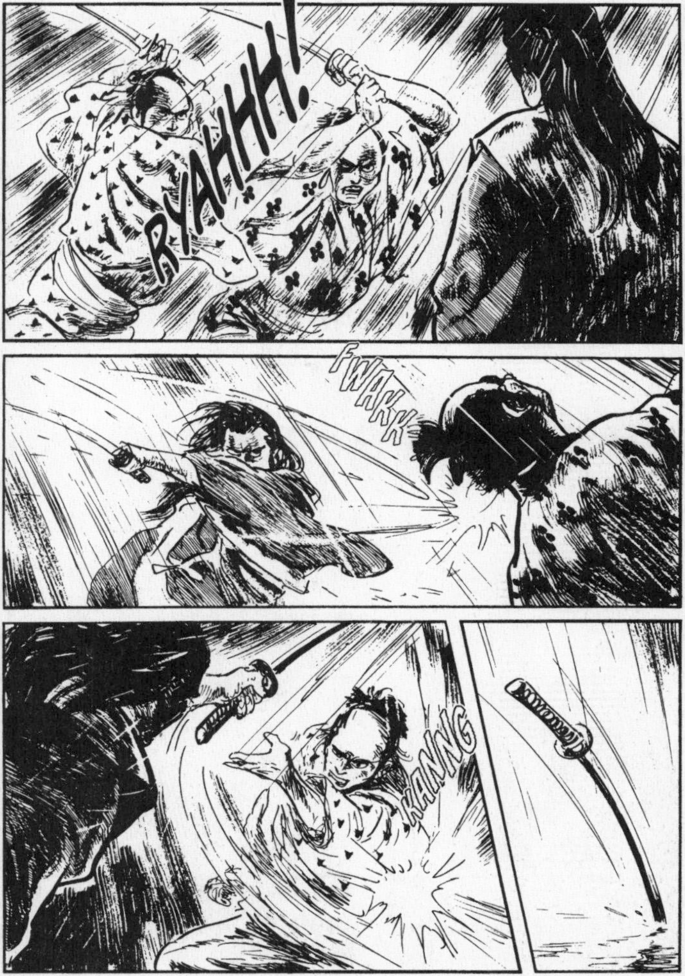
RYAHHH!
FWAKK
KANNG

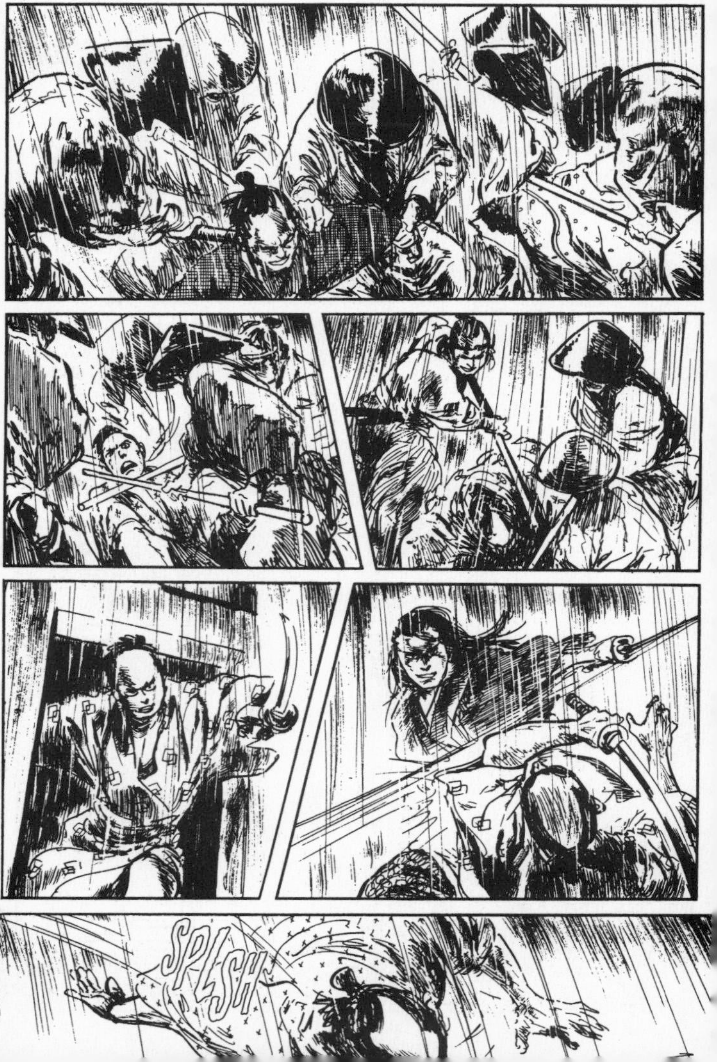
SPLSH

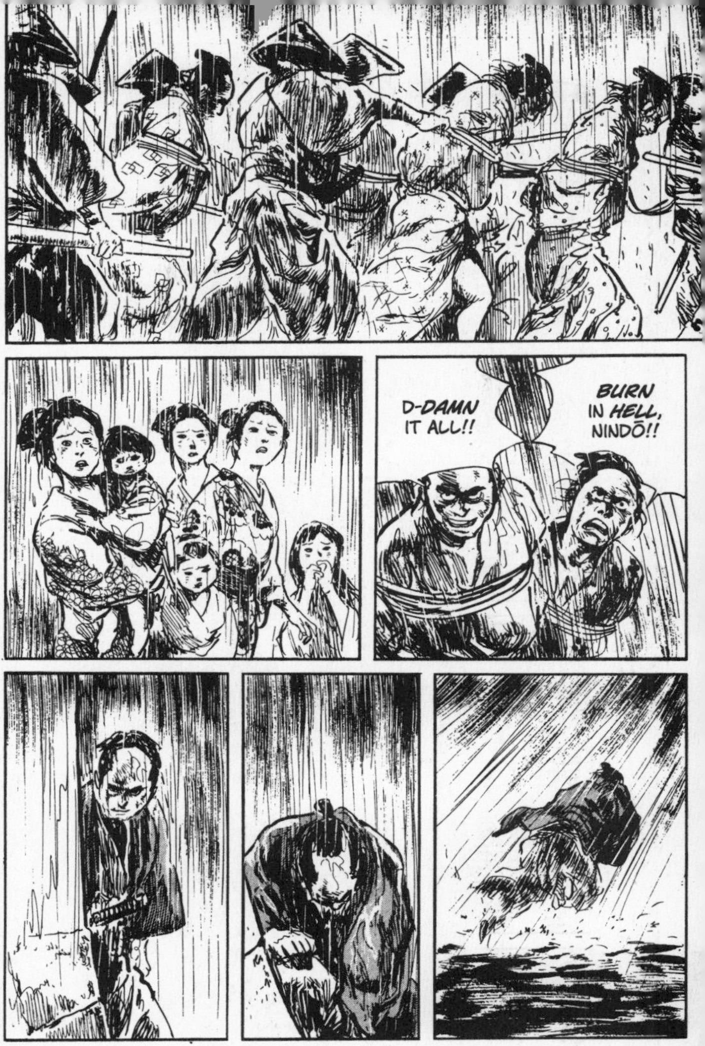
D-DAMN IT ALL!!
BURN IN HELL, NINDŌ!!

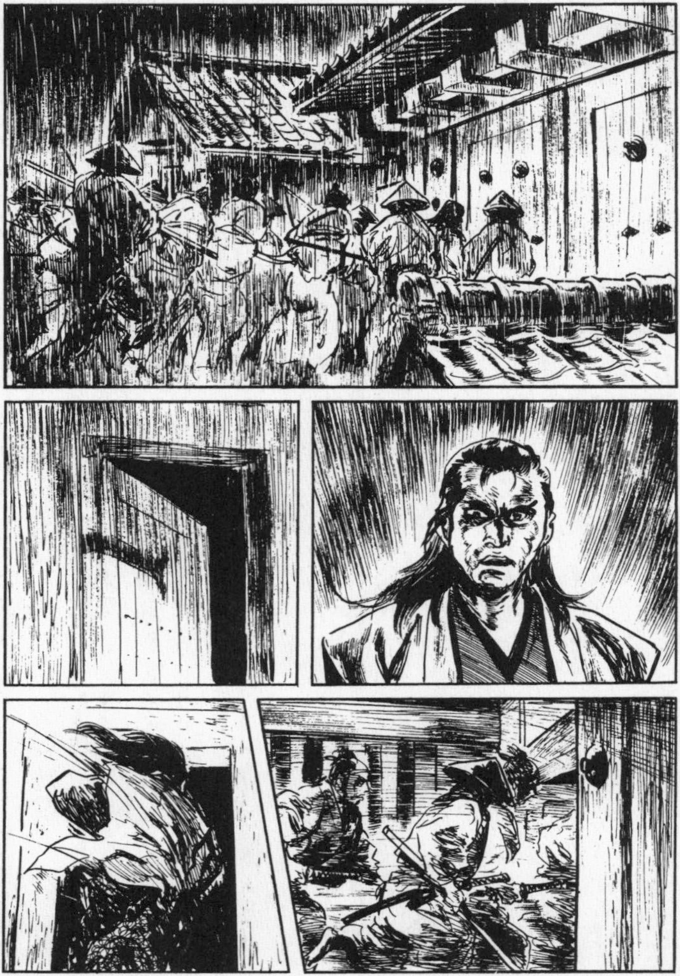

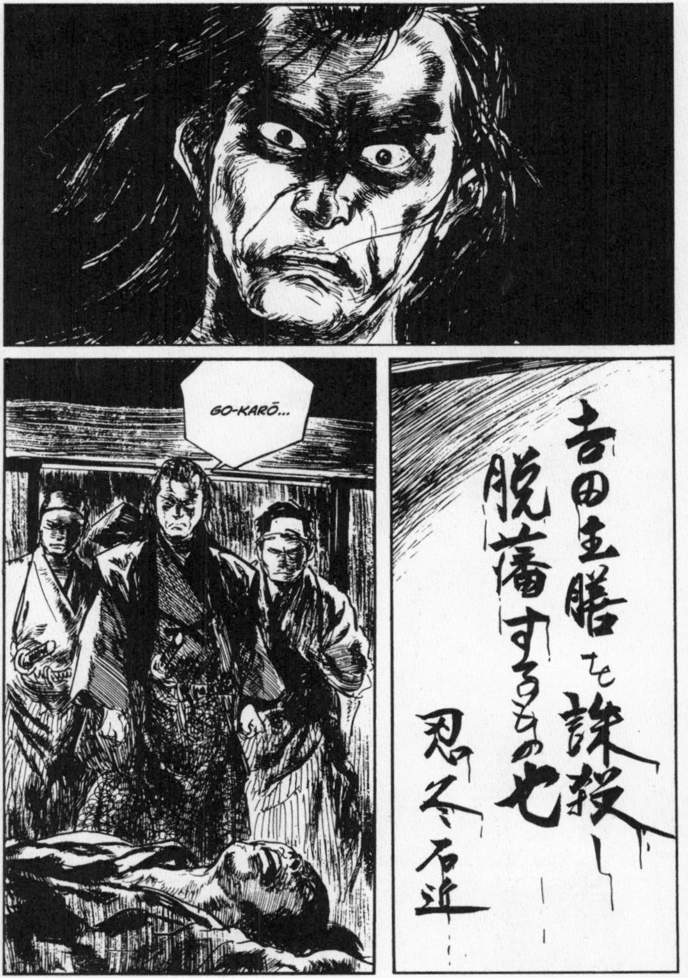
GO-KARŌ...
吉田主膳を誅殺し
脱藩するもの七
忍ノ石近

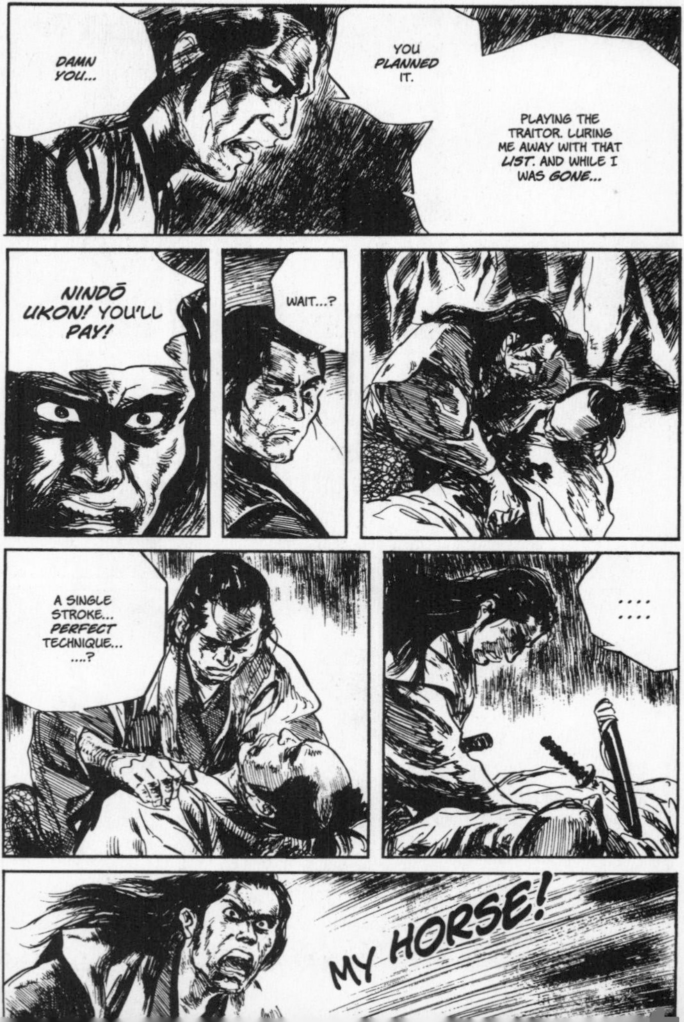
DAMN YOU...
YOU PLANNED IT.
PLAYING THE TRAITOR. LURING ME AWAY WITH THAT LIST. AND WHILE I WAS GONE...
NINDŌ UKON! YOU'LL PAY!
WAIT...?
A SINGLE STROKE... PERFECT TECHNIQUE... ...?
....
....
MY HORSE!

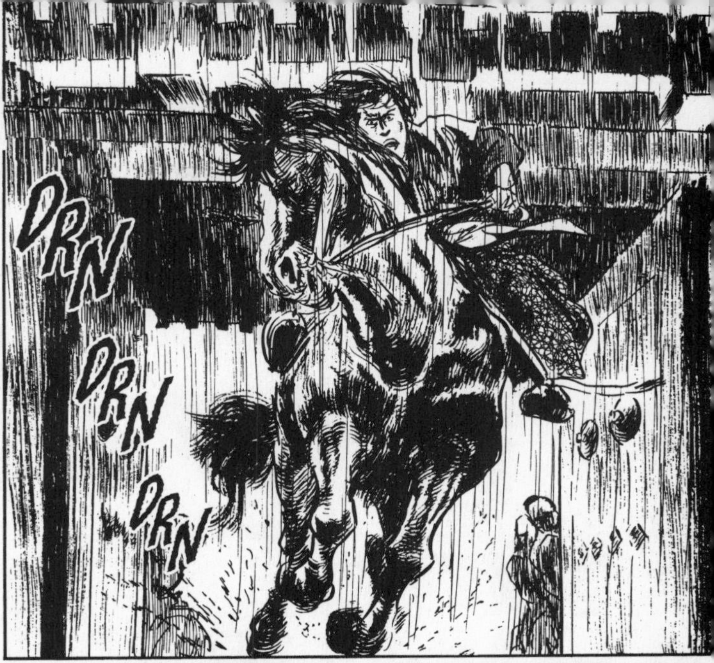
DRN
DRN
DRN

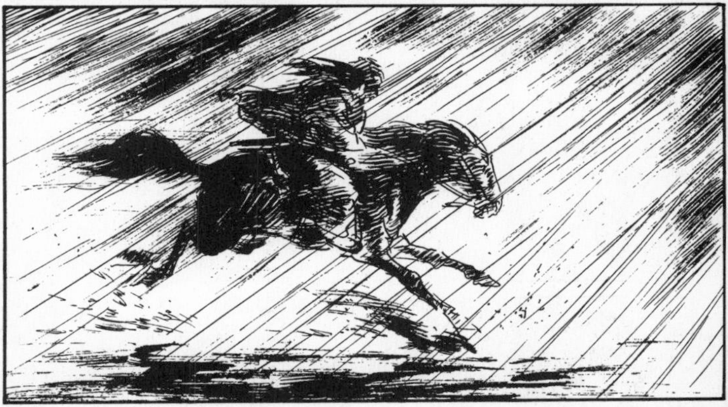

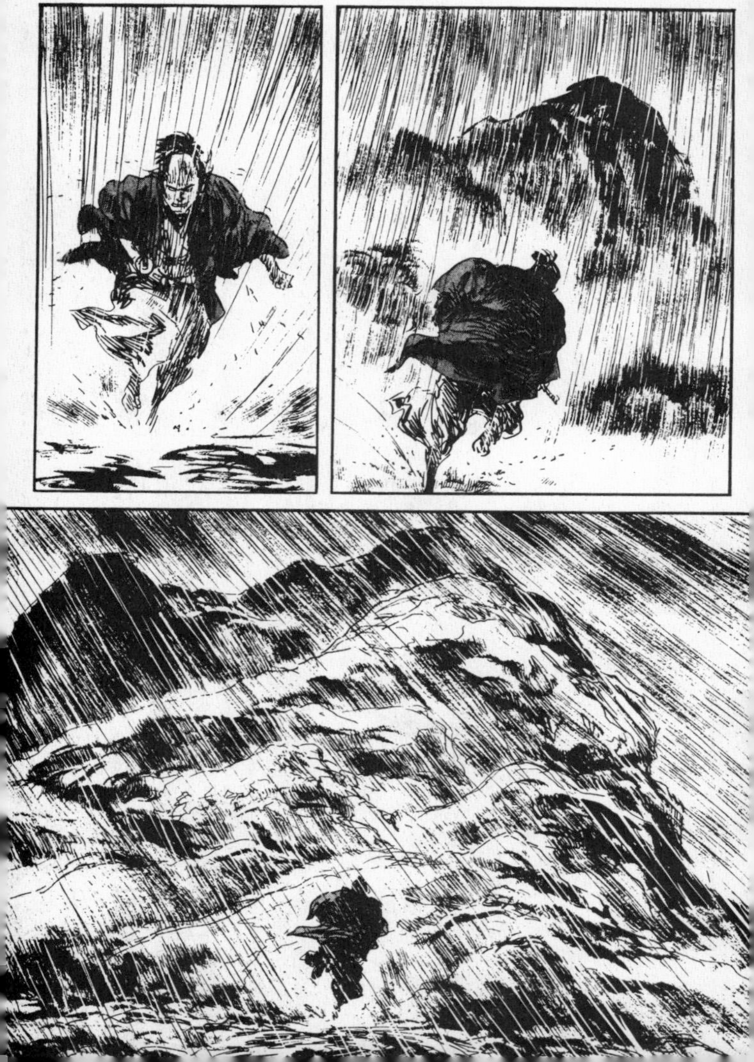

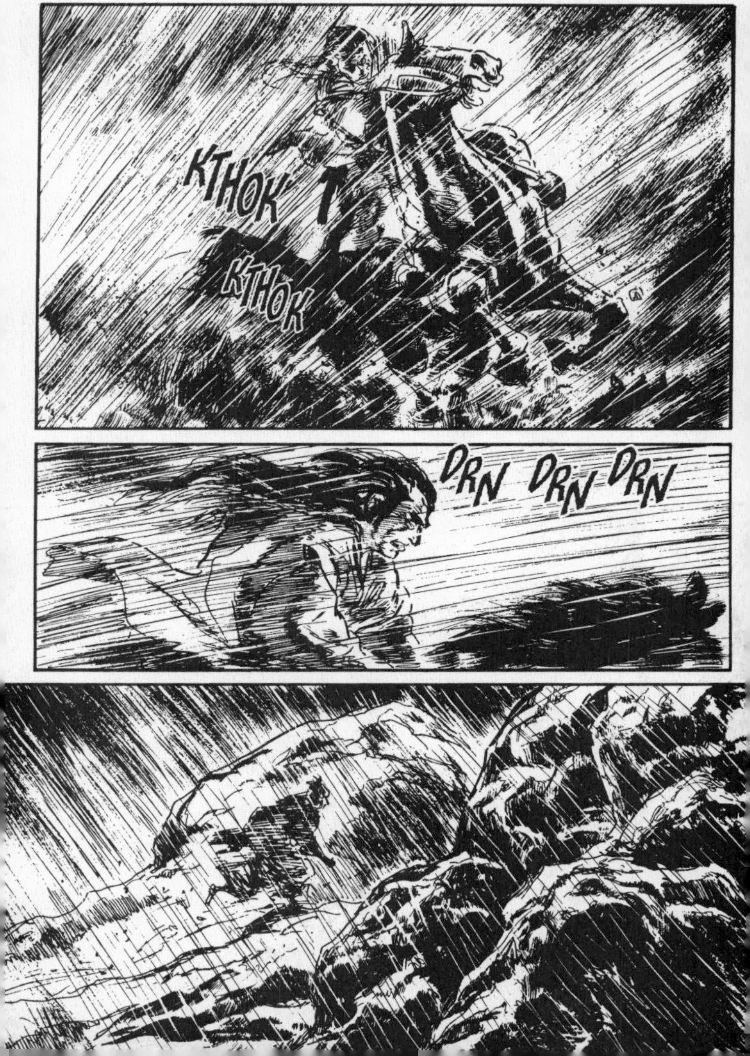
KTHOK
KTHOK
DRN DRN DRN

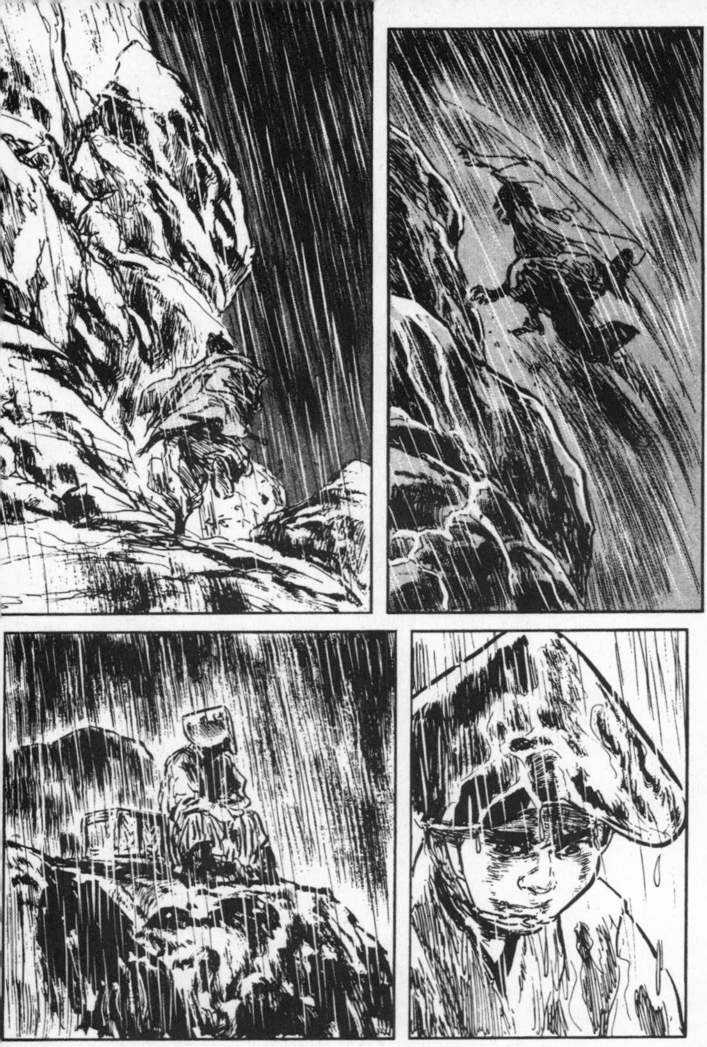

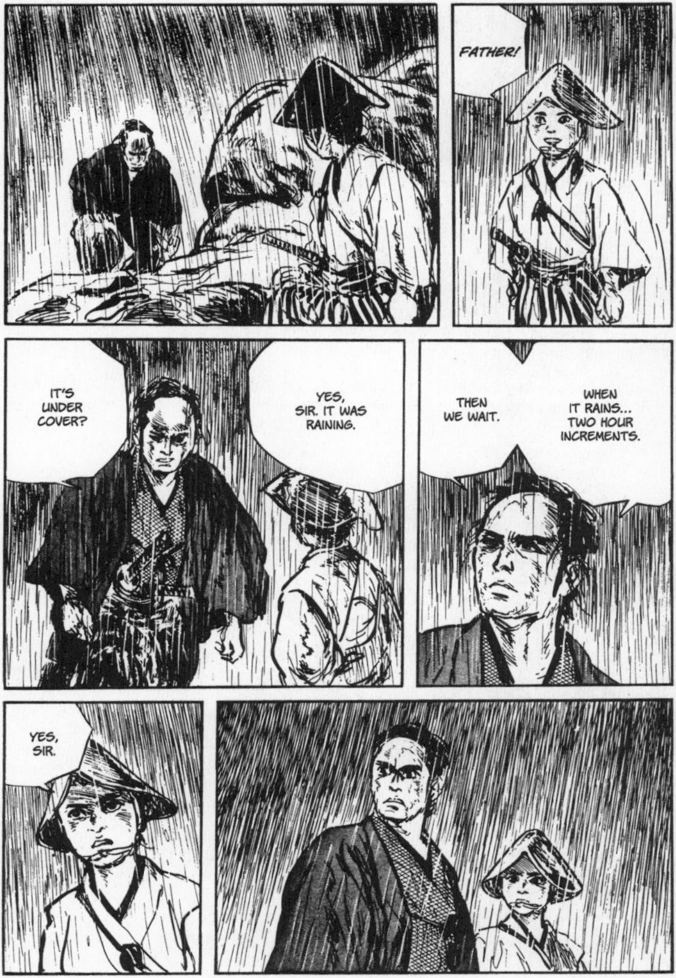
FATHER!
IT'S UNDER COVER?
YES, SIR. IT WAS RAINING.
THEN WE WAIT.
WHEN IT RAINS... TWO HOUR INCREMENTS.
YES, SIR.

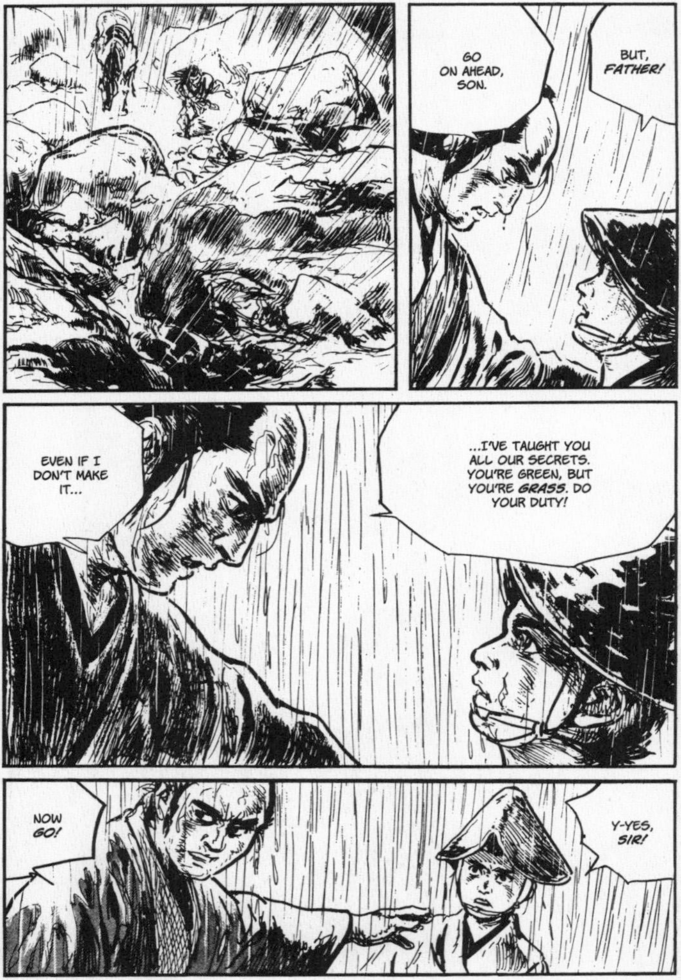
GO ON AHEAD, SON.
BUT, FATHER!
EVEN IF I DON'T MAKE IT...
...I'VE TAUGHT YOU ALL OUR SECRETS. YOU'RE GREEN, BUT YOU'RE GRASS. DO YOUR DUTY!
NOW GO!
Y-YES, SIR!

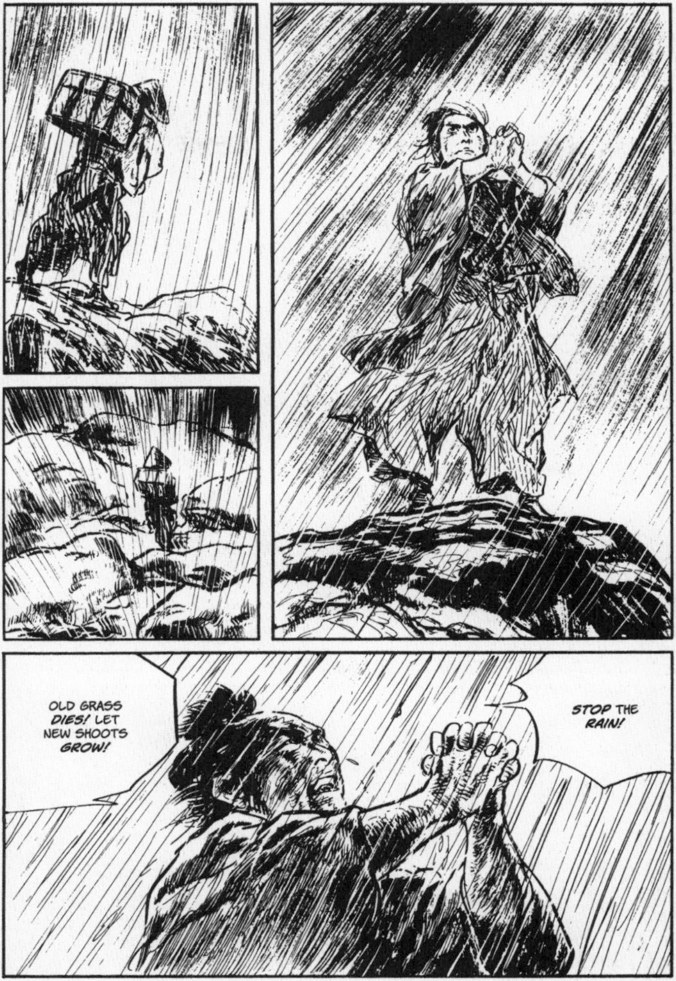
OLD GRASS DIES! LET NEW SHOOTS GROW!
STOP THE RAIN!

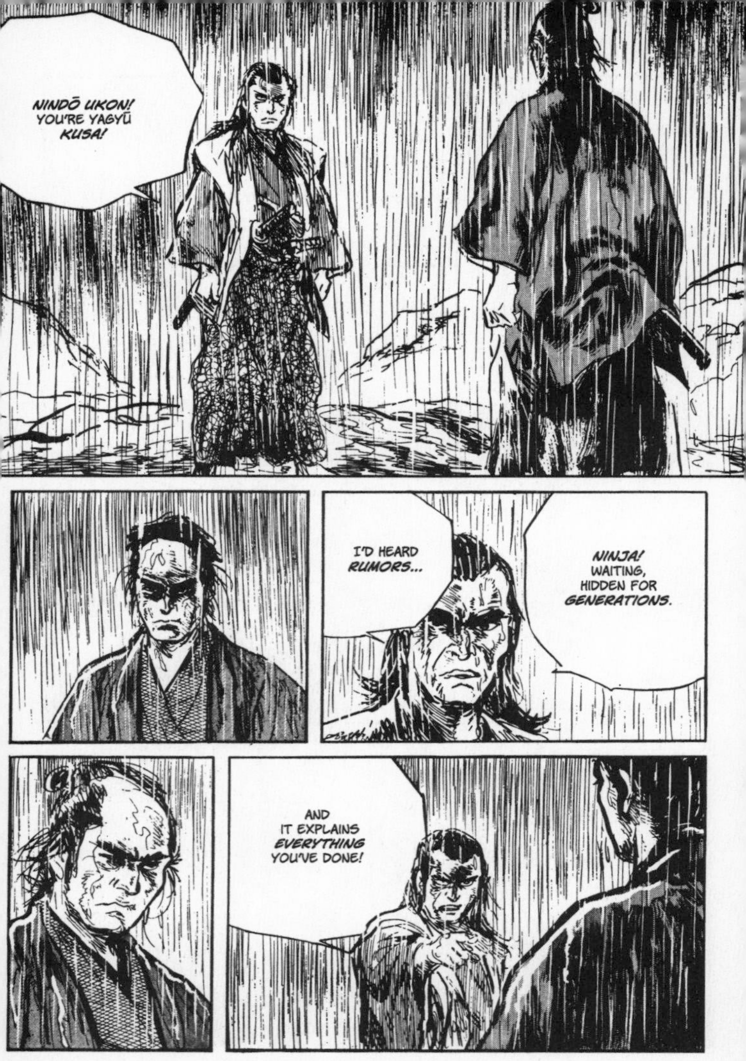

NINDŌ UKON! YOU'RE YAGYŪ KUSA!
I'D HEARD RUMORS...
NINJA! WAITING, HIDDEN FOR GENERATIONS.
AND IT EXPLAINS EVERYTHING YOU'VE DONE!

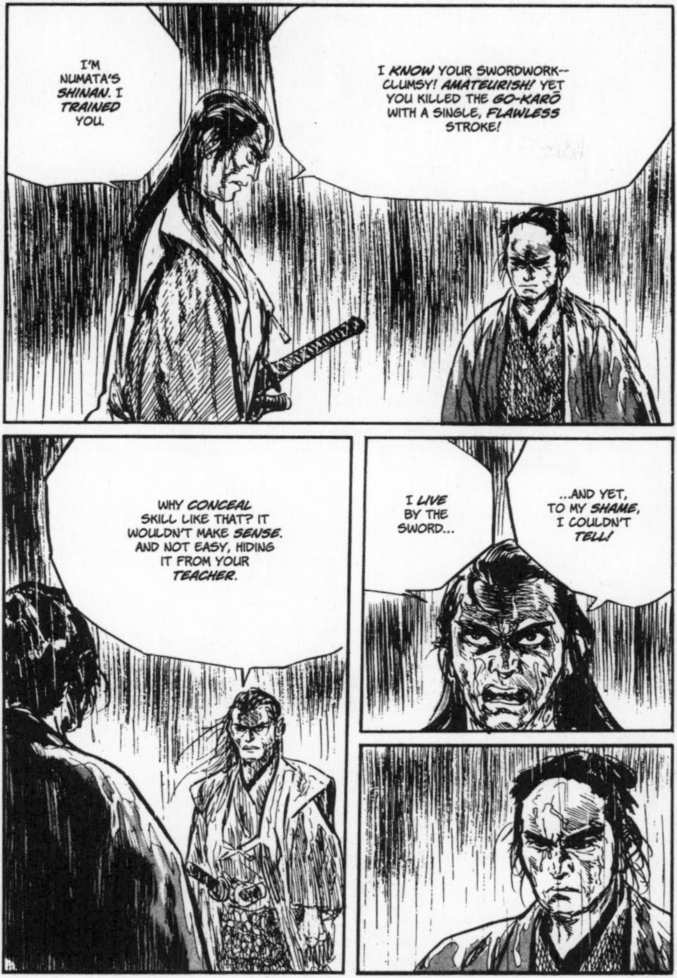
I'M NUMATA'S SHINAN. I TRAINED YOU.
I KNOW YOUR SWORDWORK-- CLUMSY! AMATEURISH! YET YOU KILLED THE GO-KARŌ WITH A SINGLE, FLAWLESS STROKE!
WHY CONCEAL SKILL LIKE THAT? IT WOULDN'T MAKE SENSE. AND NOT EASY, HIDING IT FROM YOUR TEACHER.
I LIVE BY THE SWORD...
...AND YET, TO MY SHAME, I COULDN'T TELL!

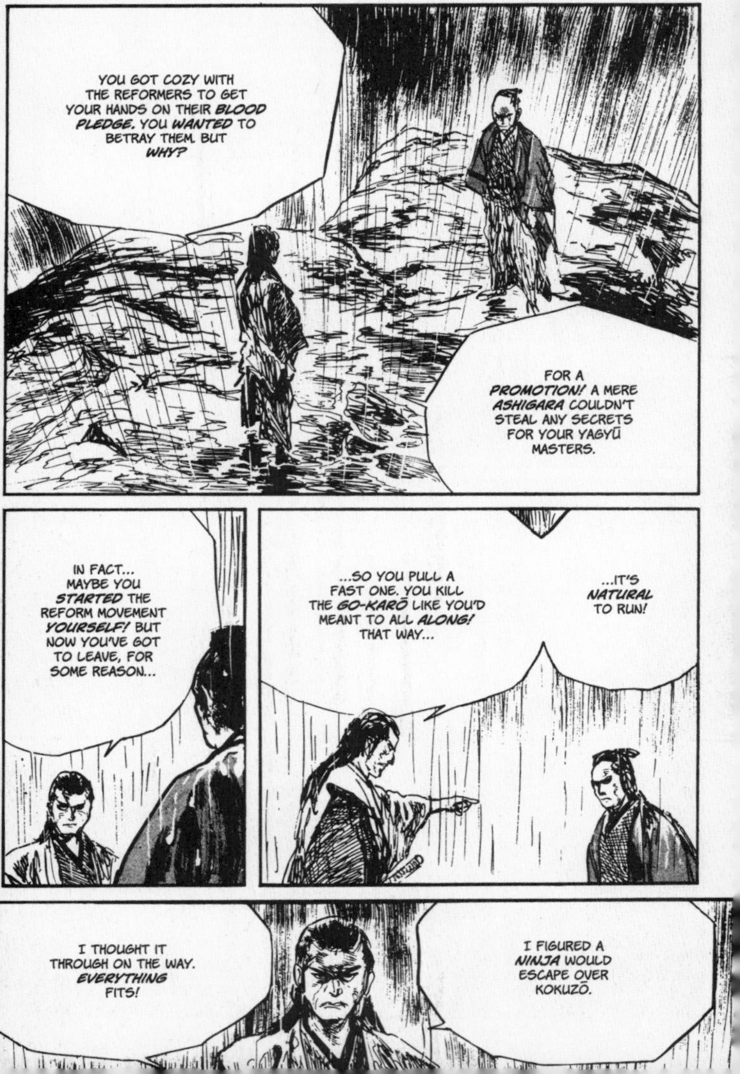
YOU GOT COZY WITH THE REFORMERS TO GET YOUR HANDS ON THEIR BLOOD PLEDGE. YOU WANTED TO BETRAY THEM. BUT WHY?
FOR A PROMOTION! A MERE ASHIGARA COULDN'T STEAL ANY SECRETS FOR YOUR YAGYŪ MASTERS.
IN FACT... MAYBE YOU STARTED THE REFORM MOVEMENT YOURSELF! BUT NOW YOU'VE GOT TO LEAVE, FOR SOME REASON...
...SO YOU PULL A FAST ONE. YOU KILL THE GO-KARŌ LIKE YOU'D MEANT TO ALL ALONG! THAT WAY...
...IT'S NATURAL TO RUN!
I THOUGHT IT THROUGH ON THE WAY. EVERYTHING FITS!
I FIGURED A NINJA WOULD ESCAPE OVER KOKUZŌ.

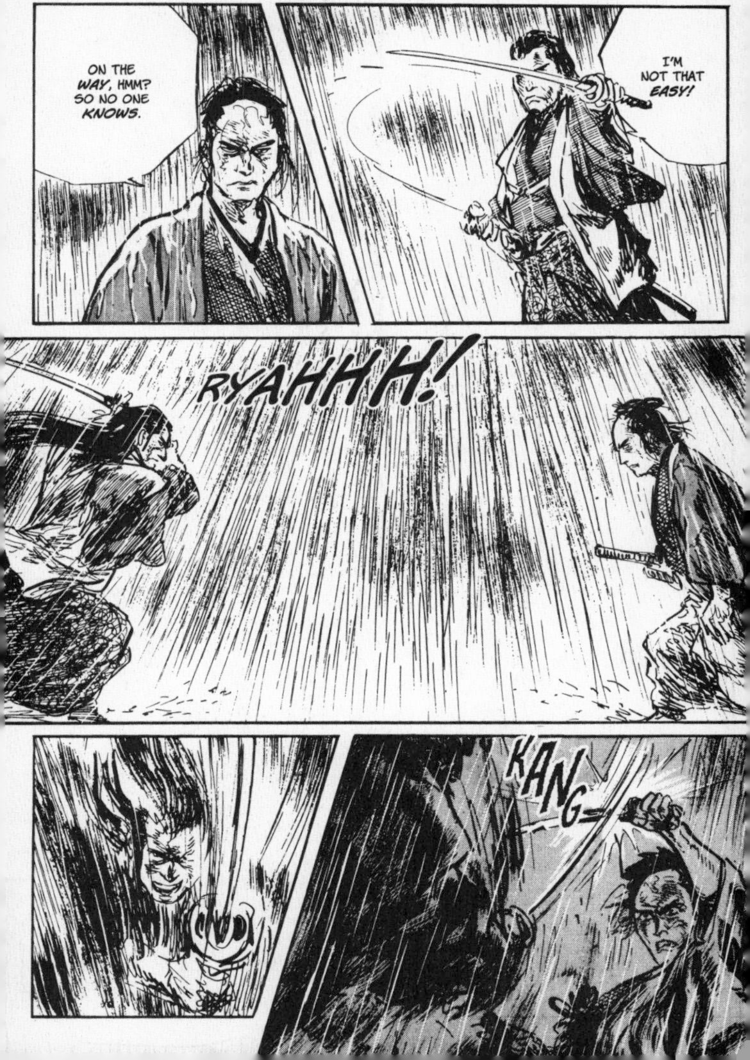
ON THE WAY, HMM? SO NO ONE KNOWS.
I'M NOT THAT EASY!
RYAHHHH!
KANG

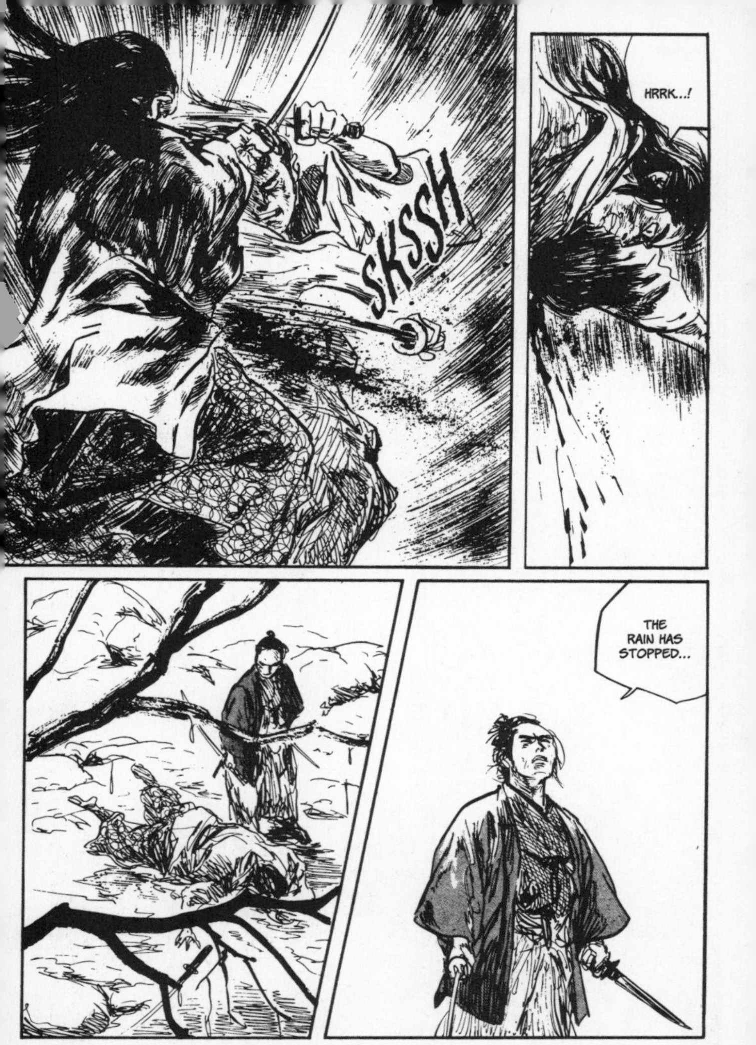
SKSSH
HRRK...!
THE RAIN HAS STOPPED...

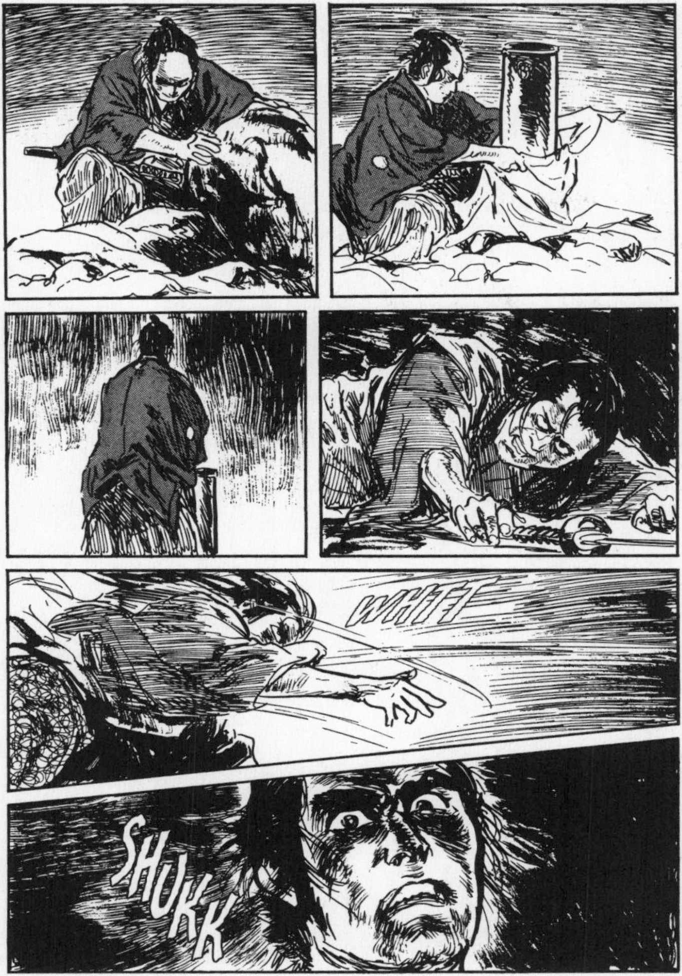
WHIT
SHUKK

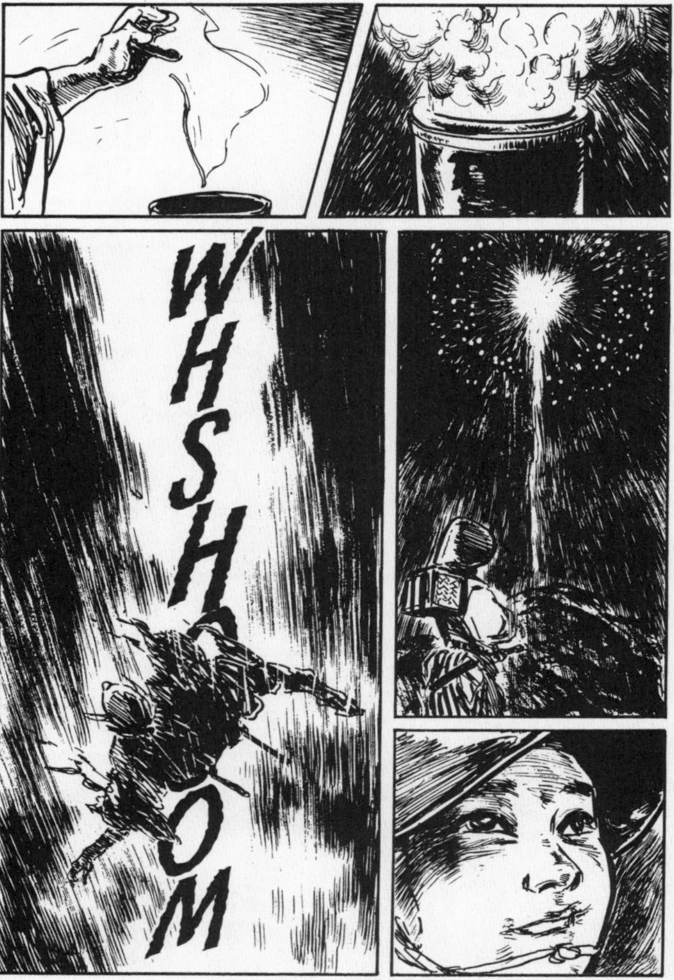
WHSHOOM

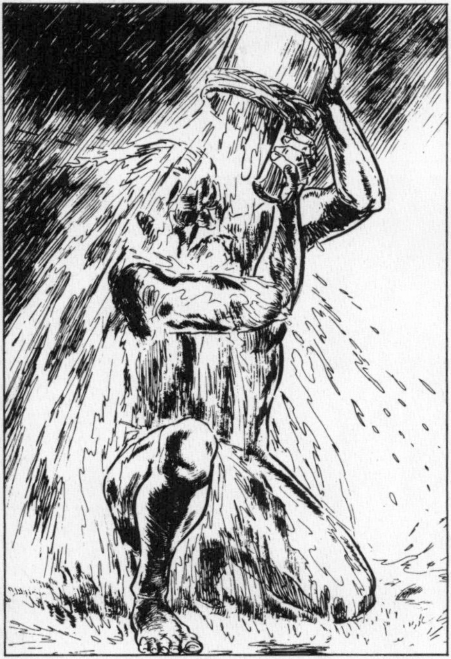

the hundred and
twenty-ninth

Struggle in the Dark

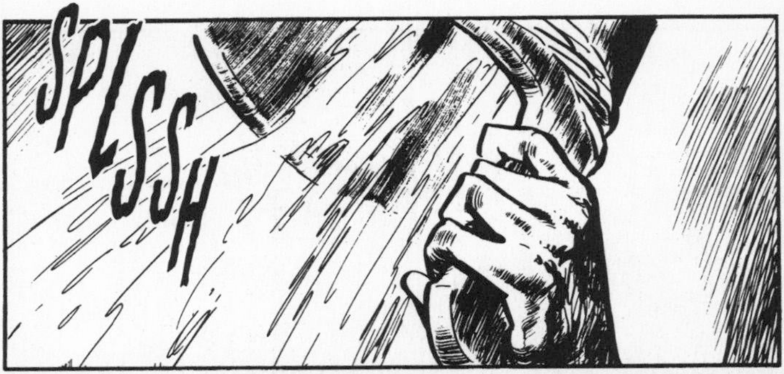
SPLSSH
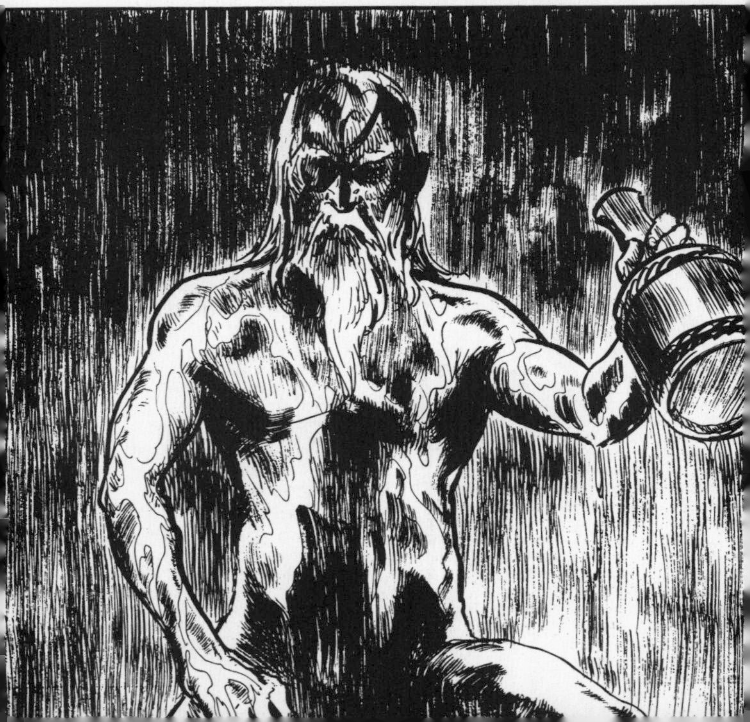

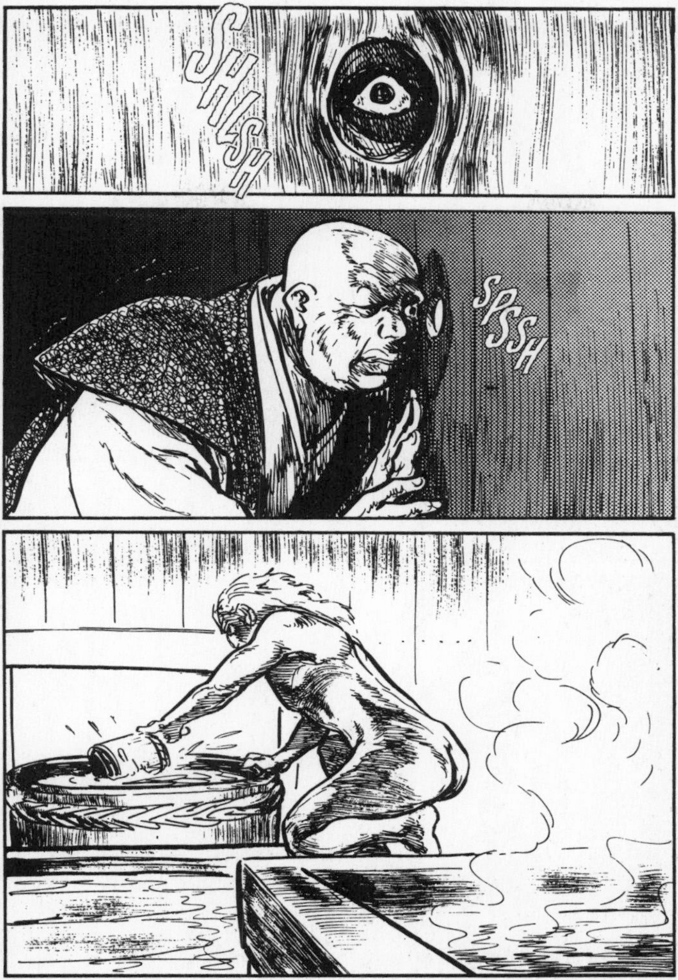
SHLSH
SPSSH

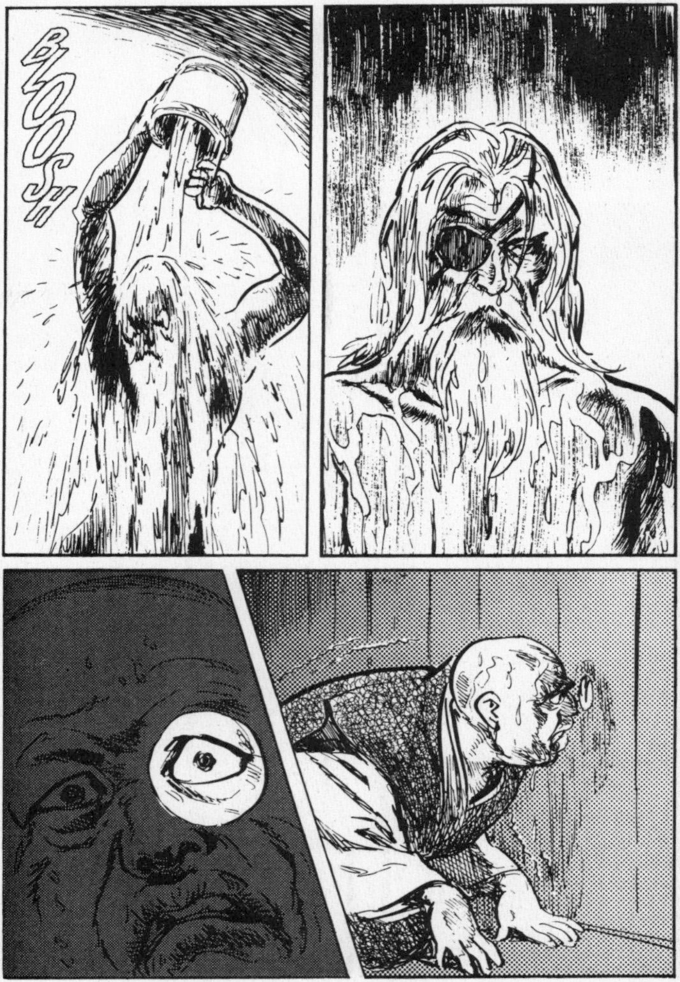
BLOOSH

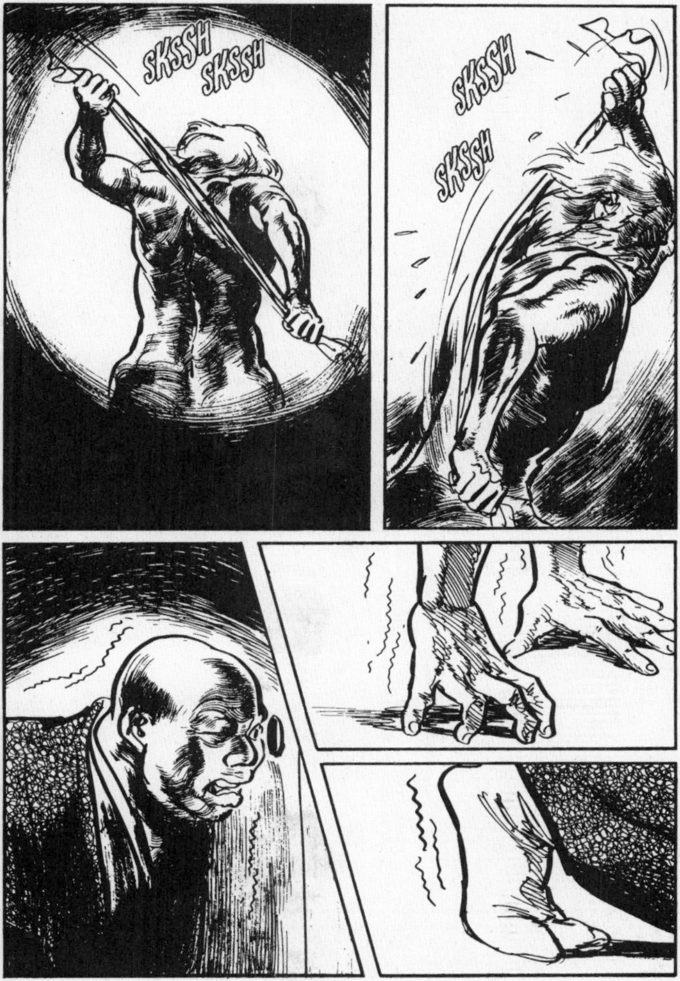
SKSSH
SKSSH
SKSSH
SKSSH

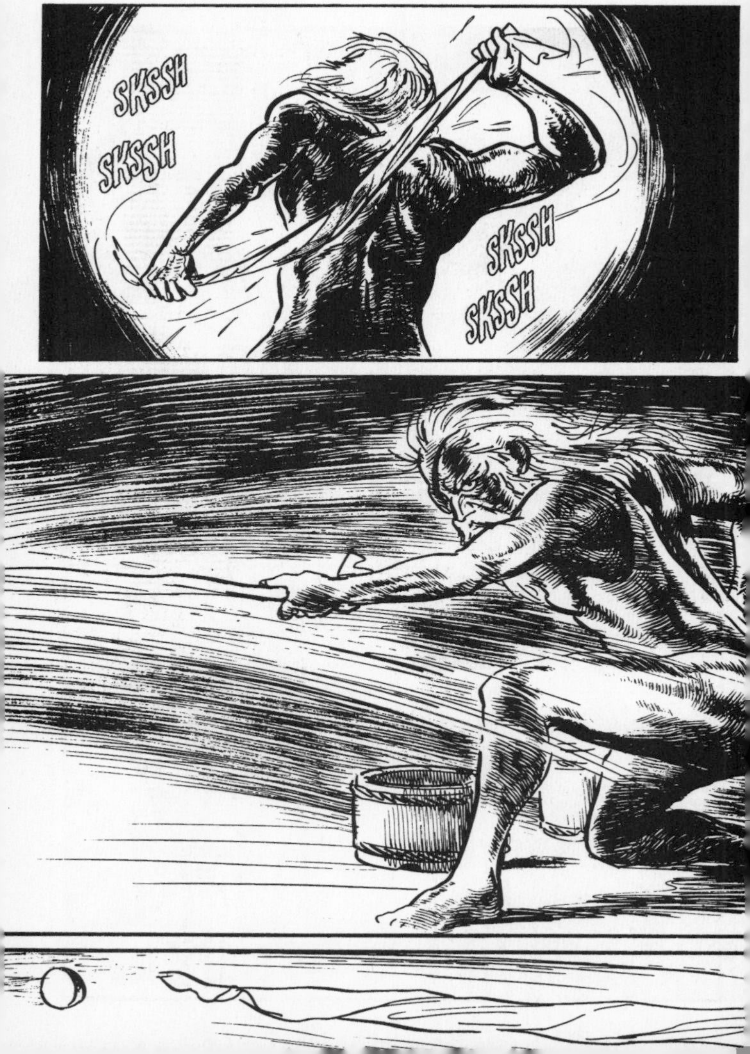
SKSSH
SKSSH
SKSSH
SKSSH

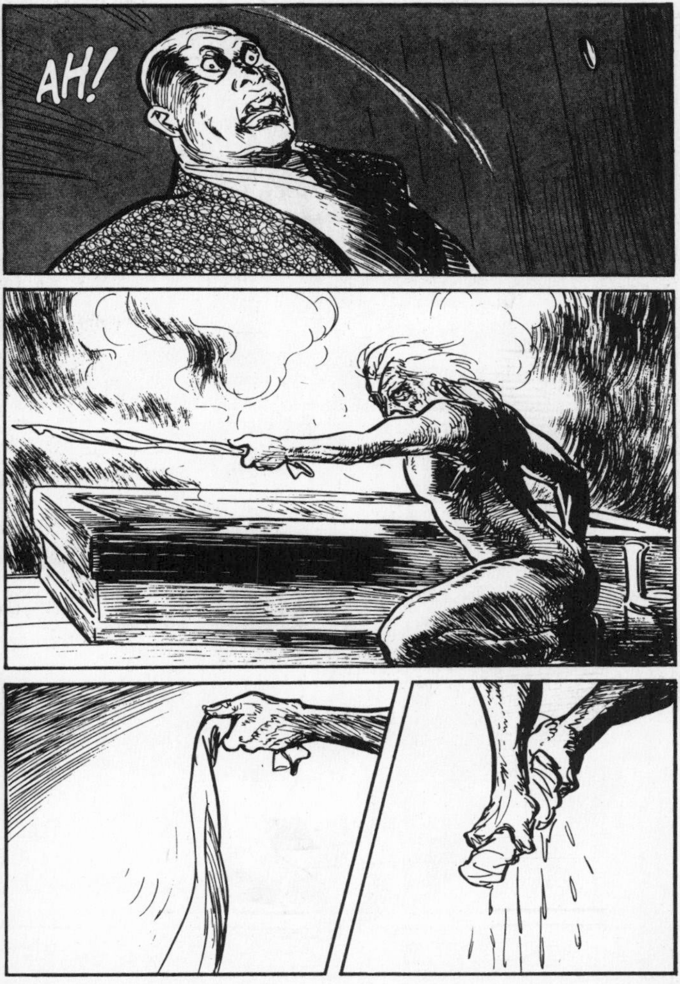
AH!

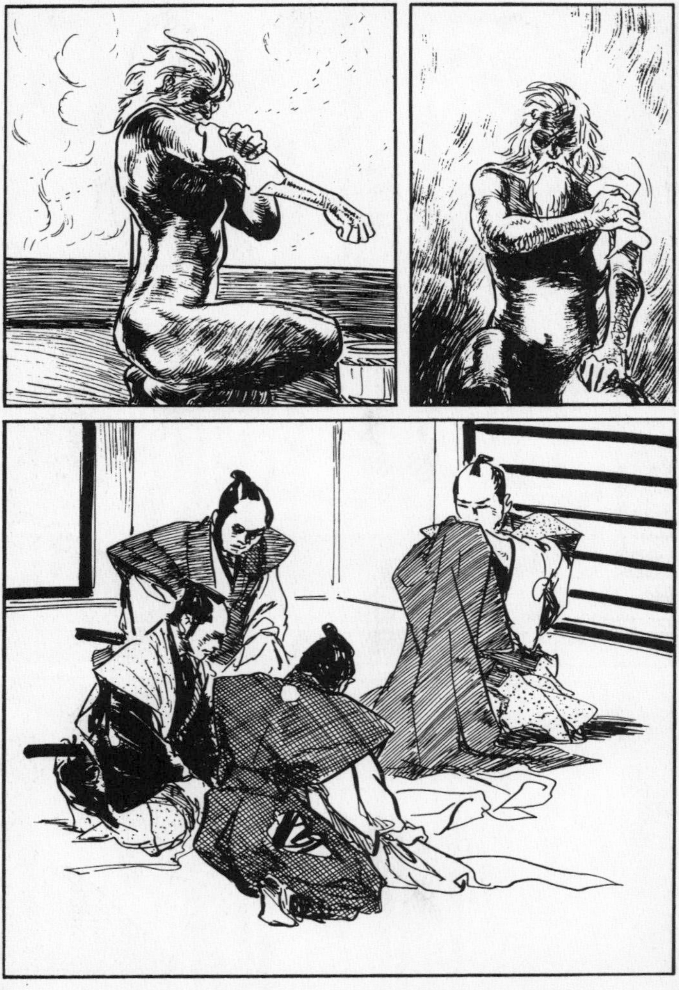

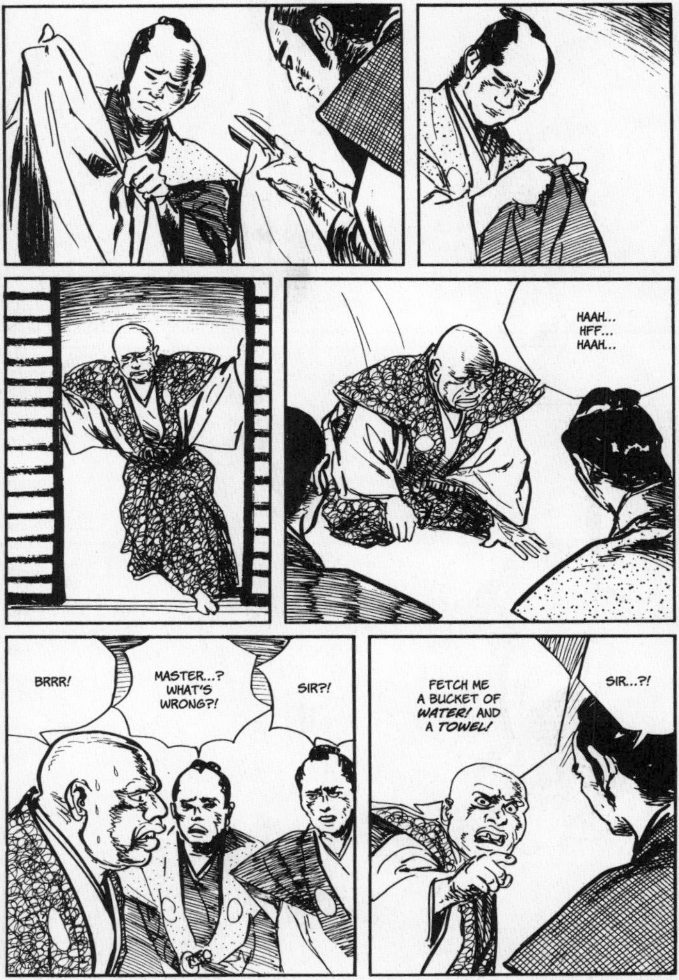
HAAH... HFF... HAAH...
BRRR!
MASTER...? WHAT'S WRONG?!
SIR?!
FETCH ME A BUCKET OF WATER! AND A TOWEL!
SIR...?!

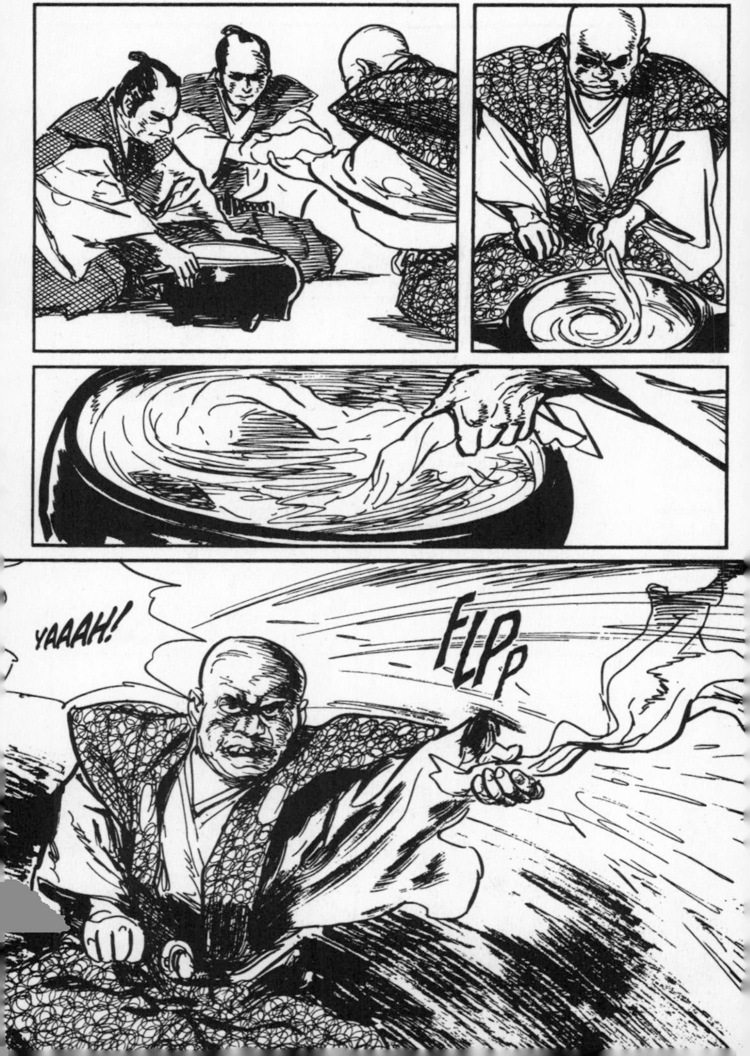
YAAAH!
FLPP

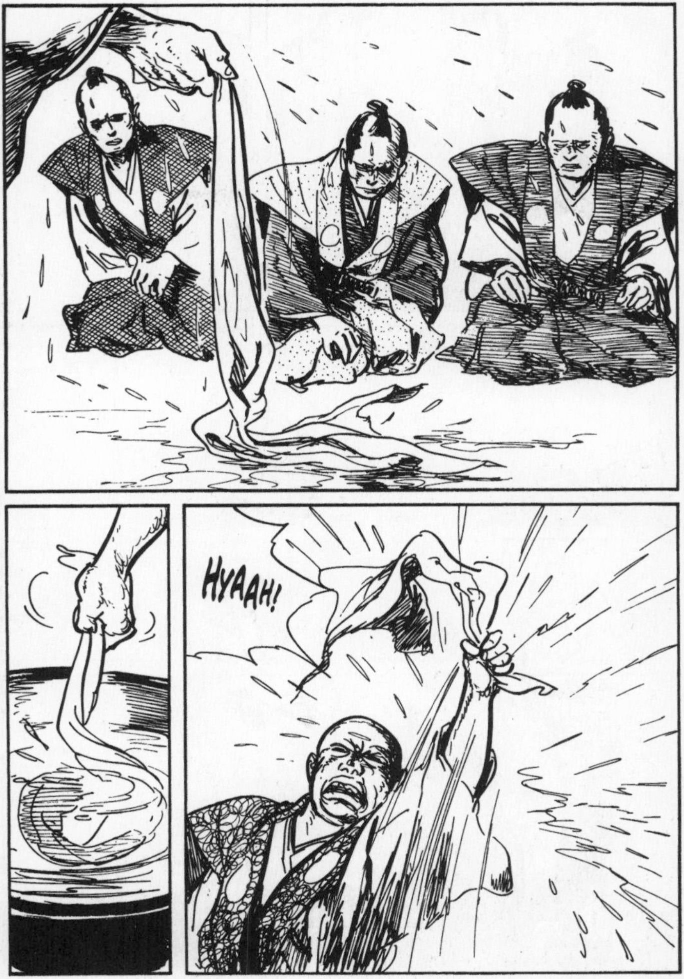
HYAAH!

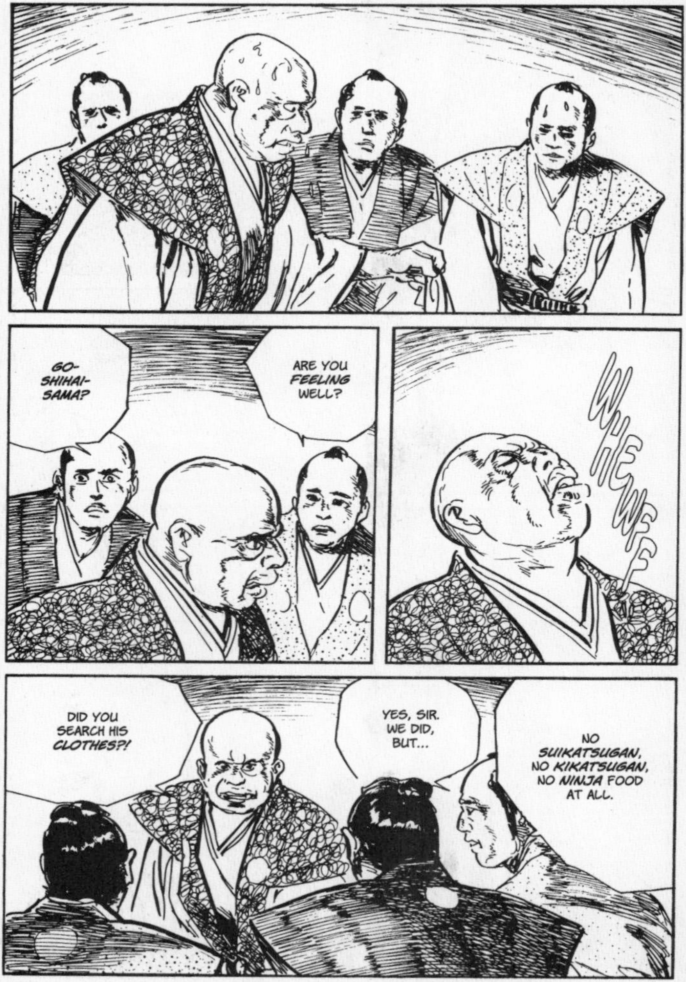
GO-SHIHAI-SAMA?
ARE YOU FEELING WELL?
WHEW
DID YOU SEARCH HIS CLOTHES?!
YES, SIR. WE DID, BUT...
NO SUIKATSUGAN, NO KIKATSUGAN, NO NINJA FOOD AT ALL.

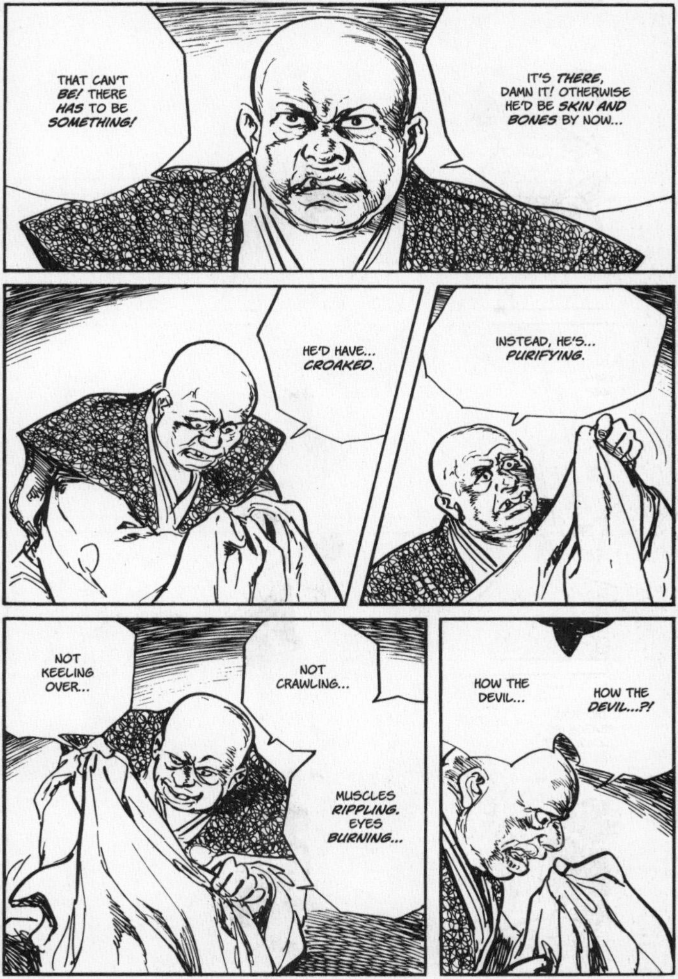
THAT CAN'T BE! THERE HAS TO BE SOMETHING!
IT'S THERE, DAMN IT! OTHERWISE HE'D BE SKIN AND BONES BY NOW...
HE'D HAVE... CROAKED.
INSTEAD, HE'S... PURIFYING.
NOT KEELING OVER...
NOT CRAWLING...
MUSCLES RIPPLING. EYES BURNING...
HOW THE DEVIL...
HOW THE DEVIL...?!

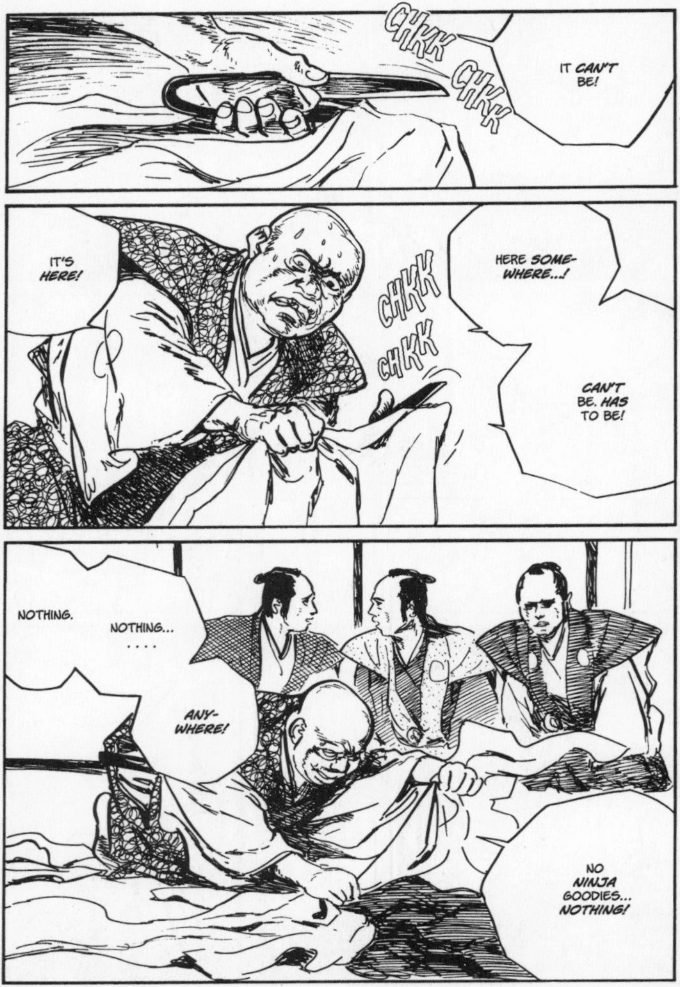
CHKK
CHKK
IT *CAN'T* BE!
IT'S *HERE!*
HERE *SOME-WHERE...!*
CHKK
CHKK
CAN'T BE. *HAS* TO BE!
NOTHING.
NOTHING...
....
ANY-WHERE!
NO *NINJA* GOODIES... *NOTHING!*

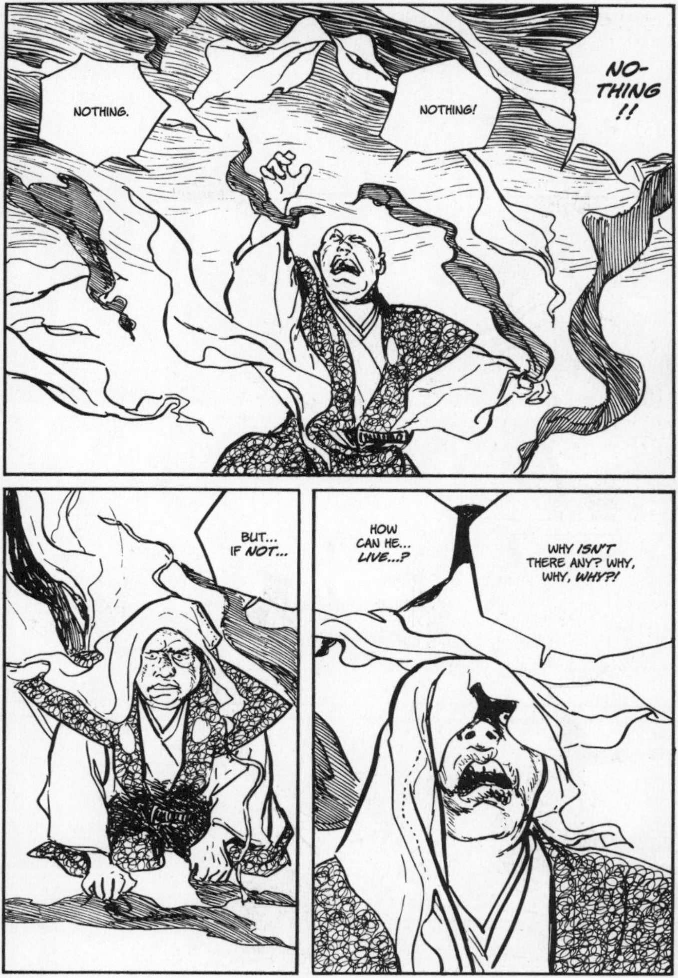
NOTHING.
NOTHING!
NO-THING!!
BUT... IF NOT...
HOW CAN HE... LIVE...?
WHY ISN'T THERE ANY? WHY, WHY, WHY?!

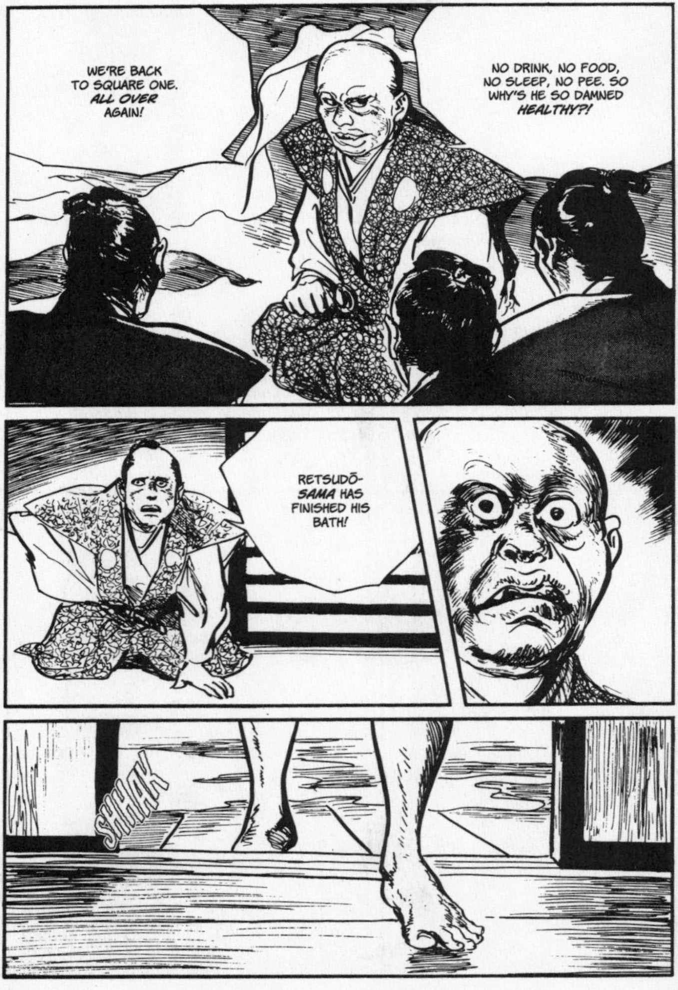
WE'RE BACK TO SQUARE ONE. ALL OVER AGAIN!
NO DRINK, NO FOOD, NO SLEEP, NO PEE. SO WHY'S HE SO DAMNED HEALTHY?!
RETSUDŌ-SAMA HAS FINISHED HIS BATH!
SHHAK

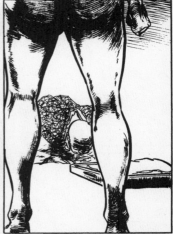

RETSUDŌ-
SAMA. I HAD
YOU PURIFY FOR
OUR LORD'S
PILGRIMAGE TO
TŌSHŌGU,
BUT...

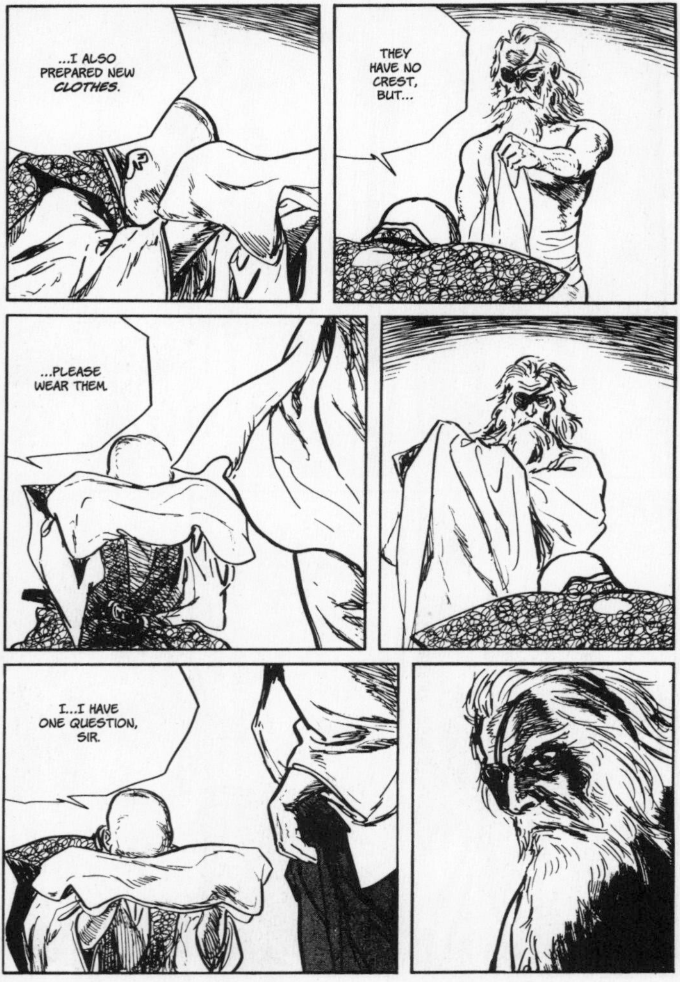
...I ALSO PREPARED NEW *CLOTHES*.
THEY HAVE NO CREST, BUT...
...PLEASE WEAR THEM.
I...I HAVE ONE QUESTION, SIR.

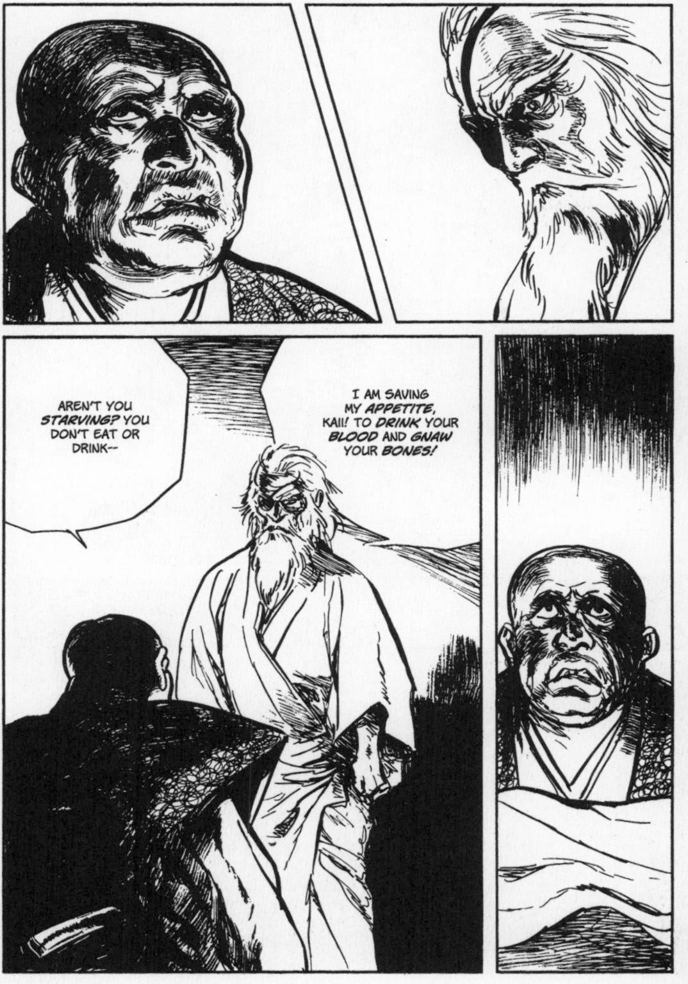
AREN'T YOU STARVING? YOU DON'T EAT OR DRINK--
I AM SAVING MY APPETITE, KAII! TO DRINK YOUR BLOOD AND GNAW YOUR BONES!

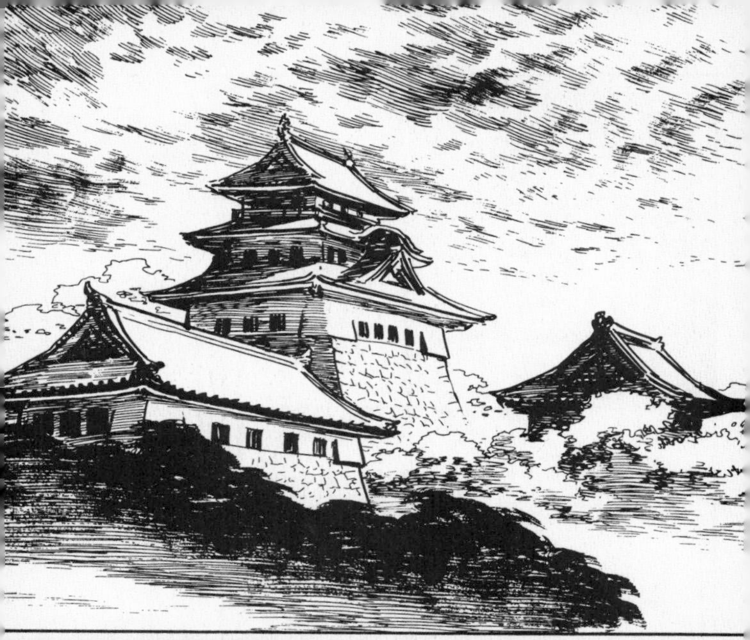

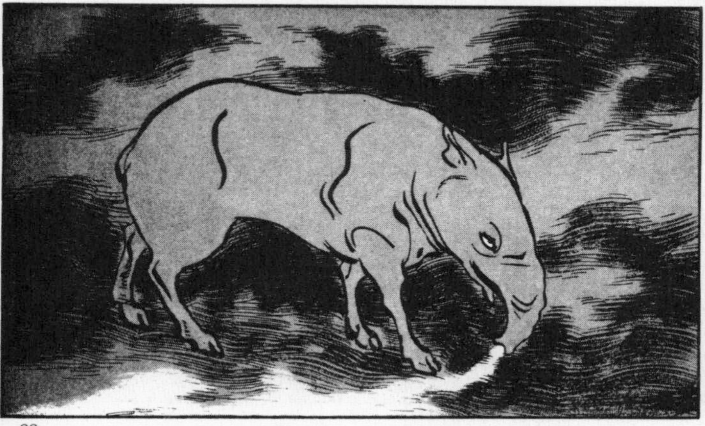

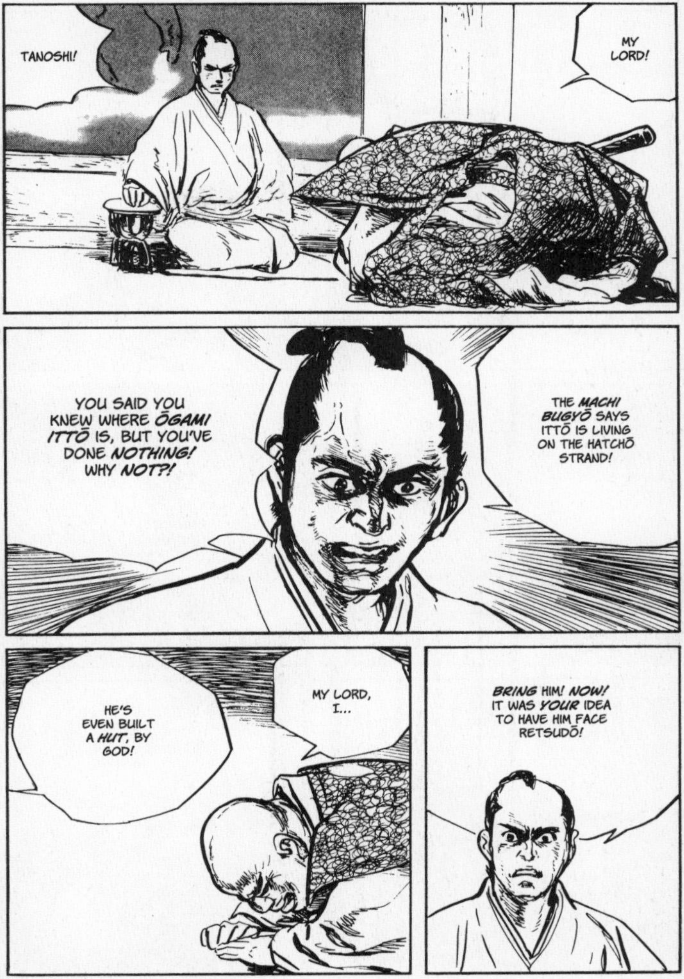
TANOSHI!
MY LORD!
YOU SAID YOU KNEW WHERE ŌGAMI ITTŌ IS, BUT YOU'VE DONE NOTHING! WHY NOT?!
THE MACHI BUGYŌ SAYS ITTŌ IS LIVING ON THE HATCHŌ STRAND!
HE'S EVEN BUILT A HUT, BY GOD!
MY LORD, I...
BRING HIM! NOW! IT WAS YOUR IDEA TO HAVE HIM FACE RETSUDŌ!

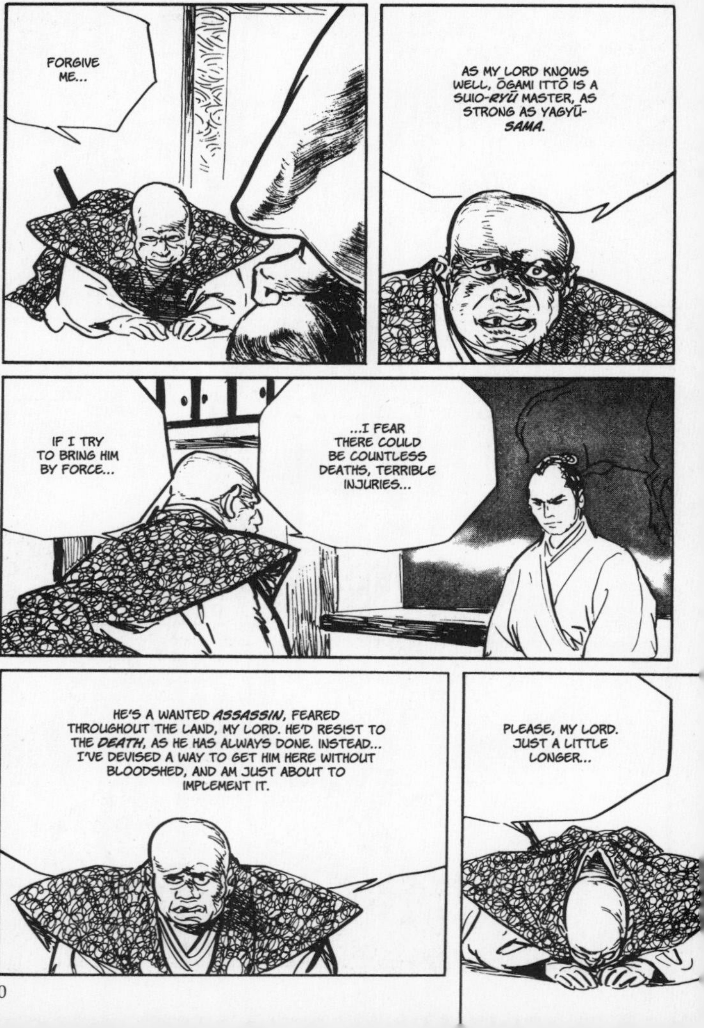

FORGIVE ME...
AS MY LORD KNOWS WELL, ŌGAMI ITTŌ IS A SUIO-*RYŪ* MASTER, AS STRONG AS YAGYŪ-*SAMA*.
IF I TRY TO BRING HIM BY FORCE...
...I FEAR THERE COULD BE COUNTLESS DEATHS, TERRIBLE INJURIES...
HE'S A WANTED *ASSASSIN*, FEARED THROUGHOUT THE LAND, MY LORD. HE'D RESIST TO THE *DEATH*, AS HE HAS ALWAYS DONE. INSTEAD... I'VE DEVISED A WAY TO GET HIM HERE WITHOUT BLOODSHED, AND AM JUST ABOUT TO IMPLEMENT IT.
PLEASE, MY LORD. JUST A LITTLE LONGER...

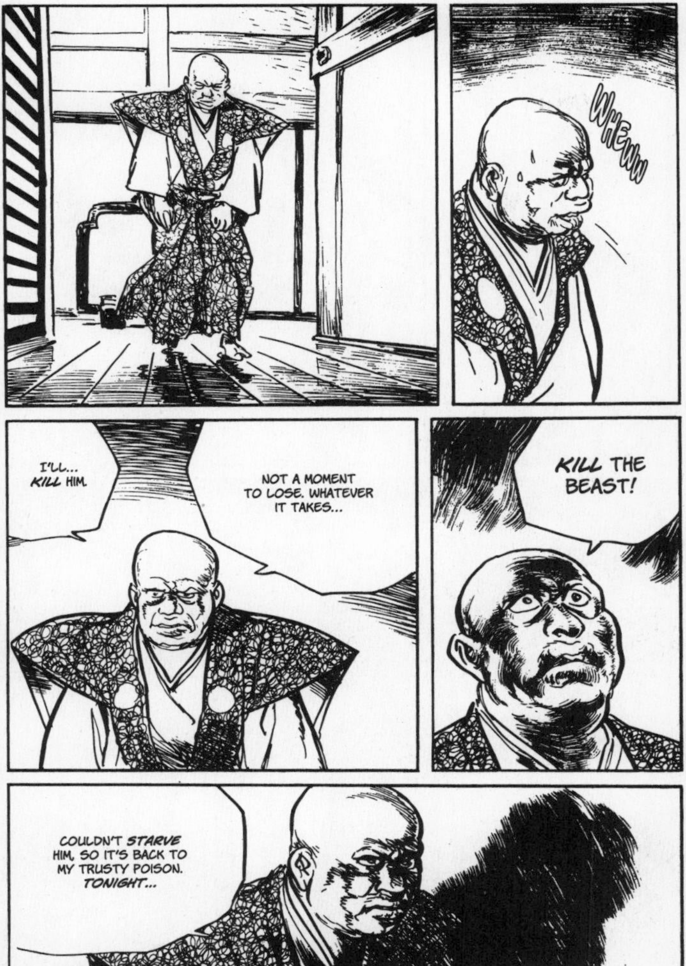
WHEWW
I'LL... KILL HIM.
NOT A MOMENT TO LOSE. WHATEVER IT TAKES...
KILL THE BEAST!
COULDN'T STARVE HIM, SO IT'S BACK TO MY TRUSTY POISON. TONIGHT...

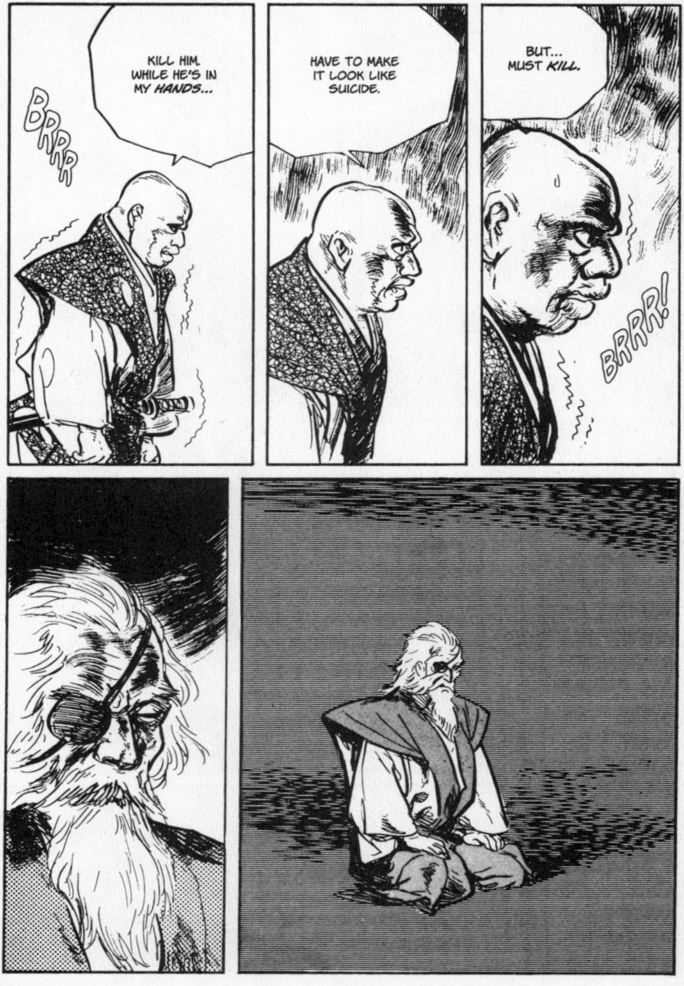
BRRR
KILL HIM. WHILE HE'S IN MY *HANDS...*
HAVE TO MAKE IT LOOK LIKE SUICIDE.
BUT... MUST *KILL.*
BRRR!

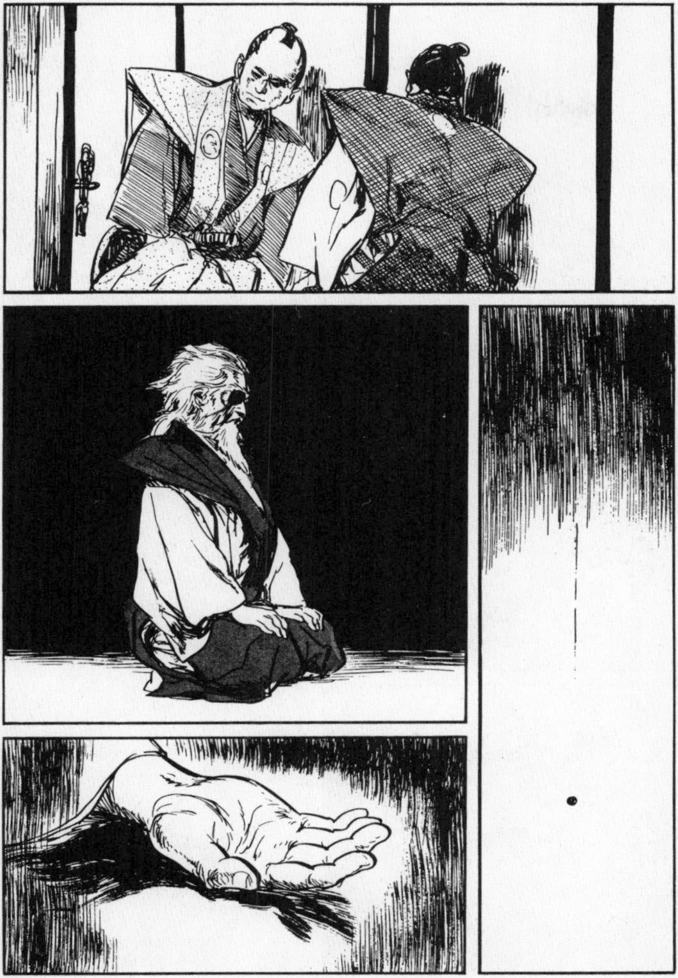

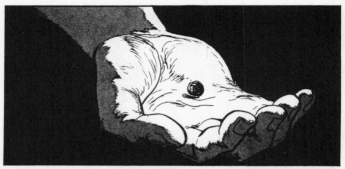

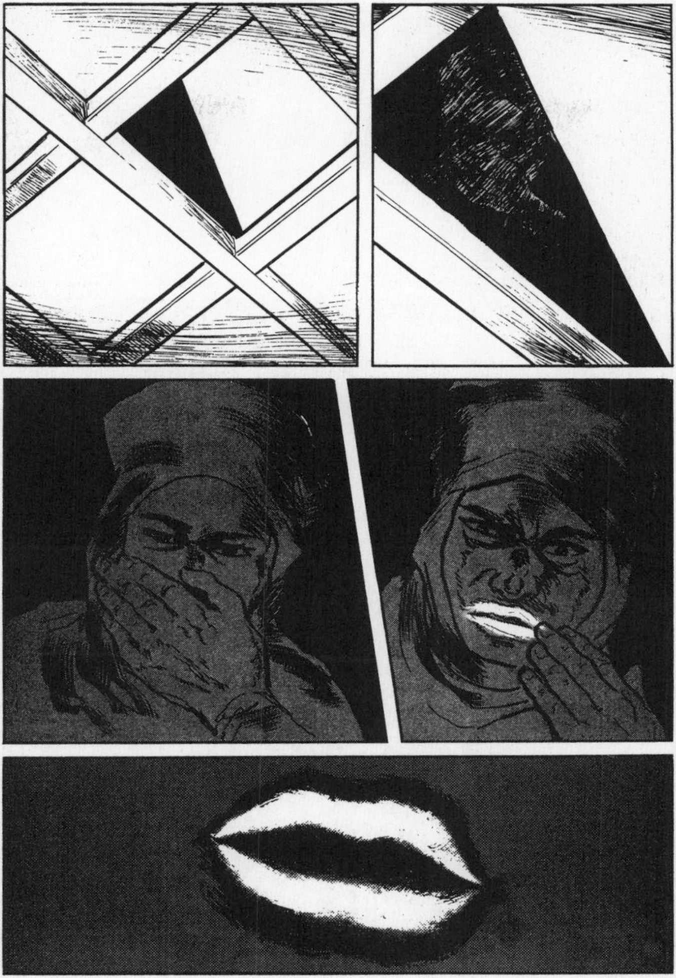

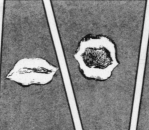

"ABE...
QUESTIONED...
IN SHŌGUN'S
CHAMBER...

"OUTCOME...

"HE
RESOLVES
TO MURDER
RETSUDŌ-
SAMA...

"WITH
POISON.
TONIGHT.

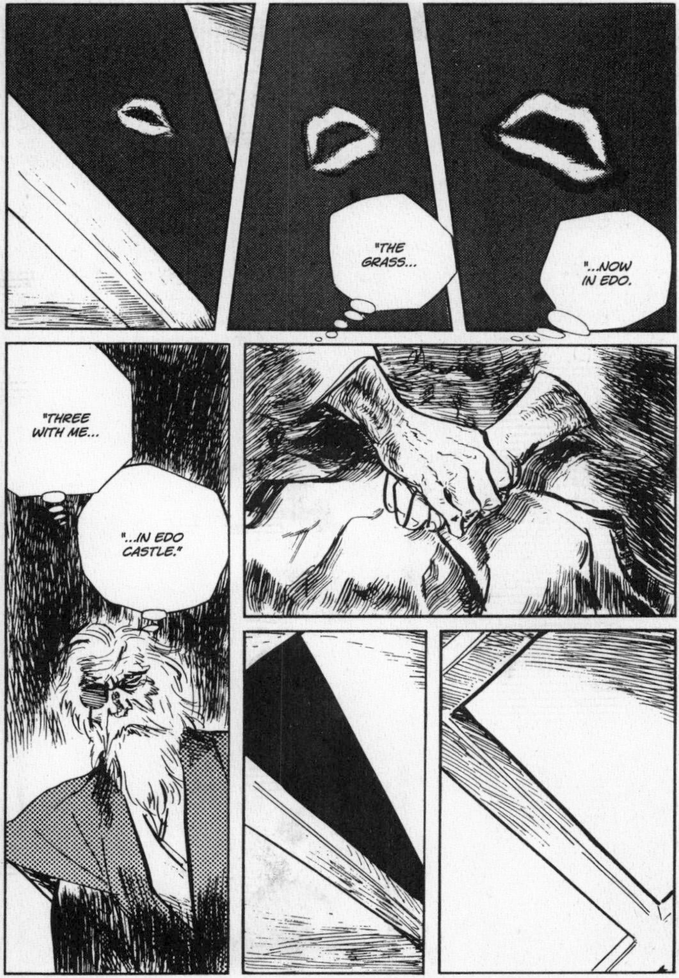
"THE GRASS...
"...NOW IN EDO.
"THREE WITH ME...
"...IN EDO CASTLE."

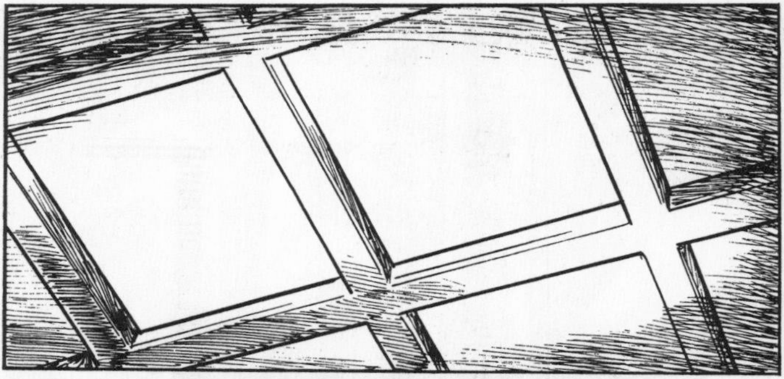

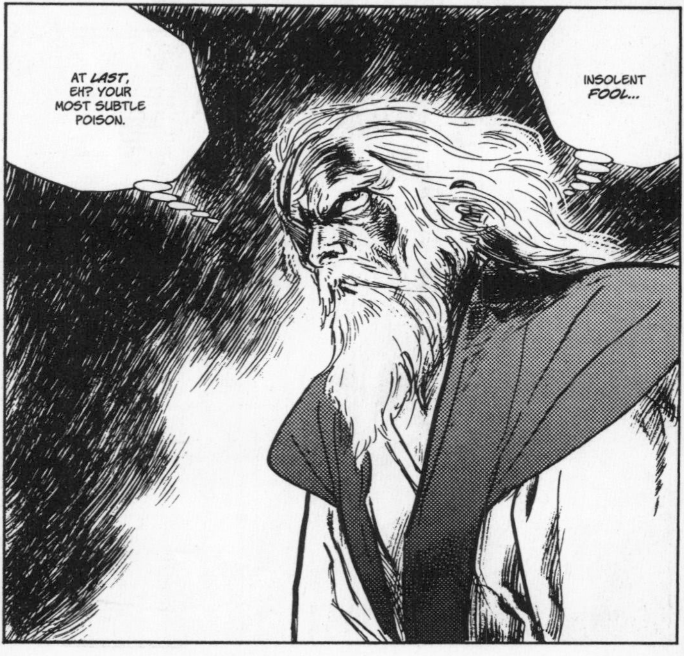
AT *LAST*, EH? YOUR MOST SUBTLE POISON.
INSOLENT *FOOL...*

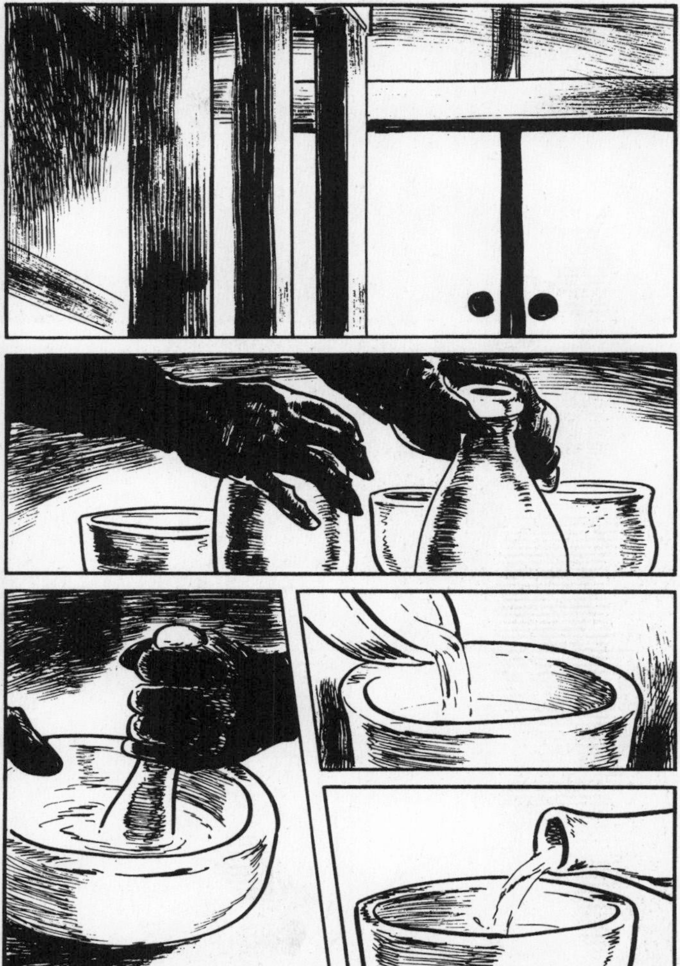

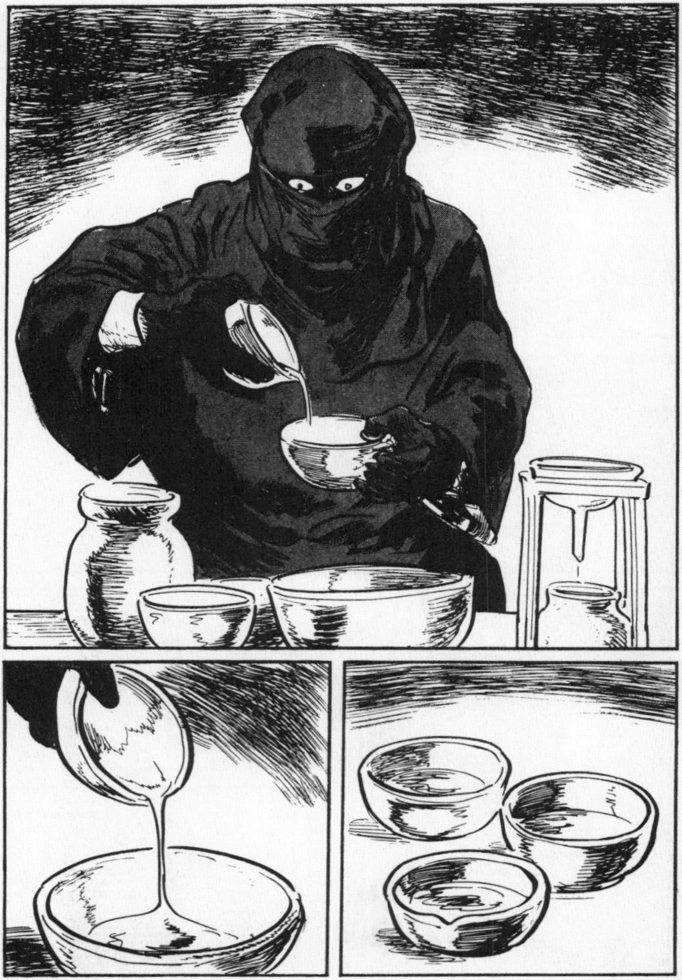

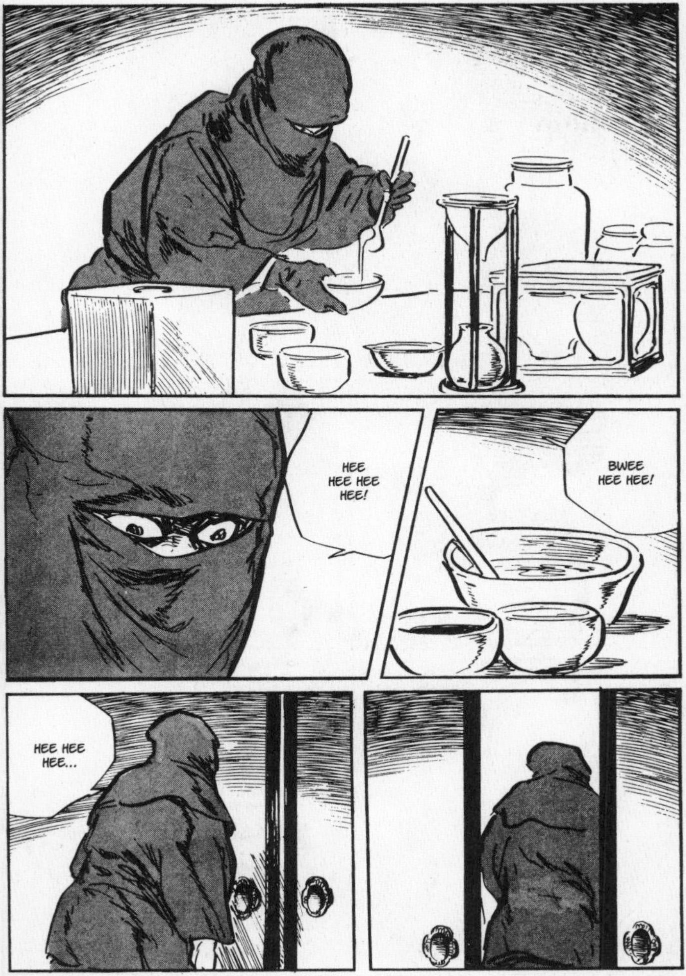
HEE HEE HEE HEE!
BWEE HEE HEE!
HEE HEE HEE...

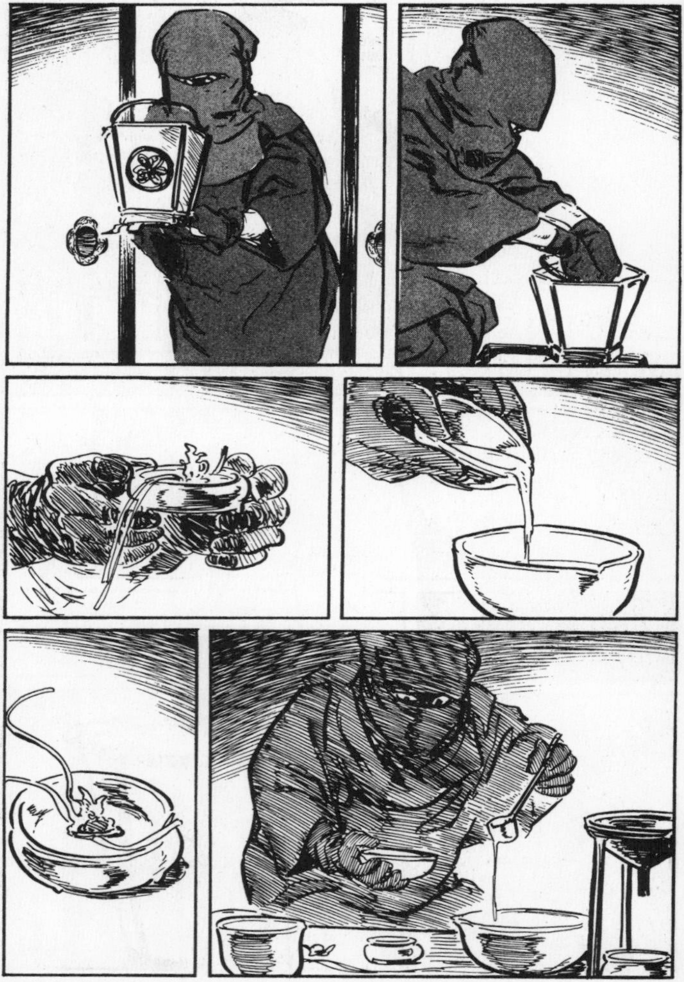

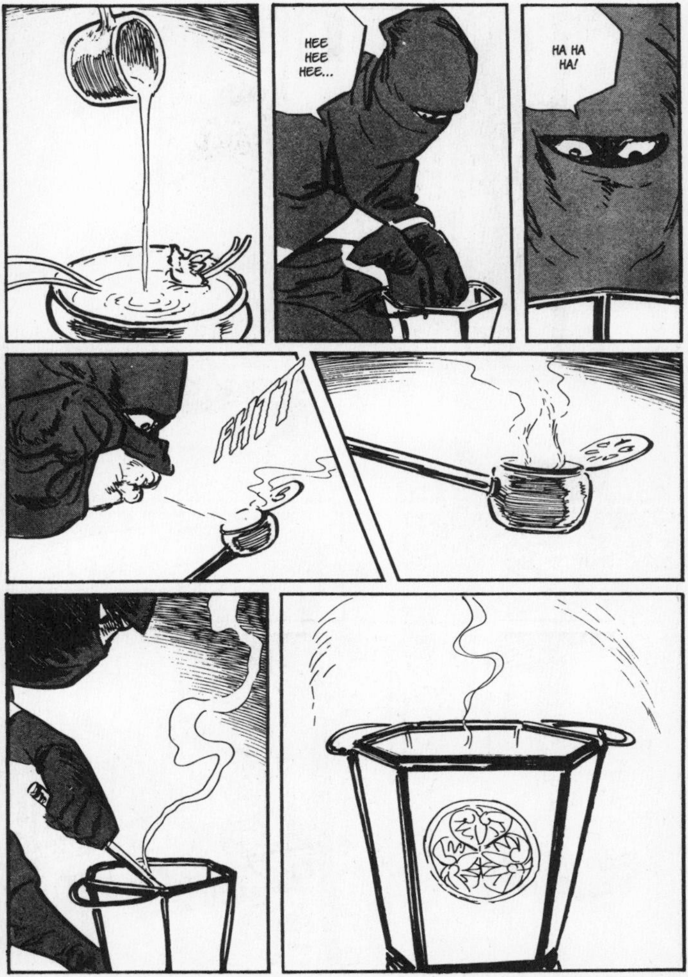
HEE
HEE
HEE...
HA HA
HA!
FHTT

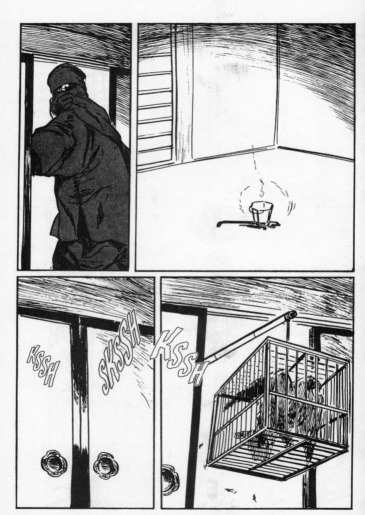

KSSH

SKSSH

KSSH

104

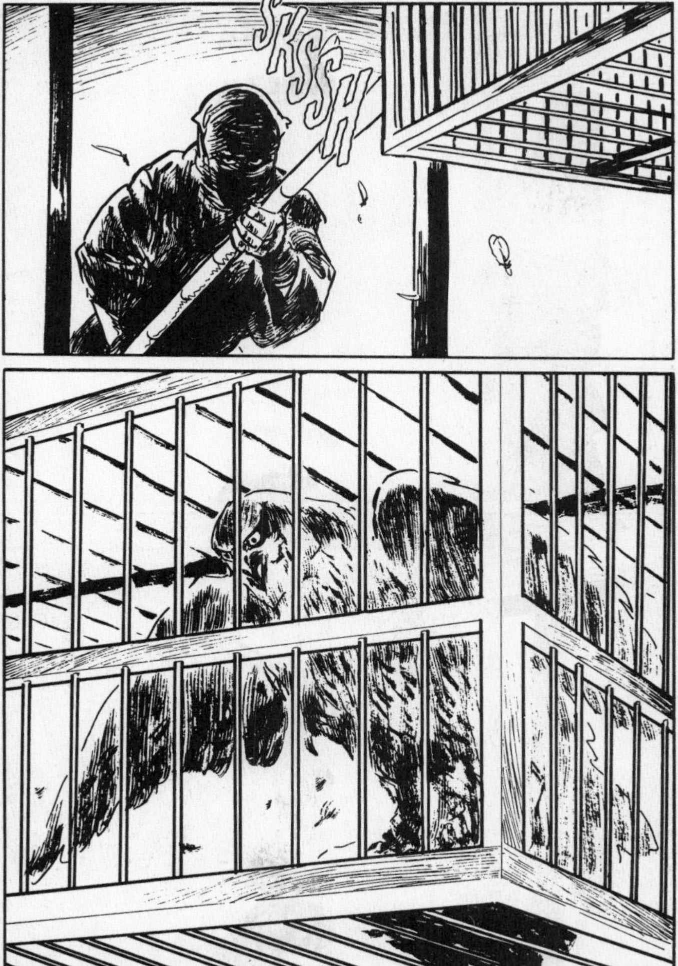
SKSSH

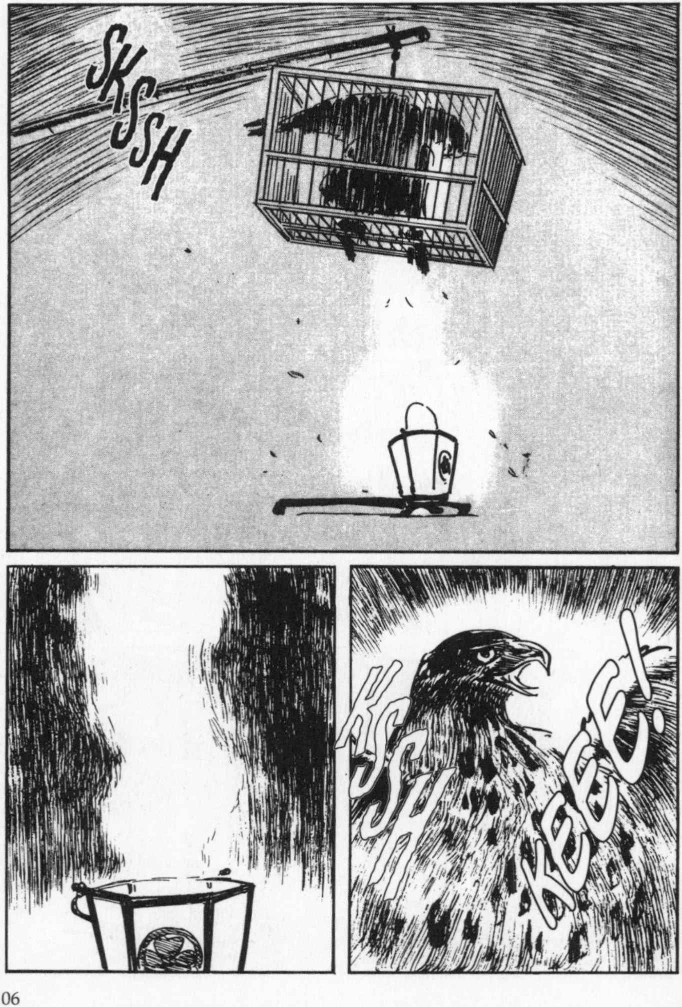
SKSSH
KSSH
KEEE!

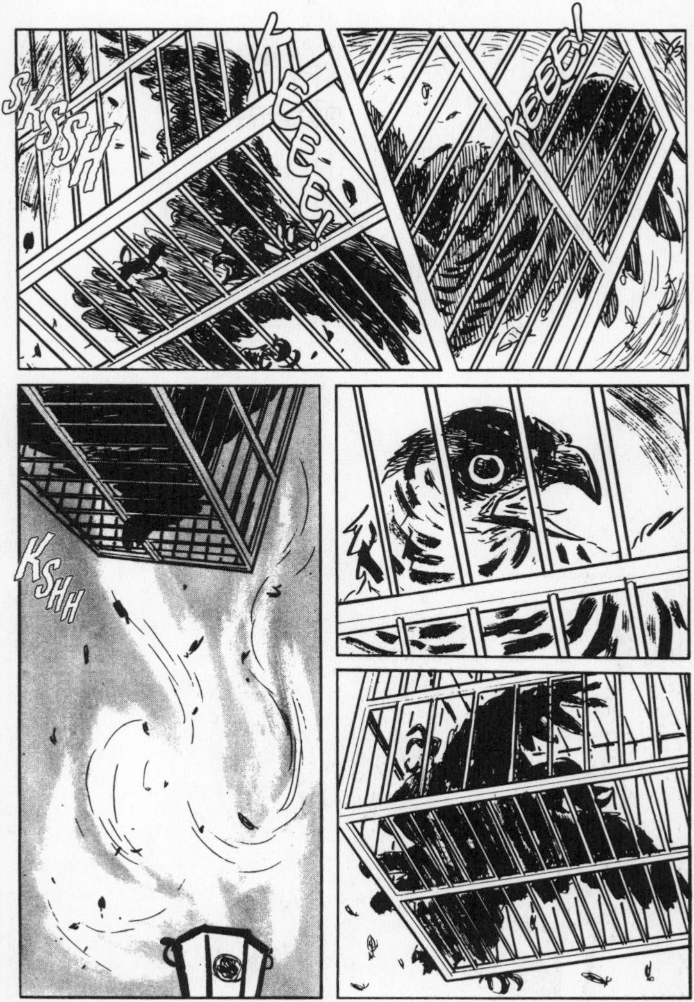
SKSSH
KEEEE!
KEEEE!
KSHH

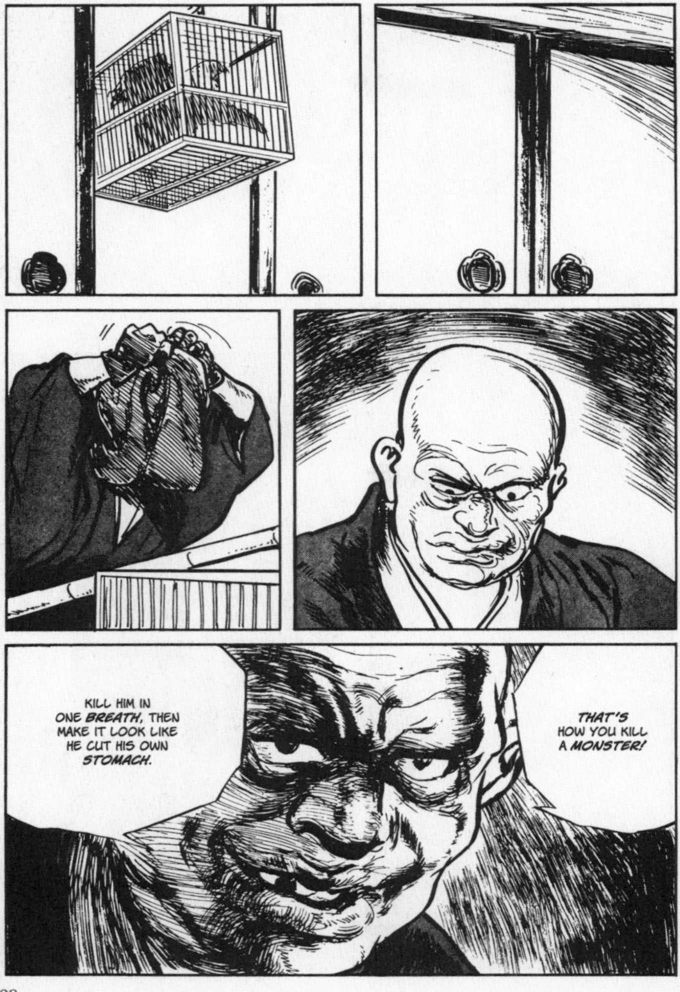
KILL HIM IN ONE BREATH, THEN MAKE IT LOOK LIKE HE CUT HIS OWN STOMACH.
THAT'S HOW YOU KILL A MONSTER!

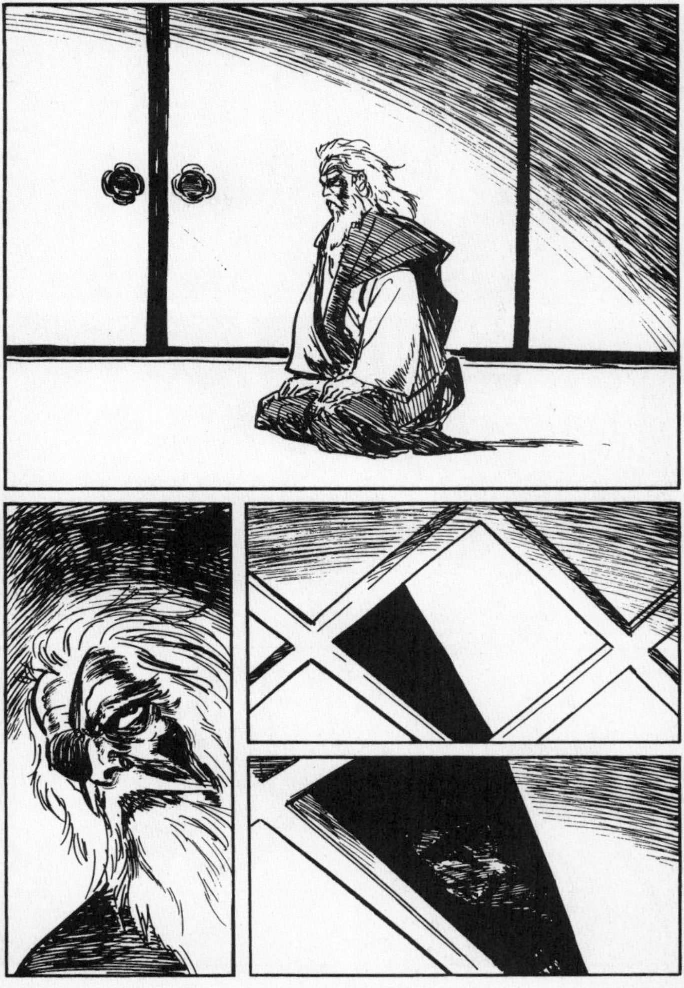

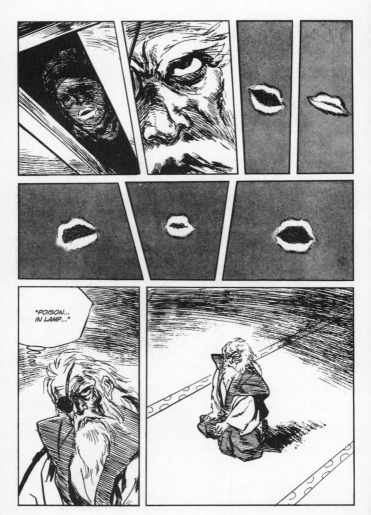

"POISON...
IN LAMP..."

110

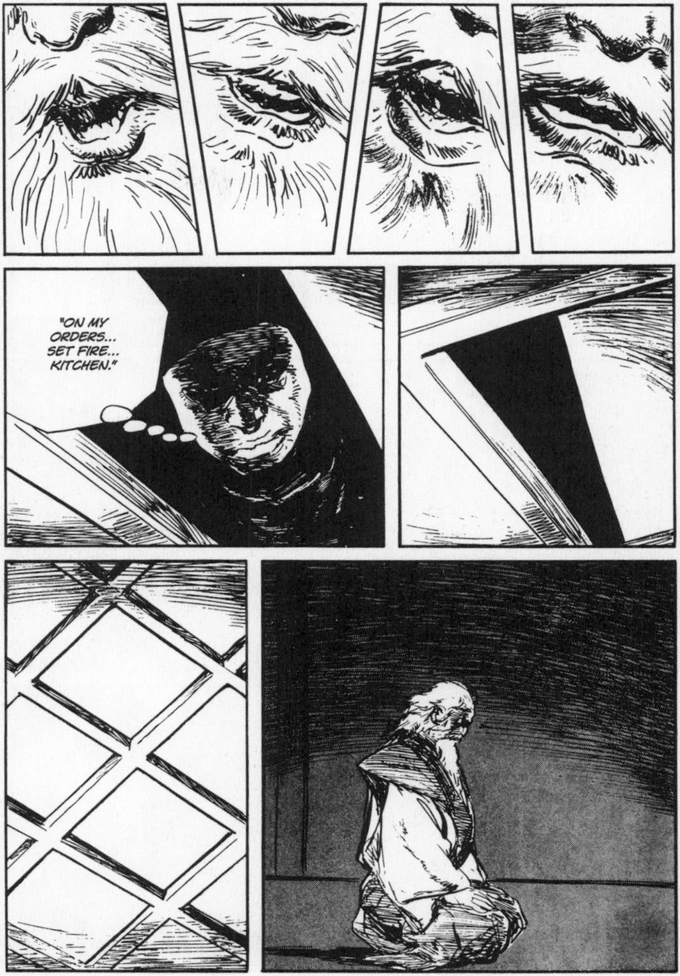
"ON MY ORDERS... SET FIRE... KITCHEN."

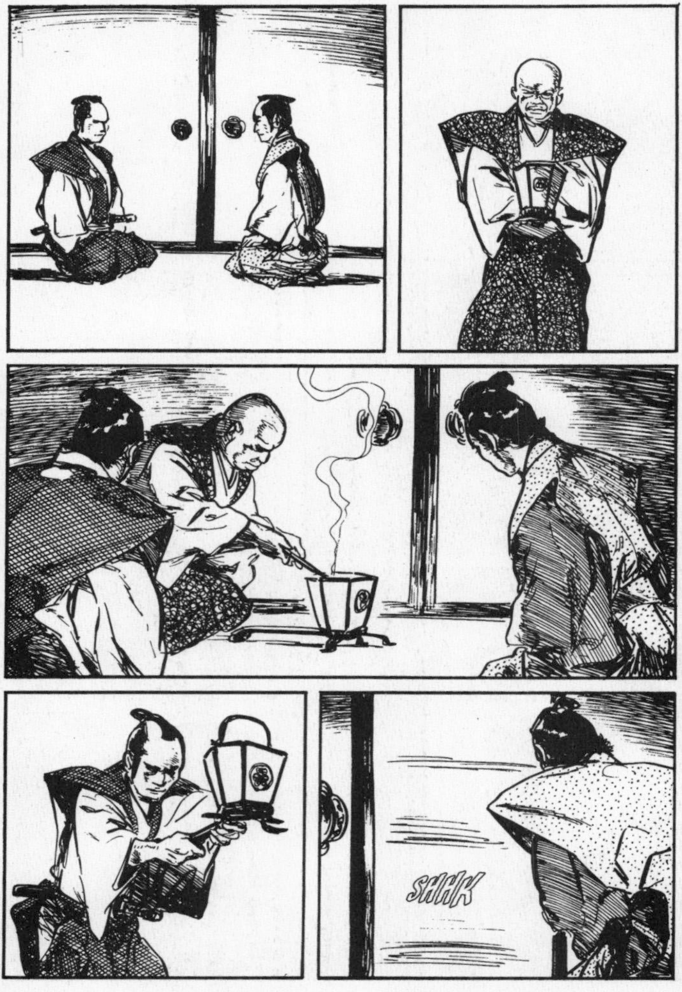
SHHK

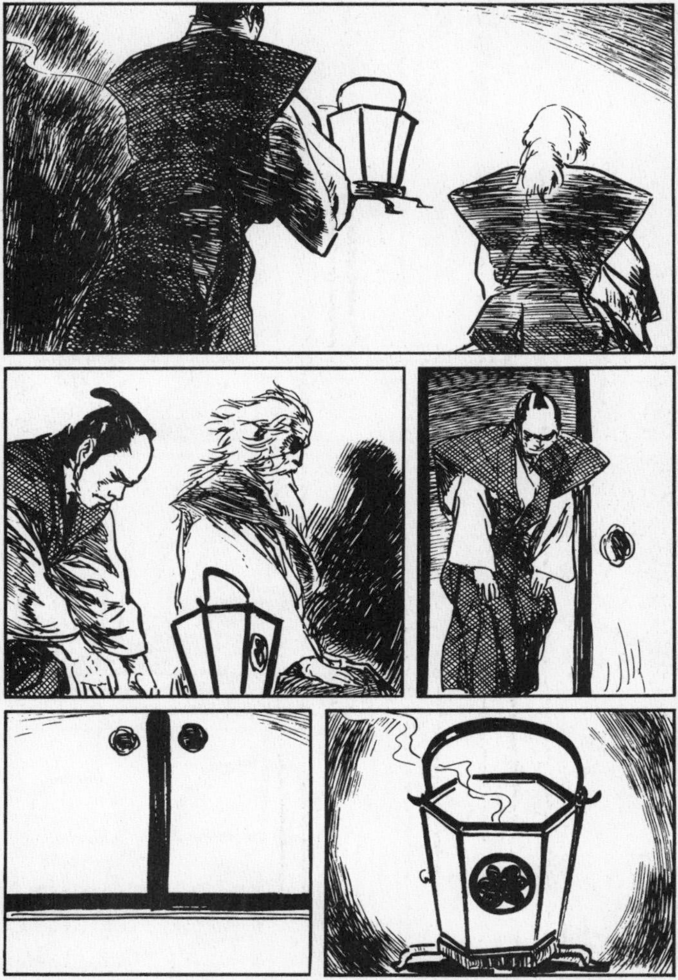

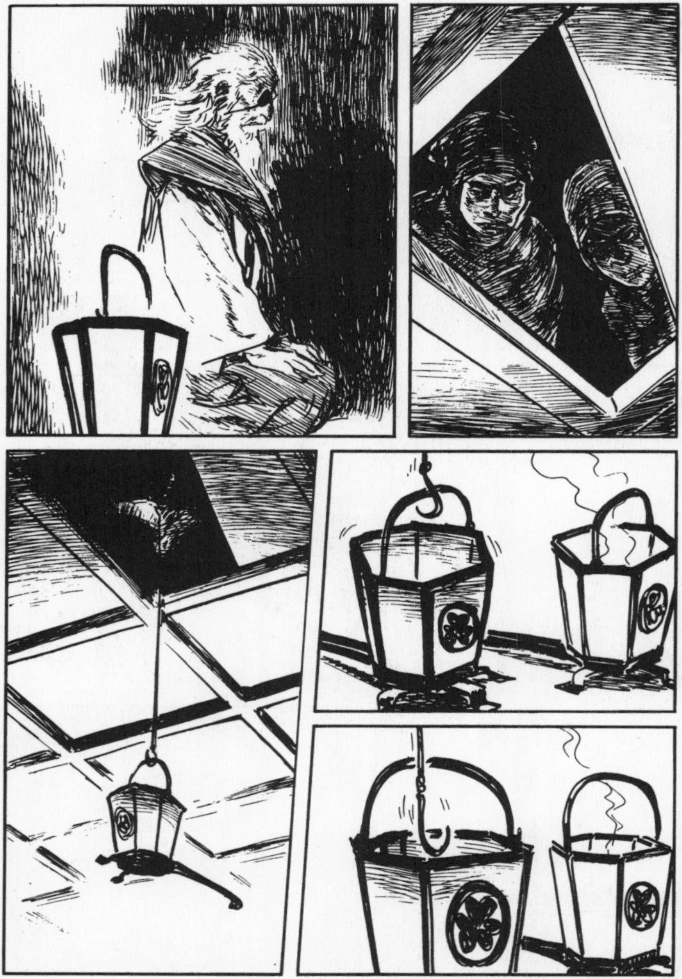

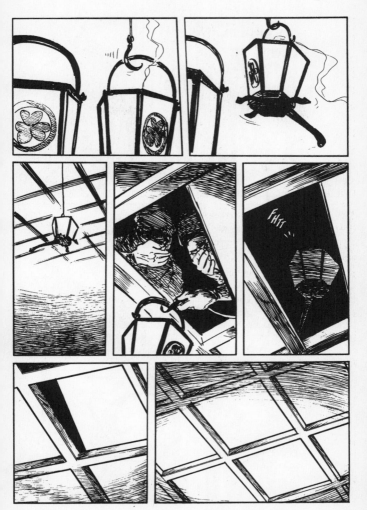

FHTT

115

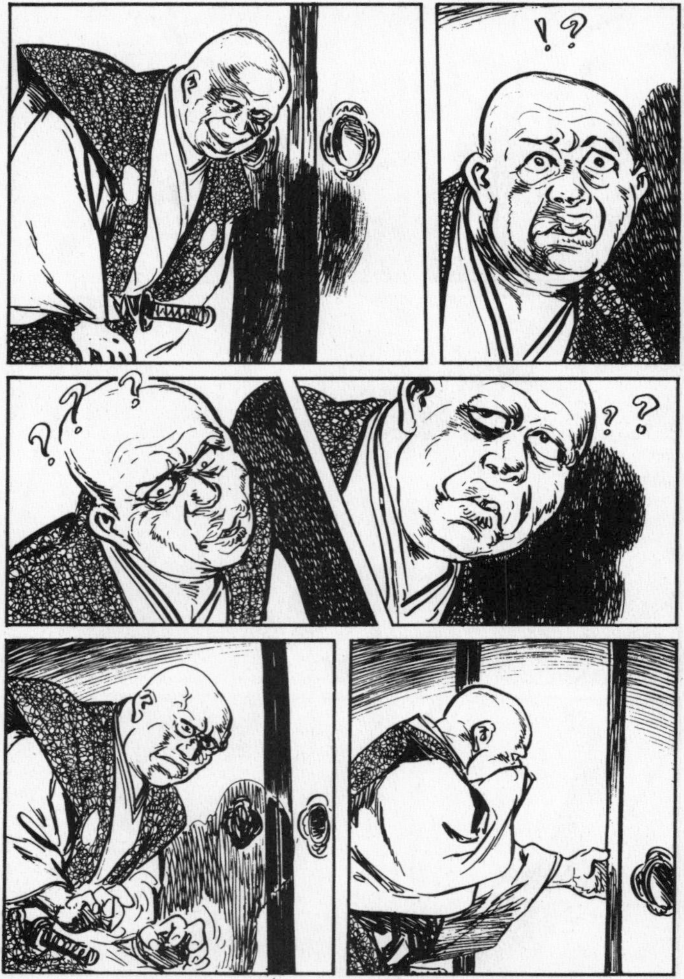
!?
???
??

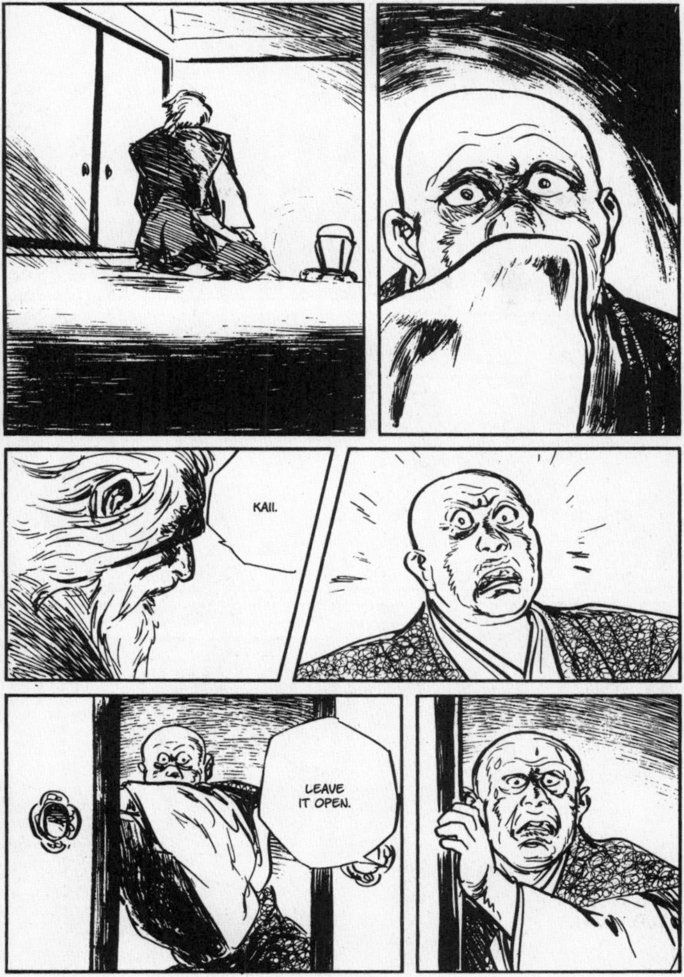
KAII.
LEAVE IT OPEN.

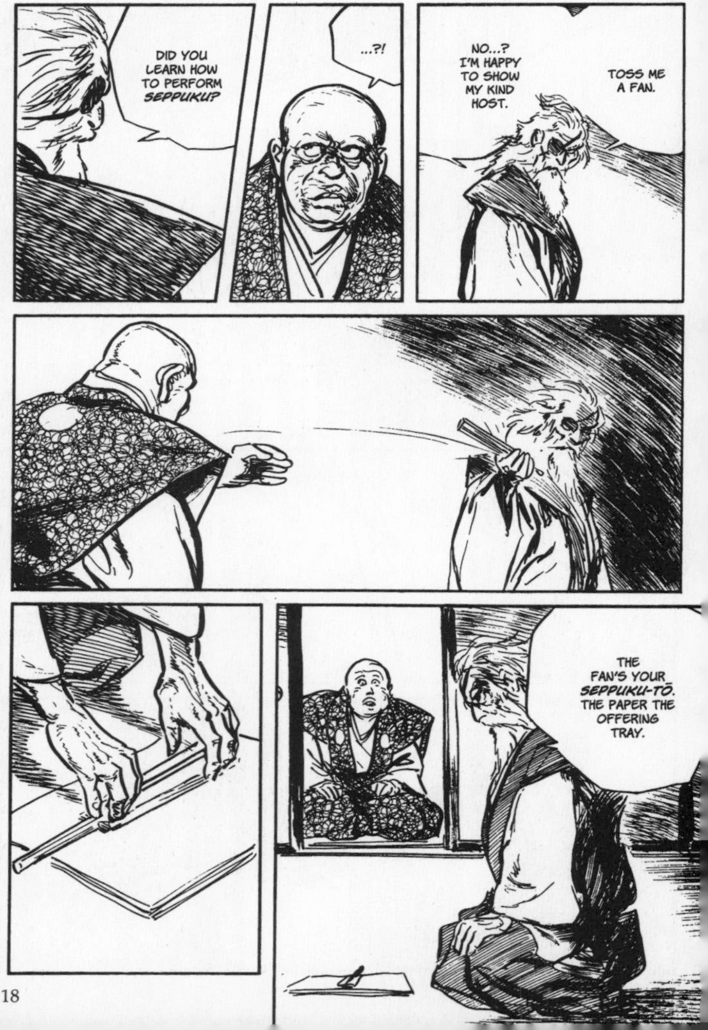
DID YOU LEARN HOW TO PERFORM *SEPPUKU?*
...?!
NO...? I'M HAPPY TO SHOW MY KIND HOST.
TOSS ME A FAN.
THE FAN'S YOUR *SEPPUKU-TŌ*. THE PAPER THE OFFERING TRAY.

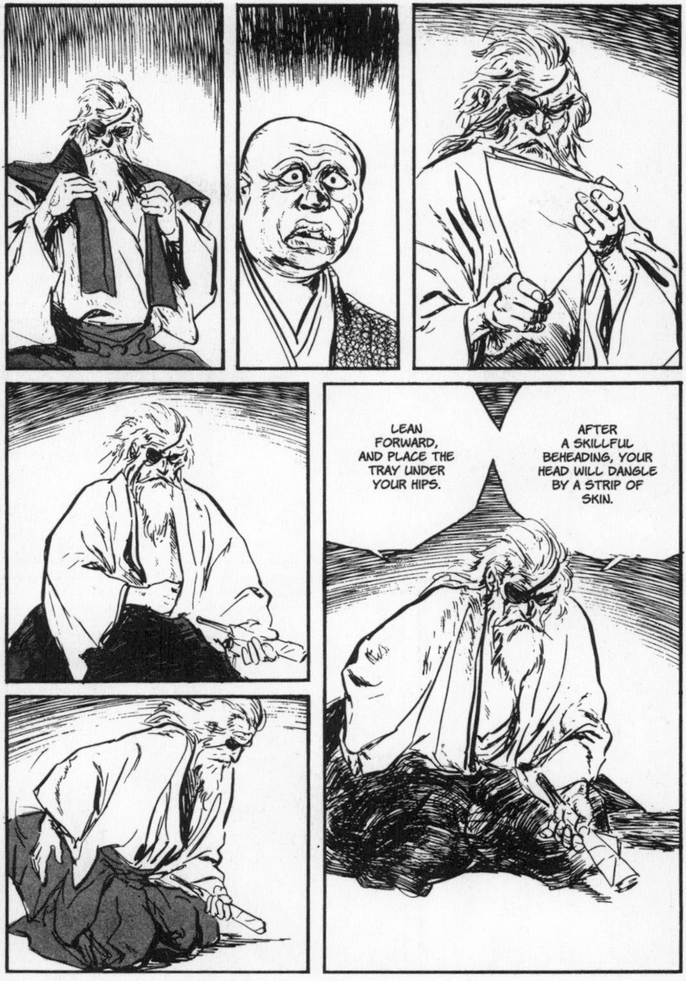
LEAN FORWARD, AND PLACE THE TRAY UNDER YOUR HIPS.
AFTER A SKILLFUL BEHEADING, YOUR HEAD WILL DANGLE BY A STRIP OF SKIN.

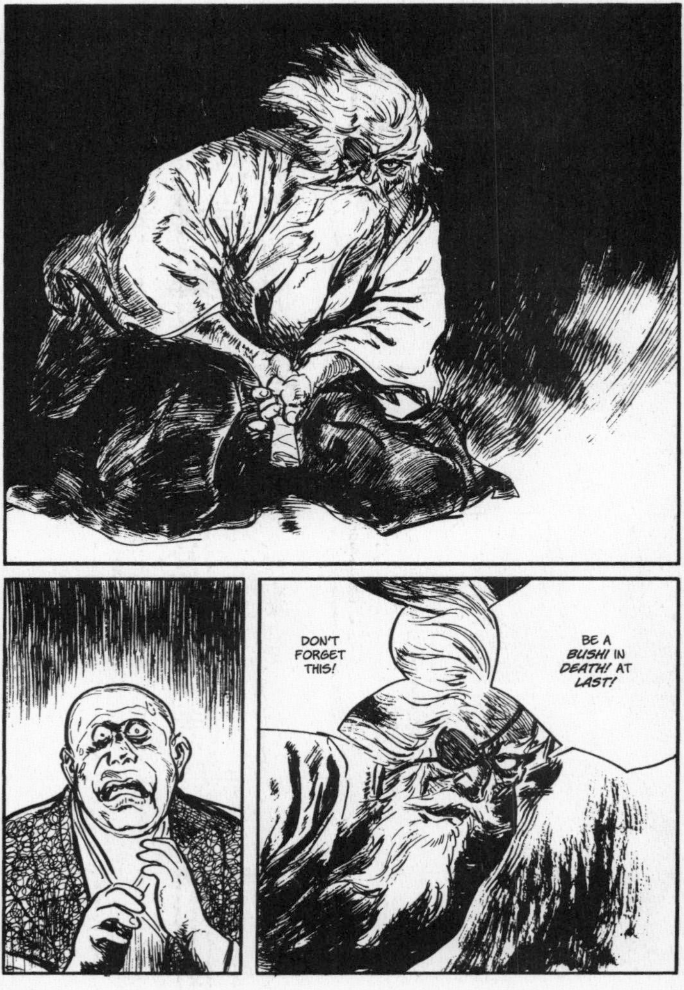
DON'T FORGET THIS!
BE A *BUSHI* IN *DEATH!* AT *LAST!*

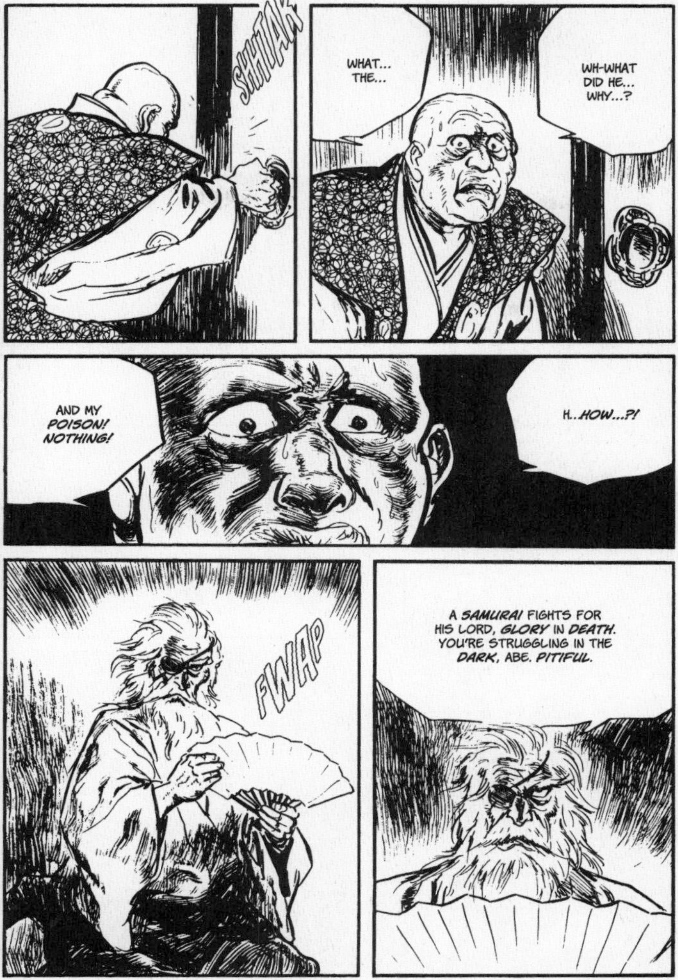
SHITAK
WHAT... THE...
WH-WHAT DID HE... WHY...?
AND MY POISON! NOTHING!
H...HOW...?!
FWAP
A SAMURAI FIGHTS FOR HIS LORD, GLORY IN DEATH. YOU'RE STRUGGLING IN THE DARK, ABE. PITIFUL.

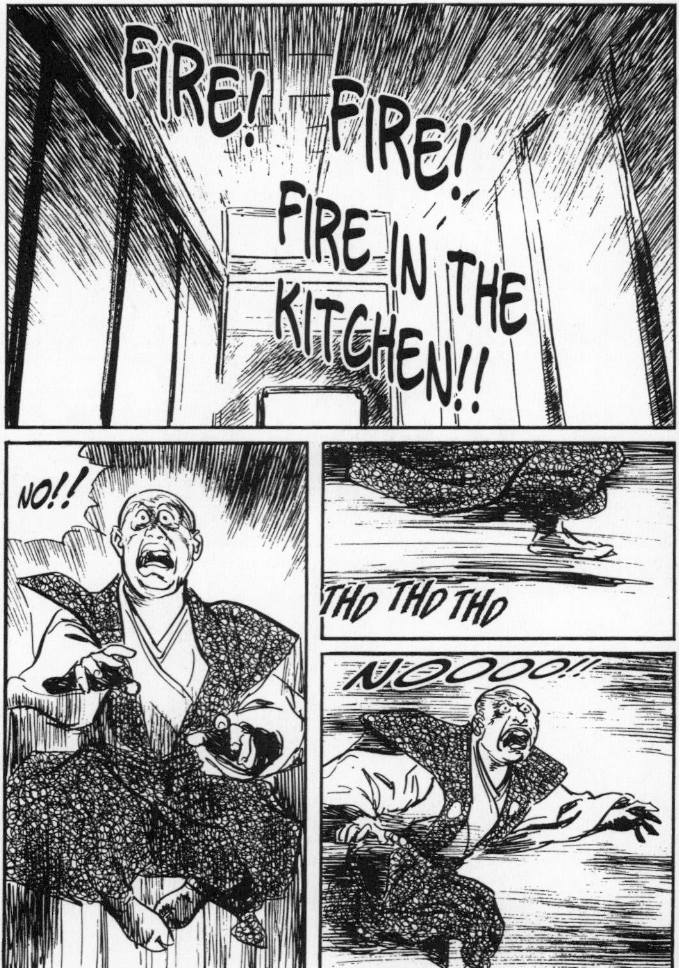
FIRE! FIRE!
FIRE IN THE KITCHEN!!
NO!!
THD THD THD
NOOOO!!

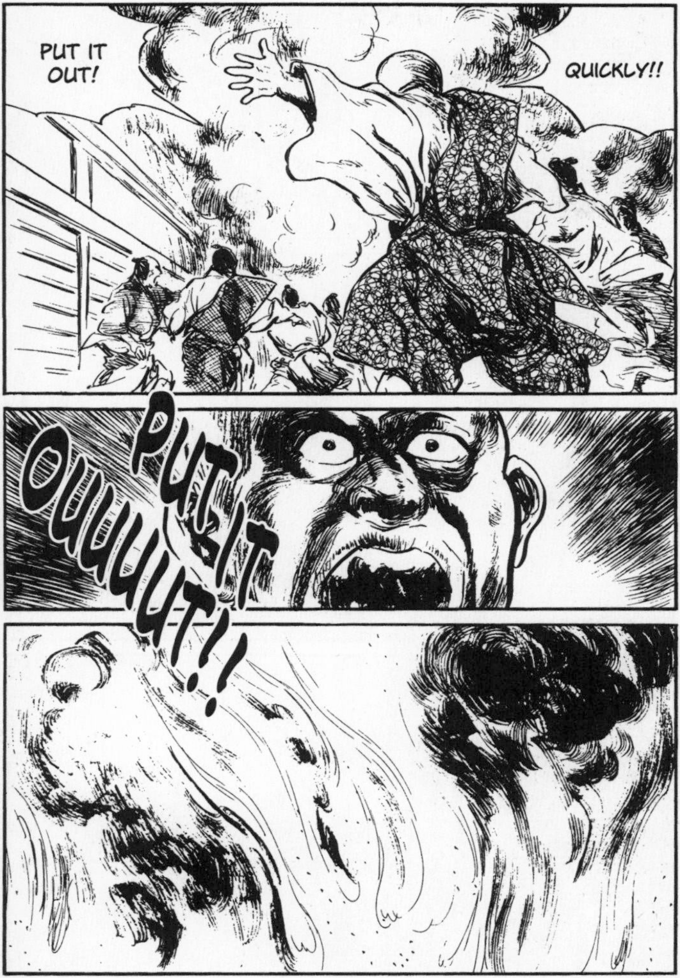
PUT IT OUT!
QUICKLY!!
PUT IT OUUUUUT!!

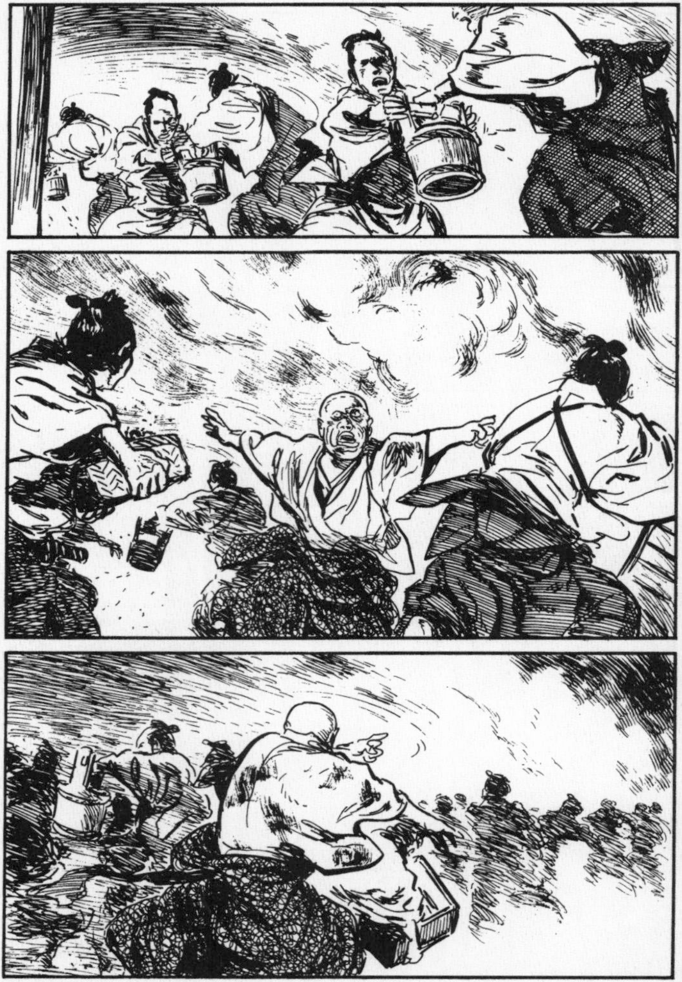

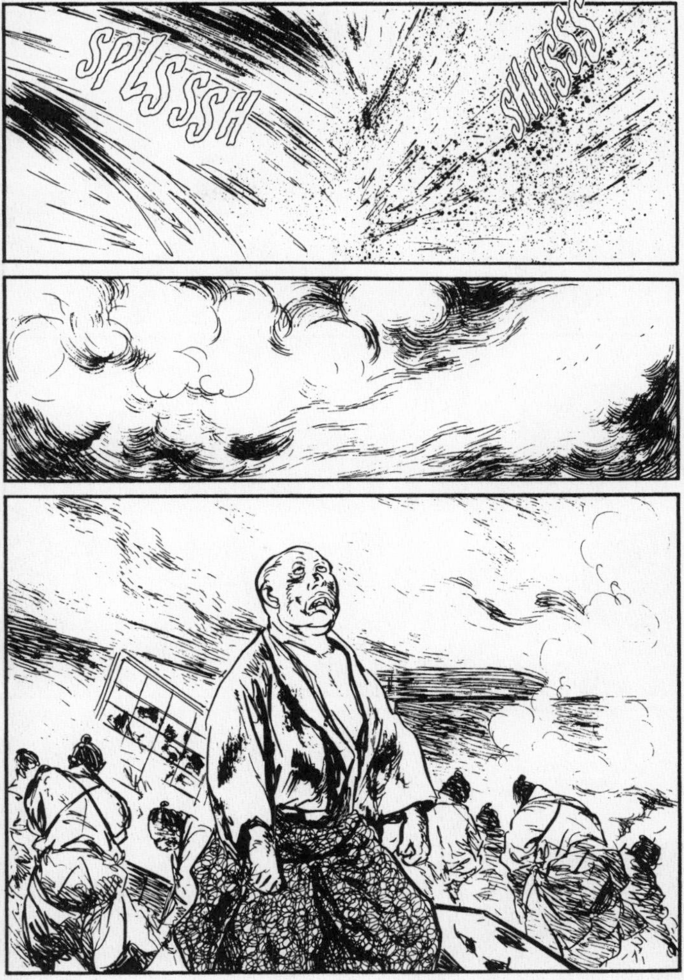
SPLSSSH
SHHSSS

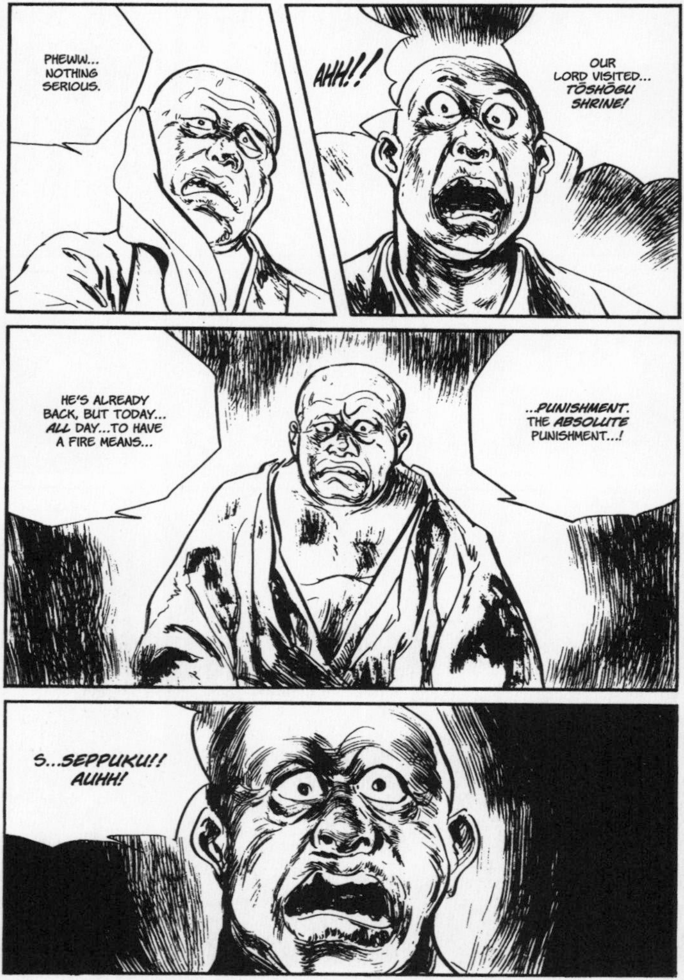
PHEWW... NOTHING SERIOUS.
AHH!!
OUR LORD VISITED... *TŌSHŌGU SHRINE!*
HE'S ALREADY BACK, BUT TODAY... *ALL* DAY...TO HAVE A FIRE MEANS...
...*PUNISHMENT*. THE *ABSOLUTE* PUNISHMENT...!
S...SEPPUKU!! AUHH!

the hundred and thirtieth

Song of the Spirit

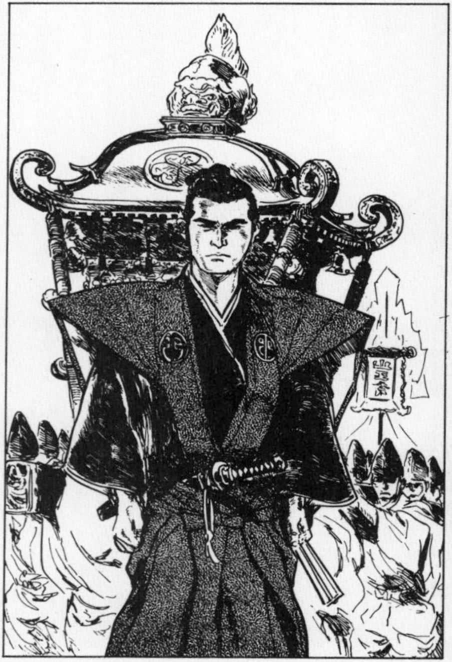

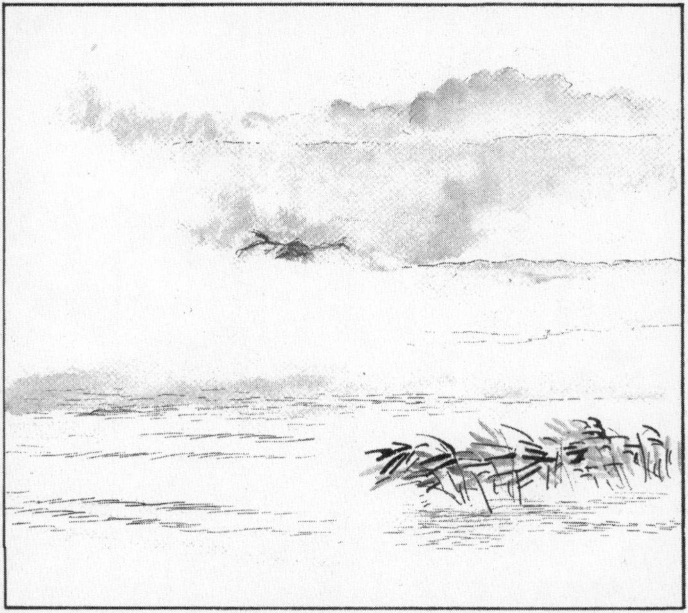

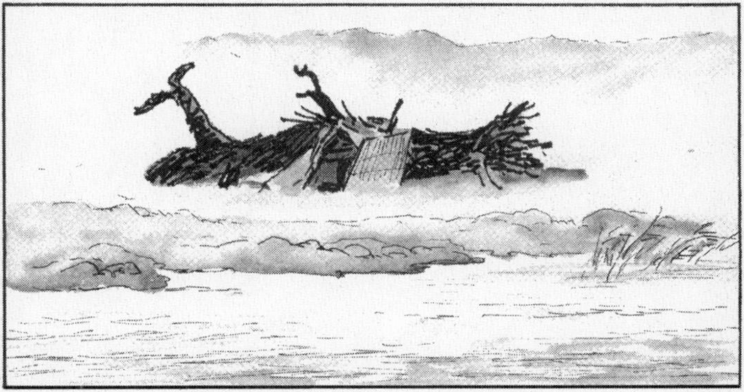

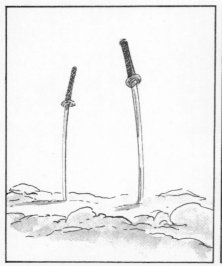

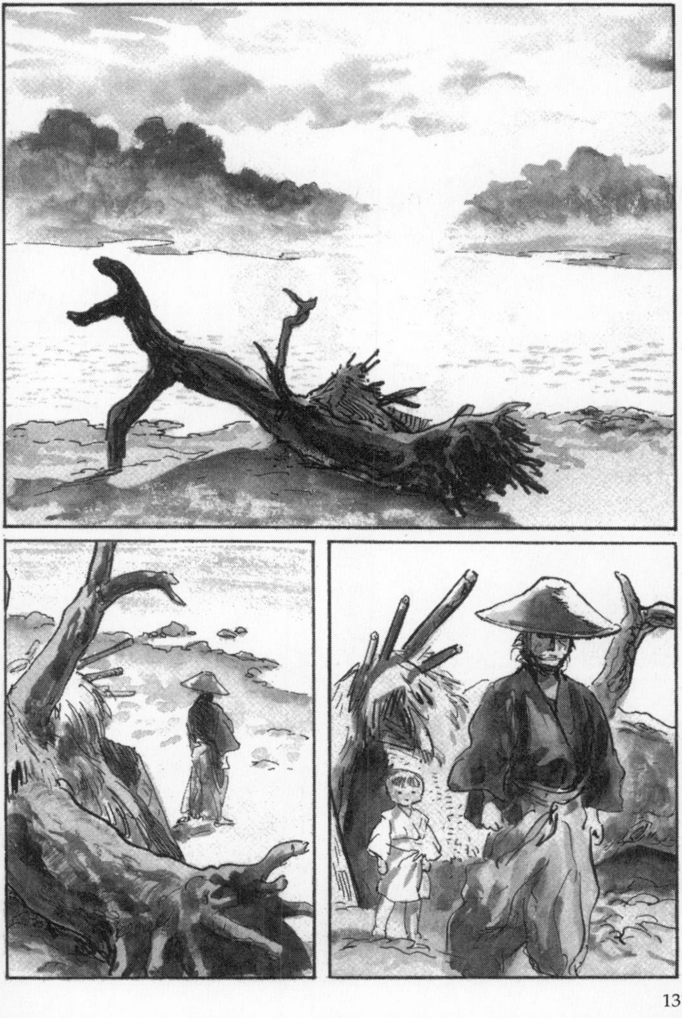

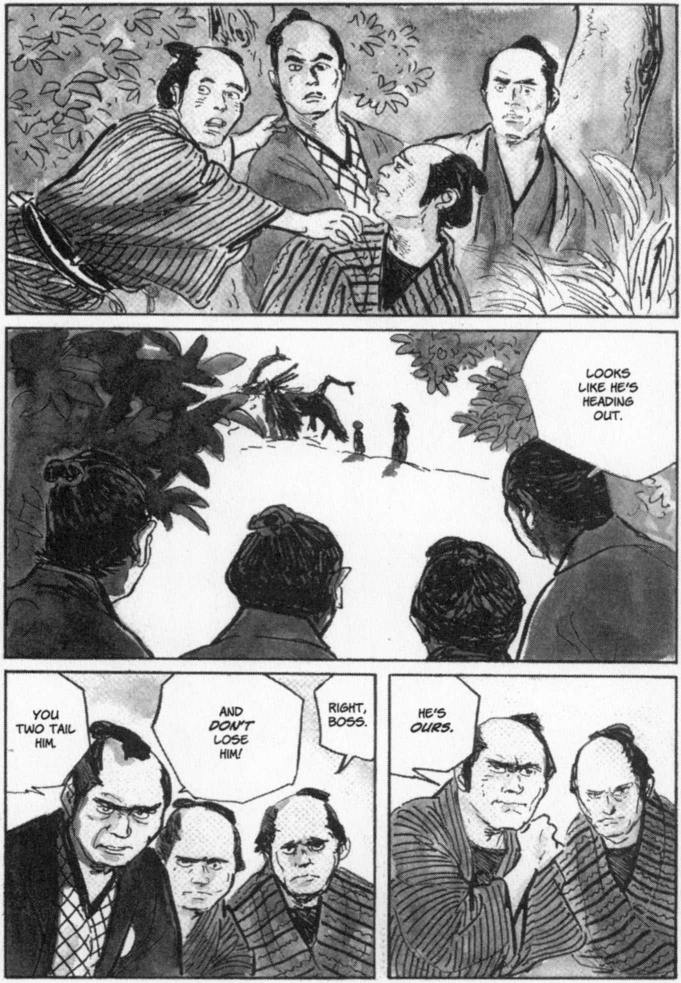
LOOKS LIKE HE'S HEADING OUT.
YOU TWO TAIL HIM.
AND *DON'T* LOSE HIM!
RIGHT, BOSS.
HE'S *OURS.*

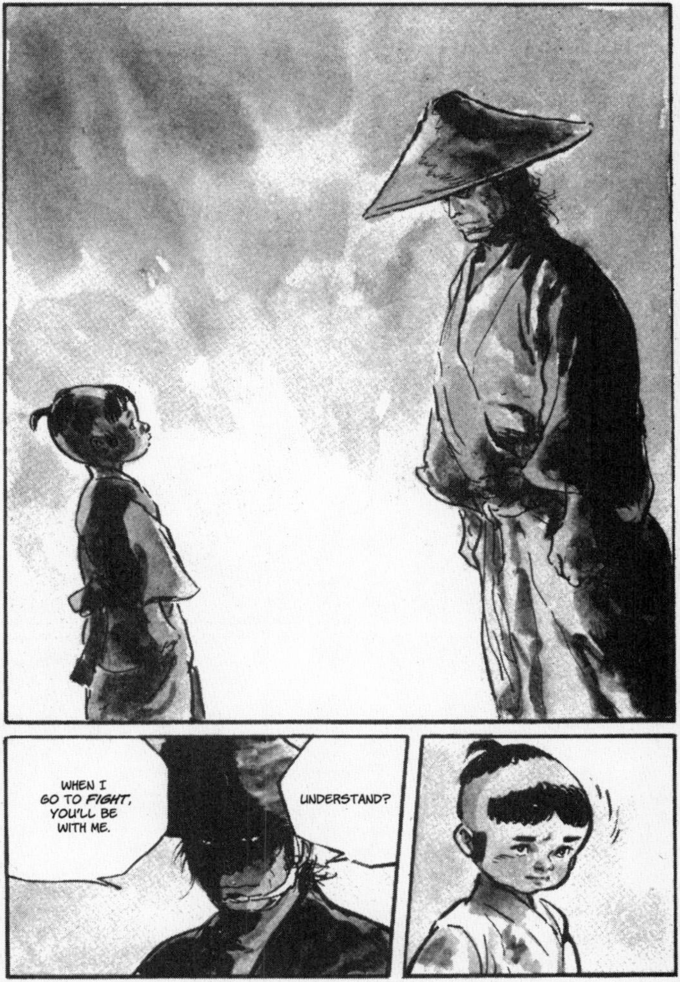
WHEN I GO TO *FIGHT*, YOU'LL BE WITH ME.
UNDERSTAND?

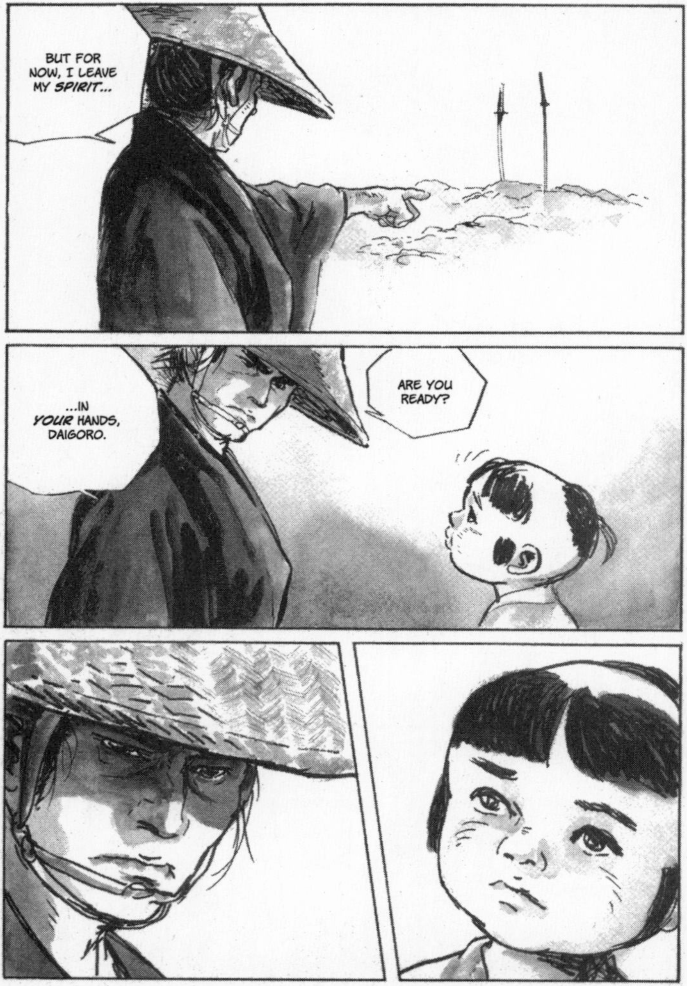
BUT FOR NOW, I LEAVE MY *SPIRIT*...
...IN *YOUR* HANDS, DAIGORO.
ARE YOU READY?

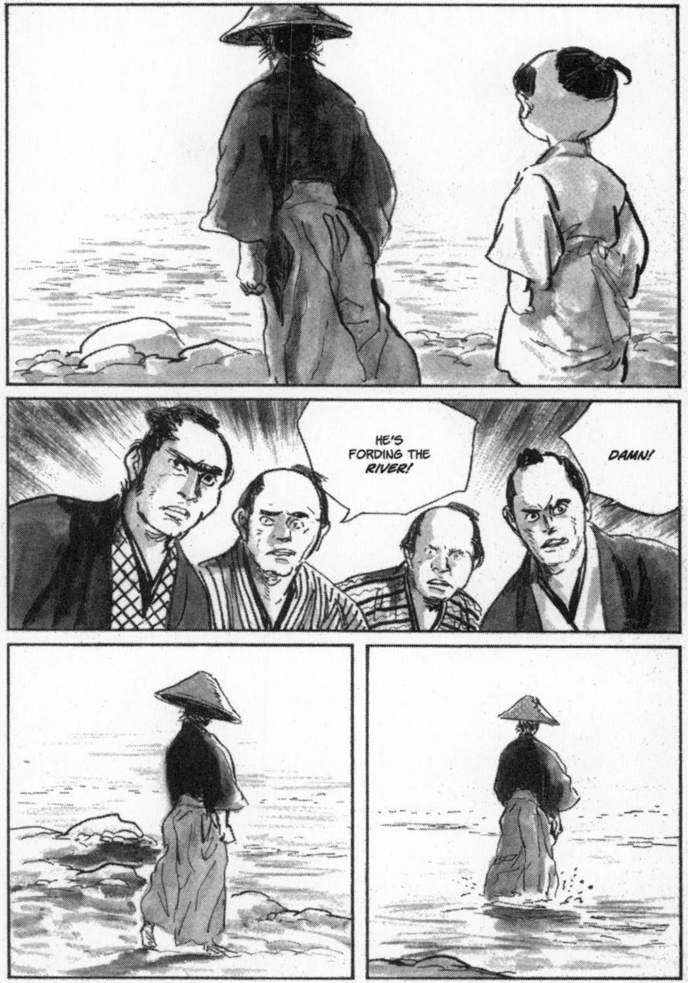
HE'S FORDING THE *RIVER!*
DAMN!

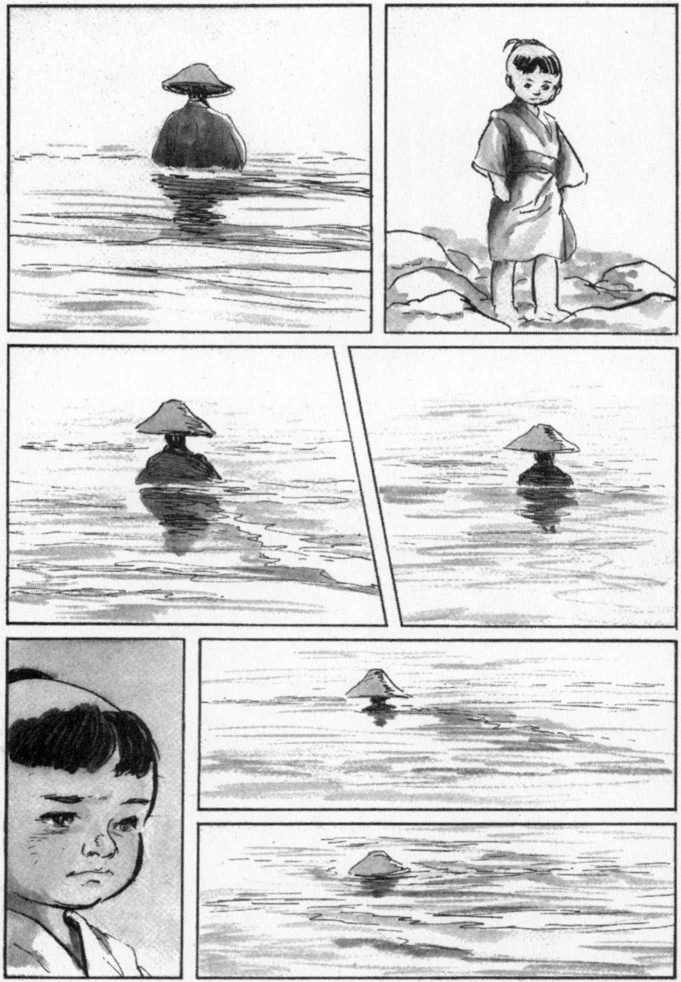

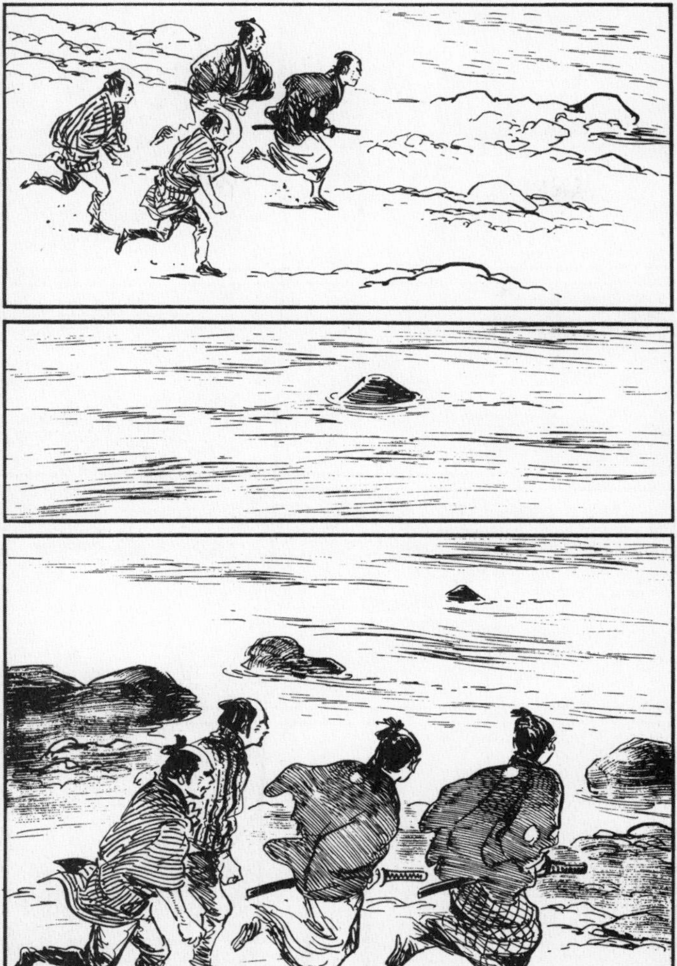

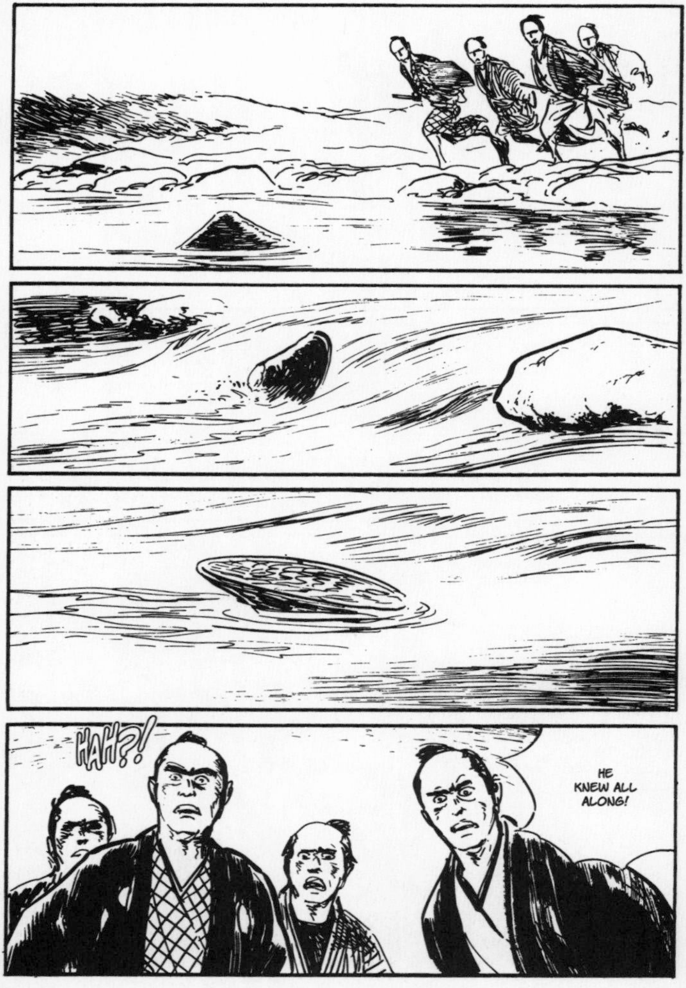
HAH?!
HE KNEW ALL ALONG!

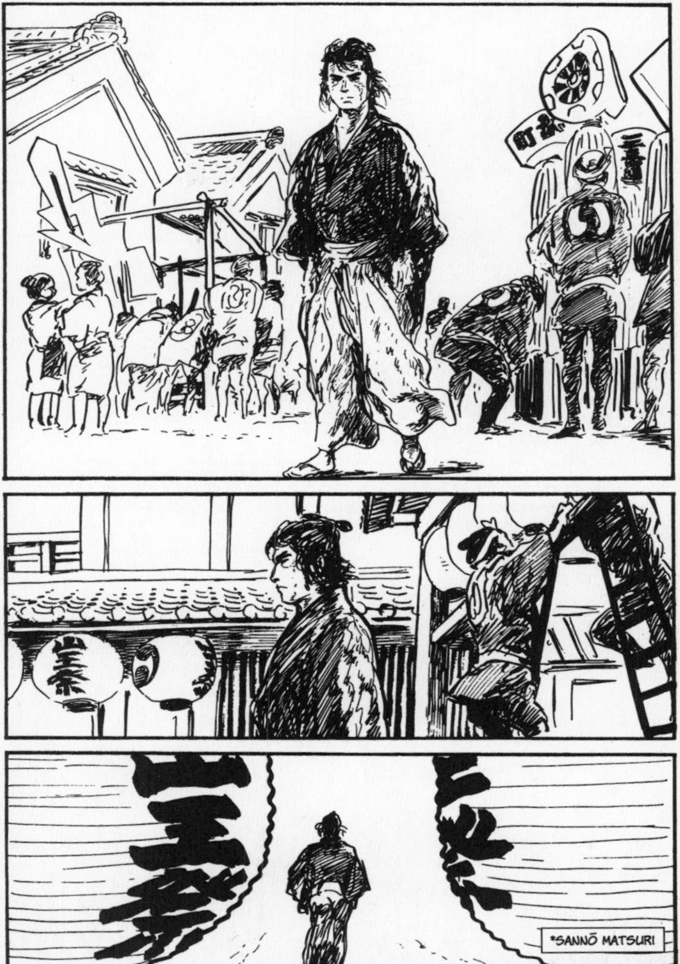
*SANNŌ MATSURI

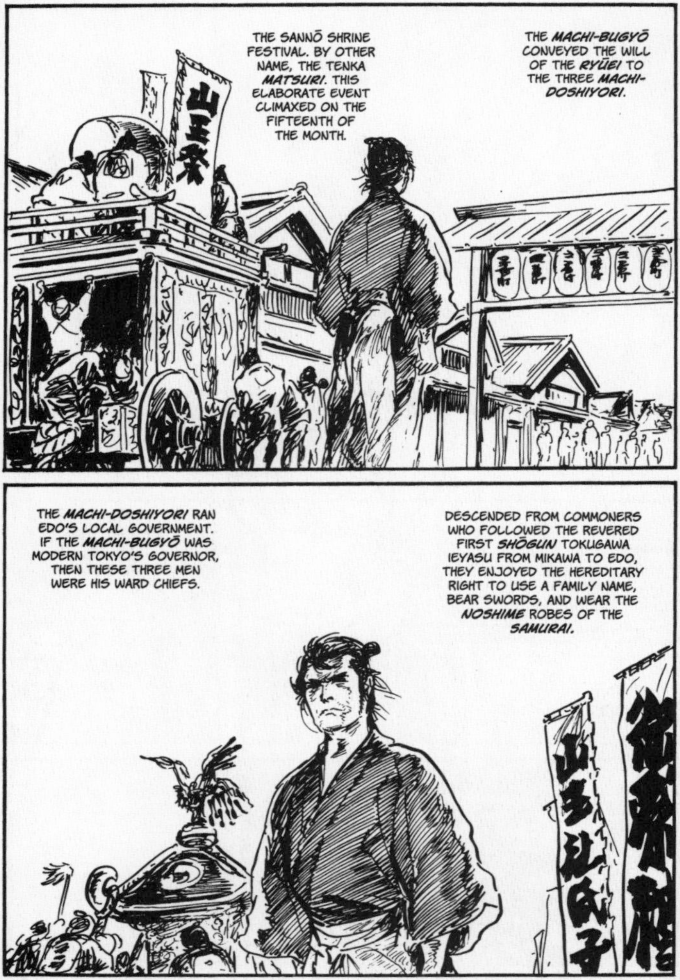
THE SANNŌ SHRINE FESTIVAL. BY OTHER NAME, THE TENKA *MATSURI*. THIS ELABORATE EVENT CLIMAXED ON THE FIFTEENTH OF THE MONTH.
山王祭
THE *MACHI-BUGYŌ* CONVEYED THE WILL OF THE *RYŪEI* TO THE THREE *MACHI-DOSHIYORI*.
THE *MACHI-DOSHIYORI* RAN EDO'S LOCAL GOVERNMENT. IF THE *MACHI-BUGYŌ* WAS MODERN TOKYO'S GOVERNOR, THEN THESE THREE MEN WERE HIS WARD CHIEFS.
DESCENDED FROM COMMONERS WHO FOLLOWED THE REVERED FIRST *SHŌGUN* TOKUGAWA IEYASU FROM MIKAWA TO EDO, THEY ENJOYED THE HEREDITARY RIGHT TO USE A FAMILY NAME, BEAR SWORDS, AND WEAR THE *NOSHIME* ROBES OF THE *SAMURAI*.

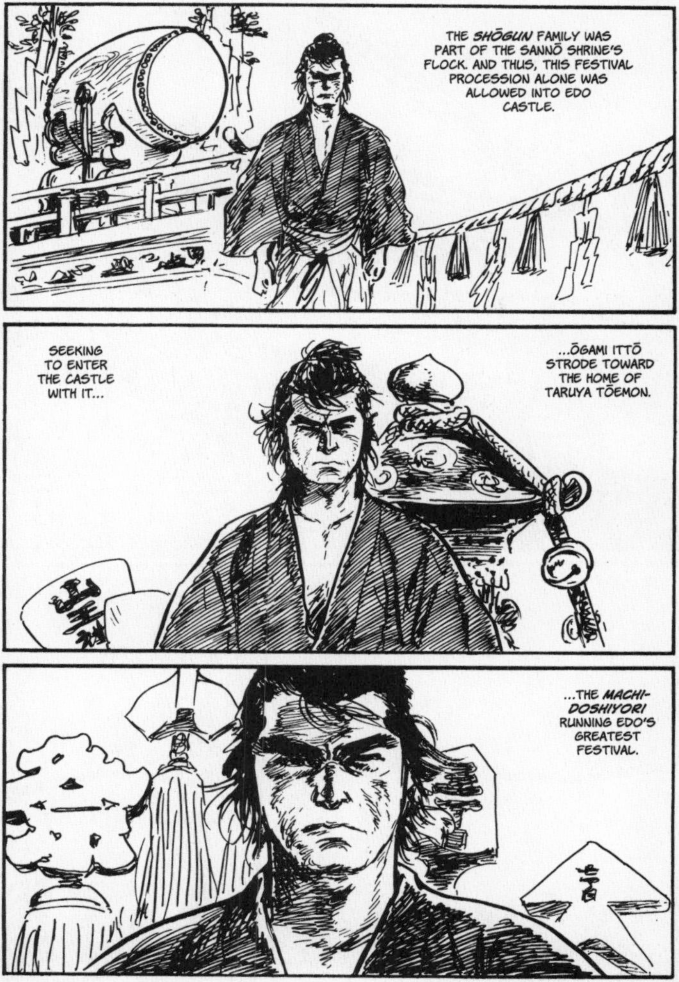
THE *SHŌGUN* FAMILY WAS PART OF THE SANNŌ SHRINE'S FLOCK. AND THUS, THIS FESTIVAL PROCESSION ALONE WAS ALLOWED INTO EDO CASTLE.
SEEKING TO ENTER THE CASTLE WITH IT...
...ŌGAMI ITTŌ STRODE TOWARD THE HOME OF TARUYA TŌEMON.
...THE *MACHI-DOSHIYORI* RUNNING EDO'S GREATEST FESTIVAL.

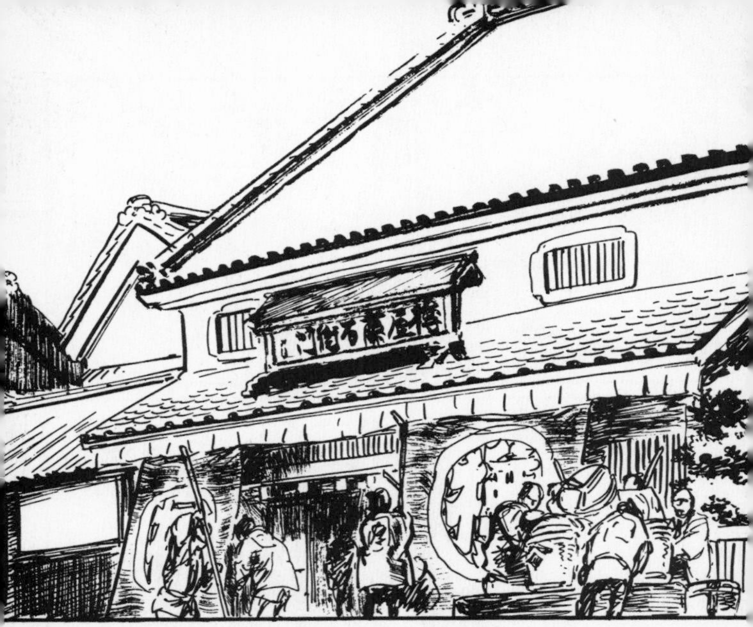

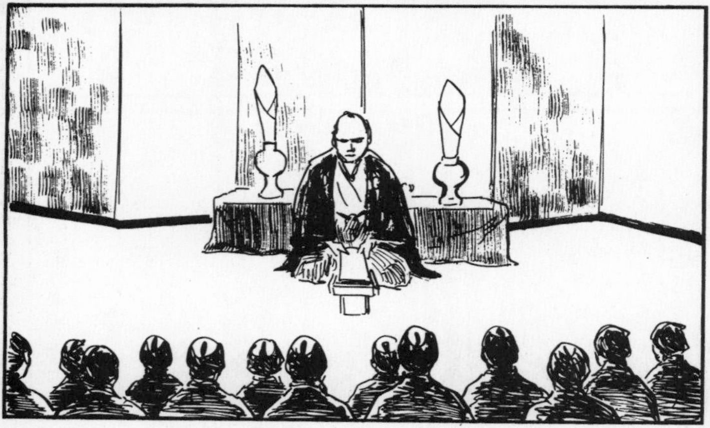

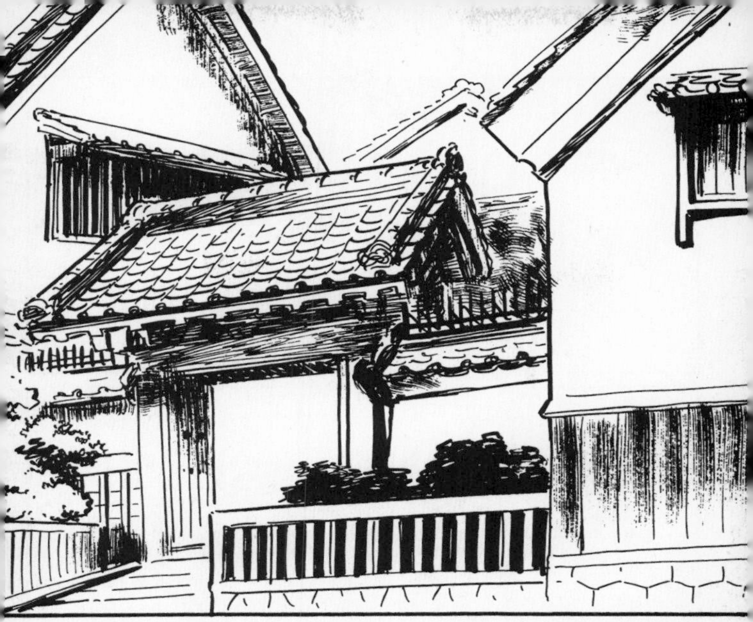
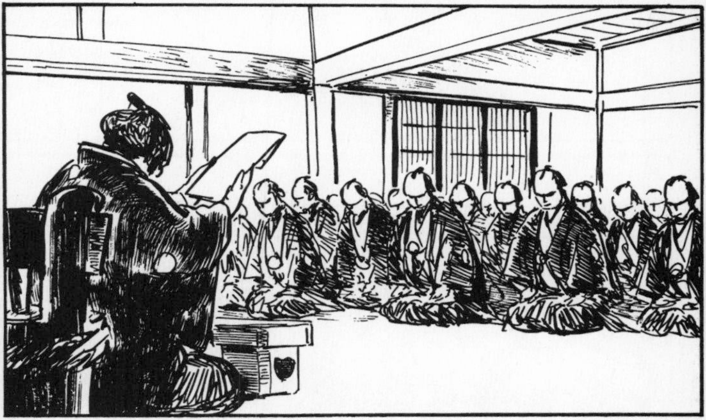

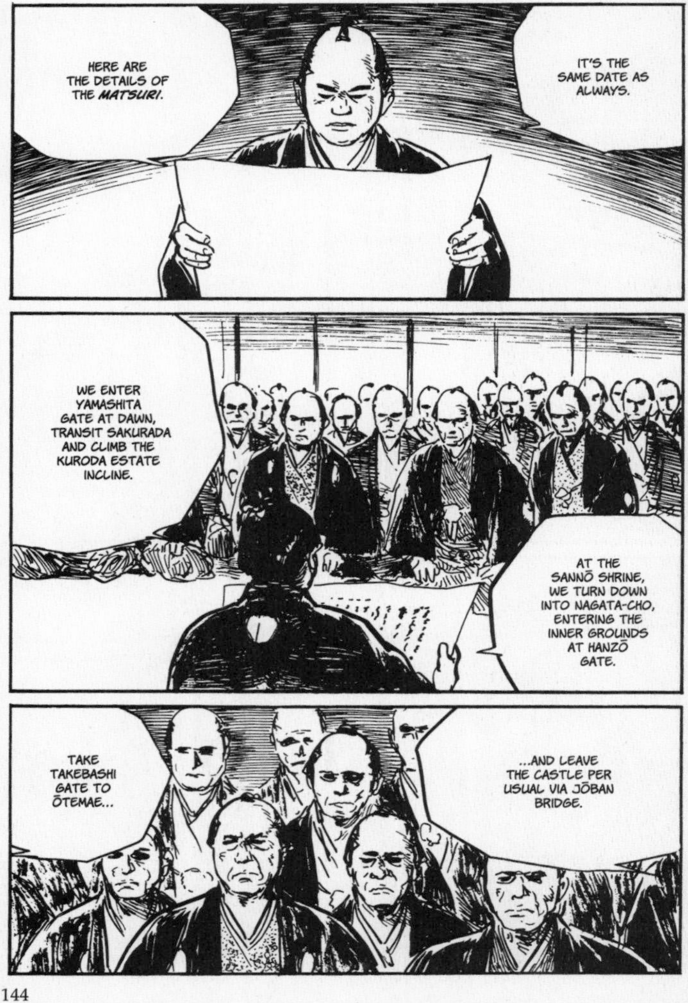
HERE ARE THE DETAILS OF THE *MATSURI*.
IT'S THE SAME DATE AS ALWAYS.
WE ENTER YAMASHITA GATE AT DAWN, TRANSIT SAKURADA AND CLIMB THE KURODA ESTATE INCLINE.
AT THE SANNŌ SHRINE, WE TURN DOWN INTO NAGATA-CHO, ENTERING THE INNER GROUNDS AT HANZŌ GATE.
TAKE TAKEBASHI GATE TO ŌTEMAE...
...AND LEAVE THE CASTLE PER USUAL VIA JŌBAN BRIDGE.

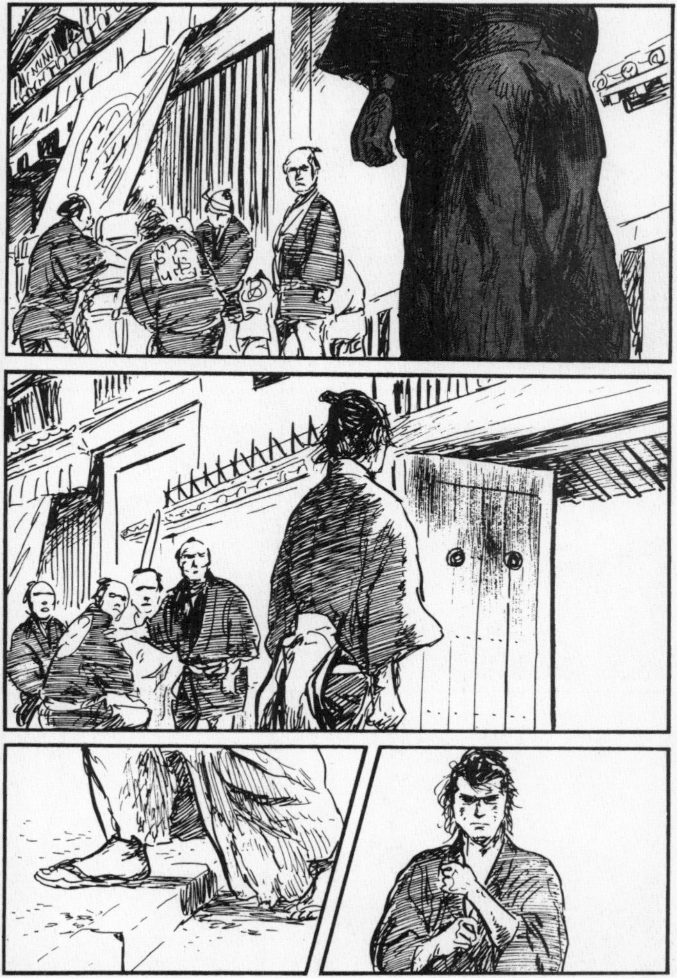

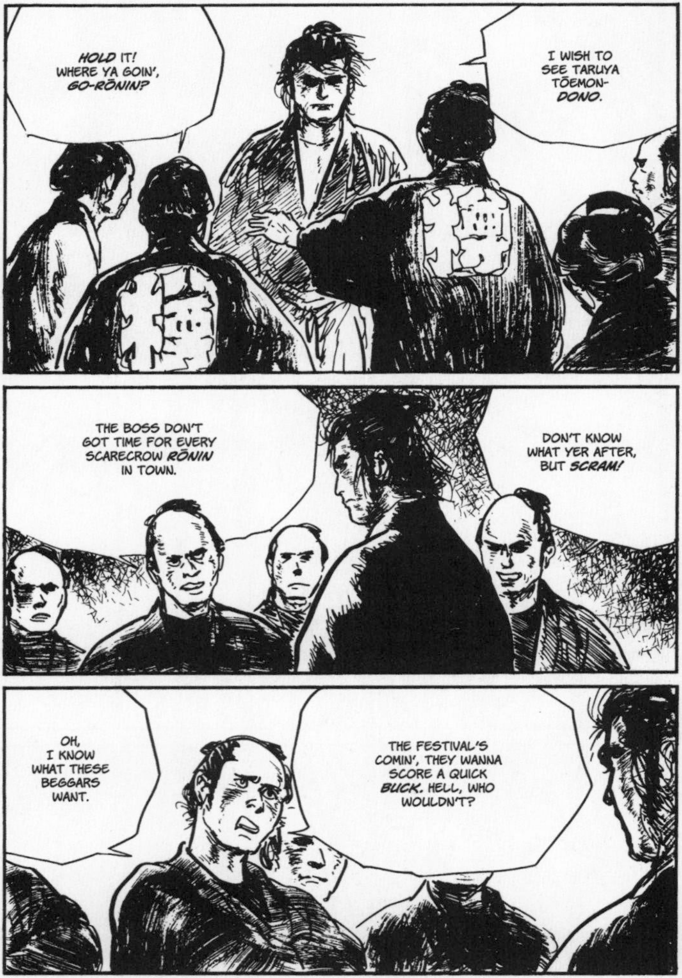
HOLD IT! WHERE YA GOIN', GO-RŌNIN?
I WISH TO SEE TARUYA TŌEMON-DONO.
THE BOSS DON'T GOT TIME FOR EVERY SCARECROW RŌNIN IN TOWN.
DON'T KNOW WHAT YER AFTER, BUT SCRAM!
OH, I KNOW WHAT THESE BEGGARS WANT.
THE FESTIVAL'S COMIN', THEY WANNA SCORE A QUICK BUCK. HELL, WHO WOULDN'T?

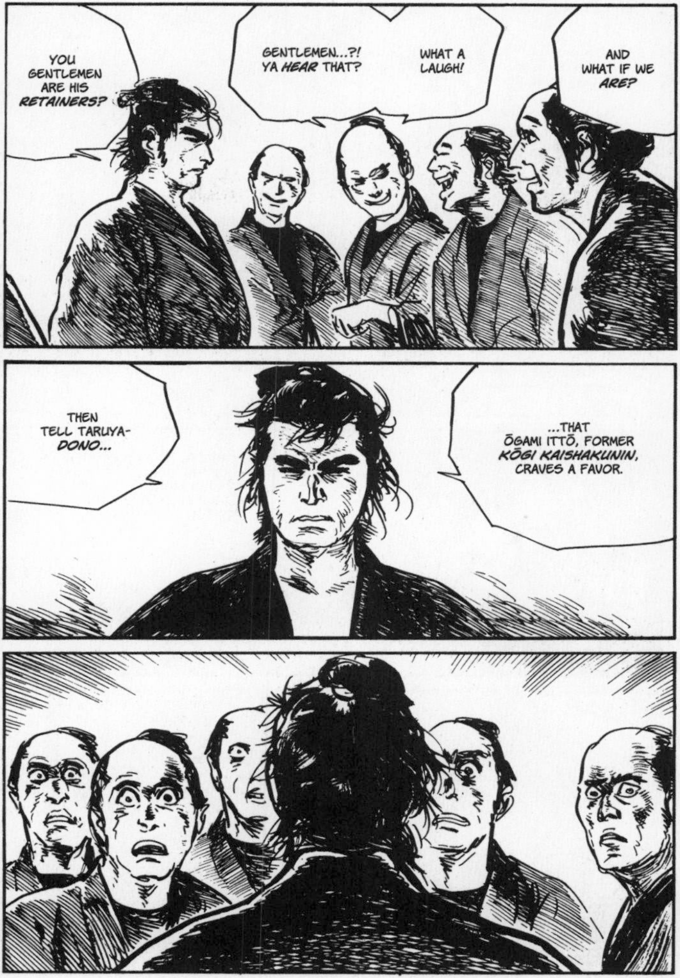
YOU GENTLEMEN ARE HIS RETAINERS?
GENTLEMEN...?! YA HEAR THAT?
WHAT A LAUGH!
AND WHAT IF WE ARE?
THEN TELL TARUYA-DONO...
...THAT ŌGAMI ITTŌ, FORMER KŌGI KAISHAKUNIN, CRAVES A FAVOR.

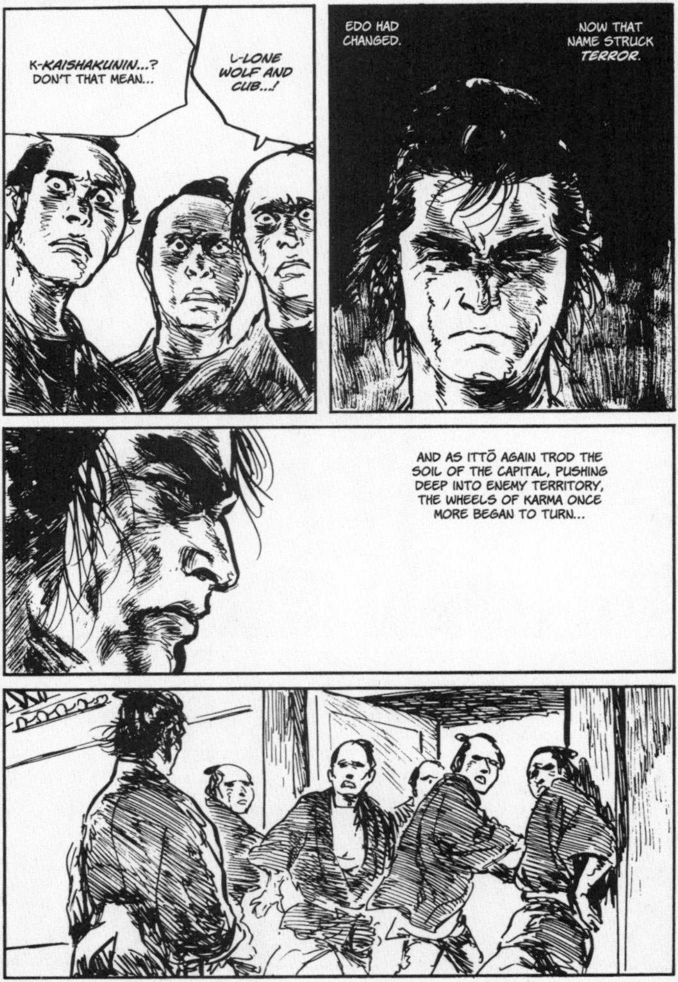
K-KAISHAKUNIN...? DON'T THAT MEAN...
L-LONE WOLF AND CUB...!
EDO HAD CHANGED.
NOW THAT NAME STRUCK TERROR.
AND AS ITTŌ AGAIN TROD THE SOIL OF THE CAPITAL, PUSHING DEEP INTO ENEMY TERRITORY, THE WHEELS OF KARMA ONCE MORE BEGAN TO TURN...

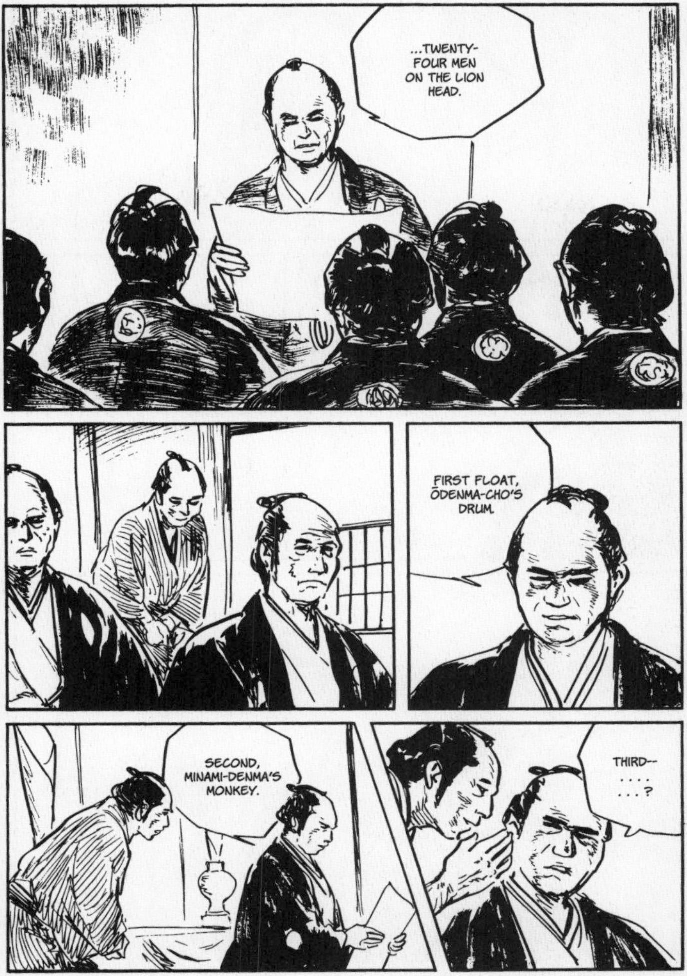
...TWENTY-FOUR MEN ON THE LION HEAD.
FIRST FLOAT, ŌDENMA-CHO'S DRUM.
SECOND, MINAMI-DENMA'S MONKEY.
THIRD--
....
...?

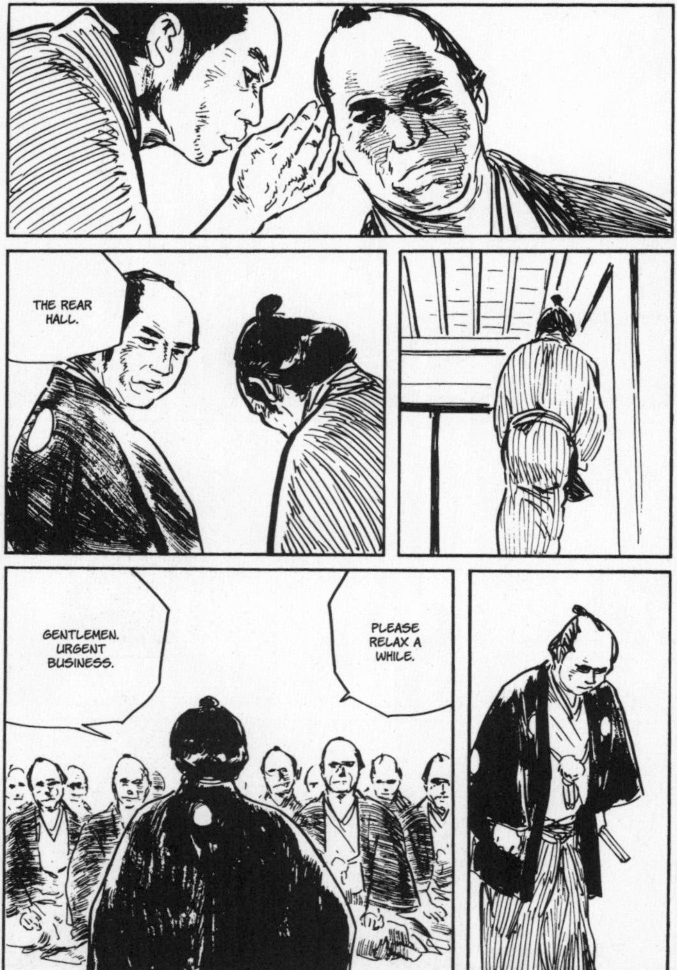
THE REAR HALL.
GENTLEMEN. URGENT BUSINESS.
PLEASE RELAX A WHILE.

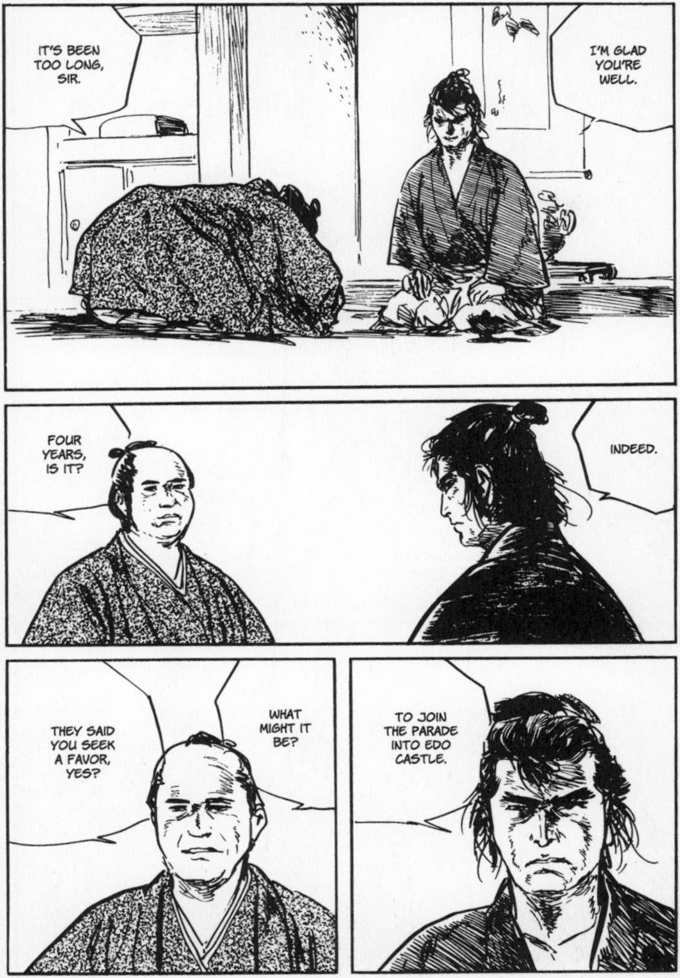
IT'S BEEN TOO LONG, SIR.
I'M GLAD YOU'RE WELL.
FOUR YEARS, IS IT?
INDEED.
THEY SAID YOU SEEK A FAVOR, YES?
WHAT MIGHT IT BE?
TO JOIN THE PARADE INTO EDO CASTLE.

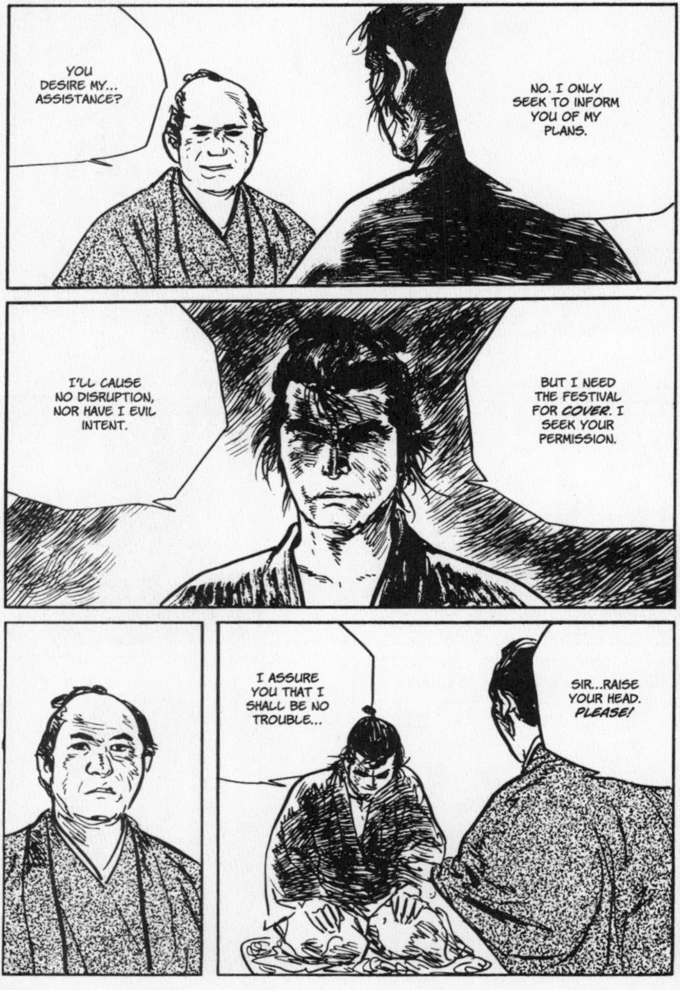
YOU DESIRE MY... ASSISTANCE?
NO. I ONLY SEEK TO INFORM YOU OF MY PLANS.
I'LL CAUSE NO DISRUPTION, NOR HAVE I EVIL INTENT.
BUT I NEED THE FESTIVAL FOR COVER. I SEEK YOUR PERMISSION.
I ASSURE YOU THAT I SHALL BE NO TROUBLE...
SIR...RAISE YOUR HEAD. PLEASE!

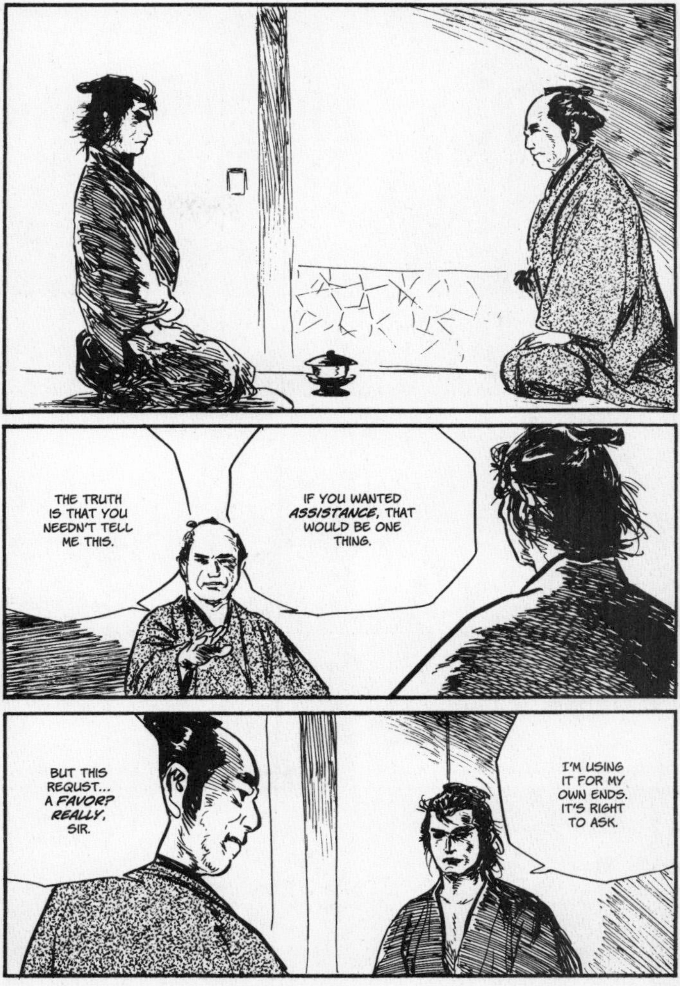
THE TRUTH IS THAT YOU NEEDN'T TELL ME THIS.
IF YOU WANTED *ASSISTANCE*, THAT WOULD BE ONE THING.
BUT THIS REQUST... A *FAVOR? REALLY*, SIR.
I'M USING IT FOR MY OWN ENDS. IT'S RIGHT TO ASK.

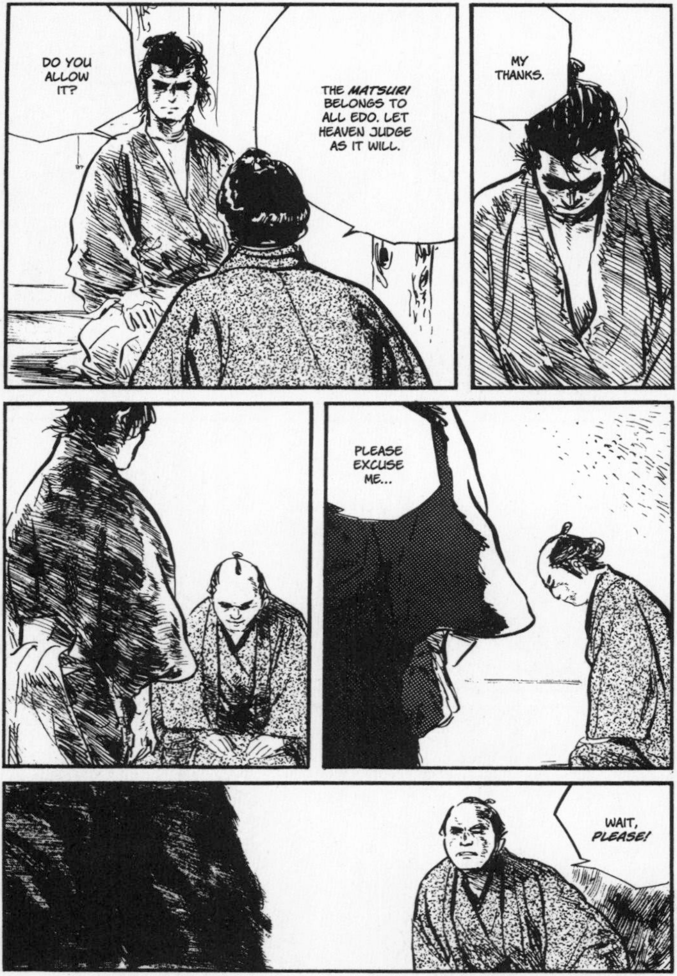
DO YOU ALLOW IT?
THE *MATSURI* BELONGS TO ALL EDO. LET HEAVEN JUDGE AS IT WILL.
MY THANKS.
PLEASE EXCUSE ME...
WAIT, *PLEASE!*

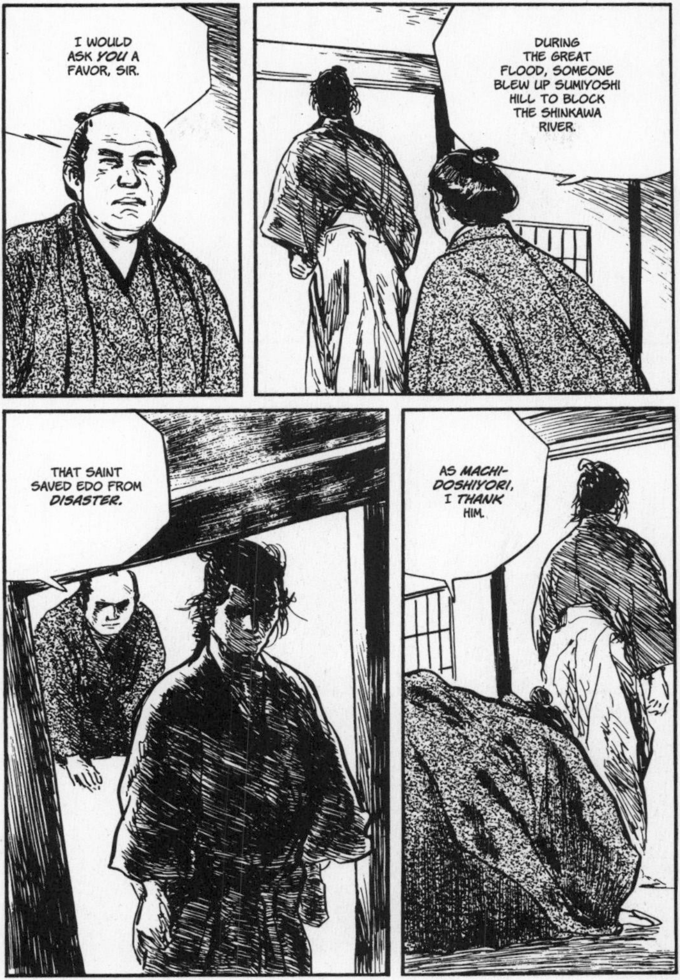
I WOULD ASK *YOU* A FAVOR, SIR.
DURING THE GREAT FLOOD, SOMEONE BLEW UP SUMIYOSHI HILL TO BLOCK THE SHINKAWA RIVER.
THAT SAINT SAVED EDO FROM *DISASTER.*
AS *MACHI-DOSHIYORI,* I *THANK* HIM.

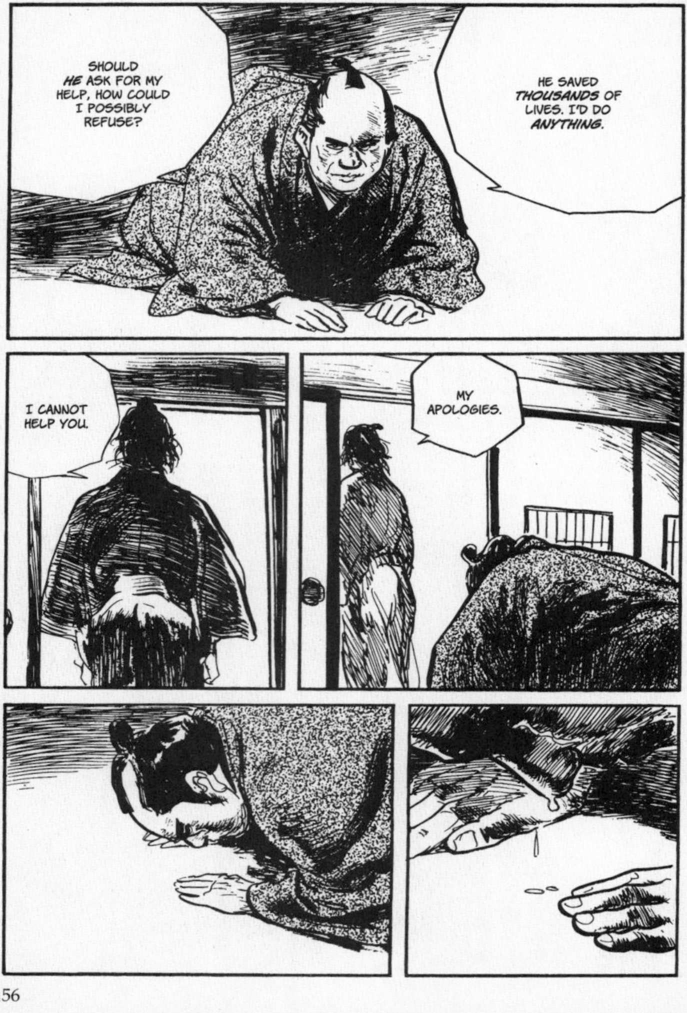
SHOULD HE ASK FOR MY HELP, HOW COULD I POSSIBLY REFUSE?
HE SAVED THOUSANDS OF LIVES. I'D DO ANYTHING.
I CANNOT HELP YOU.
MY APOLOGIES.

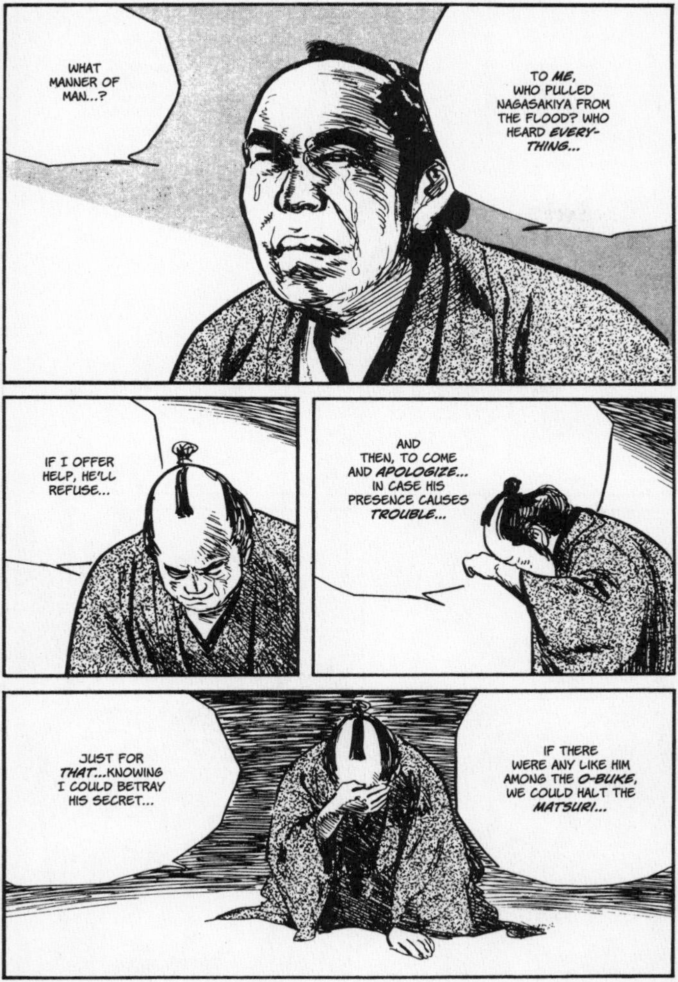
WHAT MANNER OF MAN...?
TO *ME*, WHO PULLED NAGASAKIYA FROM THE FLOOD? WHO HEARD *EVERY-THING...*
IF I OFFER HELP, HE'LL REFUSE...
AND THEN, TO COME AND *APOLOGIZE...* IN CASE HIS PRESENCE CAUSES *TROUBLE...*
JUST FOR *THAT*...KNOWING I COULD BETRAY HIS SECRET...
IF THERE WERE ANY LIKE HIM AMONG THE *O-BUKE*, WE COULD HALT THE *MATSURI...*

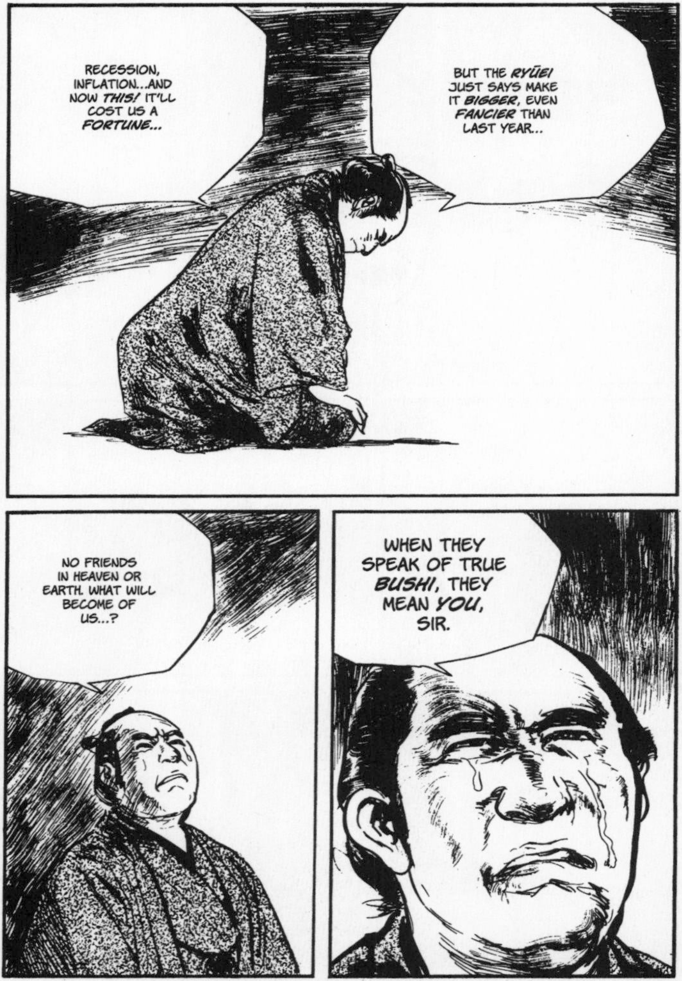
RECESSION, INFLATION...AND NOW *THIS!* IT'LL COST US A *FORTUNE*...
BUT THE *RYŪEI* JUST SAYS MAKE IT *BIGGER*, EVEN *FANCIER* THAN LAST YEAR...
NO FRIENDS IN HEAVEN OR EARTH. WHAT WILL BECOME OF US...?
WHEN THEY SPEAK OF TRUE *BUSHI*, THEY MEAN *YOU*, SIR.

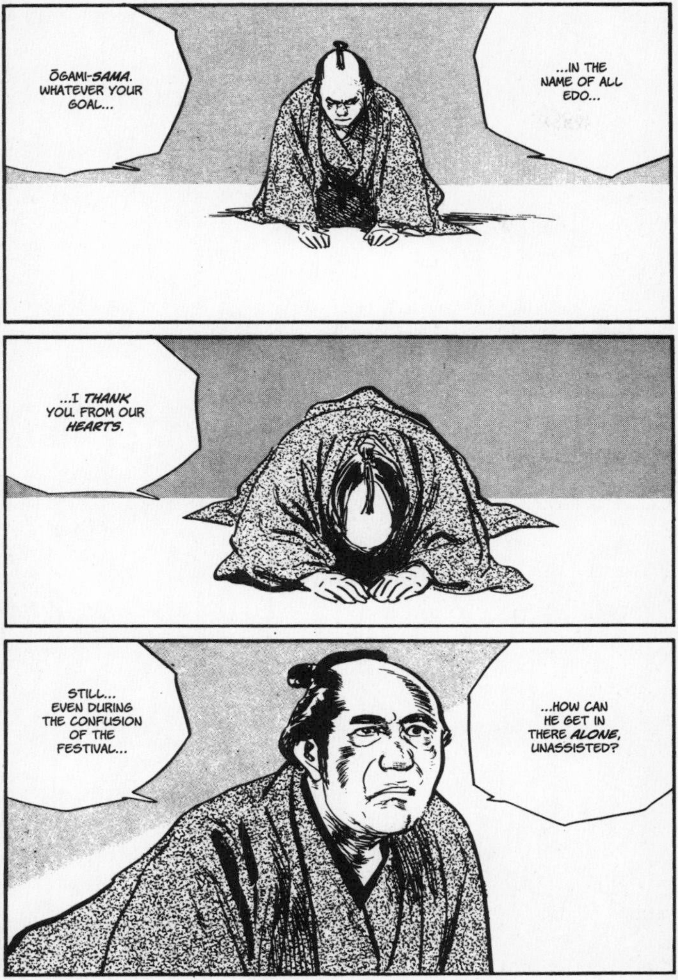
ŌGAMI-*SAMA*. WHATEVER YOUR GOAL...
...IN THE NAME OF ALL EDO...
...I *THANK* YOU. FROM OUR *HEARTS*.
STILL... EVEN DURING THE CONFUSION OF THE FESTIVAL...
...HOW CAN HE GET IN THERE *ALONE*, UNASSISTED?

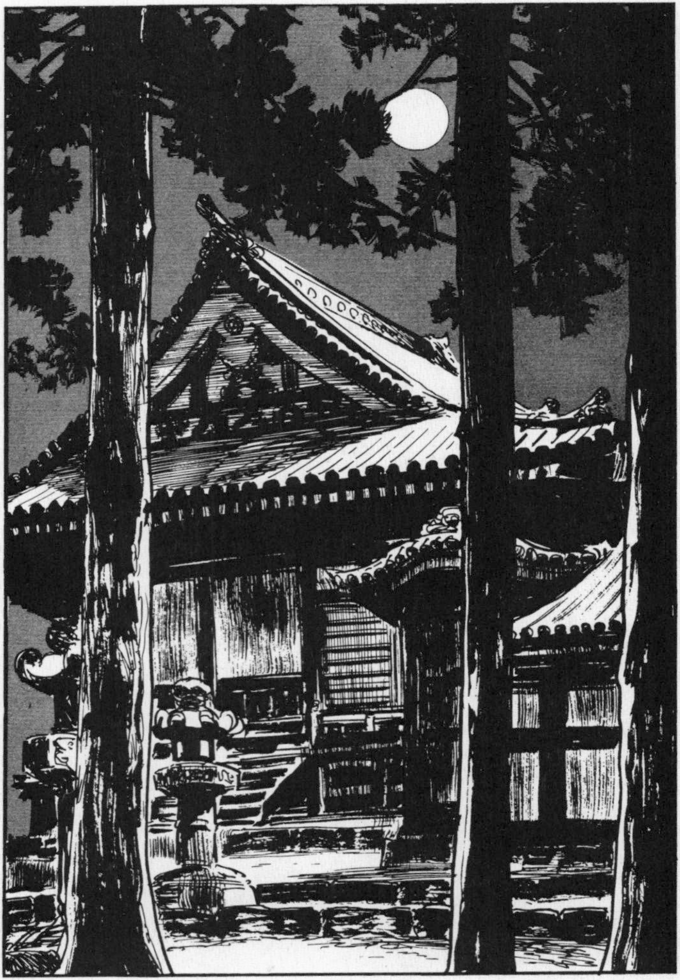

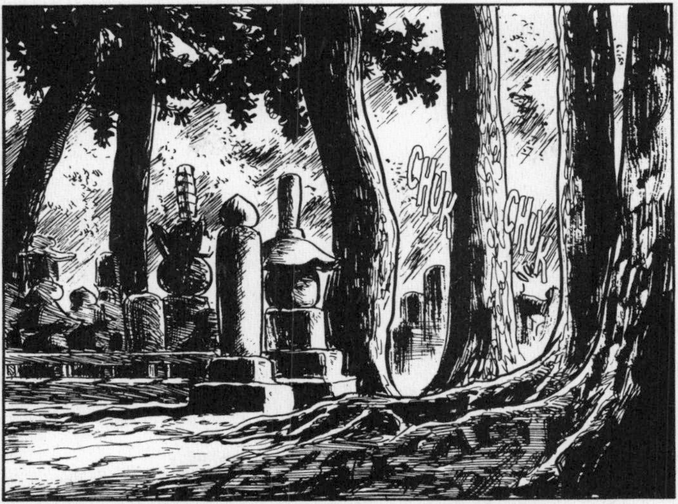
CHUK
CHUK
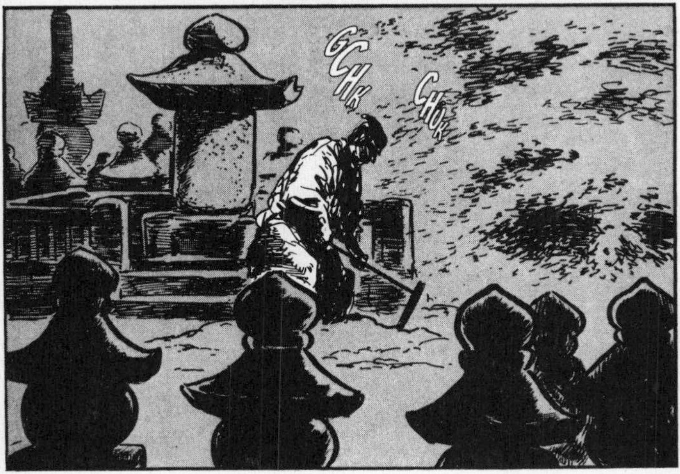
GCHK
CHOK

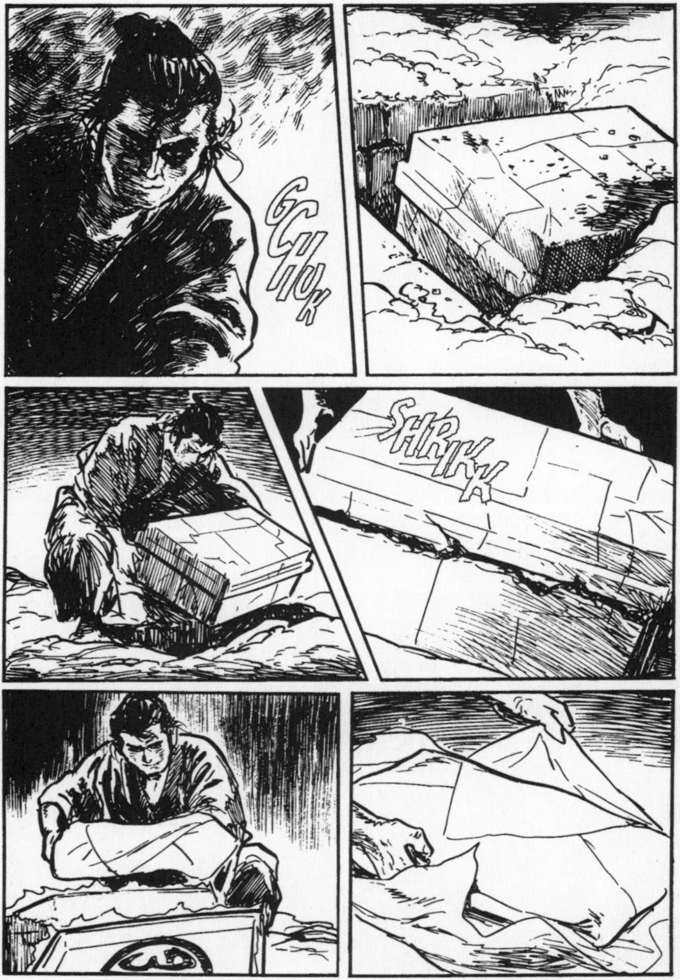
GCHUK
SHRIKK

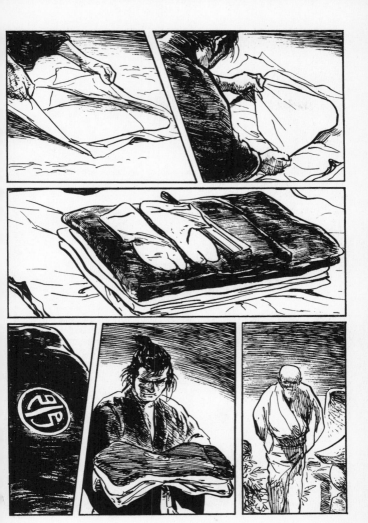

163

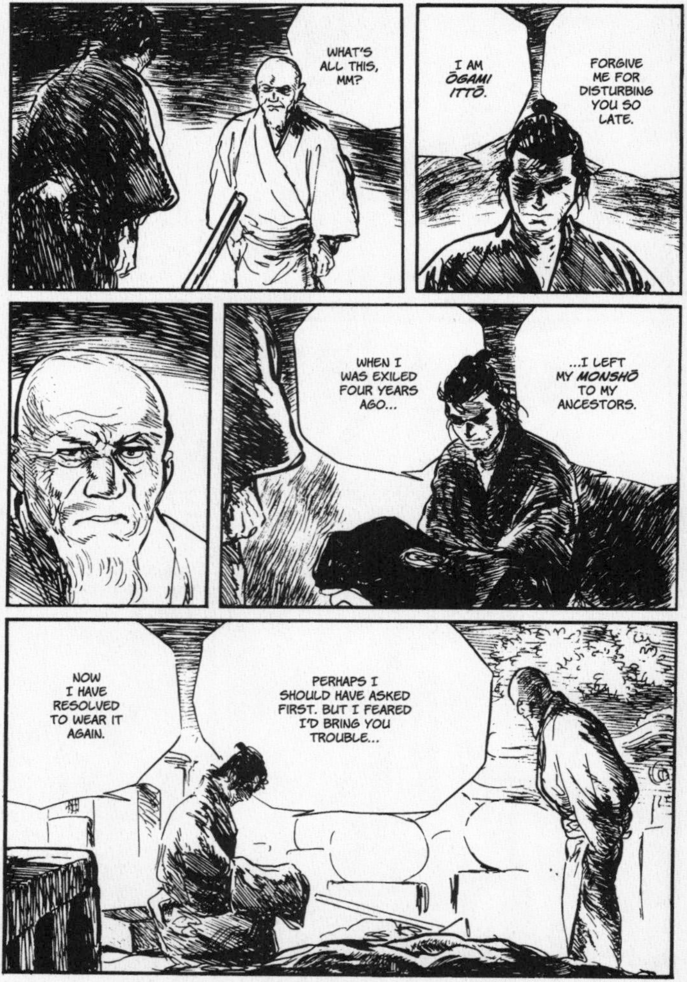
WHAT'S ALL THIS, MM?
I AM ŌGAMI ITTŌ.
FORGIVE ME FOR DISTURBING YOU SO LATE.
WHEN I WAS EXILED FOUR YEARS AGO...
...I LEFT MY MONSHŌ TO MY ANCESTORS.
NOW I HAVE RESOLVED TO WEAR IT AGAIN.
PERHAPS I SHOULD HAVE ASKED FIRST. BUT I FEARED I'D BRING YOU TROUBLE...

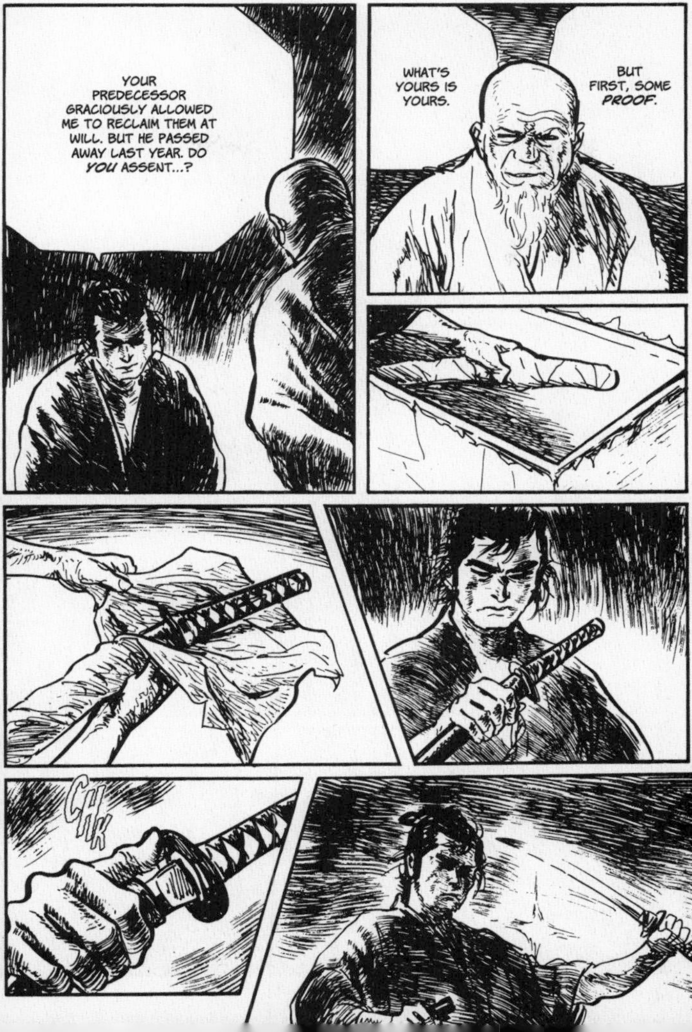
YOUR PREDECESSOR GRACIOUSLY ALLOWED ME TO RECLAIM THEM AT WILL. BUT HE PASSED AWAY LAST YEAR. DO *YOU* ASSENT...?
WHAT'S YOURS IS YOURS.
BUT FIRST, SOME *PROOF*.
CHK

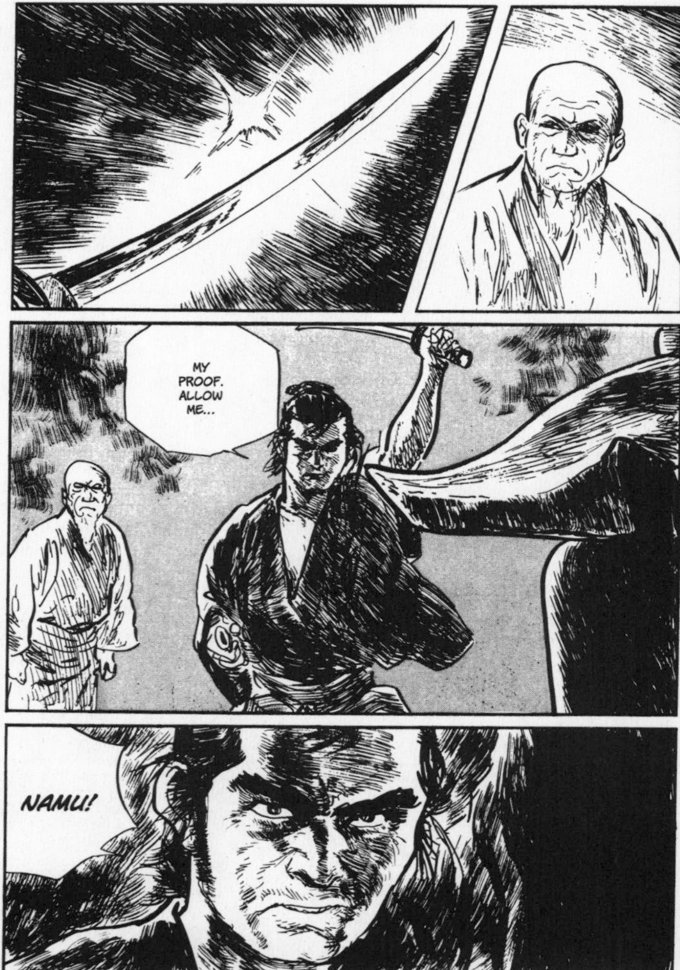
MY PROOF. ALLOW ME...
NAMU!

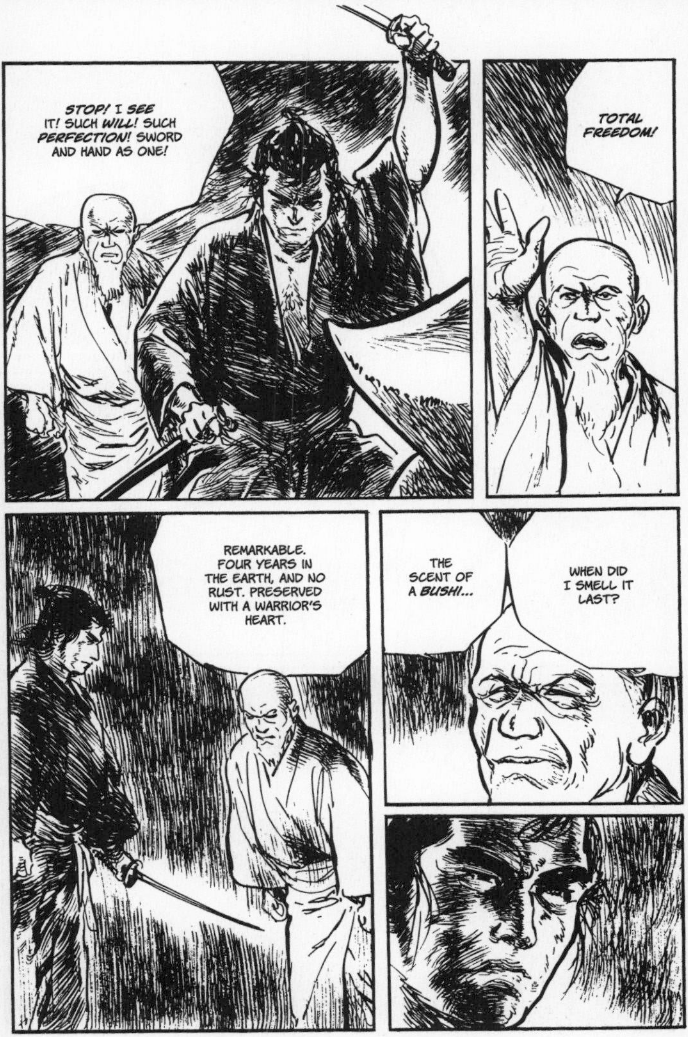
STOP! I SEE IT! SUCH WILL! SUCH PERFECTION! SWORD AND HAND AS ONE!
TOTAL FREEDOM!
REMARKABLE. FOUR YEARS IN THE EARTH, AND NO RUST. PRESERVED WITH A WARRIOR'S HEART.
THE SCENT OF A BUSHI...
WHEN DID I SMELL IT LAST?

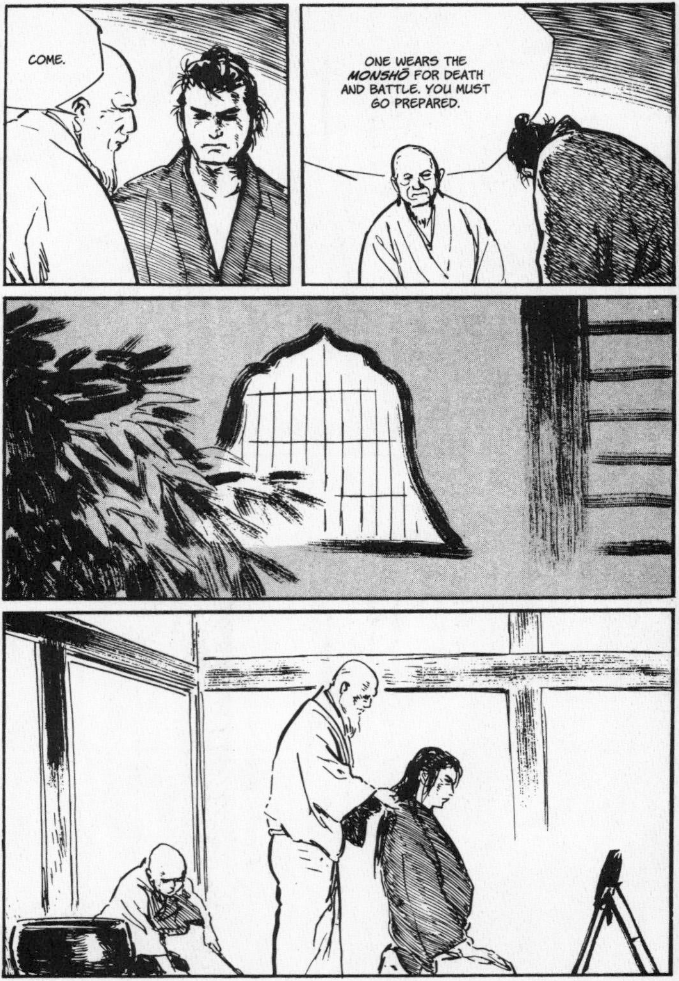
COME.
ONE WEARS THE *MONSHŌ* FOR DEATH AND BATTLE. YOU MUST GO PREPARED.

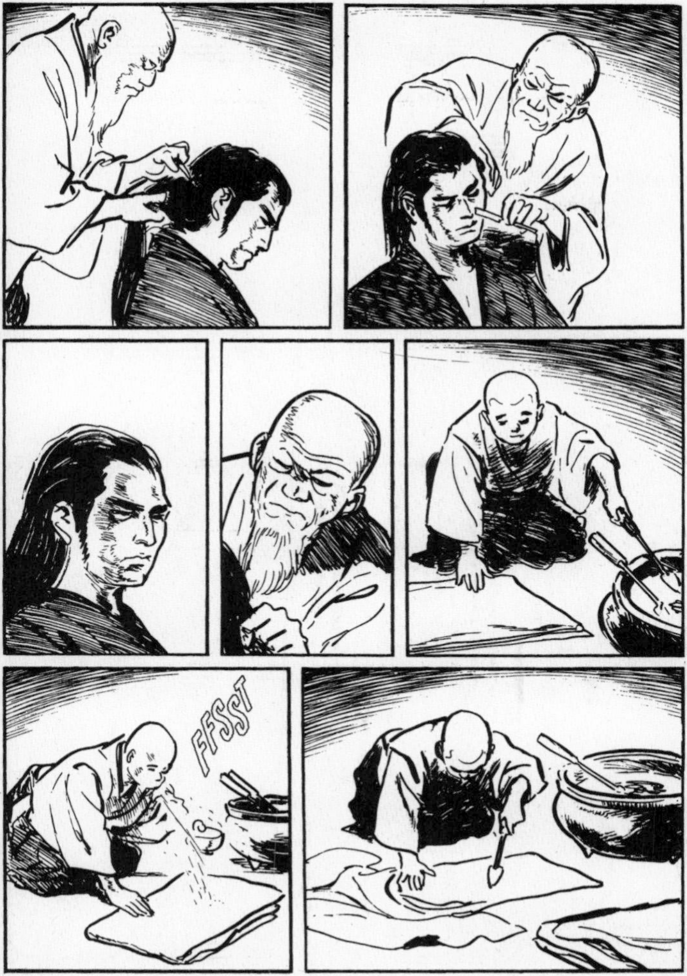
FFSST

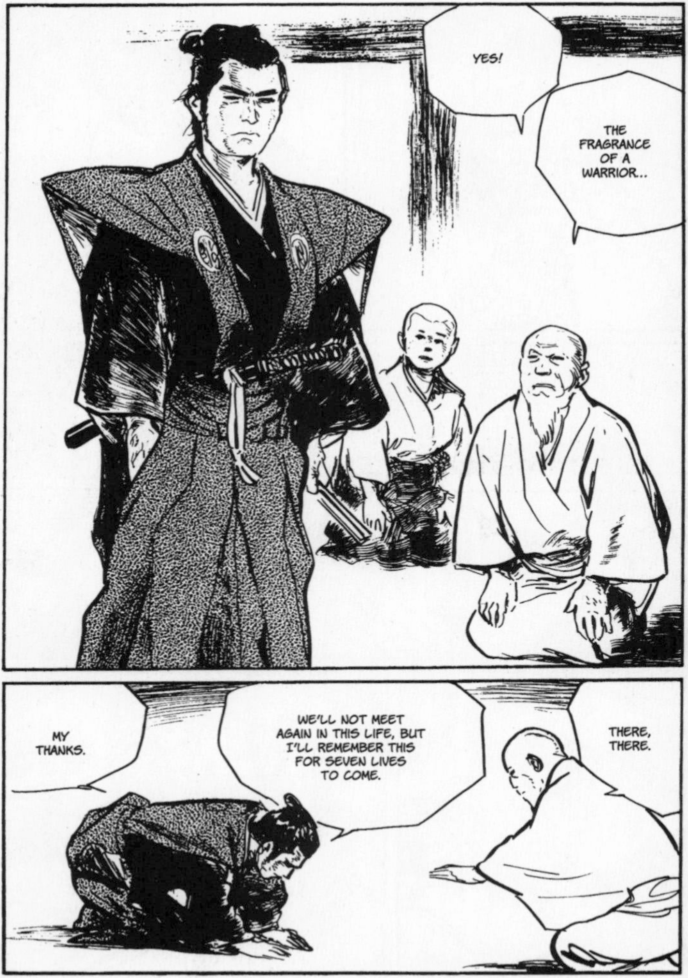
YES!
THE FRAGRANCE OF A WARRIOR...
MY THANKS.
WE'LL NOT MEET AGAIN IN THIS LIFE, BUT I'LL REMEMBER THIS FOR SEVEN LIVES TO COME.
THERE, THERE.

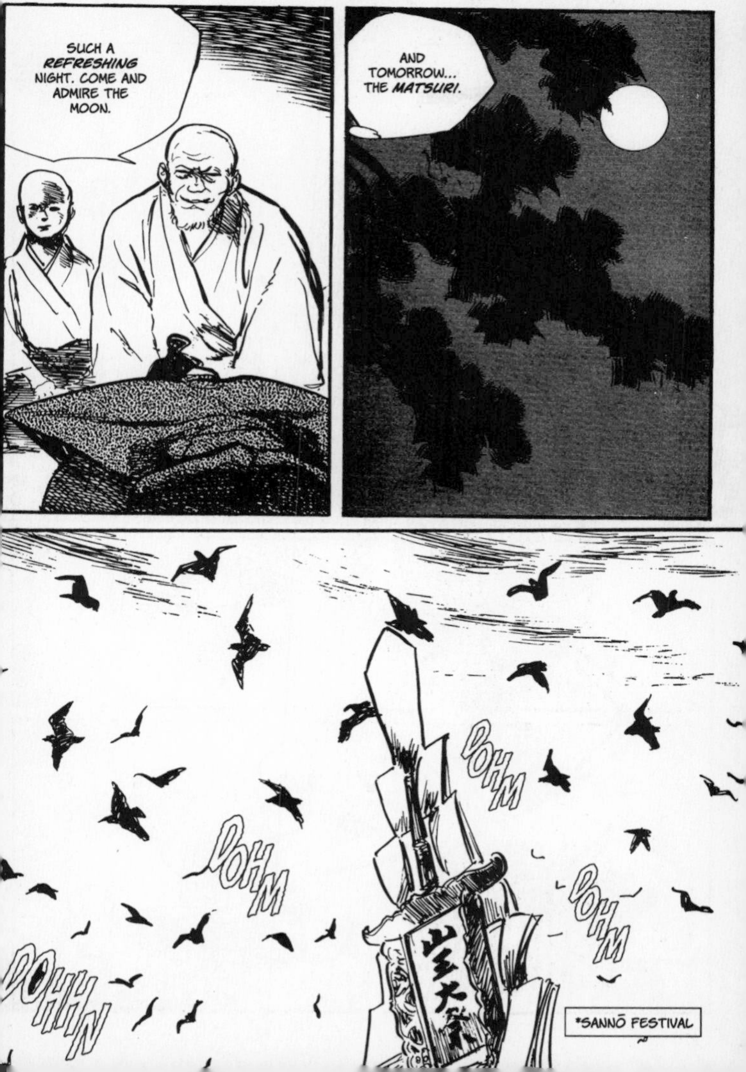
SUCH A *REFRESHING* NIGHT. COME AND ADMIRE THE MOON.
AND TOMORROW... THE *MATSURI*.
DOHM
DOHM
DOHM
DOOHHN
*SANNŌ FESTIVAL

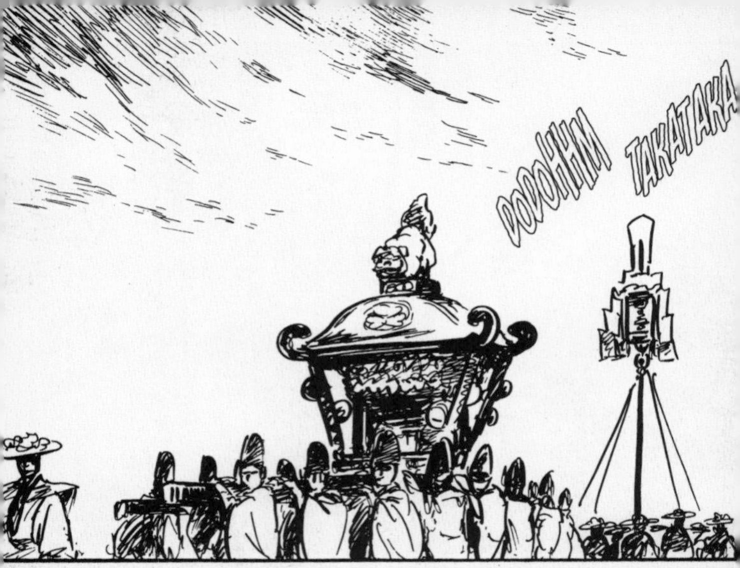
DODOHHM
TAKATAKA
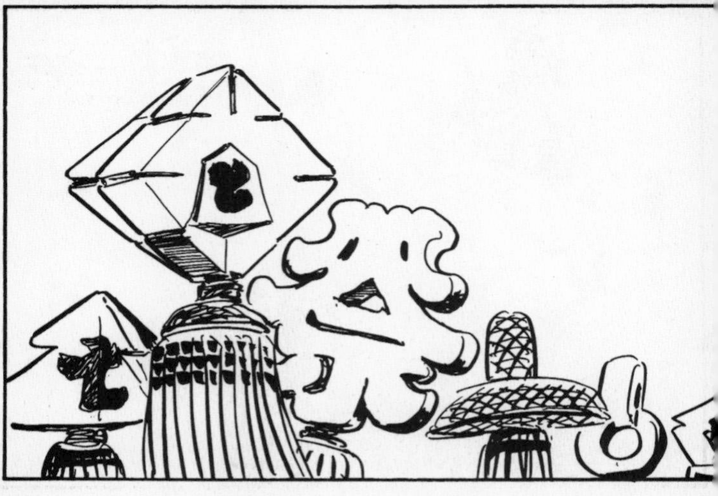

DOHNN

THE PAPIER MÂCHÉ LION WAS MADE OF PAPER PASSED DOWN FROM THE THIRD *SHŌGUN*, TOKUGAWA IEMITSU. THUS BEGAN THE TENKA *MATSURI*...

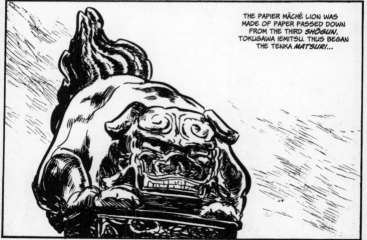

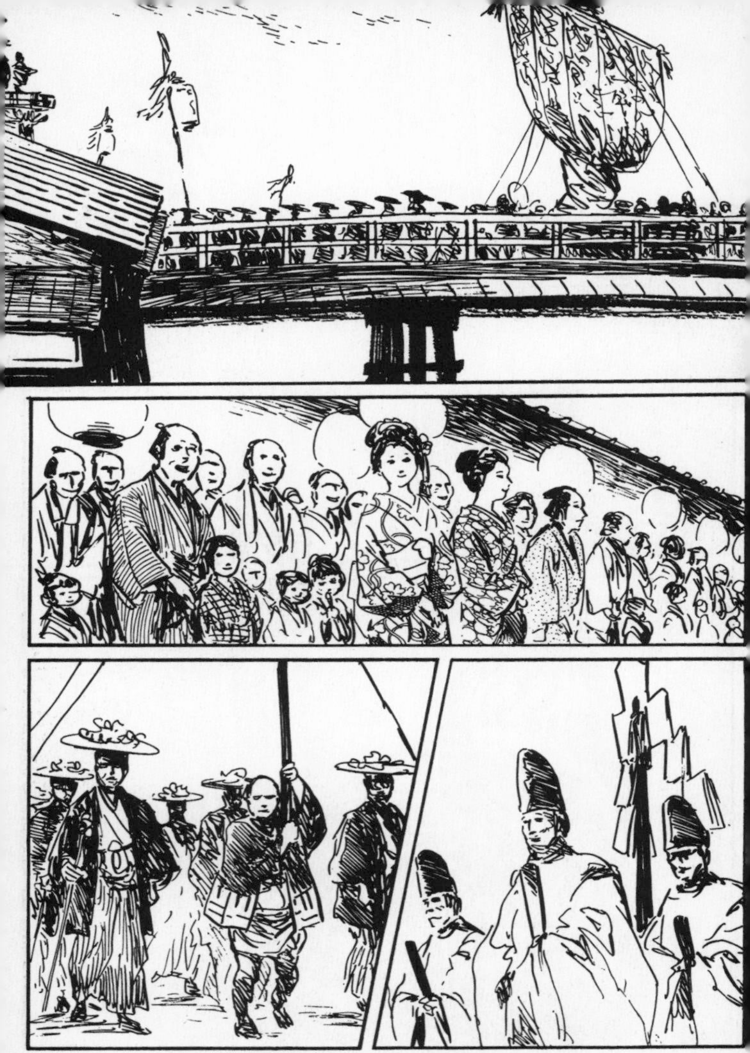

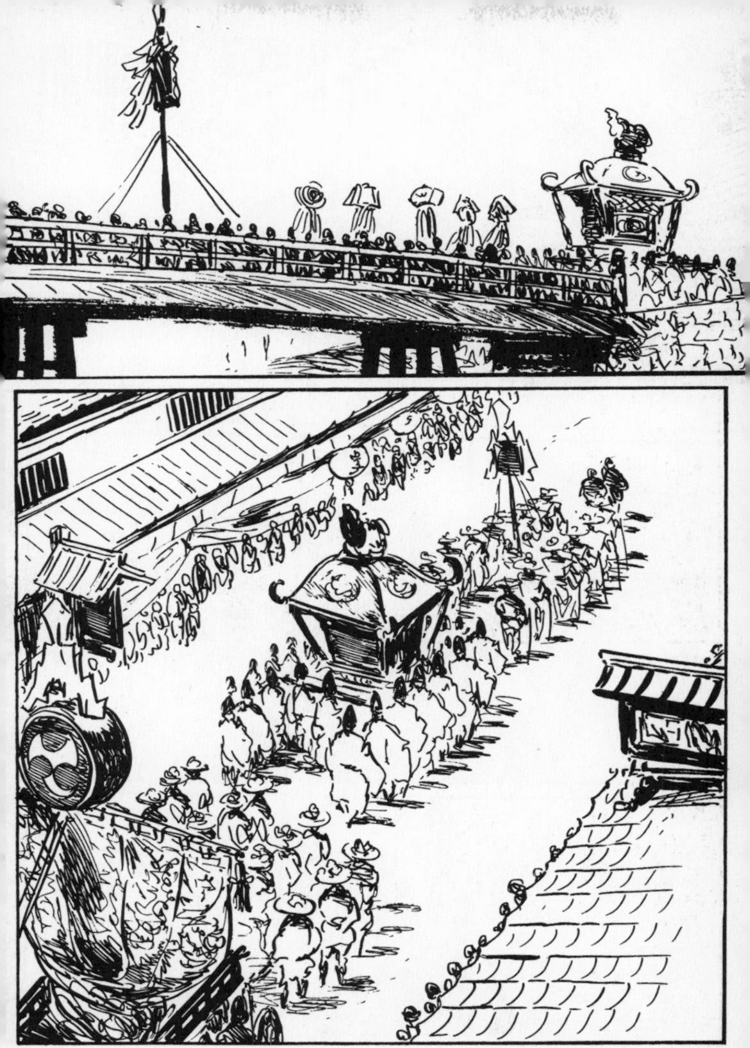

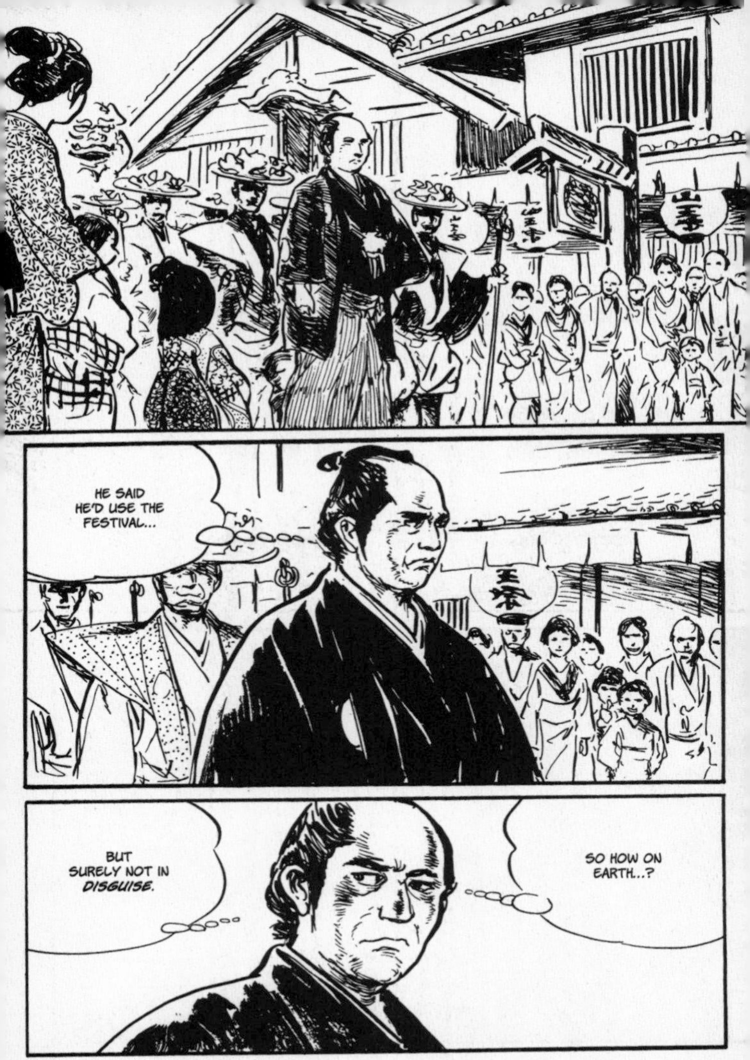
HE SAID HE'D USE THE FESTIVAL...
BUT SURELY NOT IN *DISGUISE.*
SO HOW ON EARTH...?

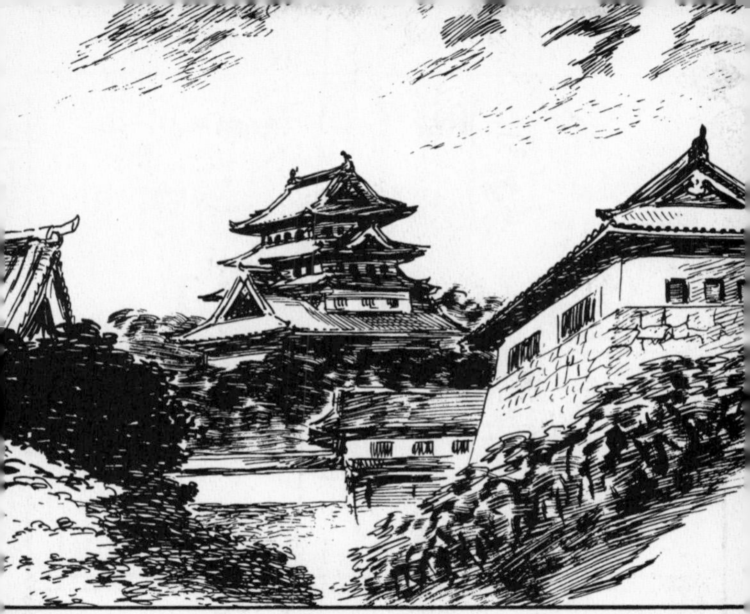

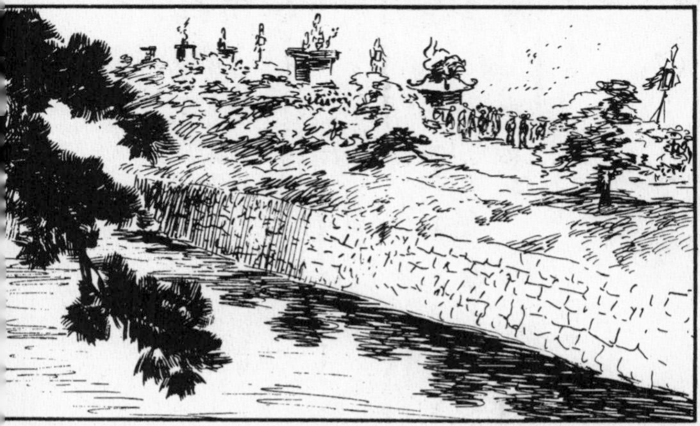

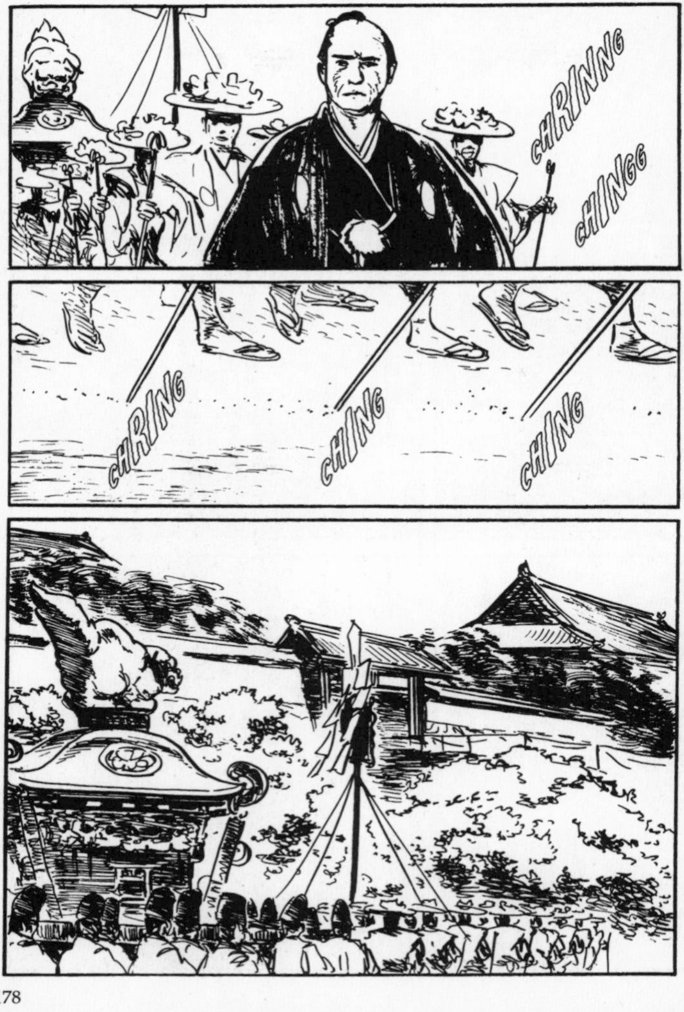

cHRINNG
cHINGG
cHRING
cHING
cHING

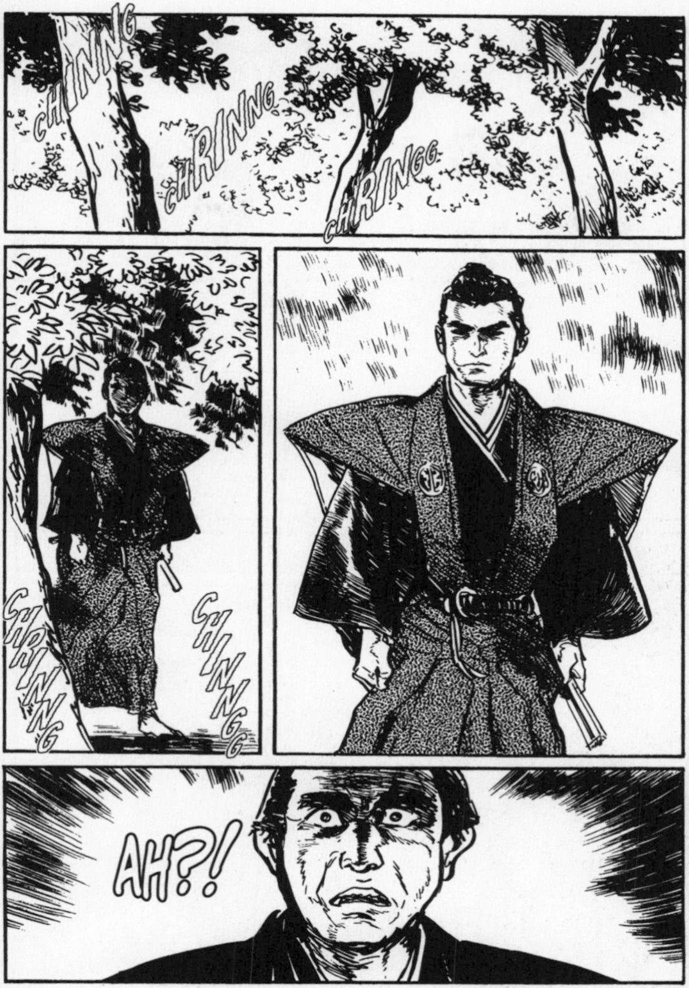
CHINNG
CHRINNG
CHRINGG
CHRINNG
CHINNGG
AH?!

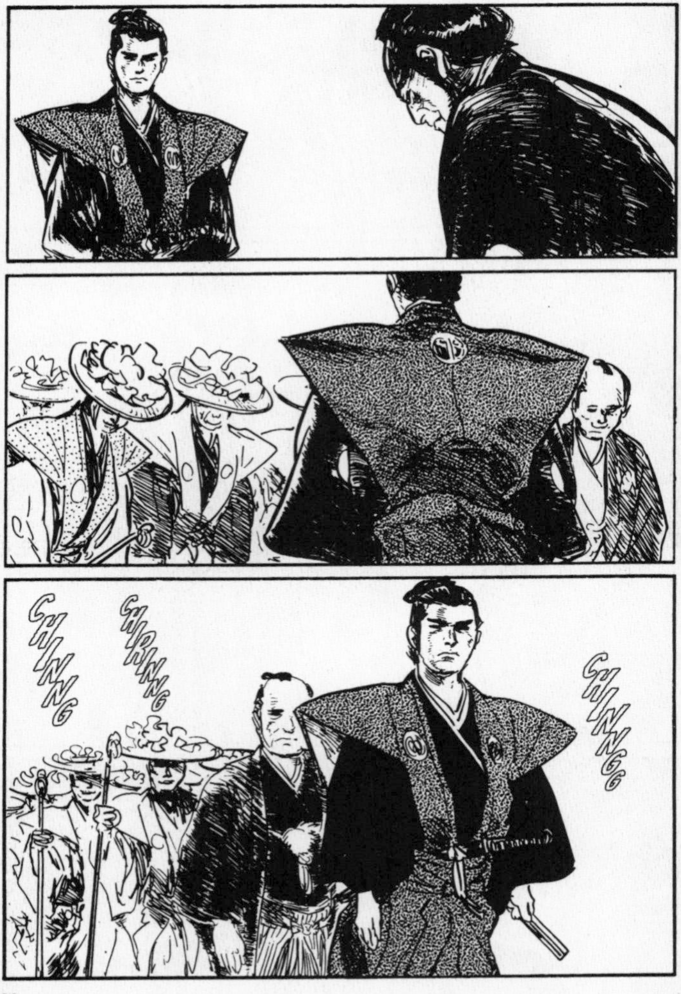
CHINNG
CHRINNG
CHINNGG

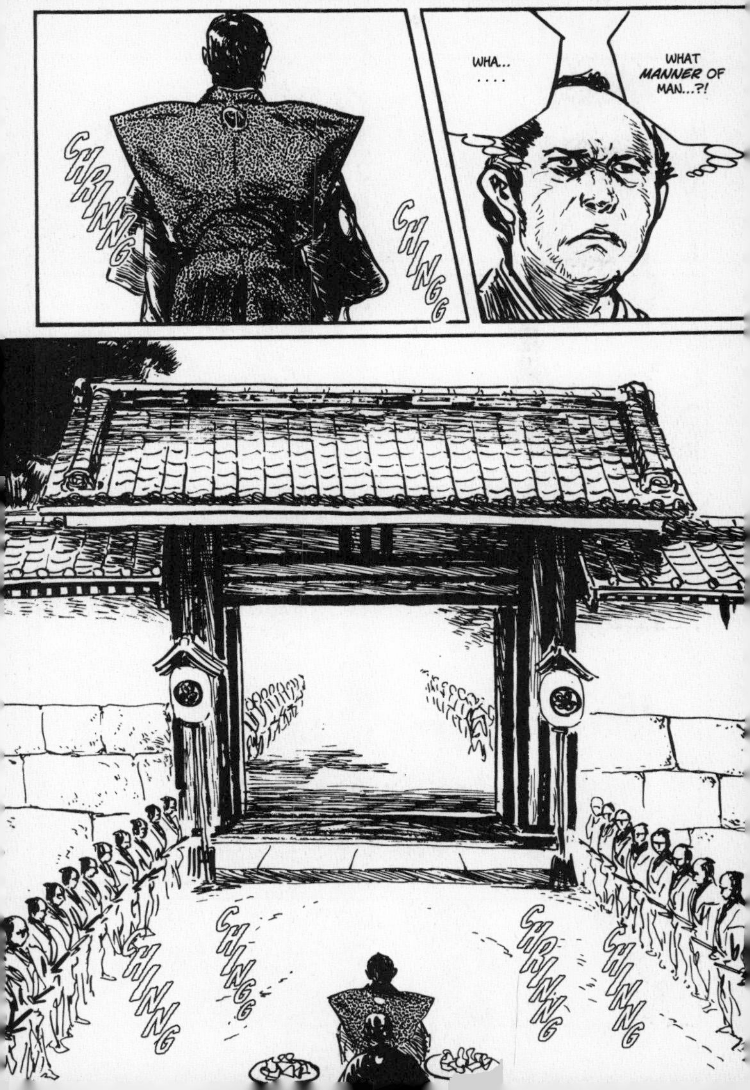
CHRINNG
CHINGG
WHA...
....
WHAT MANNER OF MAN...?!
CHINNG
CHINGG
CHRINNG
CHINNG

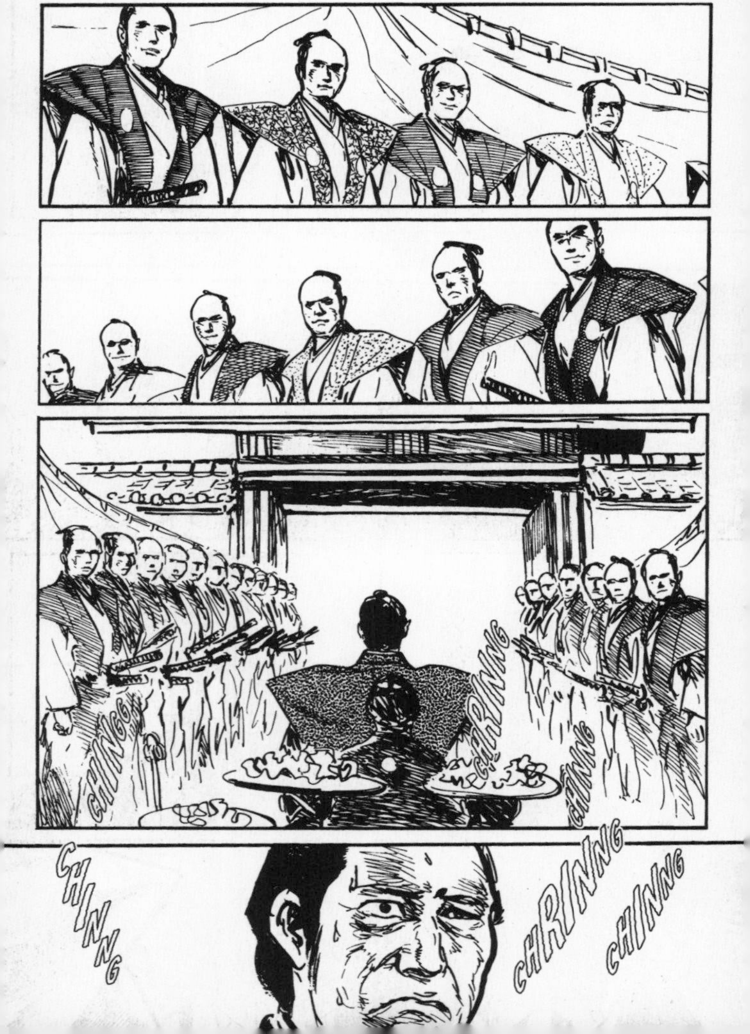

CHINGG
CHRINNG
CHINNG
CHINNG
CHINNG
CHRINNG
CHINNG

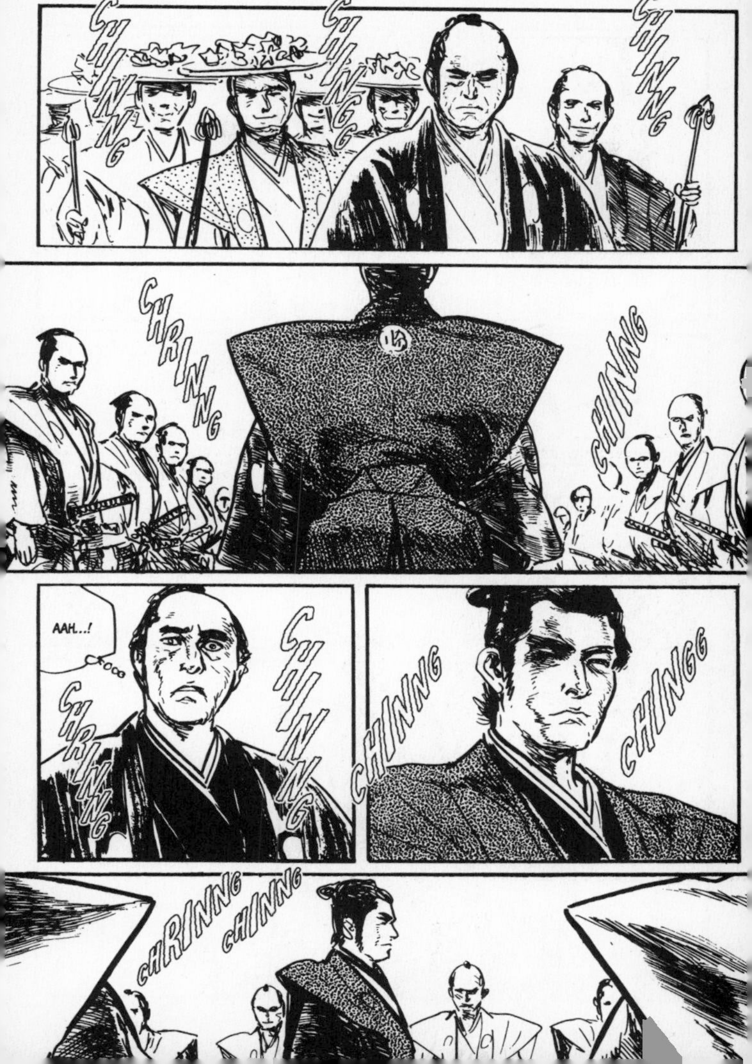
CHINNG
CHINNG
CHINNG
CHRINNG
CHINNG
AAH...!
CHRINNG
CHINNNG
CHINNG
CHINGG
CHRINNG
CHINNG

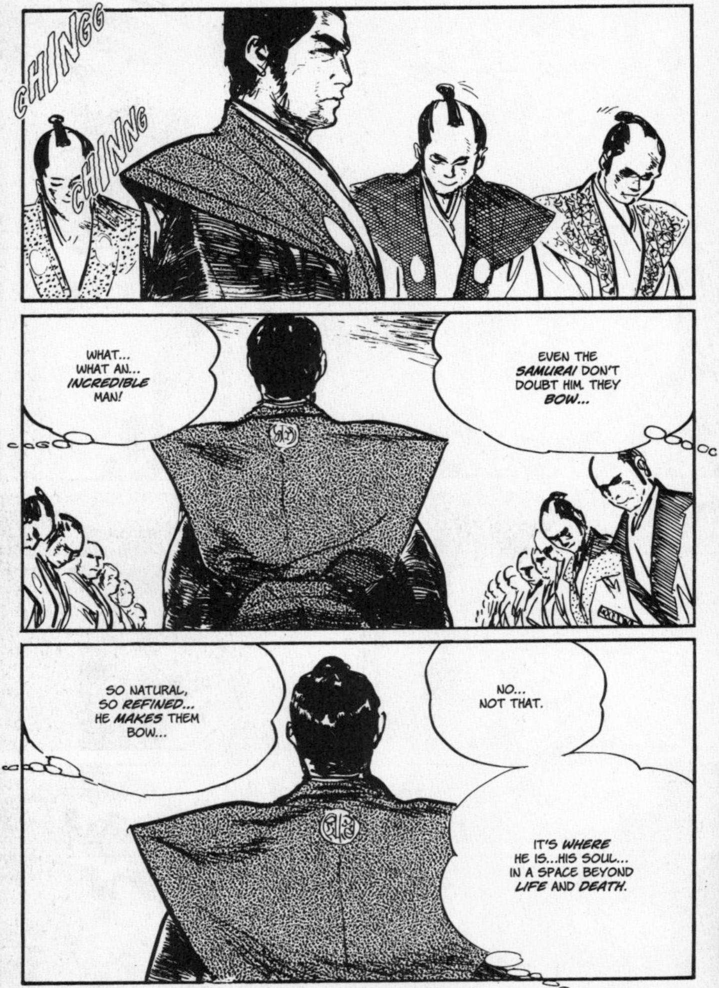
CHINGG
CHINNG
WHAT... WHAT AN... INCREDIBLE MAN!
EVEN THE SAMURAI DON'T DOUBT HIM. THEY BOW...
SO NATURAL, SO REFINED... HE MAKES THEM BOW...
NO... NOT THAT.
IT'S WHERE HE IS...HIS SOUL... IN A SPACE BEYOND LIFE AND DEATH.

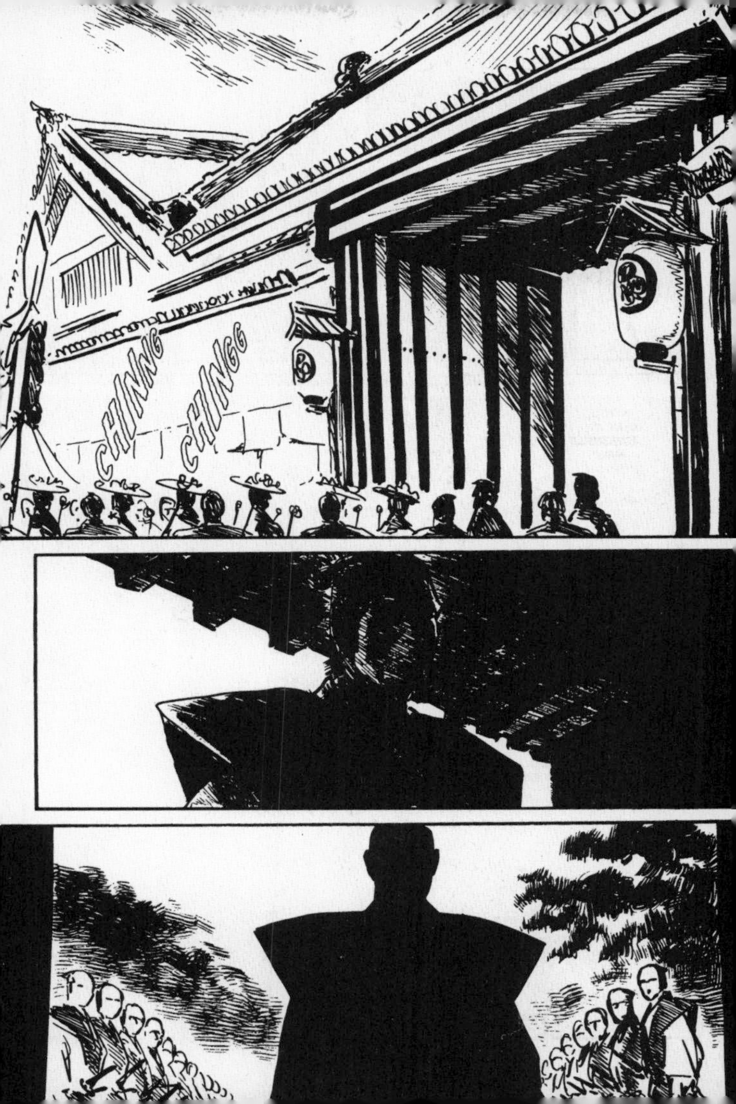
CHINNG
CHINGG

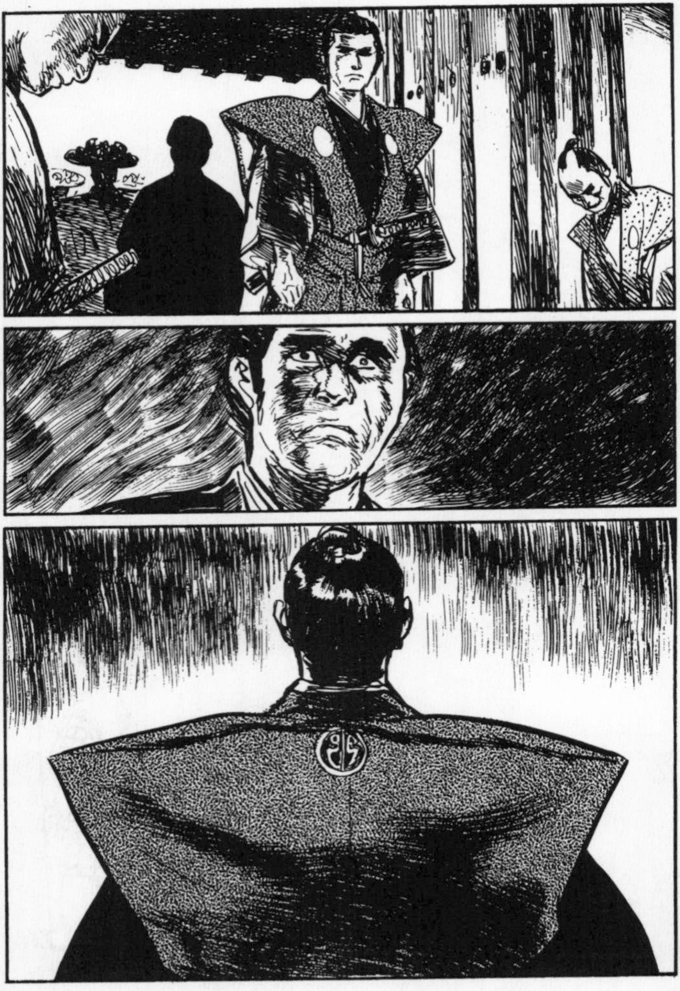

the hundred and thirty-first

Great Reversals

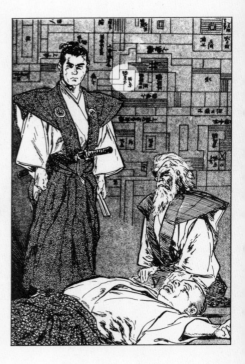

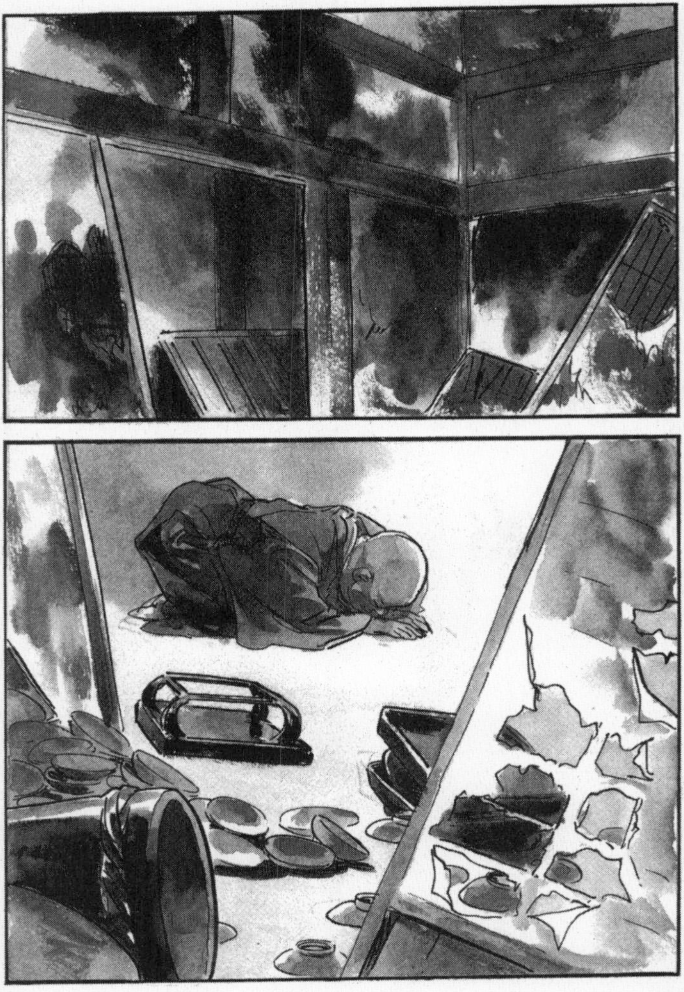

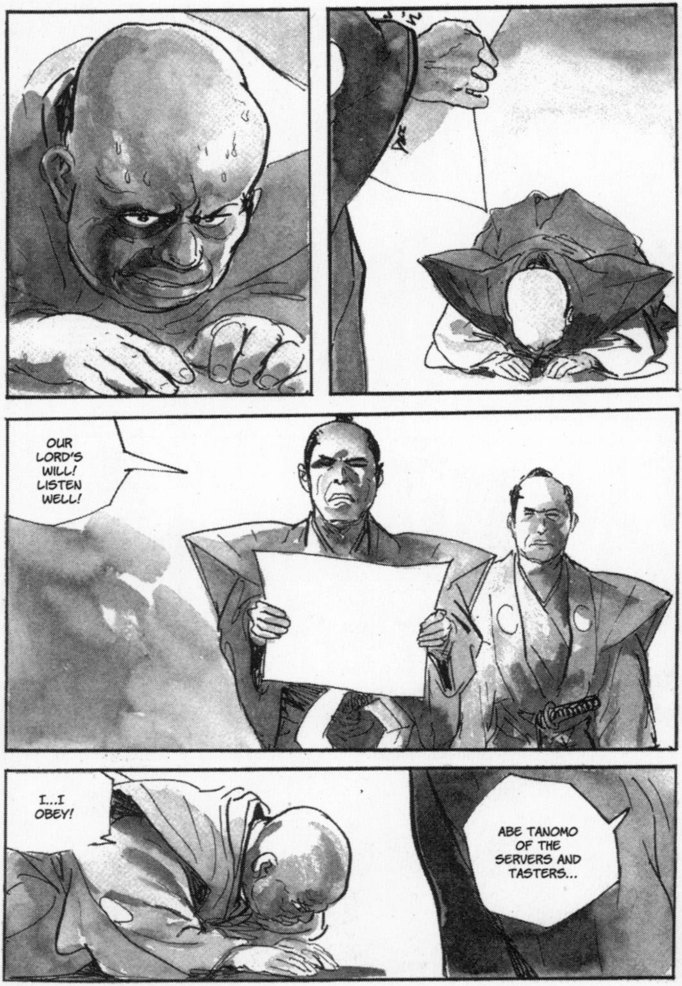
OUR LORD'S WILL! LISTEN WELL!
I...I OBEY!
ABE TANOMO OF THE SERVERS AND TASTERS...

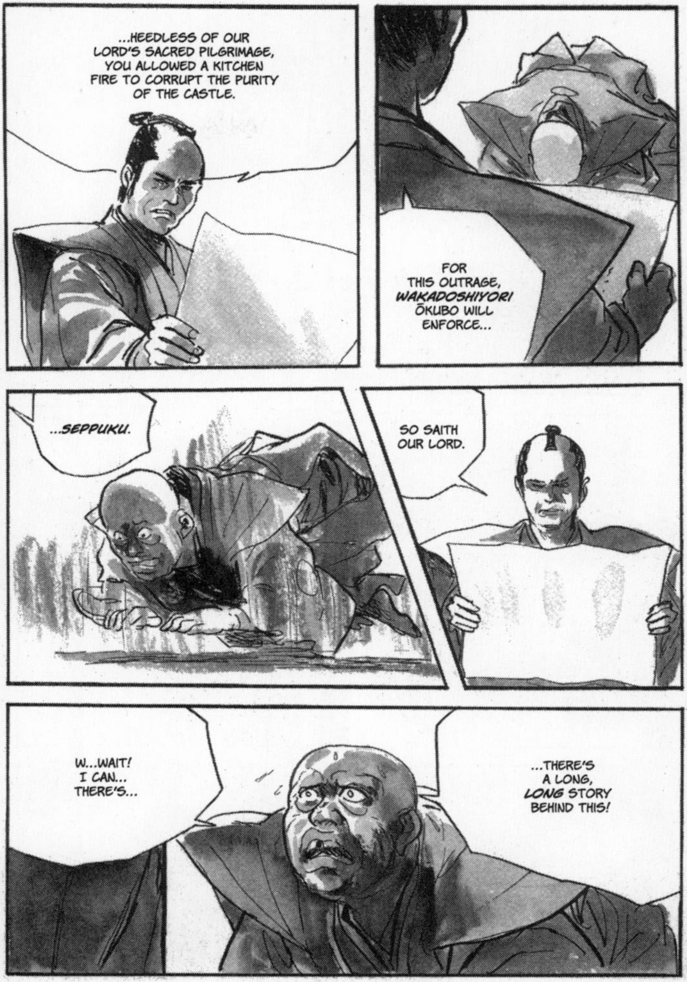
...HEEDLESS OF OUR LORD'S SACRED PILGRIMAGE, YOU ALLOWED A KITCHEN FIRE TO CORRUPT THE PURITY OF THE CASTLE.
FOR THIS OUTRAGE, *WAKADOSHIYORI* ŌKUBO WILL ENFORCE...
...*SEPPUKU*.
SO SAITH OUR LORD.
W...WAIT! I CAN... THERE'S...
...THERE'S A LONG, *LONG* STORY BEHIND THIS!

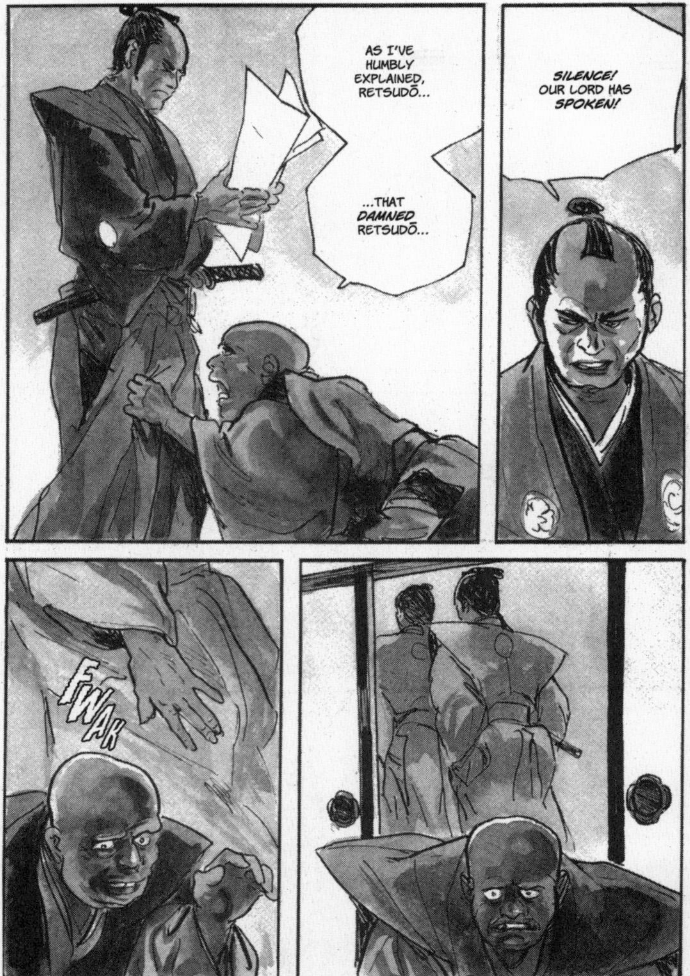
AS I'VE HUMBLY EXPLAINED, RETSUDŌ...
...THAT DAMNED RETSUDŌ...
SILENCE! OUR LORD HAS SPOKEN!
FWAK

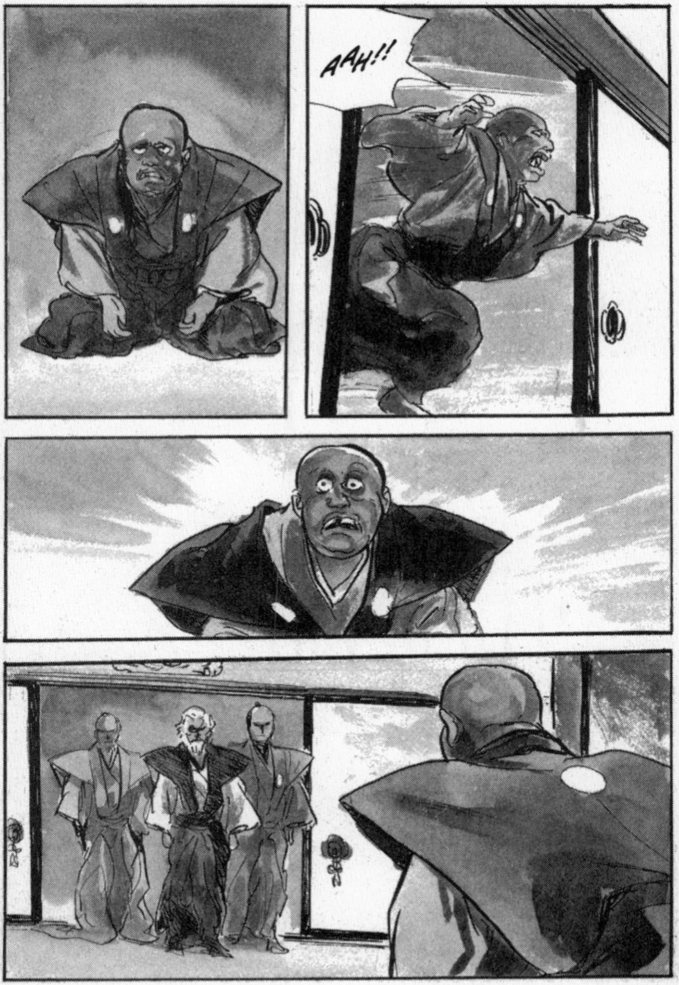
AAH!!

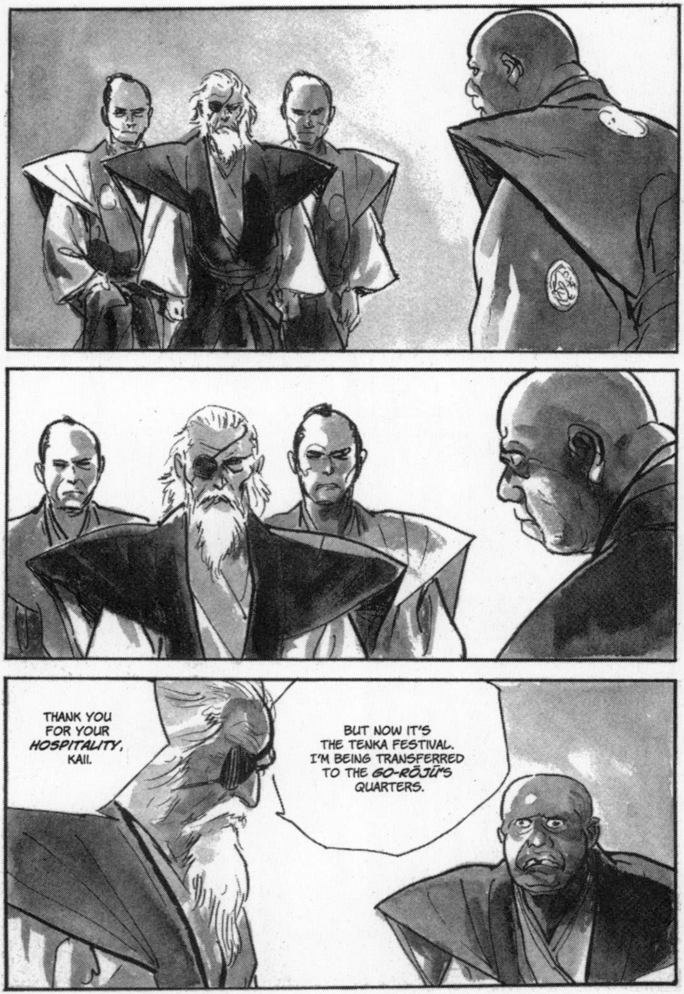
THANK YOU FOR YOUR *HOSPITALITY*, KAII.
BUT NOW IT'S THE TENKA FESTIVAL. I'M BEING TRANSFERRED TO THE *GO-RŌJŪ*'S QUARTERS.

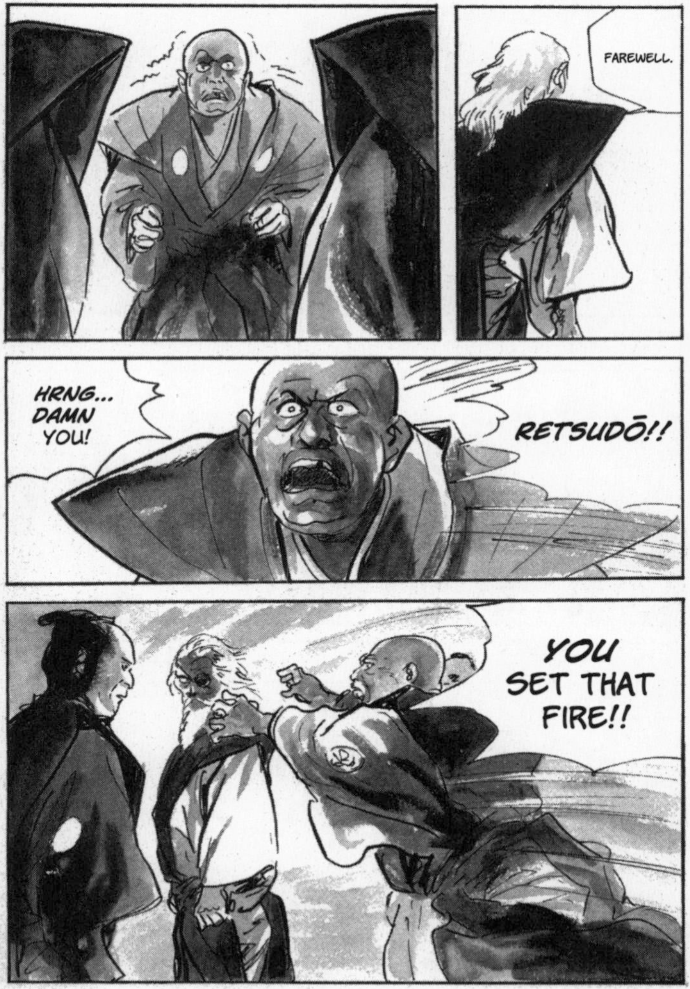
FAREWELL.
HRNG... DAMN YOU!
RETSUDŌ!!
YOU SET THAT FIRE!!

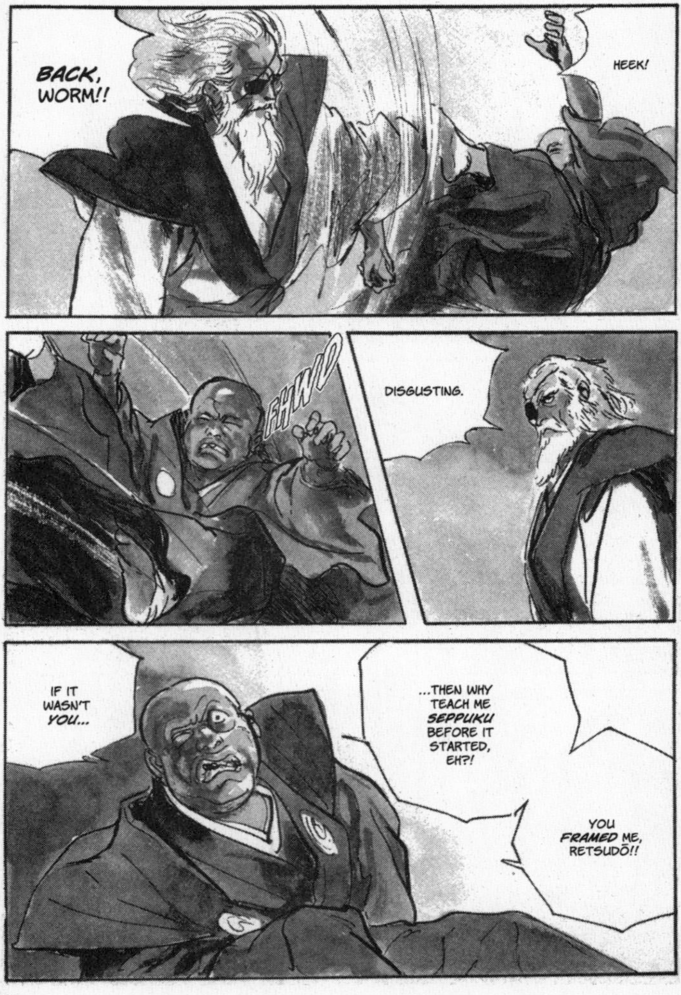

BACK, WORM!!
HEEK!
FHWO
DISGUSTING.
IF IT WASN'T YOU...
...THEN WHY TEACH ME SEPPUKU BEFORE IT STARTED, EH?!
YOU FRAMED ME, RETSUDŌ!!

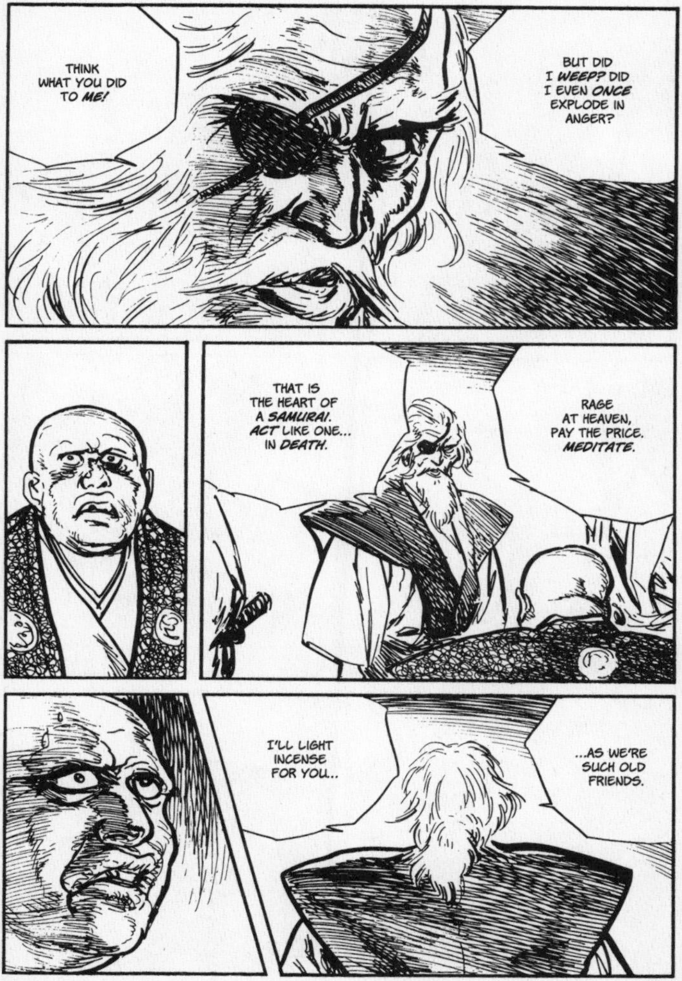
THINK WHAT YOU DID TO *ME!*
BUT DID I *WEEP?* DID I EVEN *ONCE* EXPLODE IN ANGER?
THAT IS THE HEART OF A *SAMURAI.* *ACT* LIKE ONE... IN *DEATH.*
RAGE AT HEAVEN, PAY THE PRICE. *MEDITATE.*
I'LL LIGHT INCENSE FOR YOU...
...AS WE'RE SUCH OLD FRIENDS.

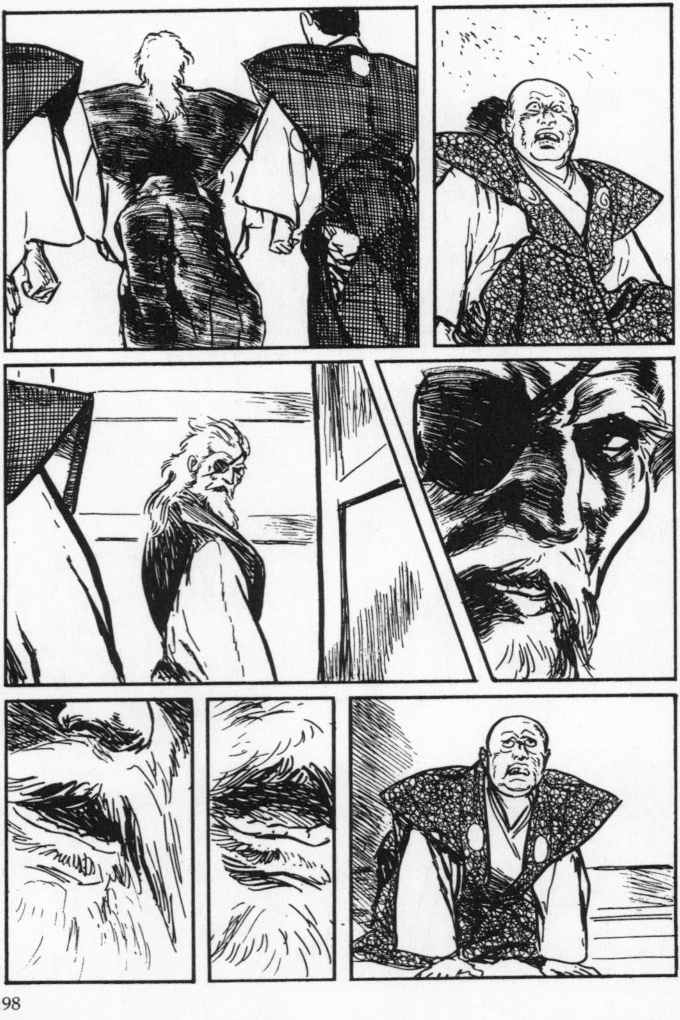

I...
LOSE.

WHO SET THE FIRE...?

WHO CARES? THE *SHŌGUN'S* SPOKEN.

IT'S OVER... I'VE *LOST*.

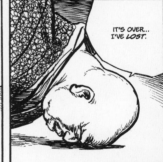

THERE'S NO...WAY... OUT...

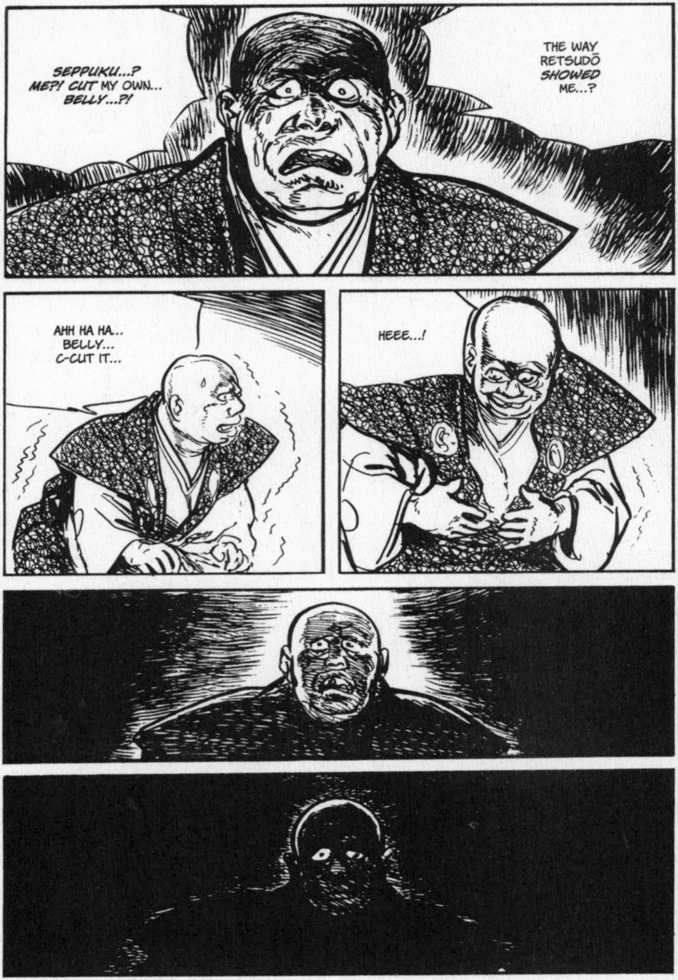
SEPPUKU...? ME?! CUT MY OWN... BELLY...?!
THE WAY RETSUDŌ SHOWED ME...?
AHH HA HA... BELLY... C-CUT IT...
HEEE...!

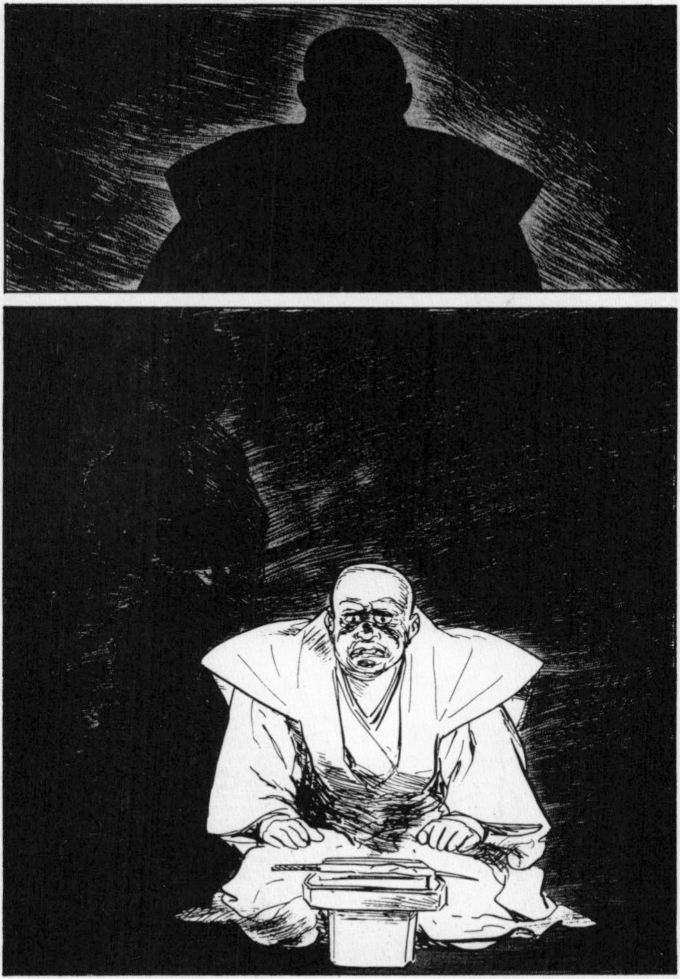

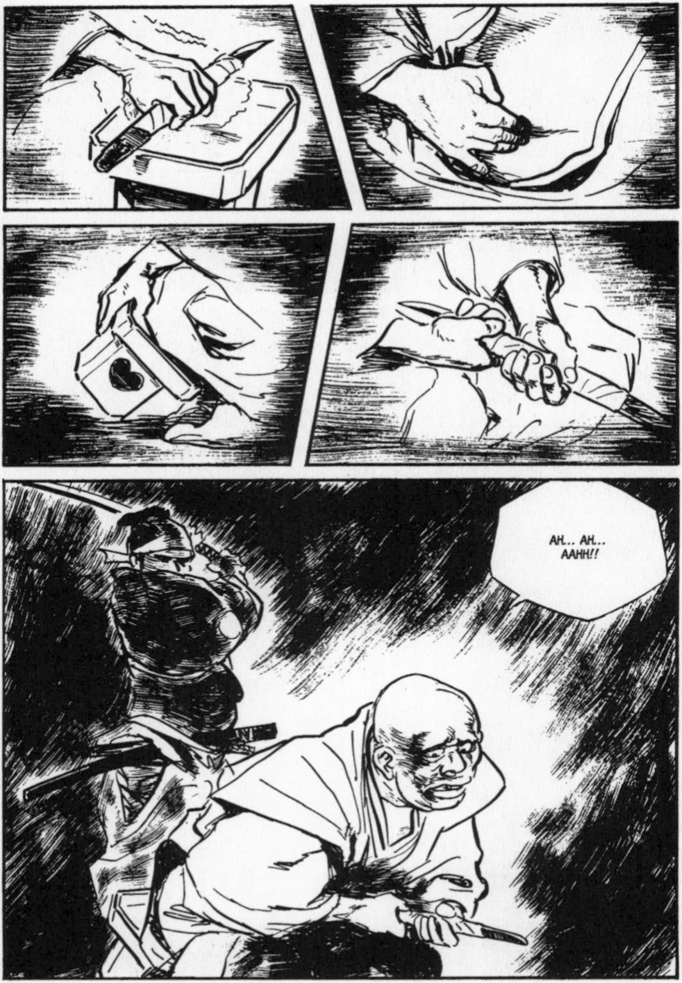
AH... AH... AAHH!!

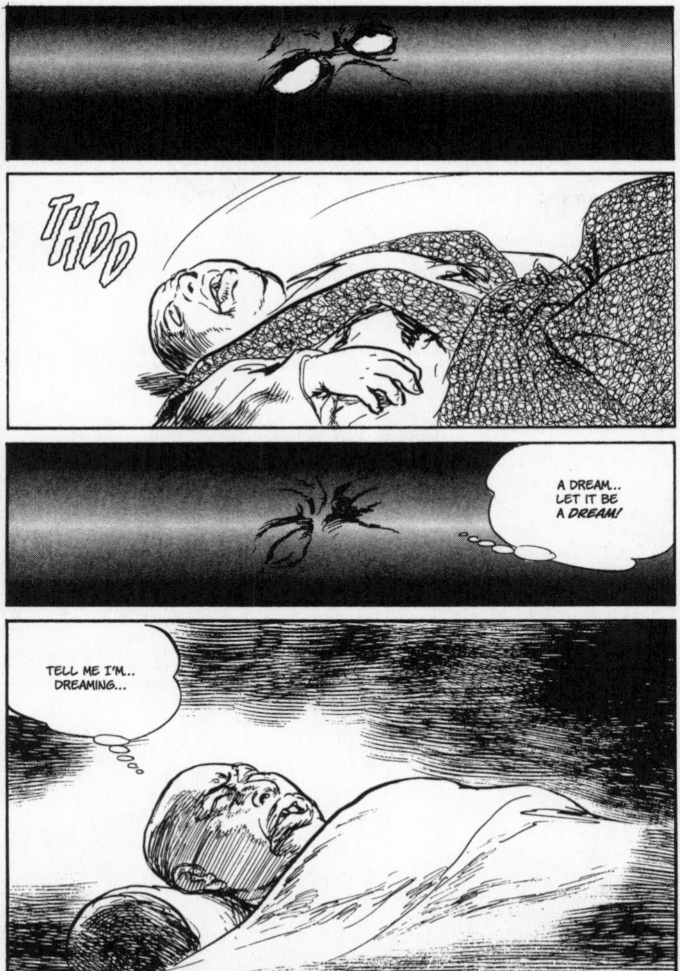
THDD
A DREAM.. LET IT BE A *DREAM!*
TELL ME I'M.. DREAMING...

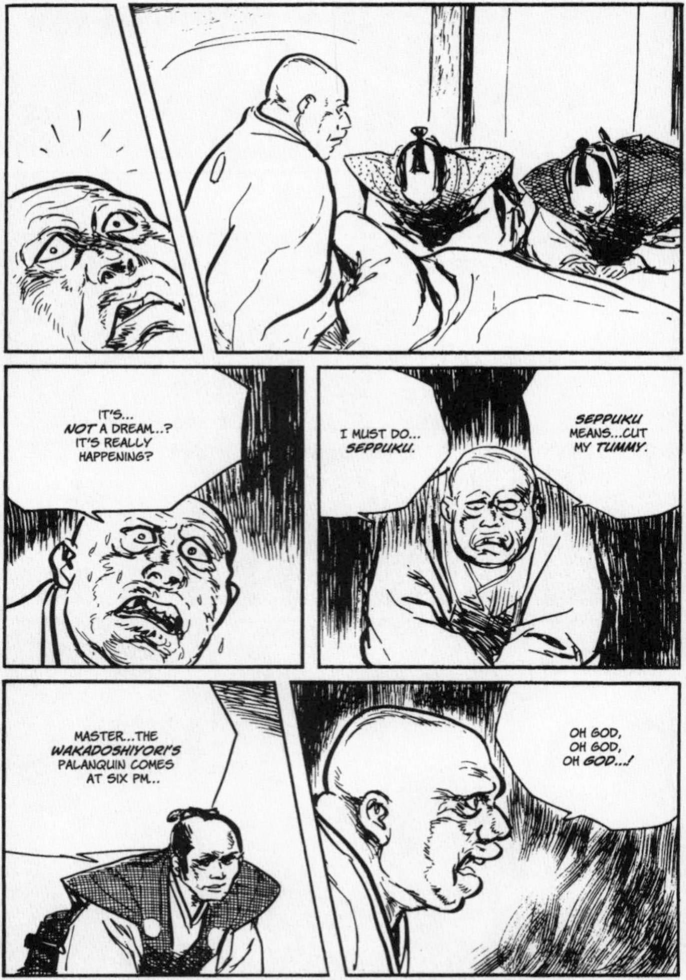
IT'S... *NOT* A DREAM...? IT'S REALLY HAPPENING?
I MUST DO... *SEPPUKU*.
SEPPUKU MEANS...CUT MY *TUMMY*.
MASTER...THE *WAKADOSHIYORI'S* PALANQUIN COMES AT SIX PM...
OH GOD, OH GOD, OH *GOD*...!

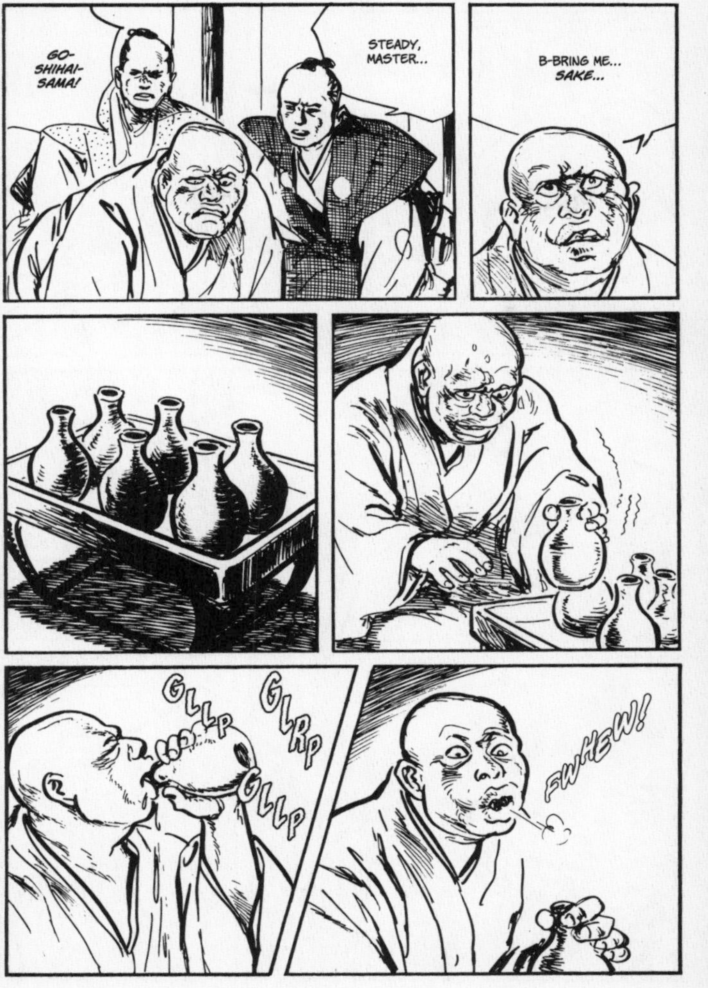
GO-SHIHAI-SAMA!
STEADY, MASTER...
B-BRING ME... SAKE...
GLLP
GLRP
GLLP
FWHEW!

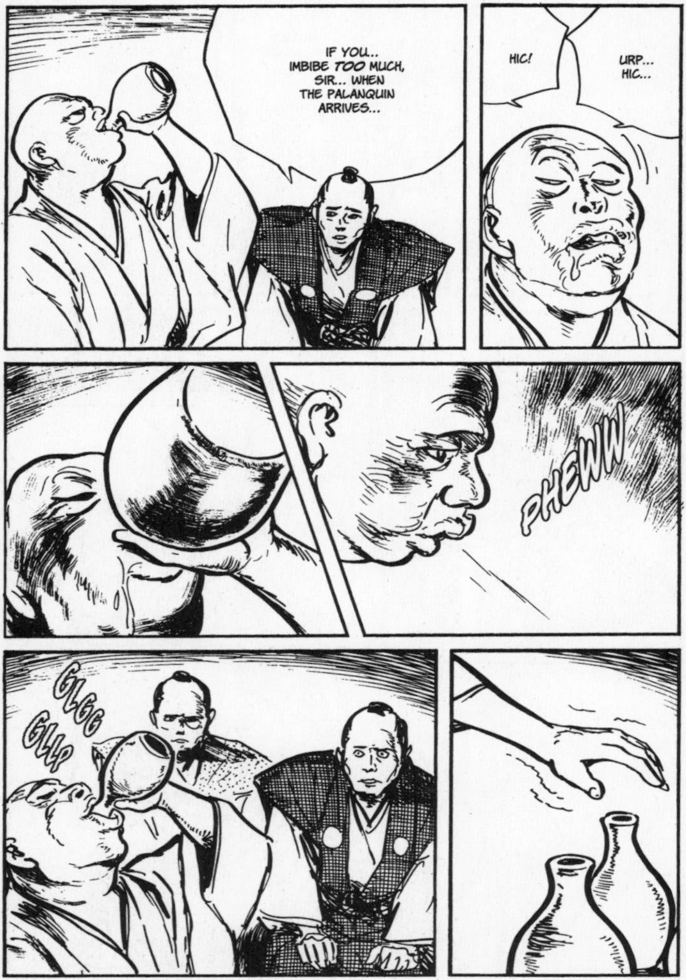
IF YOU... IMBIBE *TOO* MUCH, SIR... WHEN THE PALANQUIN ARRIVES...
HIC!
URP... HIC...
PHEWW
GLGG
GLLP

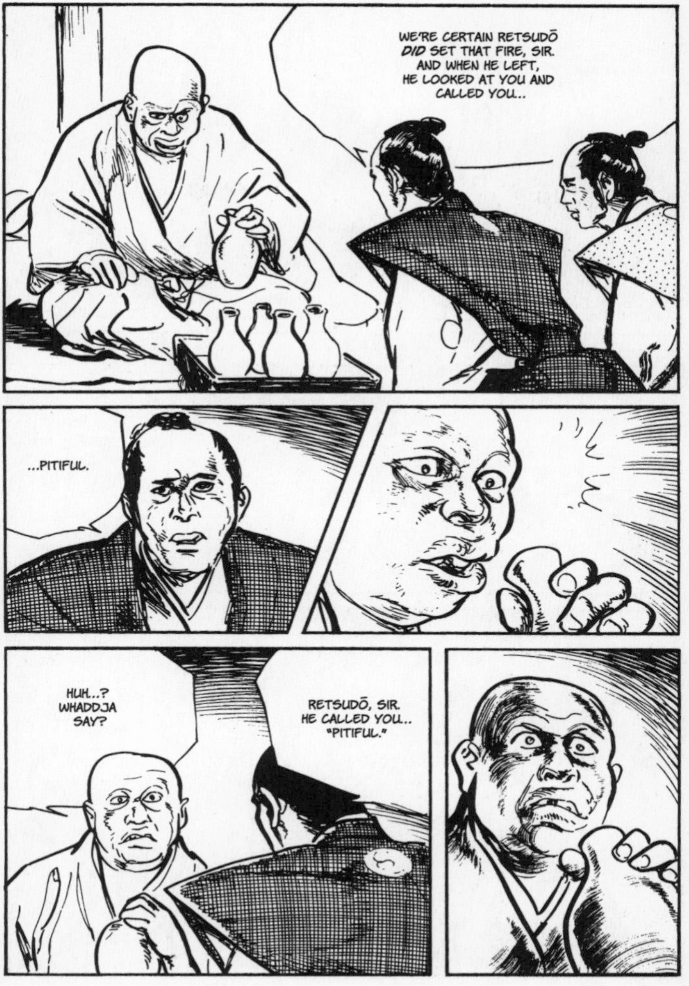
WE'RE CERTAIN RETSUDŌ *DID* SET THAT FIRE, SIR. AND WHEN HE LEFT, HE LOOKED AT YOU AND CALLED YOU..
...PITIFUL.
HUH..? WHADDJA SAY?
RETSUDŌ, SIR. HE CALLED YOU.. "PITIFUL."

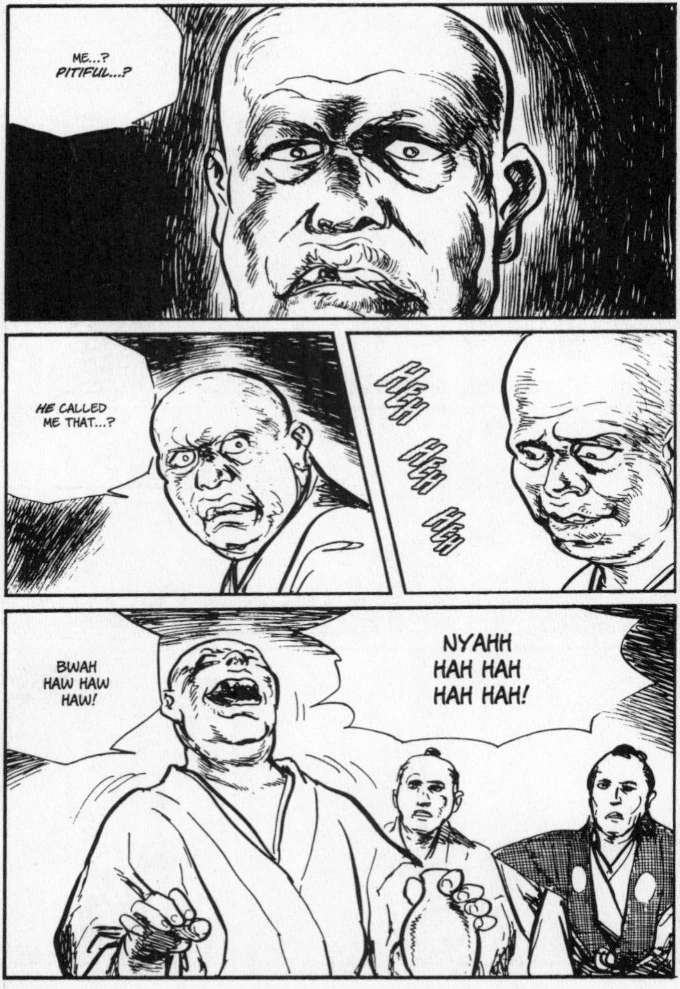
ME...? PITIFUL...?
HE CALLED ME THAT...?
HEH HEH HEH
BWAH HAW HAW HAW!
NYAHH HAH HAH HAH HAH!

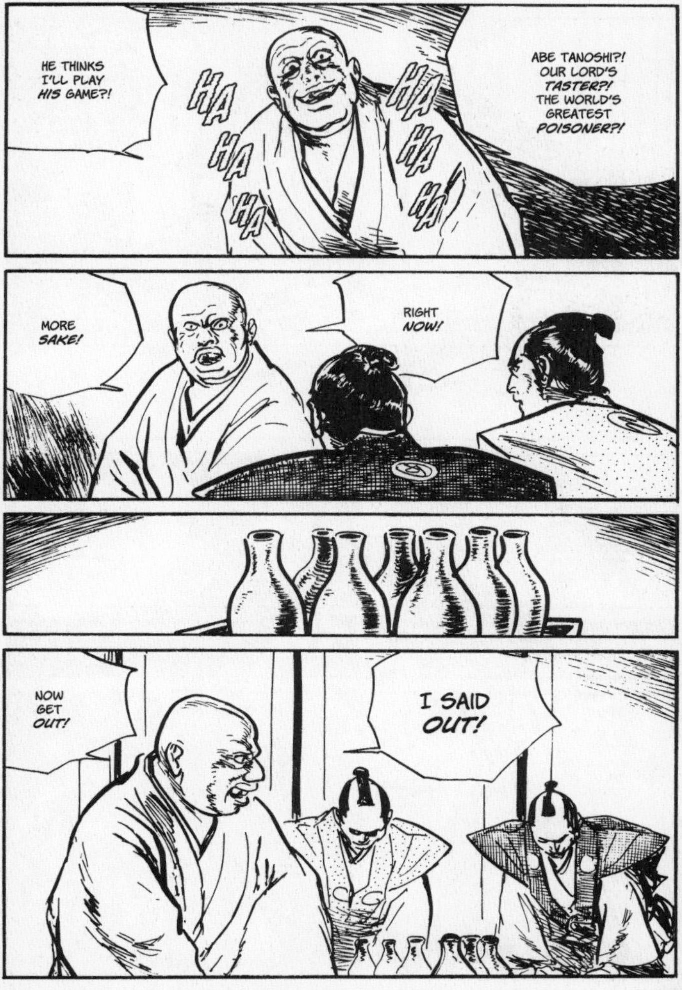
HE THINKS I'LL PLAY HIS GAME?!
HA HA HA
ABE TANOSHI?! OUR LORD'S TASTER?! THE WORLD'S GREATEST POISONER?!
HA HA HA
MORE SAKE!
RIGHT NOW!
NOW GET OUT!
I SAID OUT!

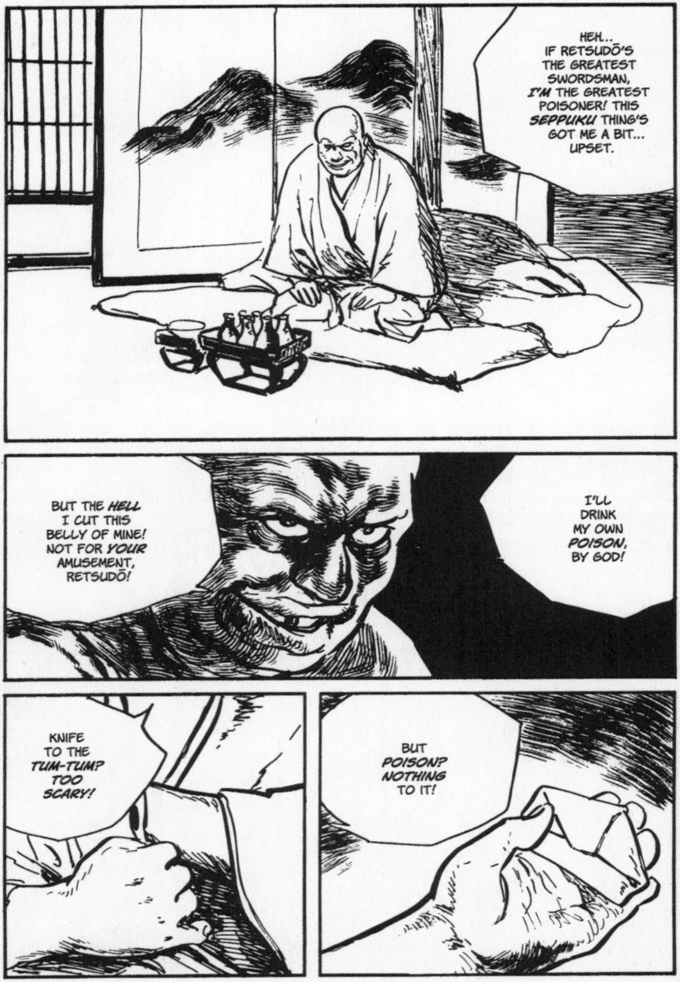
HEH..
IF RETSUDŌ'S THE GREATEST SWORDSMAN, *I'M* THE GREATEST POISONER! THIS *SEPPUKU* THING'S GOT ME A BIT... UPSET.
BUT THE *HELL* I CUT THIS BELLY OF MINE! NOT FOR *YOUR* AMUSEMENT, RETSUDŌ!
I'LL DRINK MY OWN *POISON*, BY GOD!
KNIFE TO THE *TUM-TUM?* *TOO SCARY!*
BUT *POISON?* *NOTHING* TO IT!

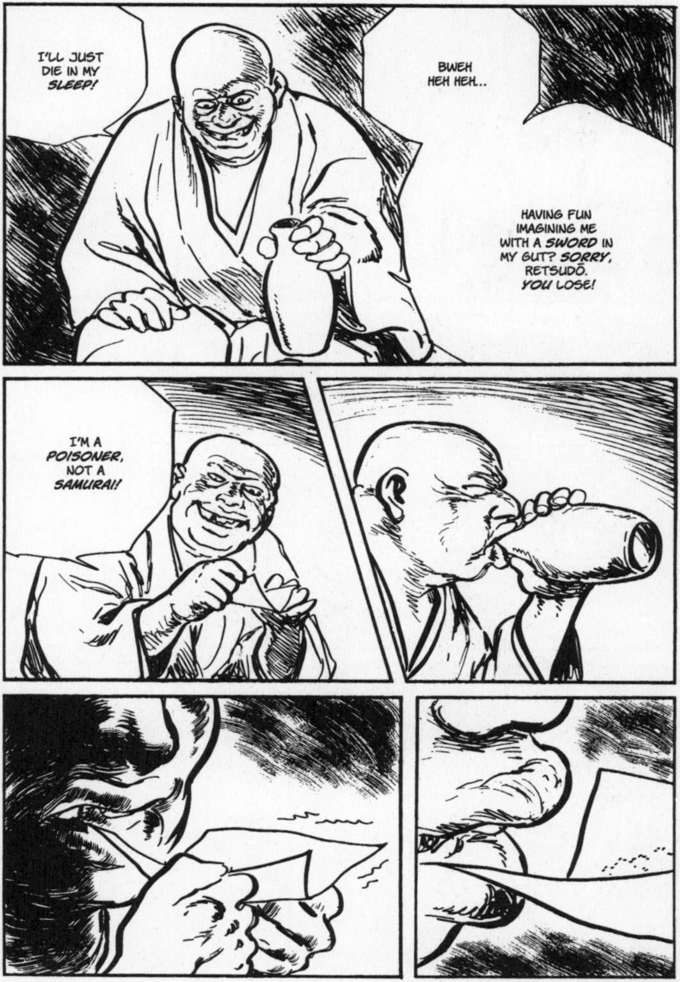
I'LL JUST DIE IN MY SLEEP!
BWEH HEH HEH...
HAVING FUN IMAGINING ME WITH A SWORD IN MY GUT? SORRY, RETSUDŌ. YOU LOSE!
I'M A POISONER, NOT A SAMURAI!

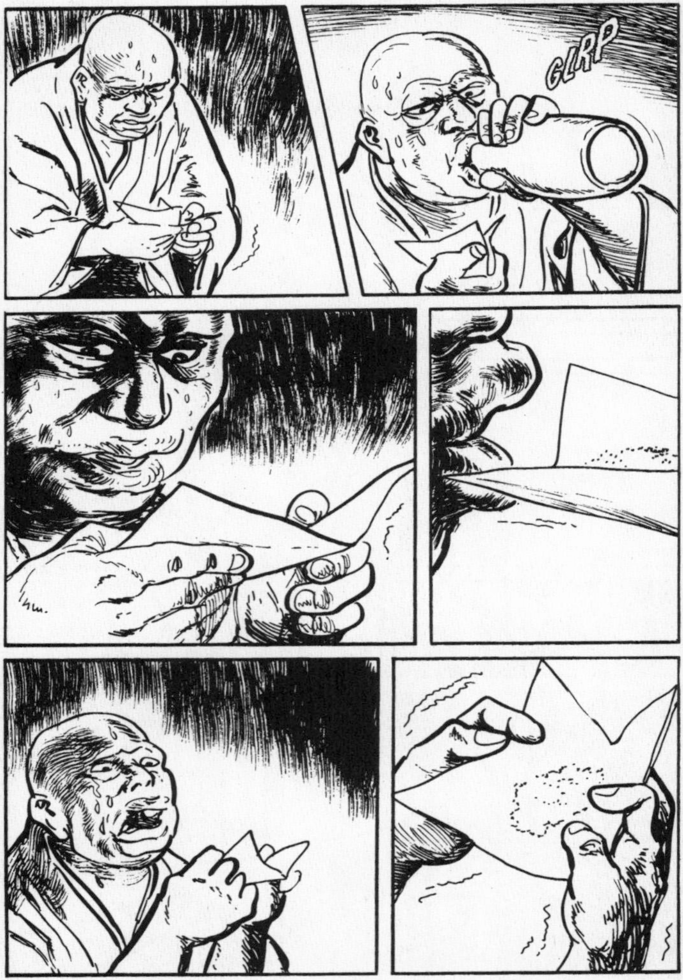
GLRP

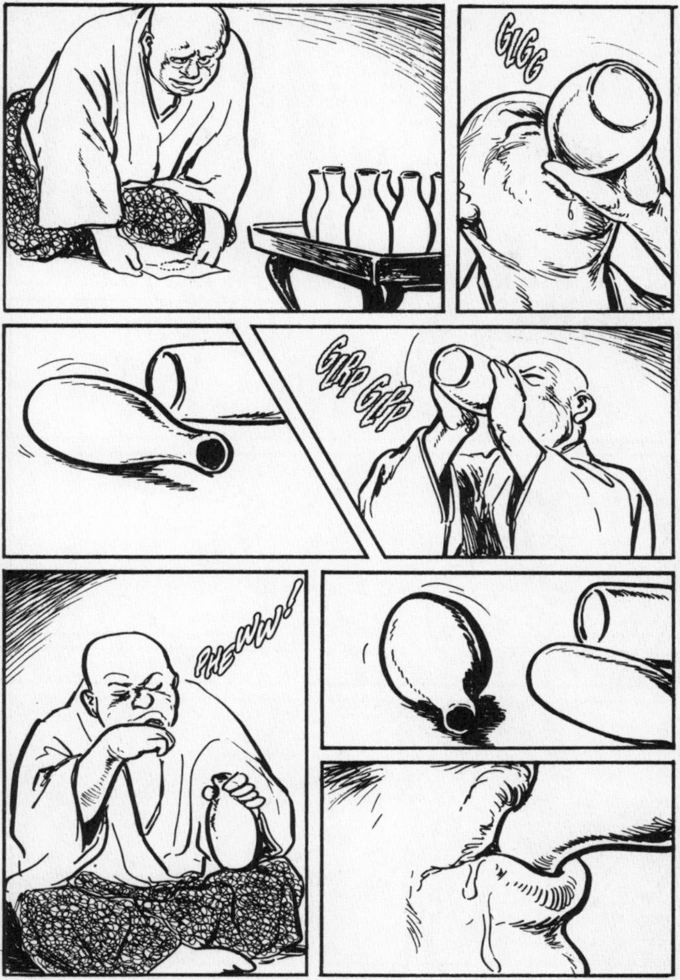
GLGG
GLRP GLRP
PHEWW!

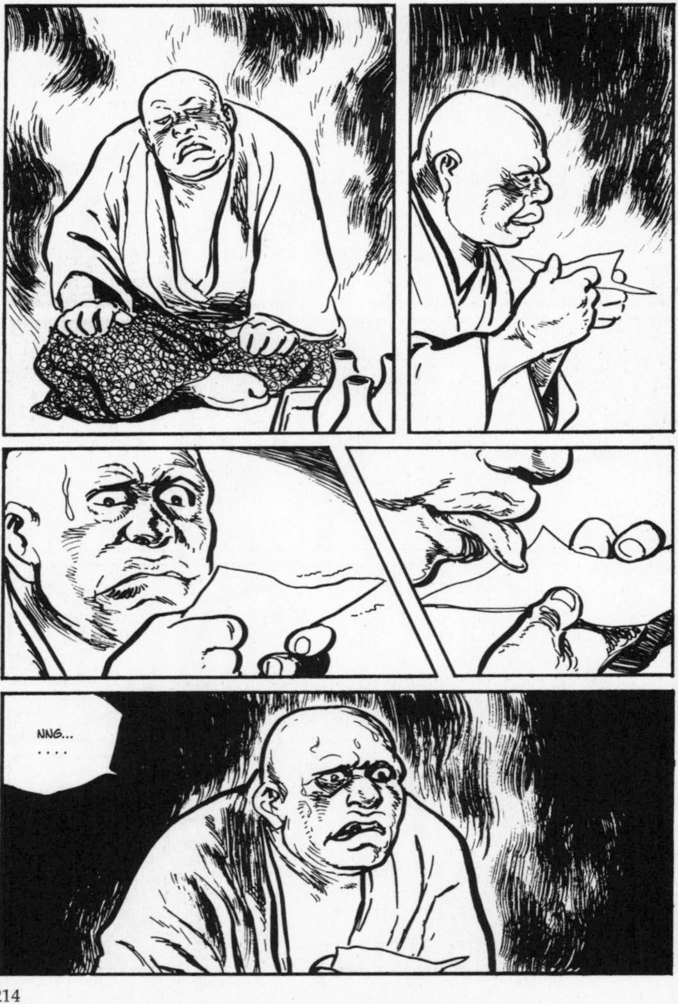
NNG...
....

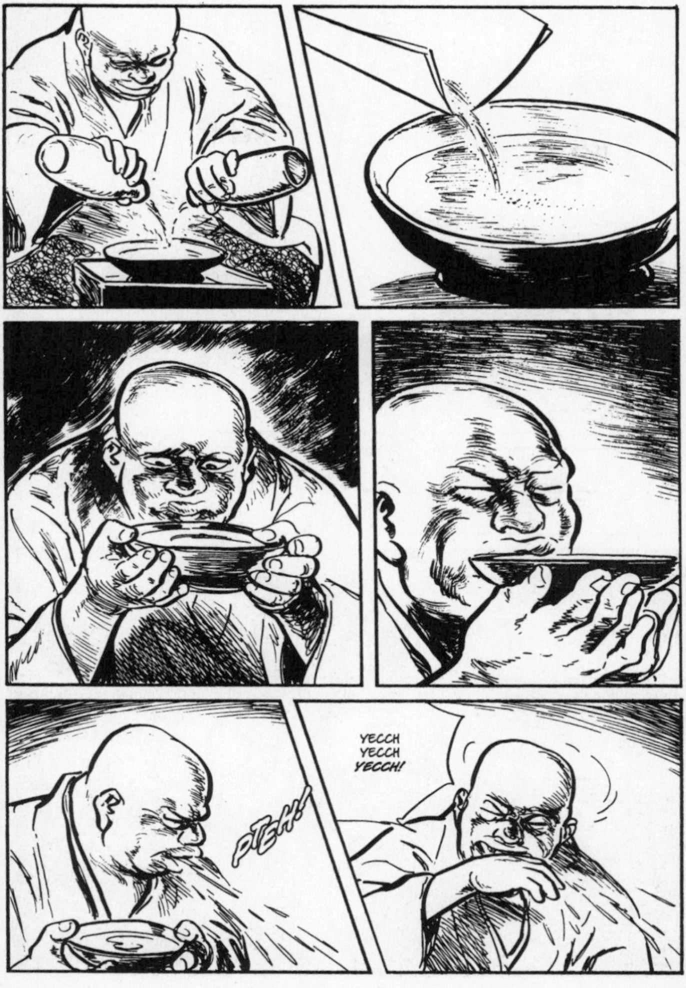
PTEH!
YECCH
YECCH
YECCH!

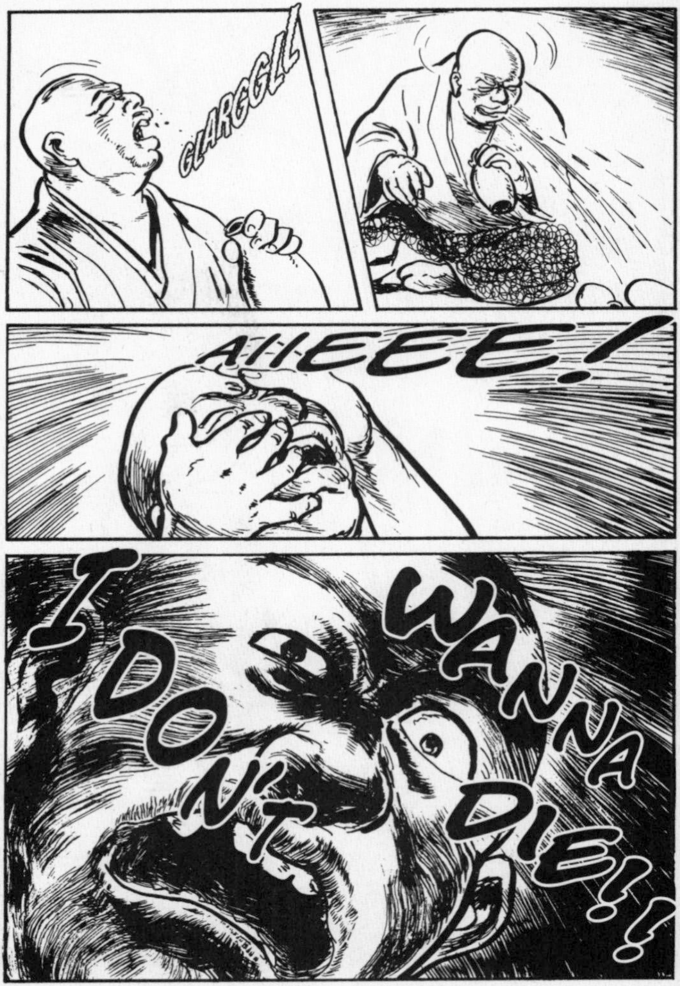
GLARGGLL
AIIEEEE!
I DON'T WANNA DIE!!!

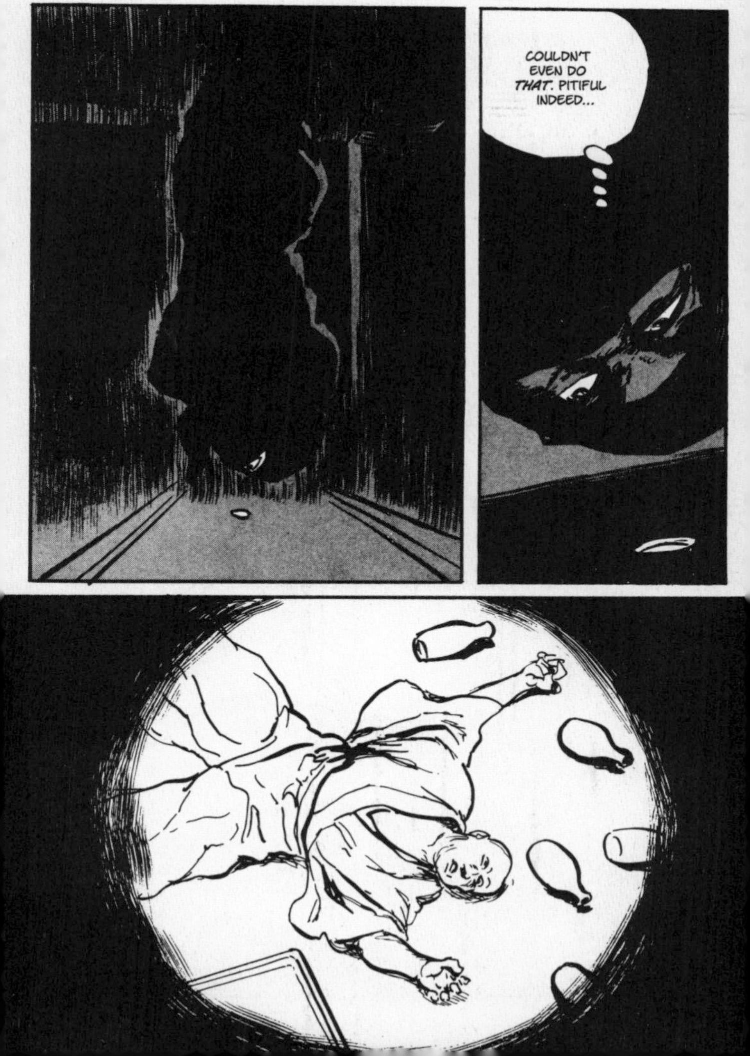
COULDN'T EVEN DO *THAT*. PITIFUL INDEED...

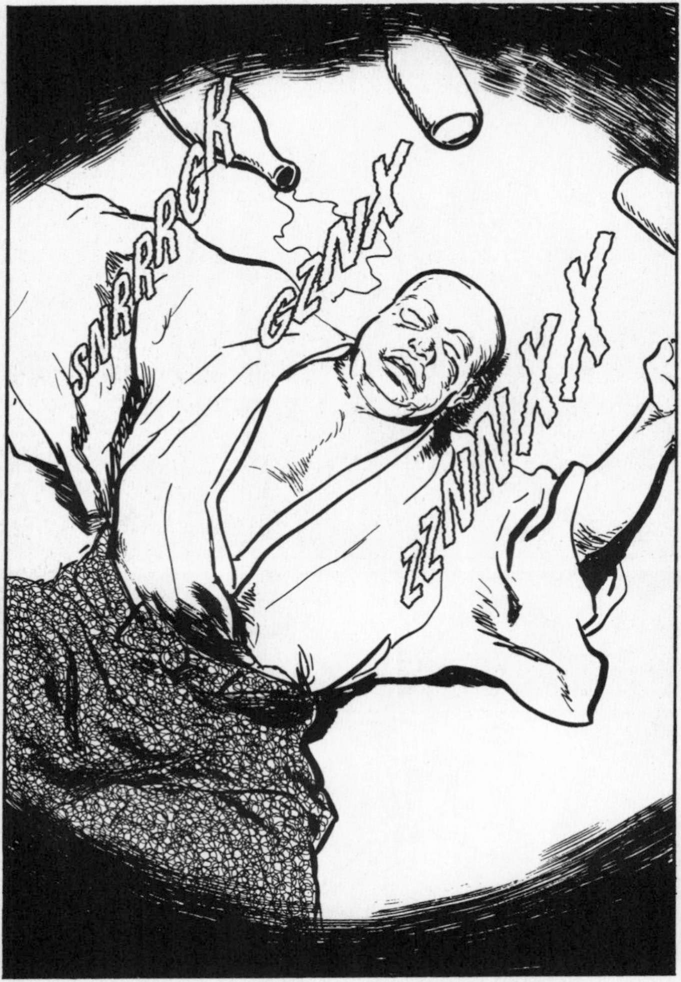
SNRRRGK
GZNX
ZZNNNXX

GZAWW
SNRRK

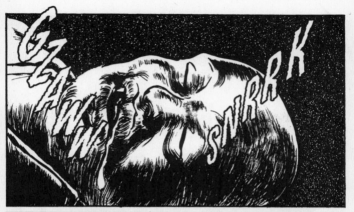

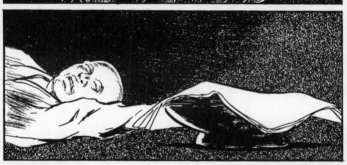

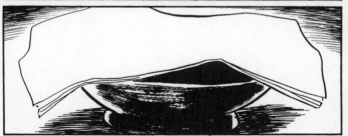

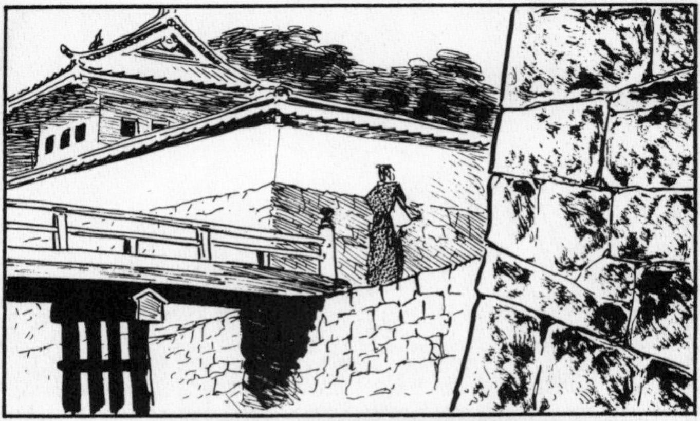

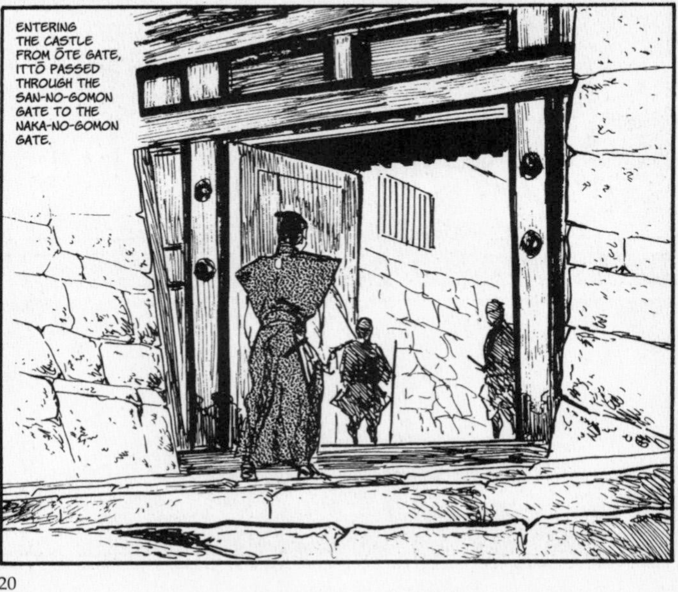
ENTERING THE CASTLE FROM ŌTE GATE, ITTŌ PASSED THROUGH THE SAN-NO-GOMON GATE TO THE NAKA-NO-GOMON GATE.

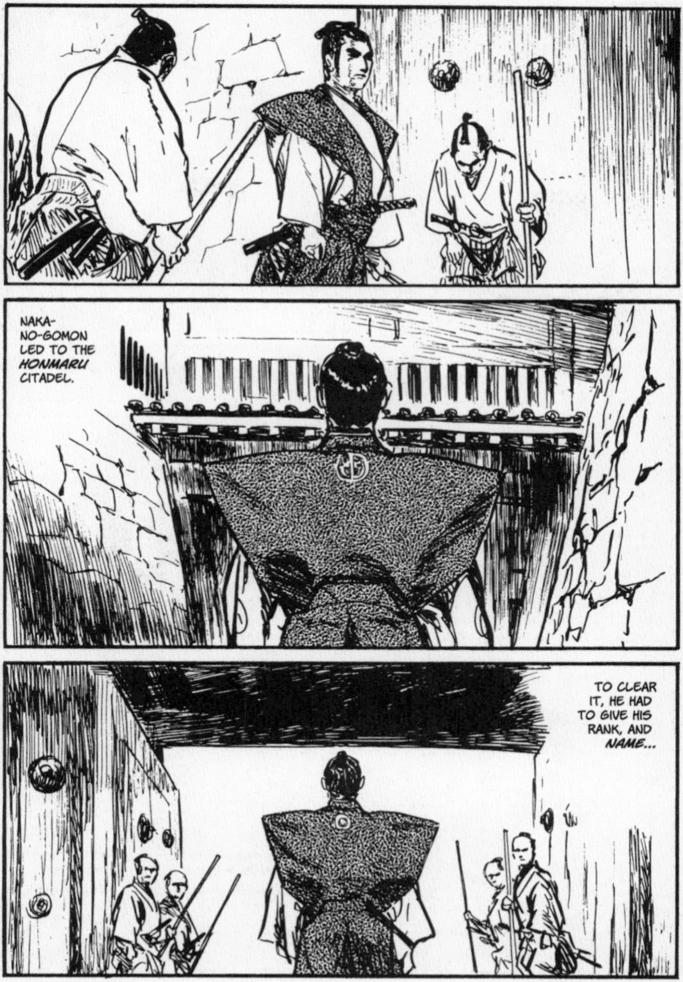
NAKA-
NO-GOMON
LED TO THE
HONMARU
CITADEL.
TO CLEAR
IT, HE HAD
TO GIVE HIS
RANK, AND
NAME...

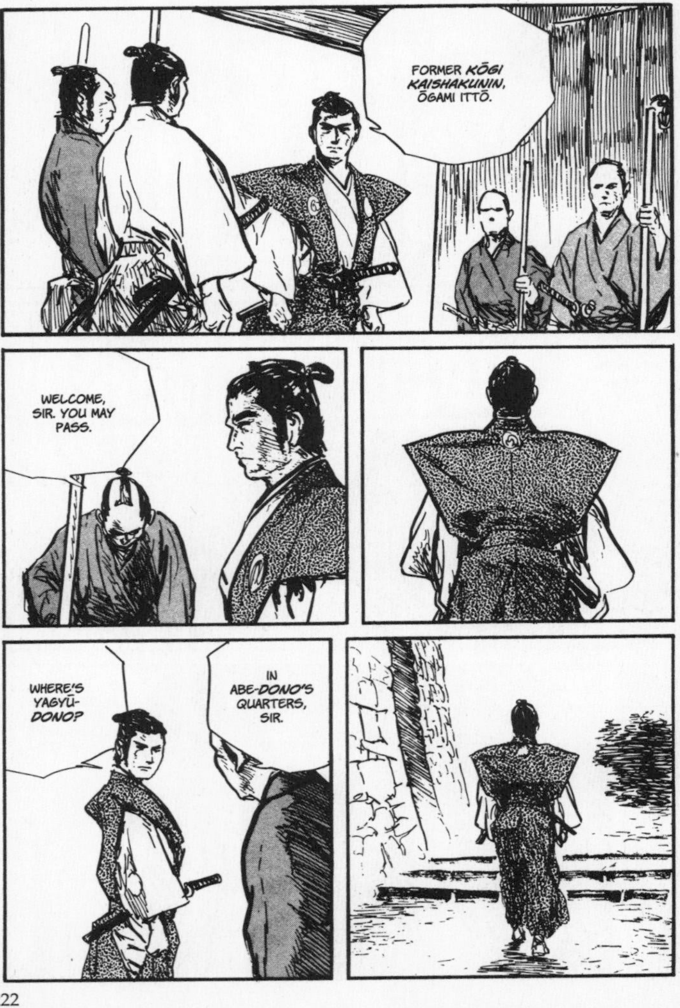
FORMER KŌGI KAISHAKUNIN, ŌGAMI ITTŌ.
WELCOME, SIR. YOU MAY PASS.
WHERE'S YAGYŪ-DONO?
IN ABE-DONO'S QUARTERS, SIR.

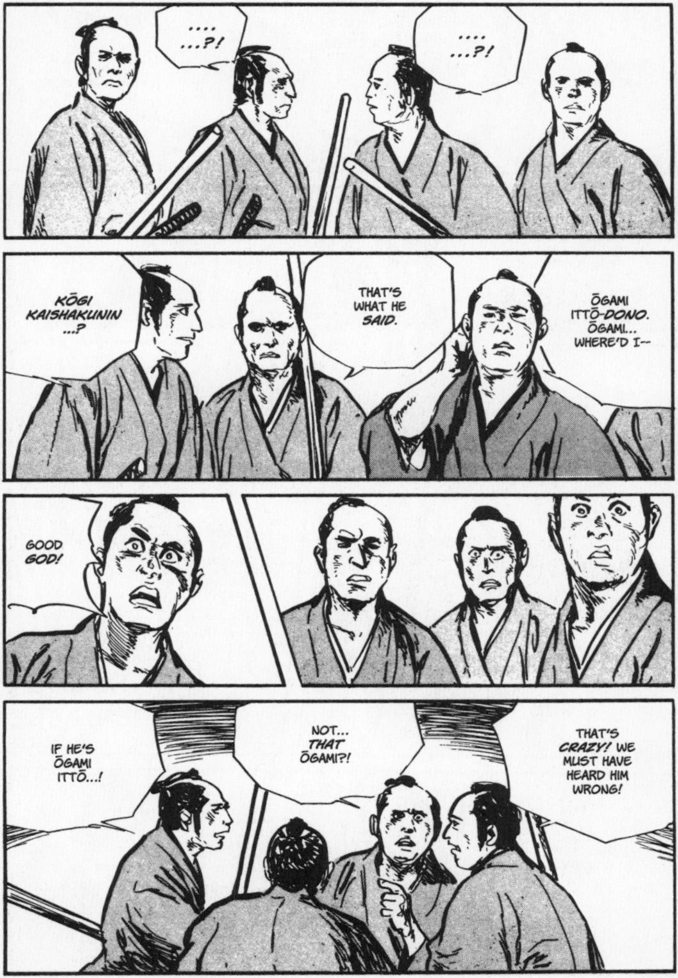
....
...?!
....
...?!
KŌGI KAISHAKUNIN ...?
THAT'S WHAT HE SAID.
ŌGAMI ITTŌ-DONO. ŌGAMI... WHERE'D I--
GOOD GOD!
IF HE'S ŌGAMI ITTŌ...!
NOT... THAT ŌGAMI?!
THAT'S CRAZY! WE MUST HAVE HEARD HIM WRONG!

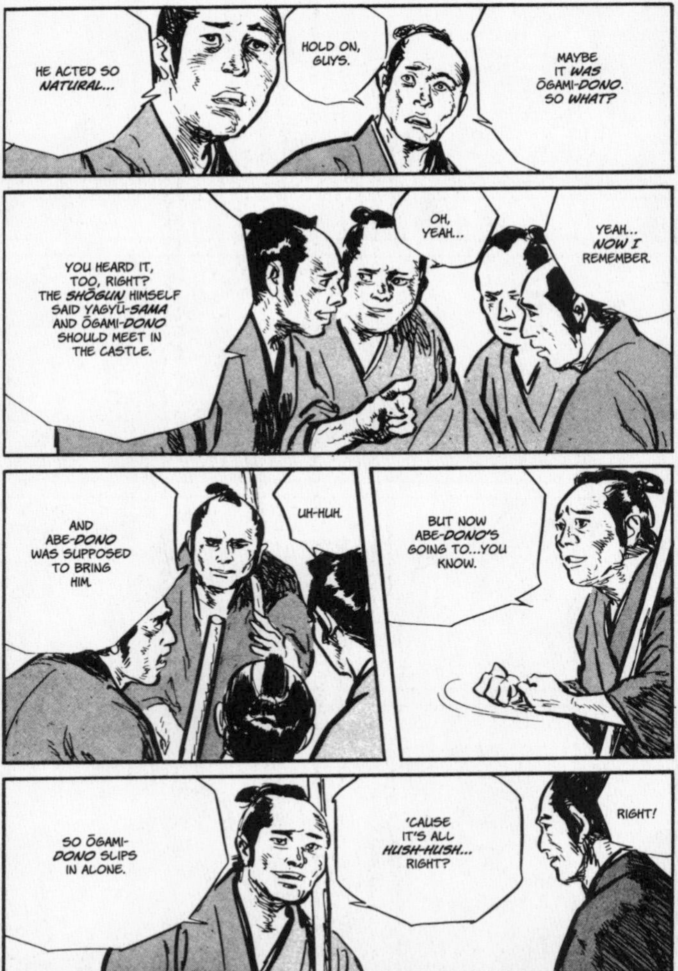
HE ACTED SO *NATURAL...*
HOLD ON, GUYS.
MAYBE IT *WAS* ŌGAMI-*DONO*. SO *WHAT?*
YOU HEARD IT, TOO, RIGHT? THE *SHŌGUN* HIMSELF SAID YAGYŪ-*SAMA* AND ŌGAMI-*DONO* SHOULD MEET IN THE CASTLE.
OH, YEAH...
YEAH... *NOW I* REMEMBER.
AND ABE-*DONO* WAS SUPPOSED TO BRING HIM.
UH-HUH.
BUT NOW ABE-*DONO'S* GOING TO...YOU KNOW.
SO ŌGAMI-*DONO* SLIPS IN ALONE.
'CAUSE IT'S ALL *HUSH-HUSH...* RIGHT?
RIGHT!

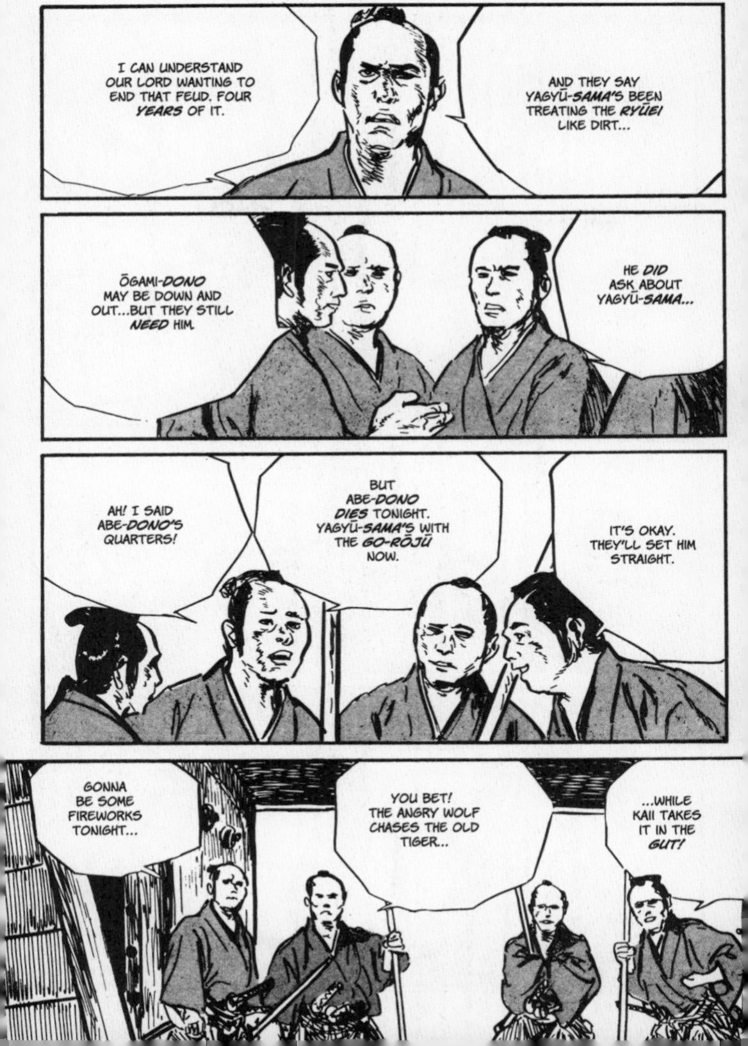
I CAN UNDERSTAND OUR LORD WANTING TO END THAT FEUD. FOUR *YEARS* OF IT.
AND THEY SAY YAGYŪ-*SAMA'S* BEEN TREATING THE *RYŪEI* LIKE DIRT...
ŌGAMI-*DONO* MAY BE DOWN AND OUT...BUT THEY STILL *NEED* HIM.
HE *DID* ASK ABOUT YAGYŪ-*SAMA*...
AH! I SAID ABE-*DONO'S* QUARTERS!
BUT ABE-*DONO* *DIES* TONIGHT. YAGYŪ-*SAMA'S* WITH THE *GO-RŌJŪ* NOW.
IT'S OKAY. THEY'LL SET HIM STRAIGHT.
GONNA BE SOME FIREWORKS TONIGHT...
YOU BET! THE ANGRY WOLF CHASES THE OLD TIGER...
...WHILE KAII TAKES IT IN THE *GUT!*

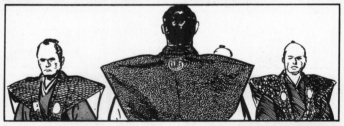

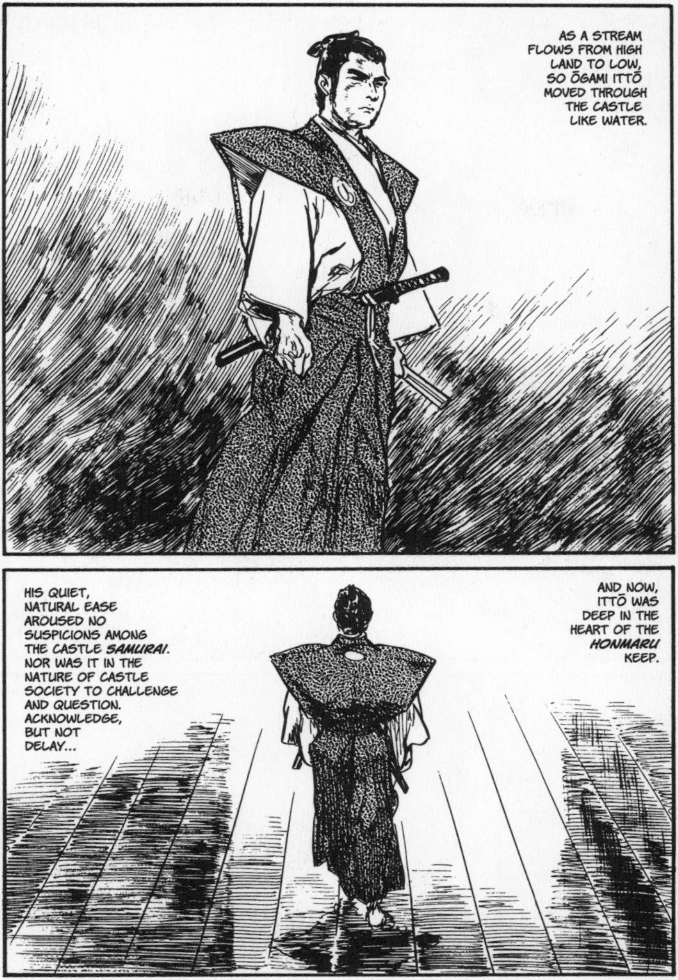
AS A STREAM FLOWS FROM HIGH LAND TO LOW, SO ŌGAMI ITTŌ MOVED THROUGH THE CASTLE LIKE WATER.
HIS QUIET, NATURAL EASE AROUSED NO SUSPICIONS AMONG THE CASTLE *SAMURAI*. NOR WAS IT IN THE NATURE OF CASTLE SOCIETY TO CHALLENGE AND QUESTION. ACKNOWLEDGE, BUT NOT DELAY...
AND NOW, ITTŌ WAS DEEP IN THE HEART OF THE *HONMARU* KEEP.

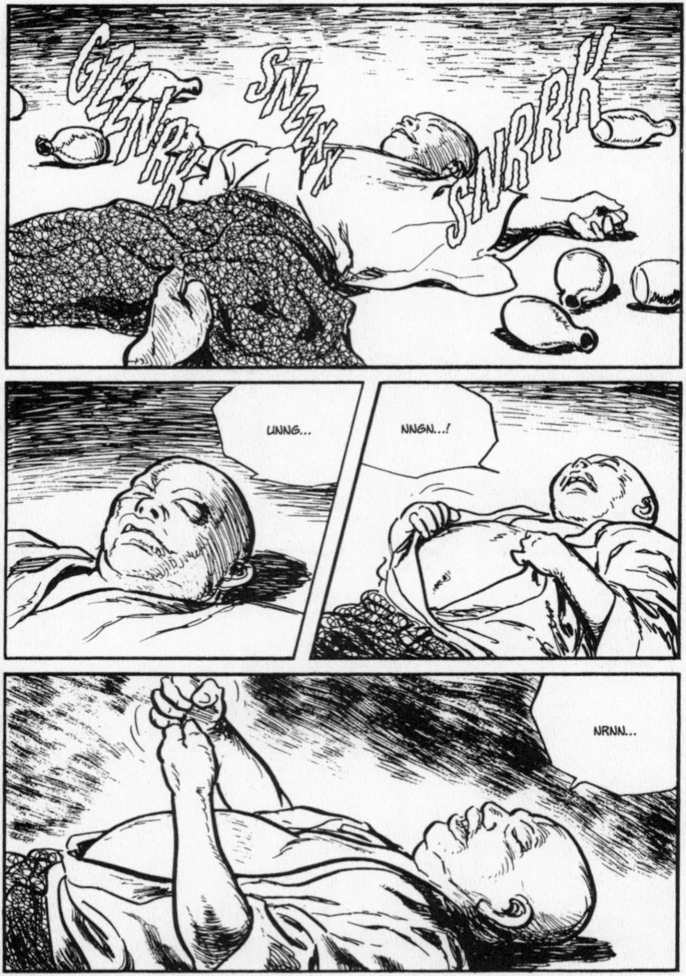
GZZNRK
SNZZXX
SNRRK!
UNNG...
NNGN...!
NRNN...

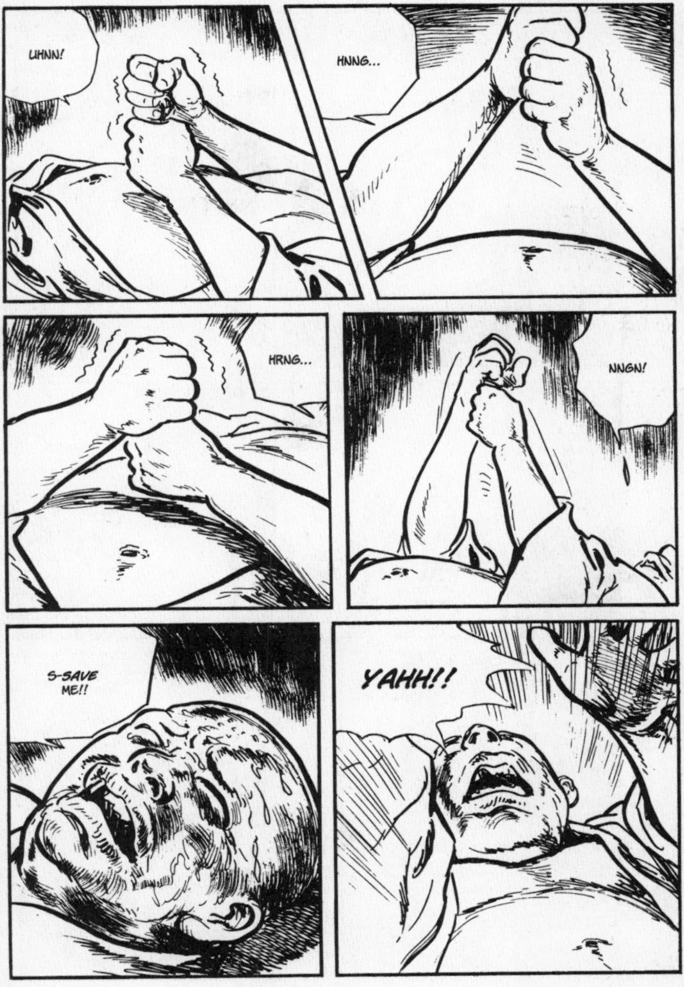
UHNN!
HNNG...
HRNG...
NNGN!
S-SAVE ME!!
YAHH!!

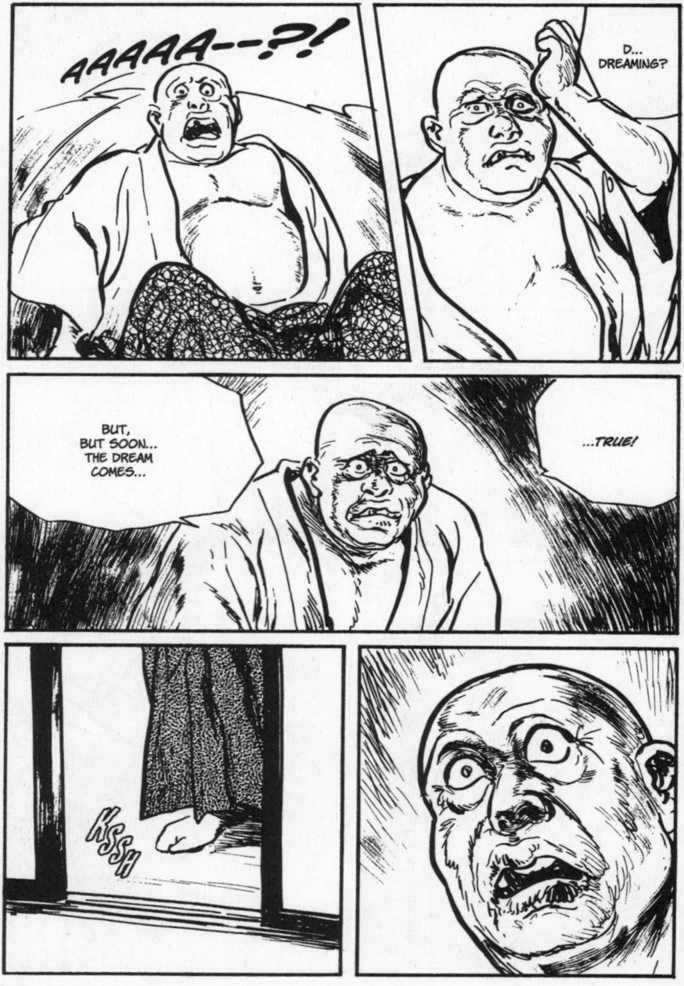
AAAAA--?!
D... DREAMING?
BUT, BUT SOON... THE DREAM COMES...
...TRUE!
KSSH

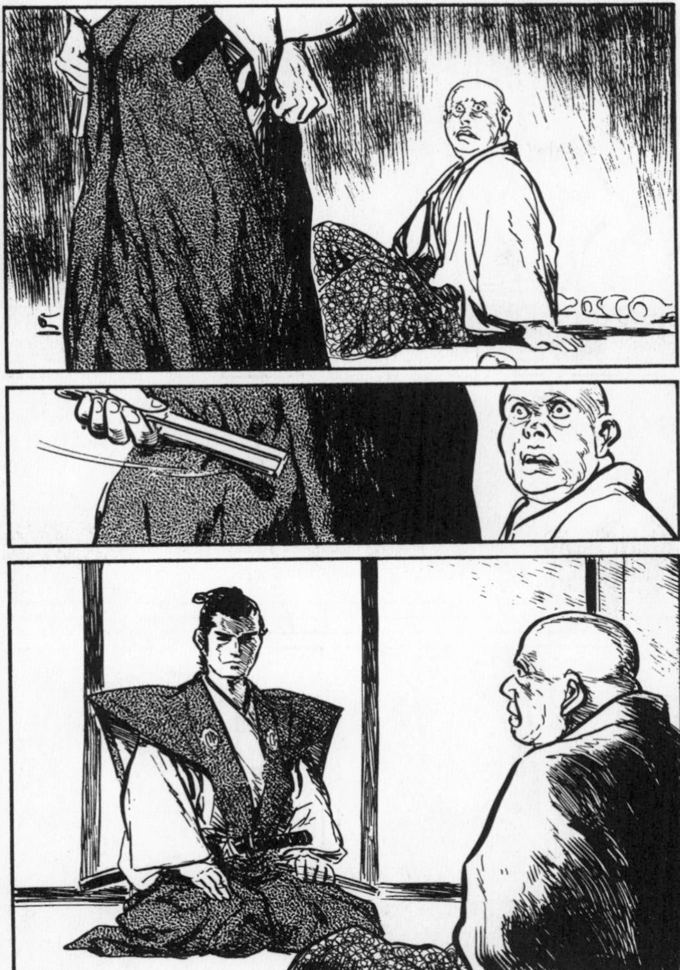

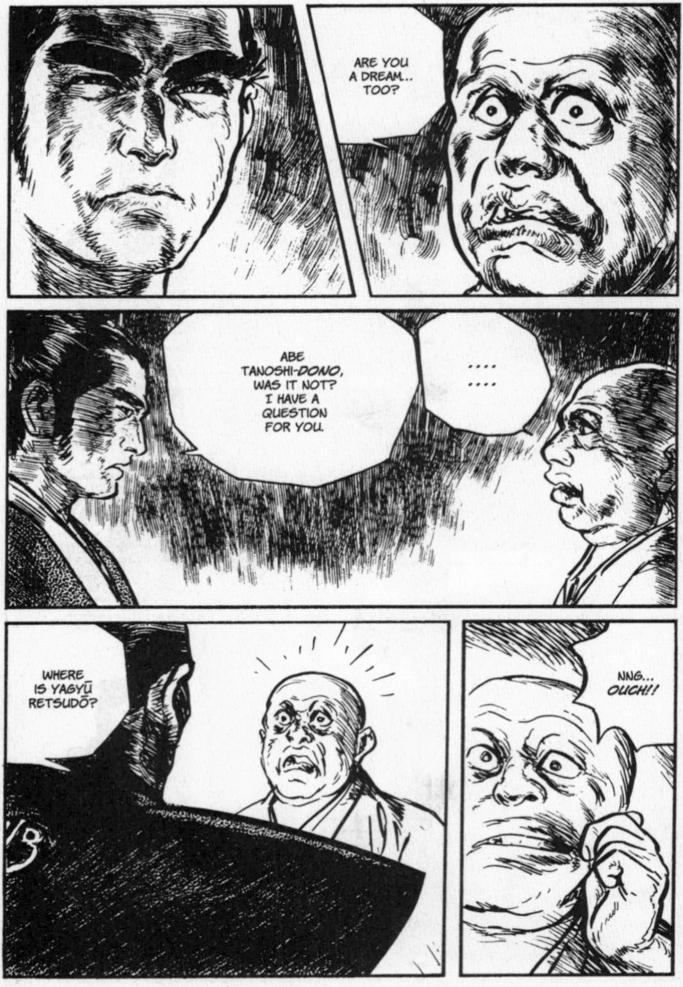
ARE YOU A DREAM.. TOO?
ABE TANOSHI-*DONO*, WAS IT NOT? I HAVE A QUESTION FOR YOU.
....
....
WHERE IS YAGYŪ RETSUDŌ?
NNG... *OUCH!!*

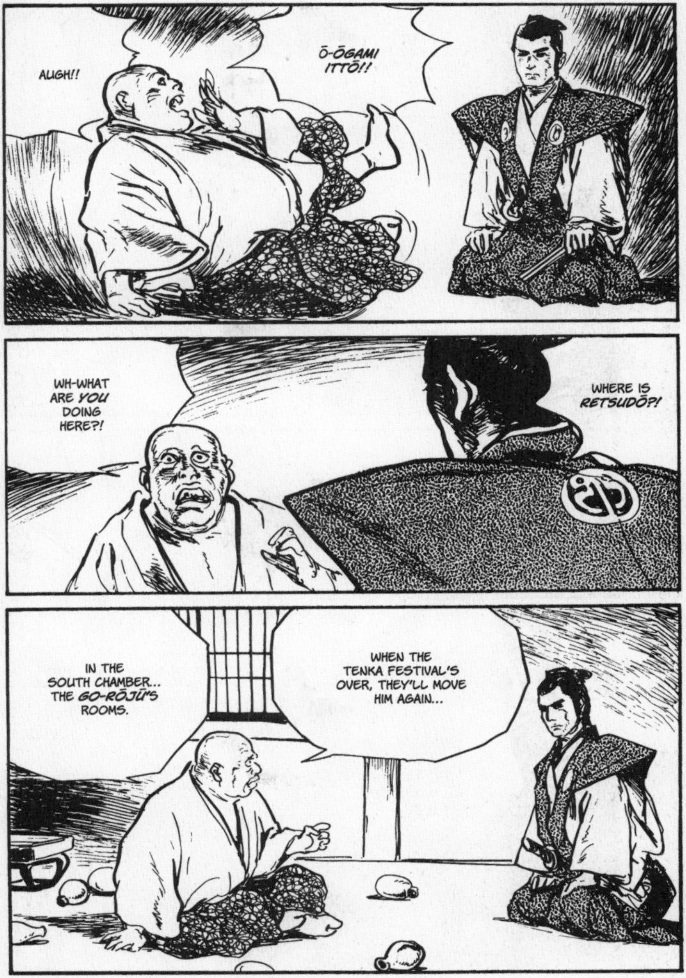
AUGH!!
Ō-ŌGAMI ITTŌ!!
WH-WHAT ARE *YOU* DOING HERE?!
WHERE IS *RETSUDŌ*?!
IN THE SOUTH CHAMBER... THE *GO-RŌJŪ'S* ROOMS.
WHEN THE TENKA FESTIVAL'S OVER, THEY'LL MOVE HIM AGAIN...

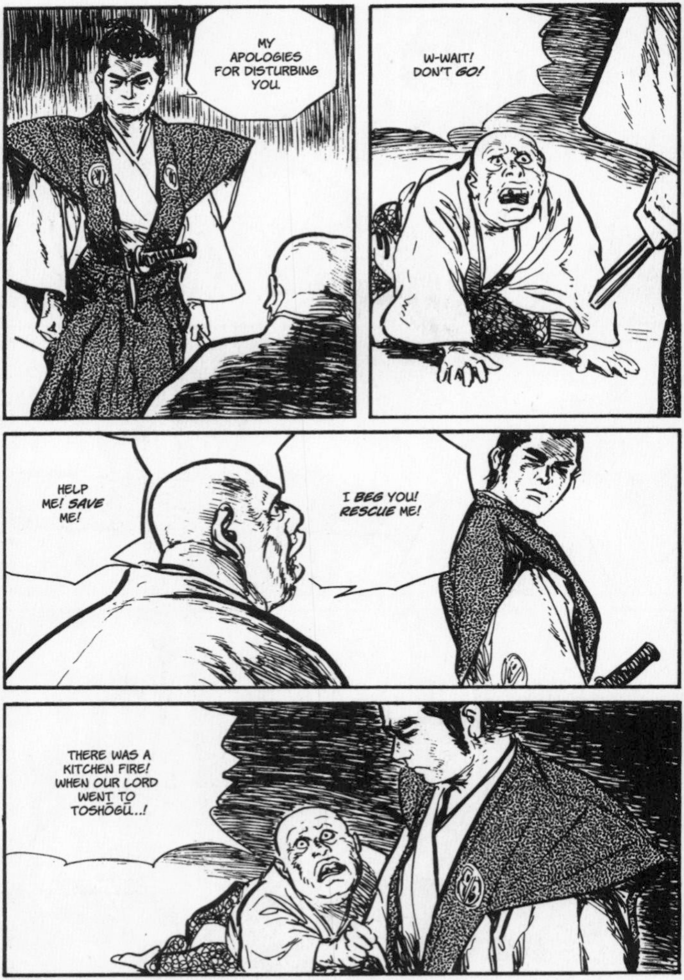
MY APOLOGIES FOR DISTURBING YOU.
W-WAIT! DON'T *GO!*
HELP ME! *SAVE* ME!
I *BEG* YOU! *RESCUE* ME!
THERE WAS A KITCHEN FIRE! WHEN OUR LORD WENT TO TOSHŌGŪ...!

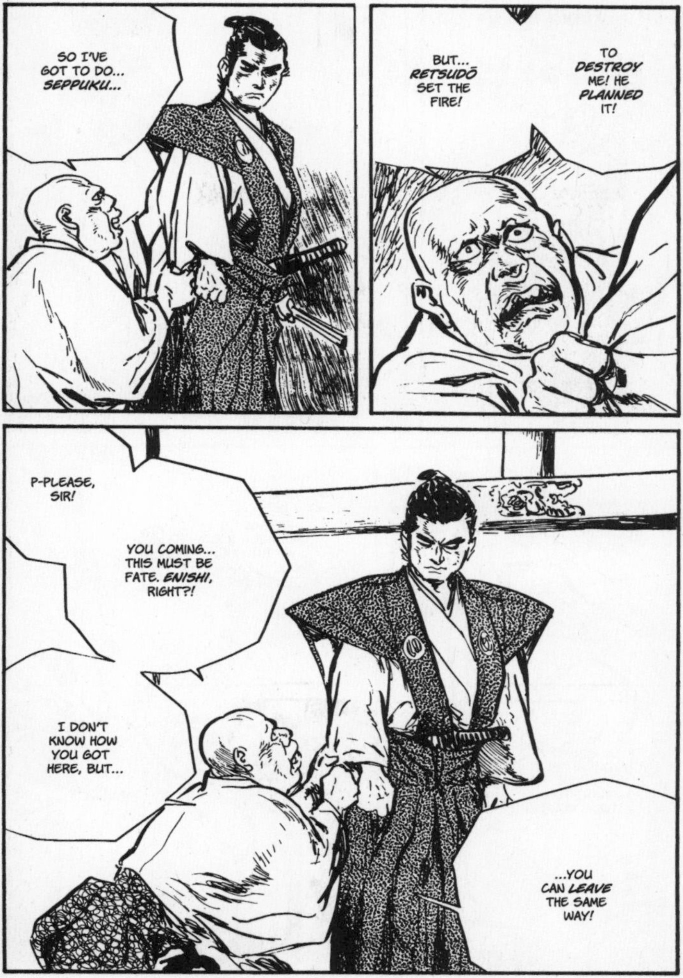
SO I'VE GOT TO DO... *SEPPUKU*...
BUT... *RETSUDŌ* SET THE FIRE!
TO *DESTROY* ME! HE *PLANNED* IT!
P-PLEASE, SIR!
YOU COMING... THIS MUST BE FATE. *ENISHI*, RIGHT?!
I DON'T KNOW HOW YOU GOT HERE, BUT...
...YOU CAN *LEAVE* THE SAME WAY!

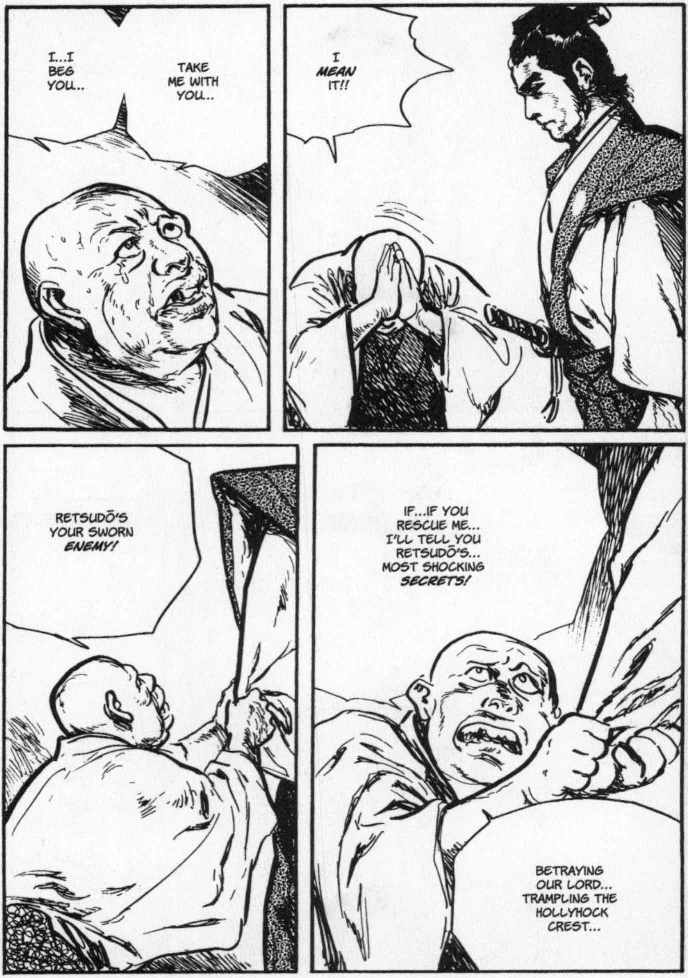
I...I BEG YOU...
TAKE ME WITH YOU...
I *MEAN* IT!!
RETSUDŌ'S YOUR SWORN *ENEMY!*
IF...IF YOU RESCUE ME... I'LL TELL YOU RETSUDŌ'S... MOST SHOCKING *SECRETS!*
BETRAYING OUR LORD... TRAMPLING THE HOLLYHOCK CREST...

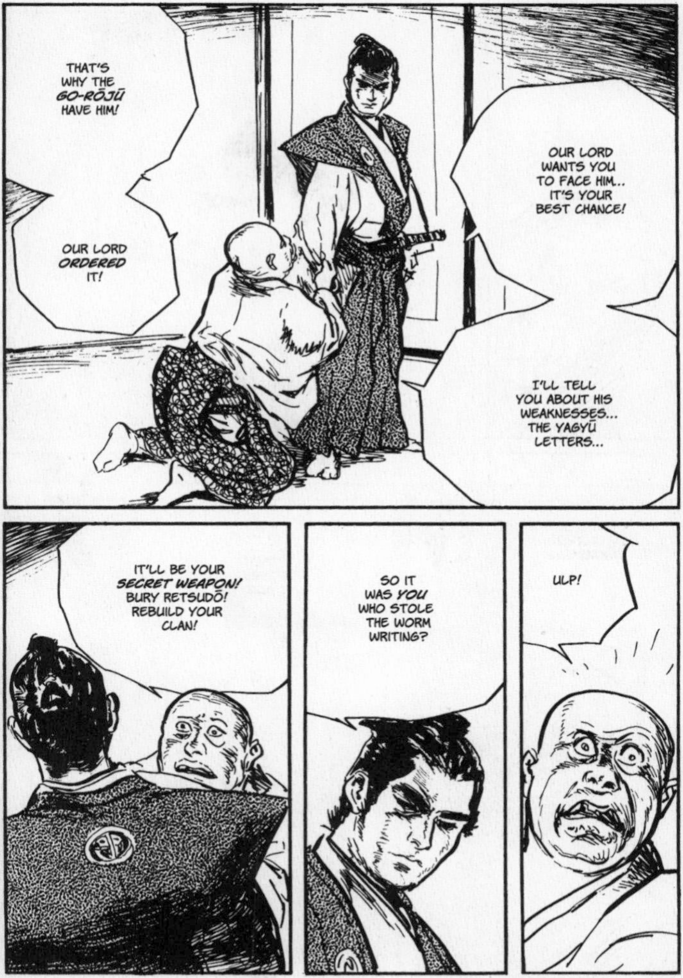
THAT'S WHY THE GO-RŌJŪ HAVE HIM!
OUR LORD ORDERED IT!
OUR LORD WANTS YOU TO FACE HIM.. IT'S YOUR BEST CHANCE!
I'LL TELL YOU ABOUT HIS WEAKNESSES... THE YAGYŪ LETTERS...
IT'LL BE YOUR SECRET WEAPON! BURY RETSUDŌ! REBUILD YOUR CLAN!
SO IT WAS YOU WHO STOLE THE WORM WRITING?
ULP!

THAT'S... RIGHT. HEH... FORGOT ABOUT THAT.

Y-YES! I *DID THAT!* BUT THERE'S *MORE!*

ALL *KINDS* OF EVIDENCE. I HAVE IT *ALL!*

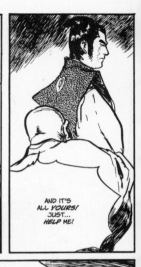

AND IT'S ALL *YOURS!* JUST... *HELP ME!*

MY APOLOGIES.

THE *PALANQUIN* IS COMING... ANY *MINUTE!*

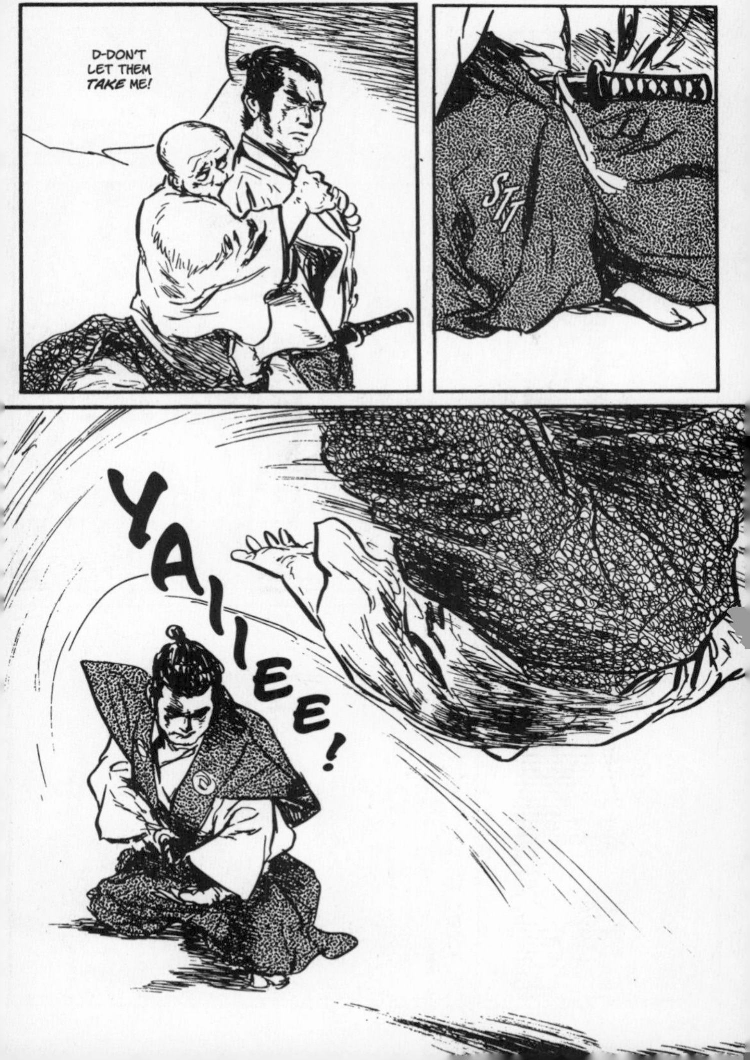
D-DON'T LET THEM *TAKE* ME!
YAIIEE!

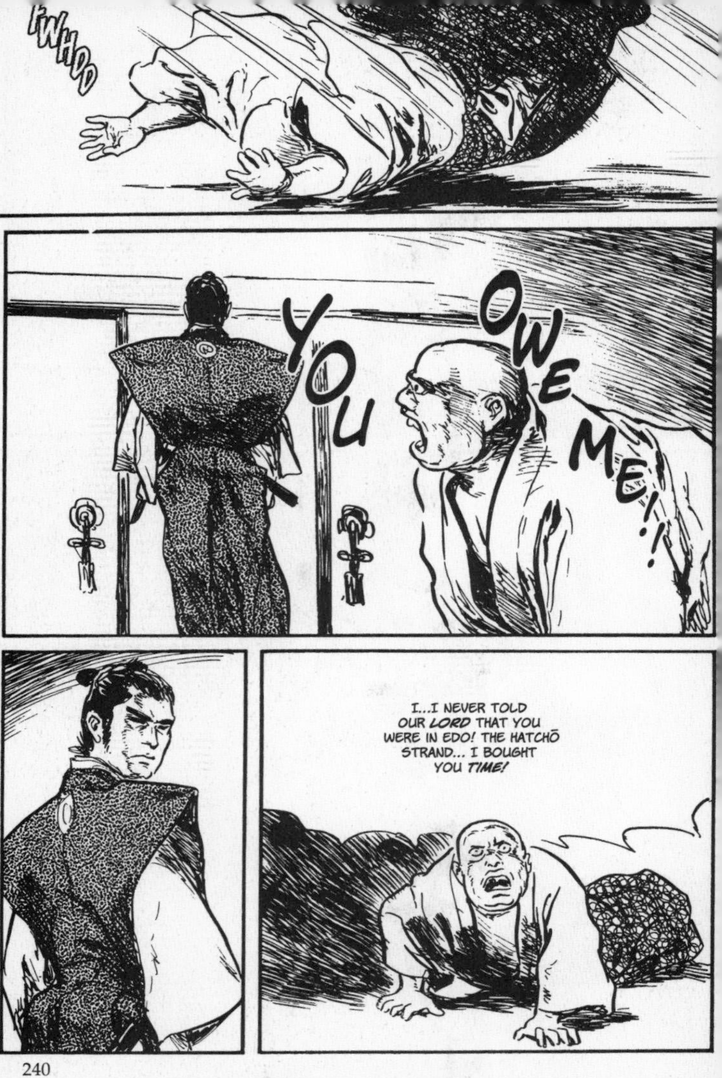

FWHOD
YOU OWE ME!!
I...I NEVER TOLD OUR *LORD* THAT YOU WERE IN EDO! THE HATCHŌ STRAND... I BOUGHT YOU *TIME!*

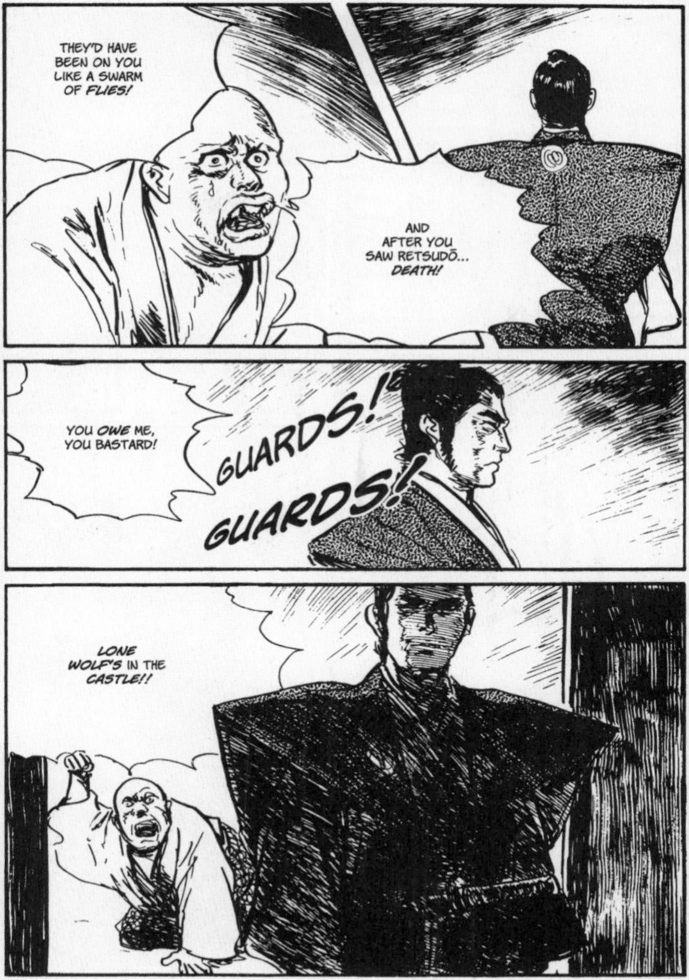
THEY'D HAVE BEEN ON YOU LIKE A SWARM OF FLIES!
AND AFTER YOU SAW RETSUDŌ... DEATH!
YOU OWE ME, YOU BASTARD!
GUARDS!!
GUARDS!!
LONE WOLF'S IN THE CASTLE!!

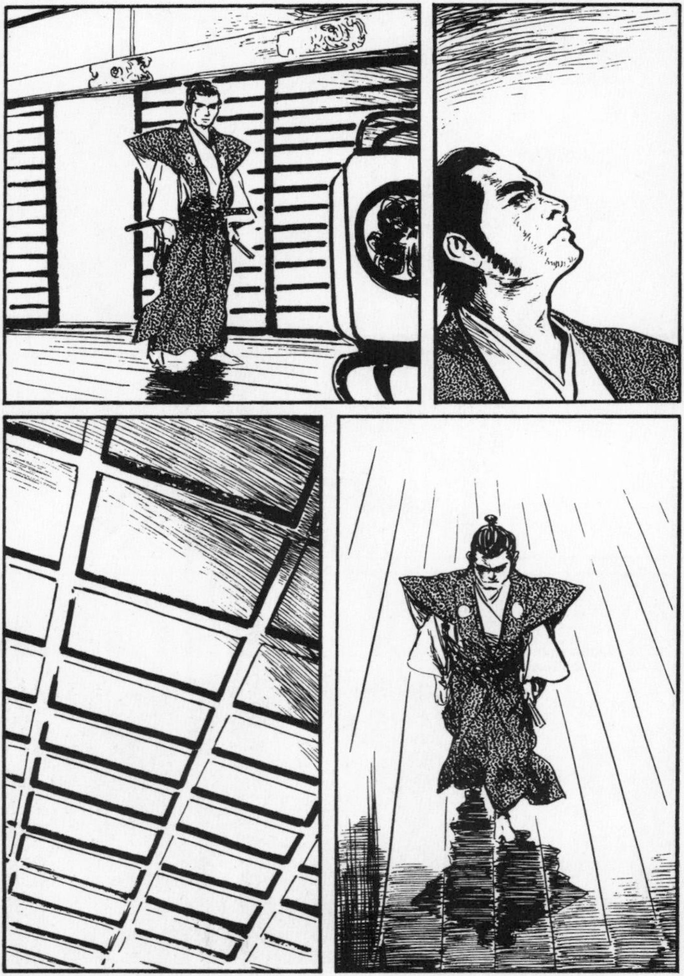

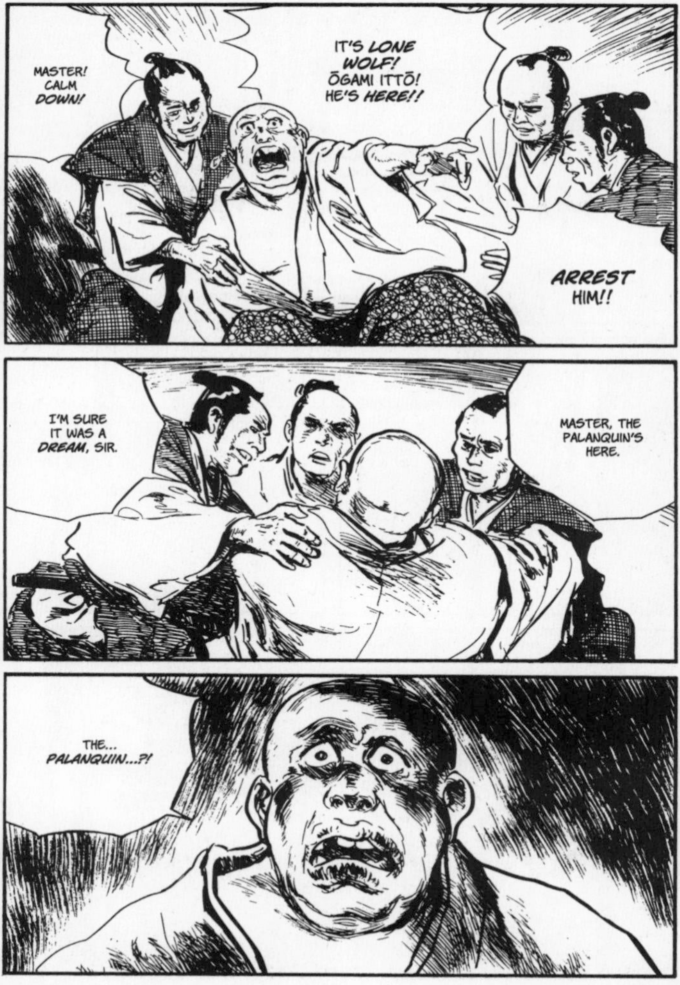
MASTER! CALM DOWN!
IT'S LONE WOLF! ŌGAMI ITTŌ! HE'S HERE!!
ARREST HIM!!
I'M SURE IT WAS A DREAM, SIR.
MASTER, THE PALANQUIN'S HERE.
THE... PALANQUIN...?!

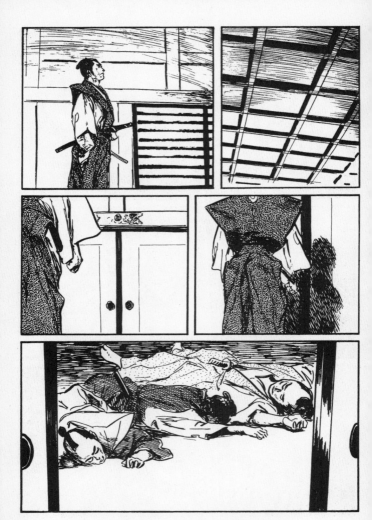

244

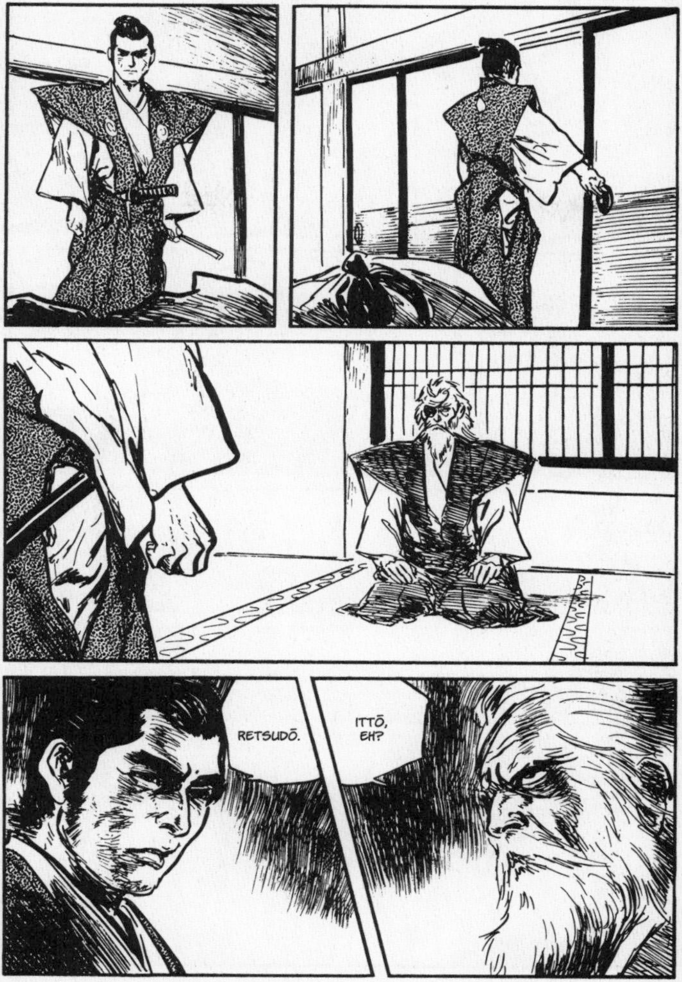

RETSUDŌ.
ITTŌ, EH?

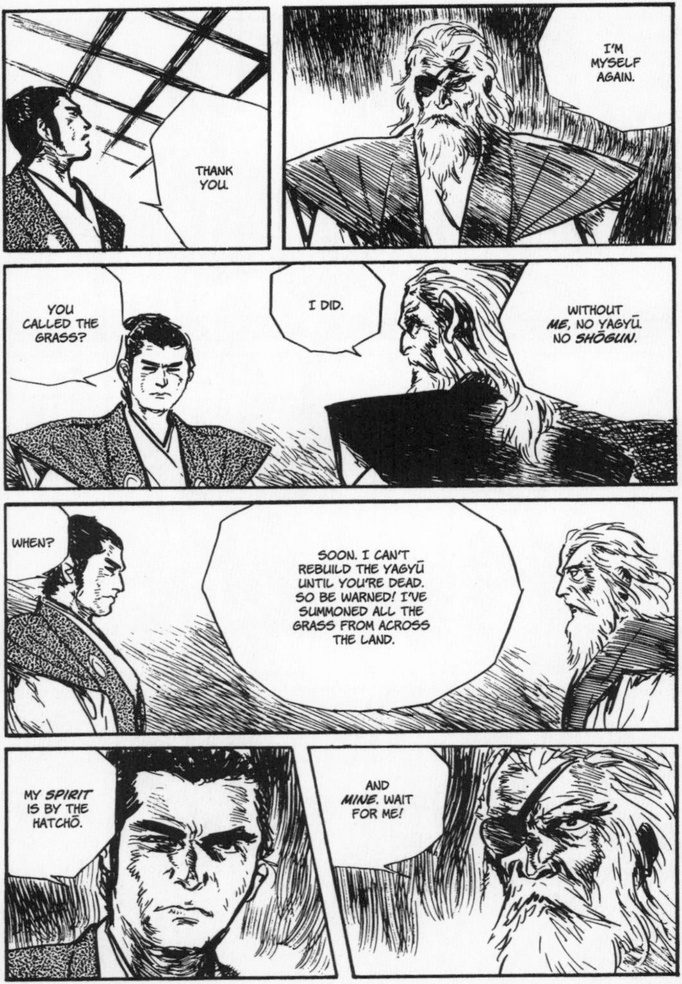
THANK YOU.
I'M MYSELF AGAIN.
YOU CALLED THE GRASS?
I DID.
WITHOUT *ME*, NO YAGYŪ. NO *SHŌGUN*.
WHEN?
SOON. I CAN'T REBUILD THE YAGYŪ UNTIL YOU'RE DEAD. SO BE WARNED! I'VE SUMMONED ALL THE GRASS FROM ACROSS THE LAND.
MY *SPIRIT* IS BY THE HATCHŌ.
AND *MINE*. WAIT FOR ME!

the hundred and thirty-second

Scarlet Summer, Silver Fall

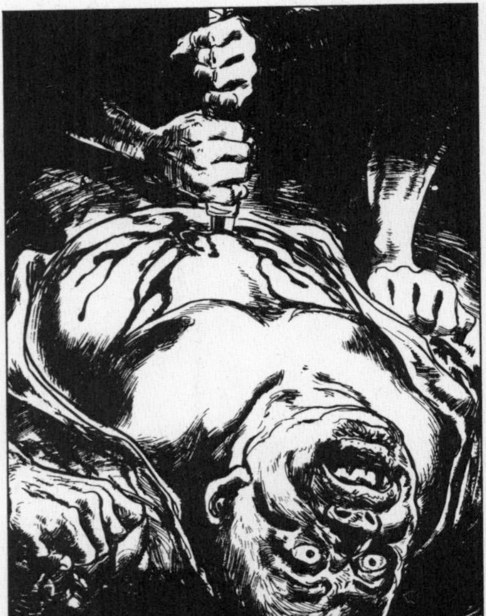

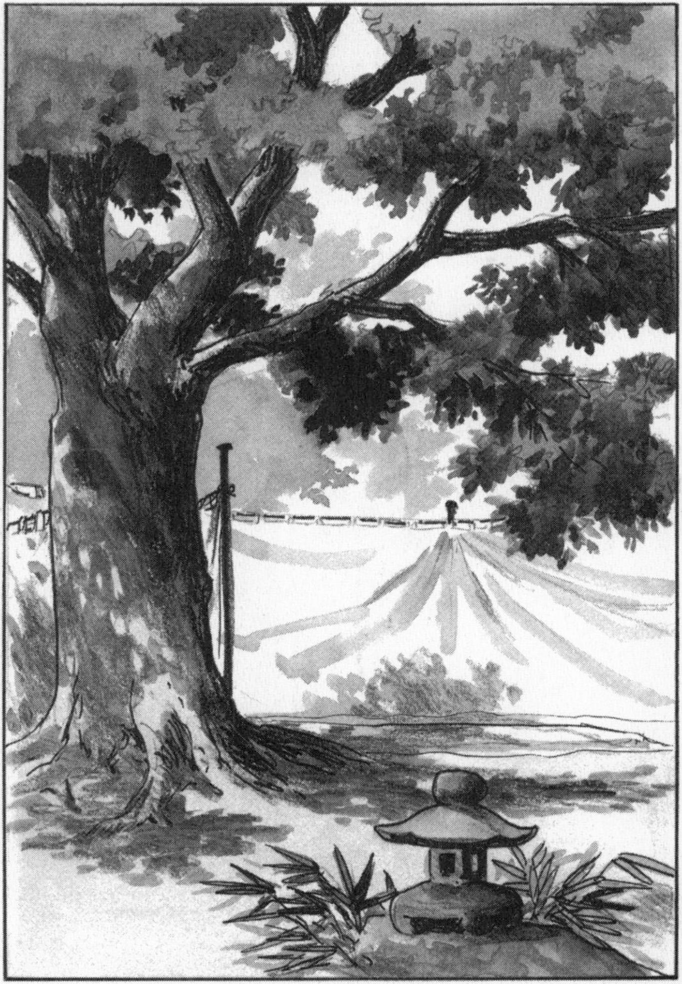

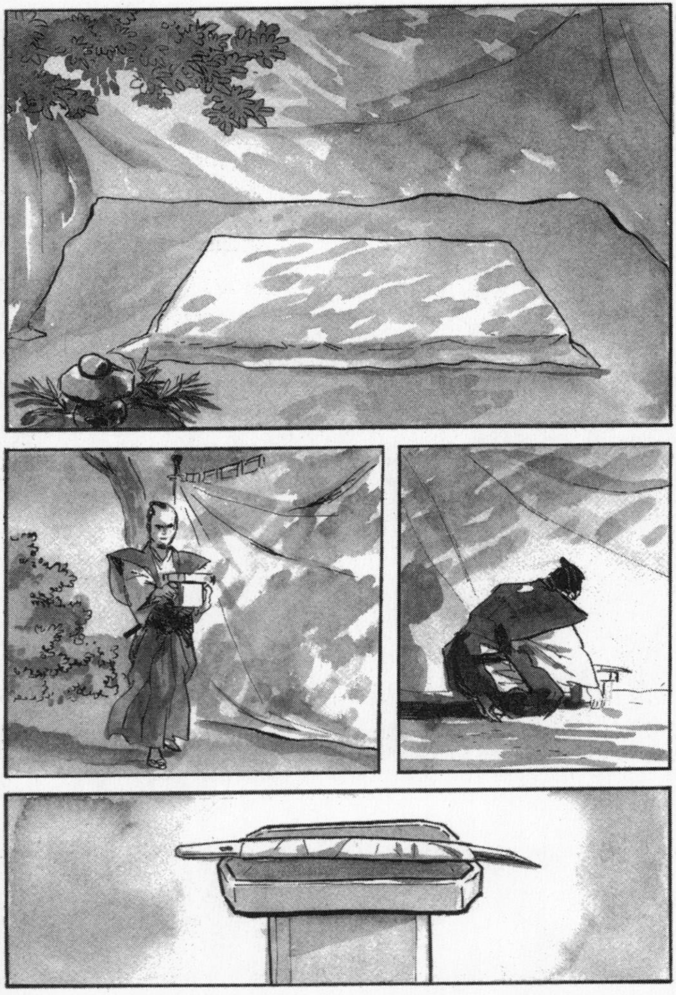

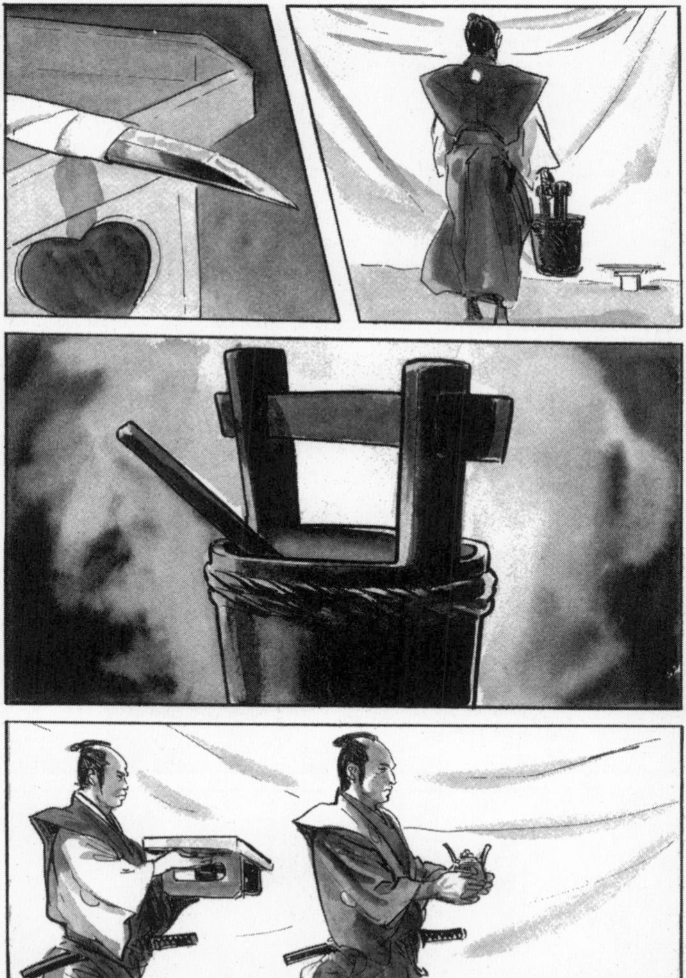

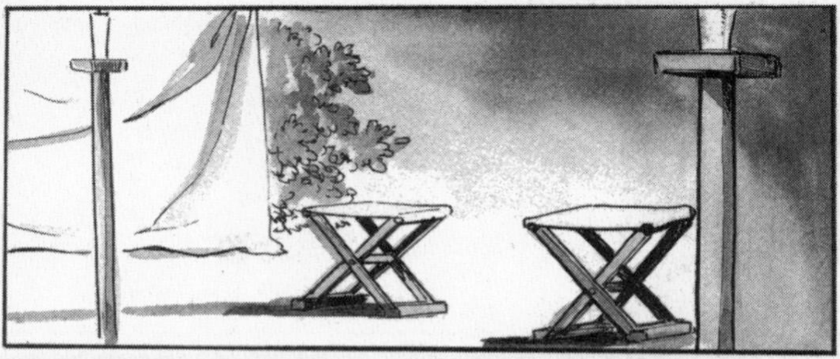

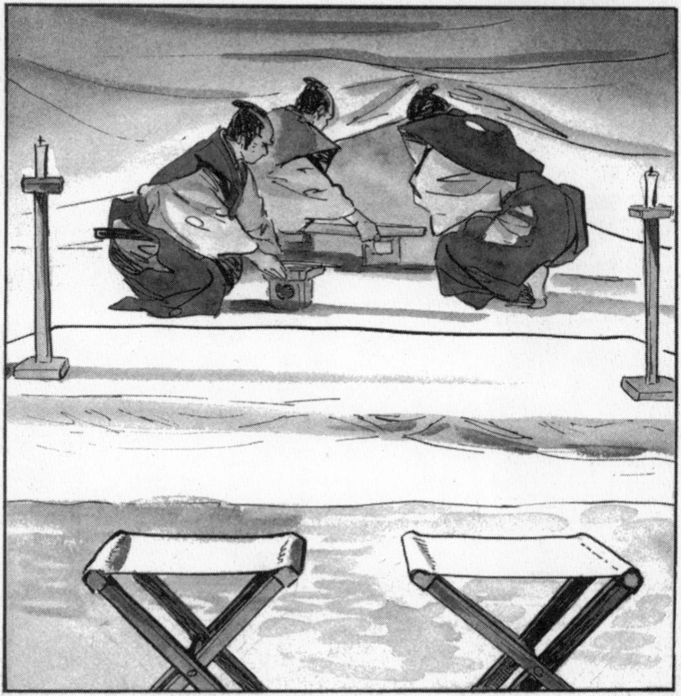

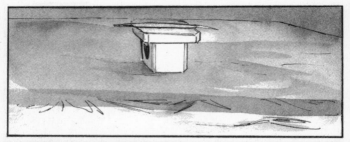

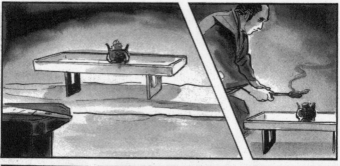

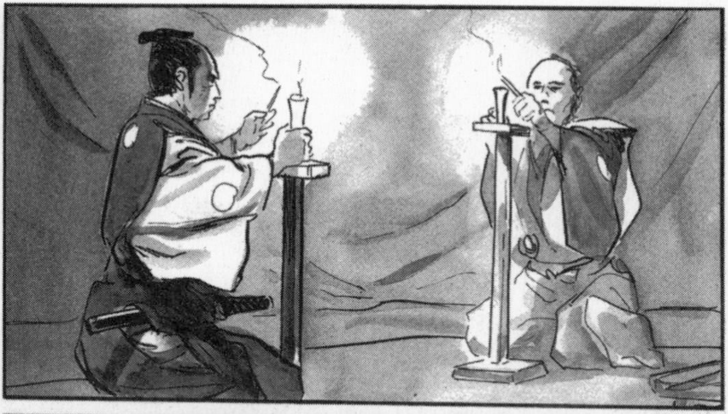

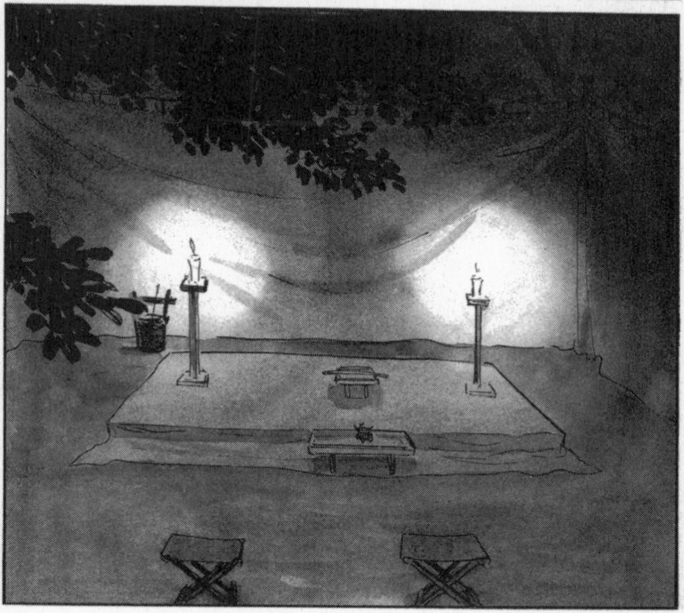

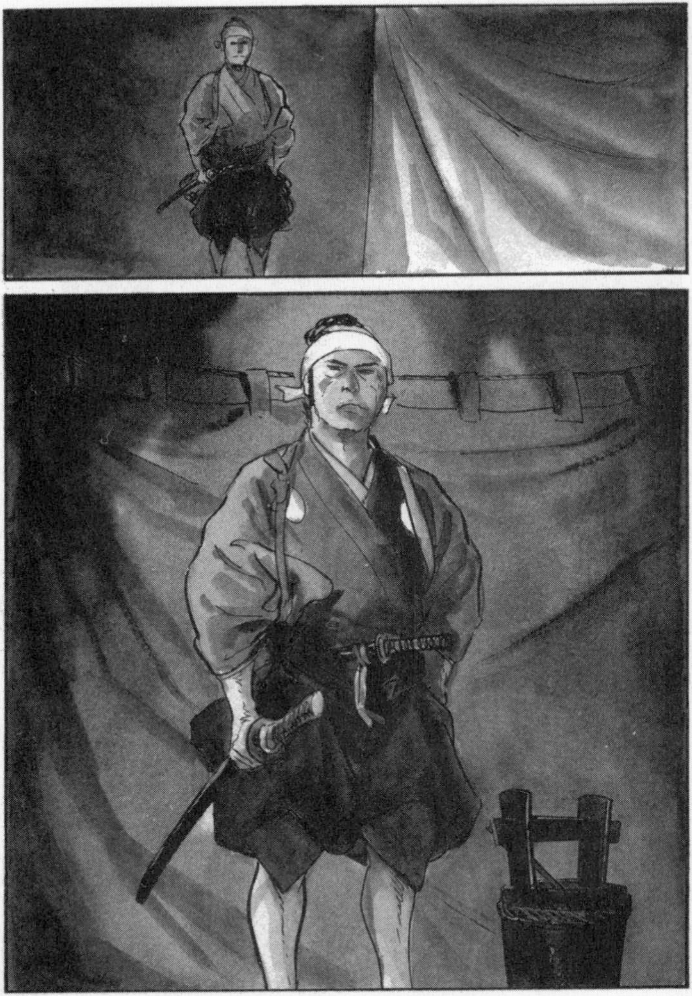

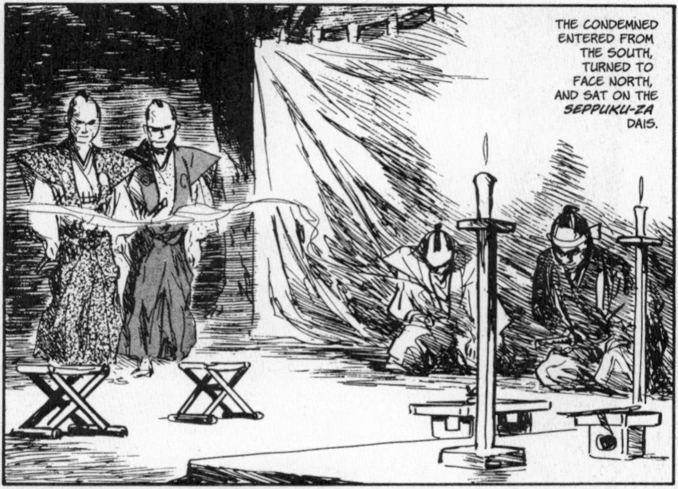
THE CONDEMNED ENTERED FROM THE SOUTH, TURNED TO FACE NORTH, AND SAT ON THE *SEPPUKU-ZA* DAIS.

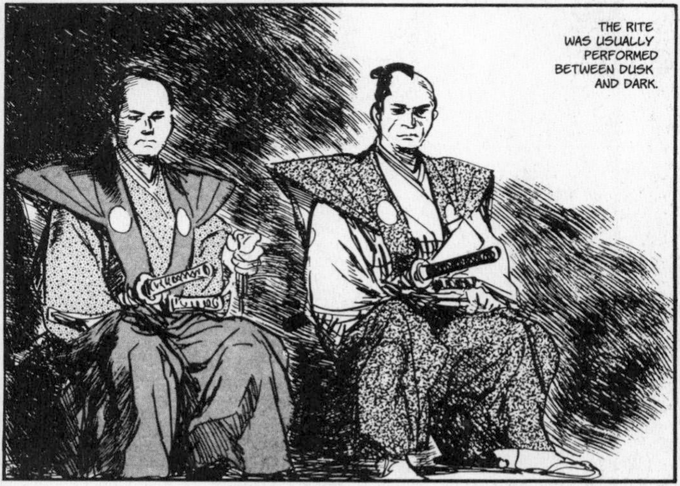
THE RITE WAS USUALLY PERFORMED BETWEEN DUSK AND DARK.

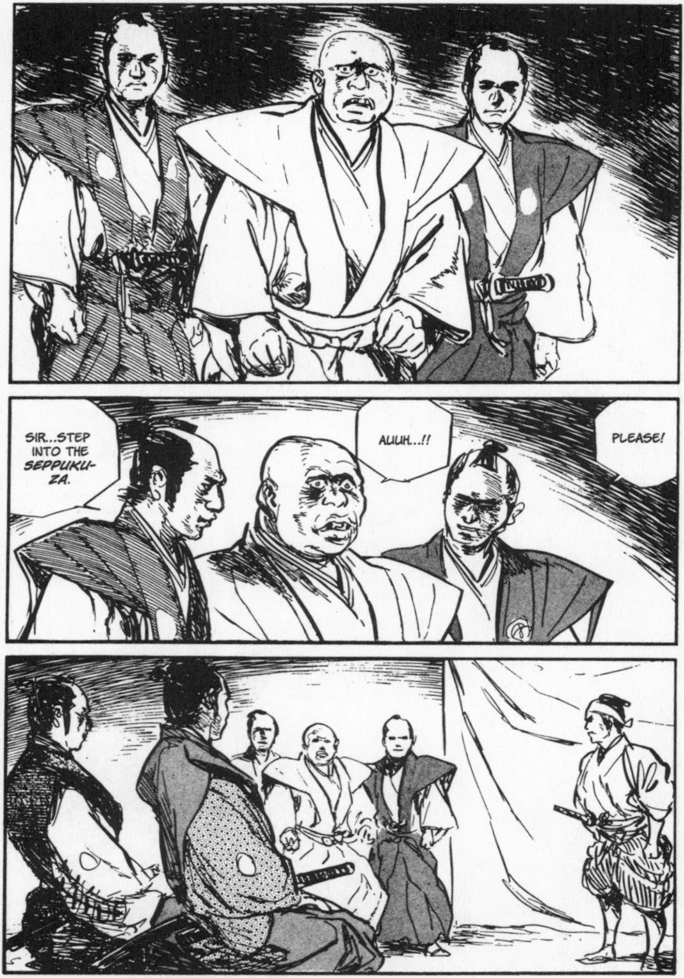
SIR...STEP INTO THE SEPPUKU-ZA.
AUUH...!!
PLEASE!

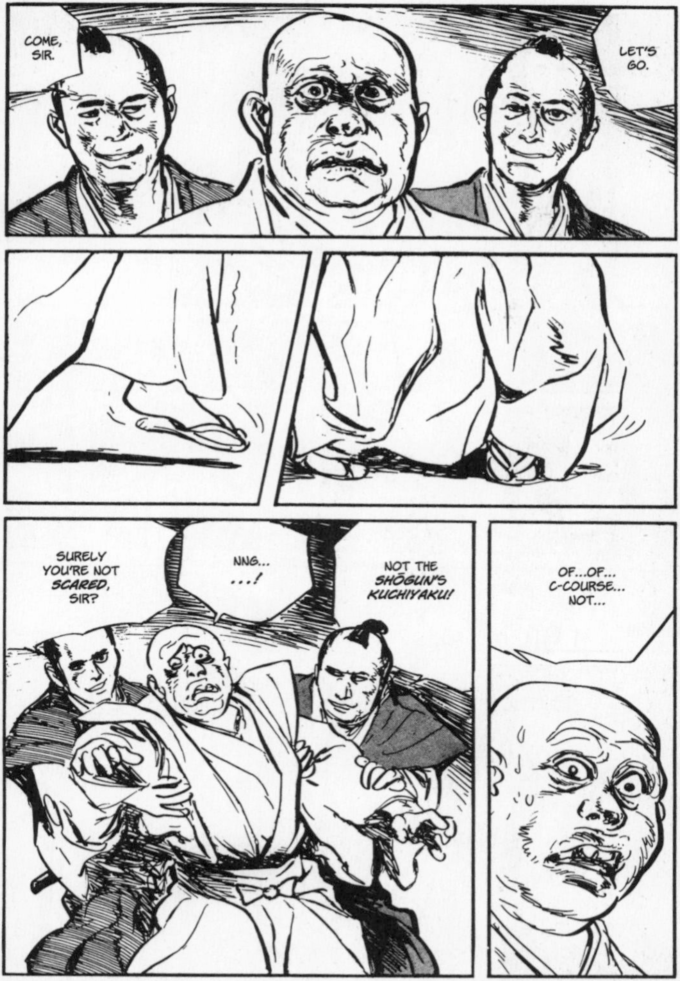
COME, SIR.
LET'S GO.
SURELY YOU'RE NOT SCARED, SIR?
NNG... ...!
NOT THE SHŌGUN'S KUCHIYAKU!
OF...OF... C-COURSE... NOT...

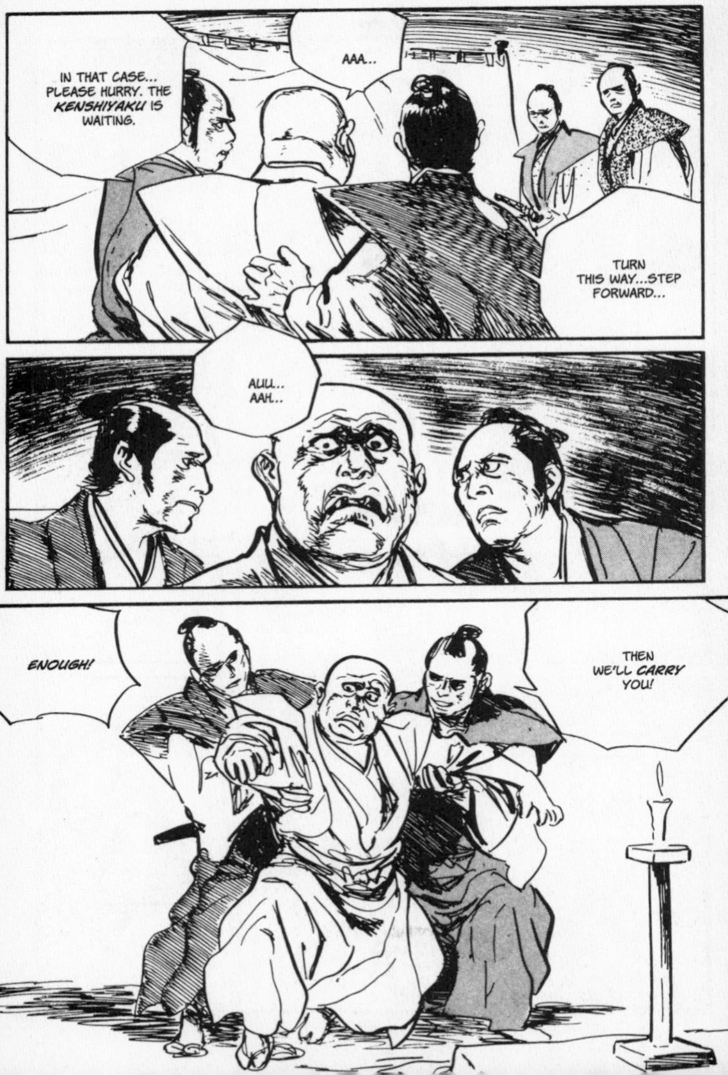
IN THAT CASE... PLEASE HURRY. THE *KENSHIYAKU* IS WAITING.
AAA...
TURN THIS WAY...STEP FORWARD...
AUU... AAH...
ENOUGH!
THEN WE'LL *CARRY* YOU!

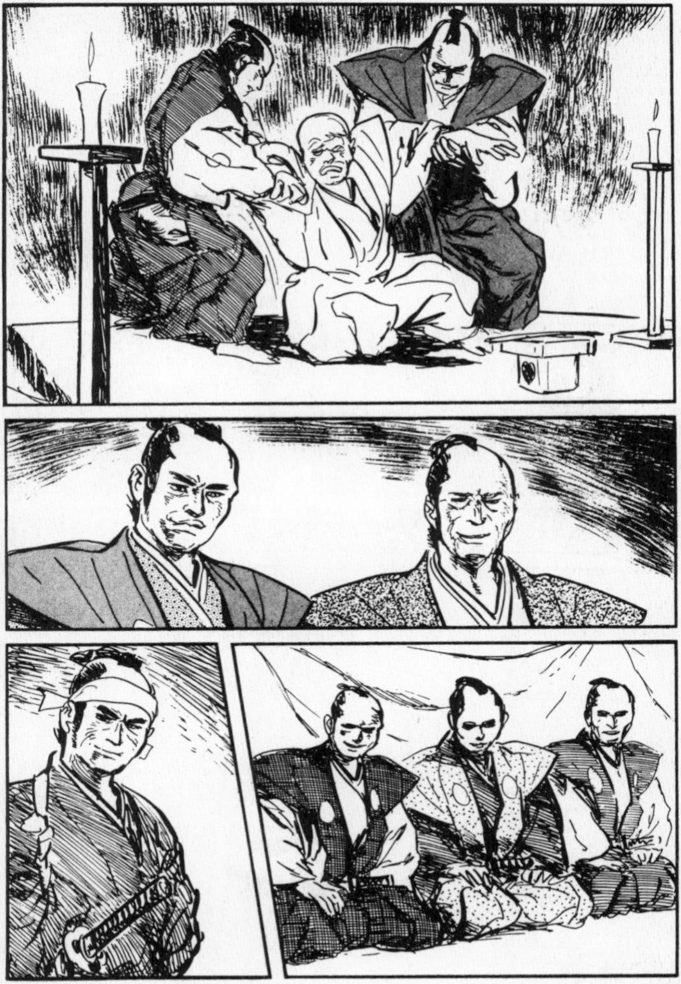

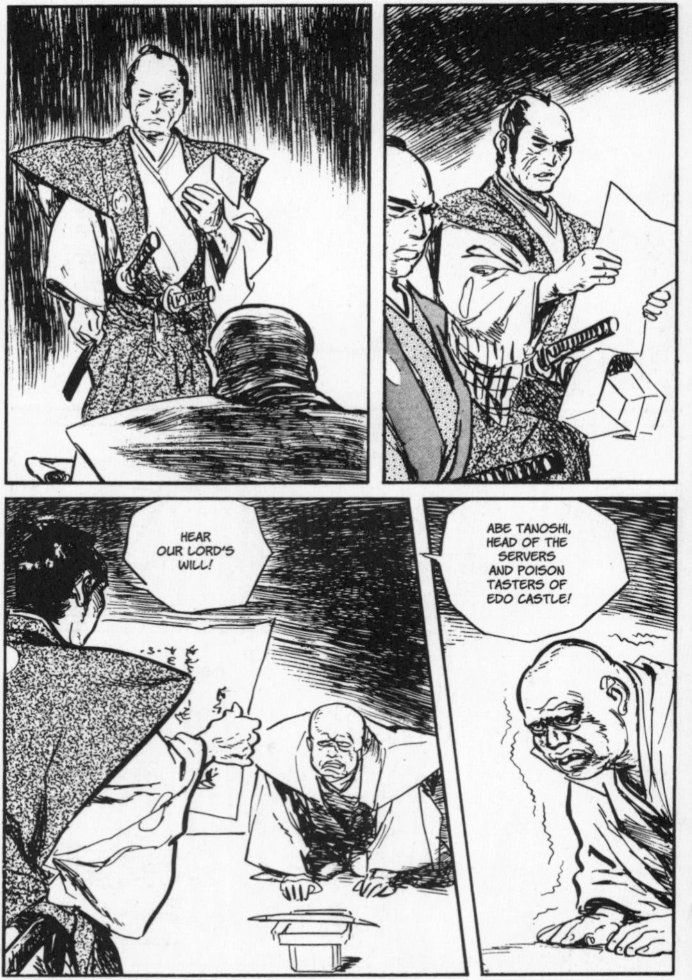
HEAR OUR LORD'S WILL!
ABE TANOSHI, HEAD OF THE SERVERS AND POISON TASTERS OF EDO CASTLE!

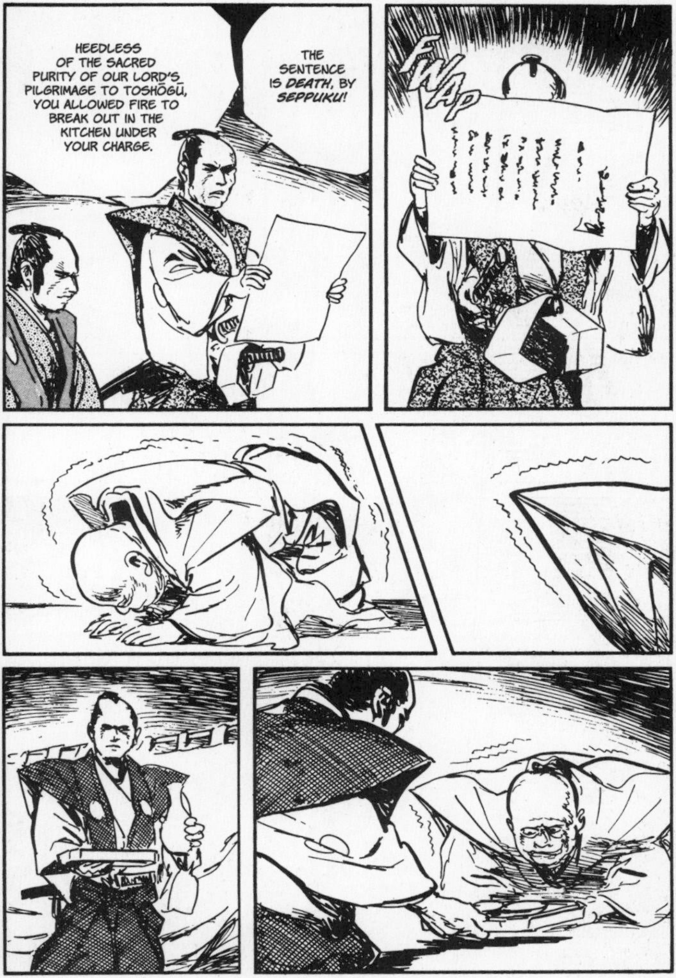
HEEDLESS OF THE SACRED PURITY OF OUR LORD'S PILGRIMAGE TO TOSHŌGŪ, YOU ALLOWED FIRE TO BREAK OUT IN THE KITCHEN UNDER YOUR CHARGE.
THE SENTENCE IS *DEATH*, BY *SEPPUKU!*
FWAP

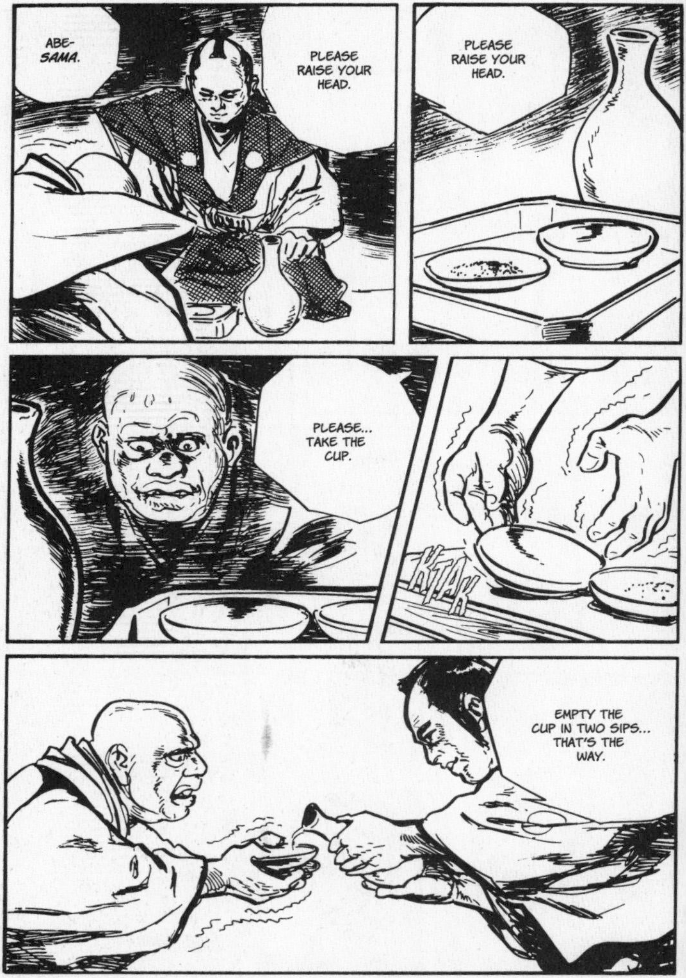
ABE-SAMA.
PLEASE RAISE YOUR HEAD.
PLEASE RAISE YOUR HEAD.
PLEASE... TAKE THE CUP.
KTAK
EMPTY THE CUP IN TWO SIPS... THAT'S THE WAY.

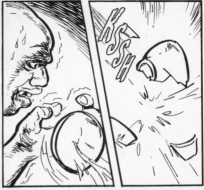

TAKE IT *AWAY!*

YES, SIR!

THIS IS *PATHETIC,* ABE TANOSHI.

265

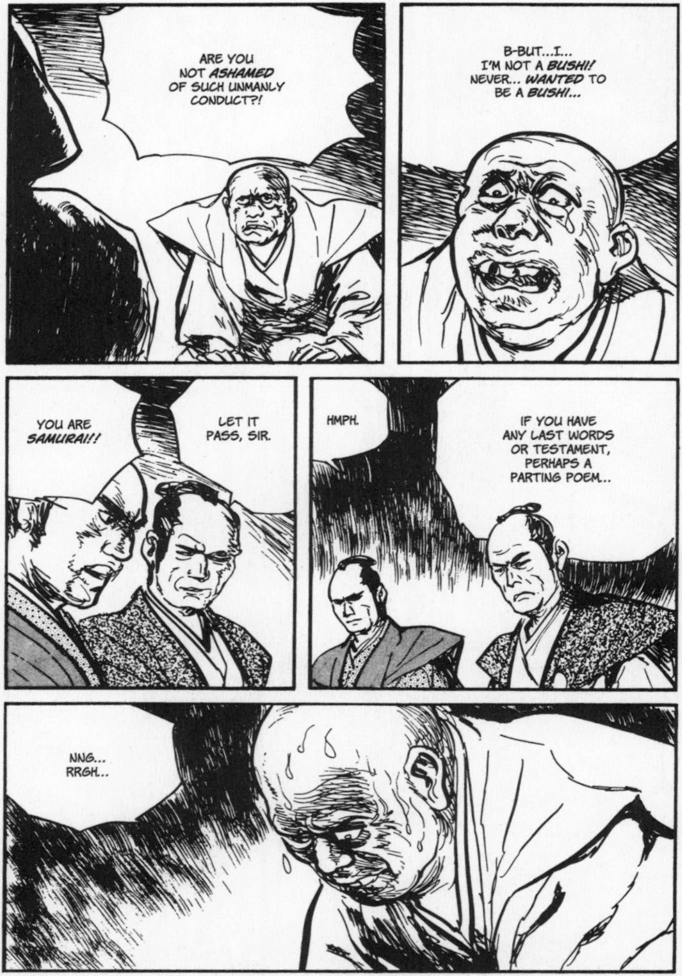
ARE YOU NOT ASHAMED OF SUCH UNMANLY CONDUCT?!
B-BUT...I... I'M NOT A BUSHI! NEVER... WANTED TO BE A BUSHI...
YOU ARE SAMURAI!!
LET IT PASS, SIR.
HMPH.
IF YOU HAVE ANY LAST WORDS OR TESTAMENT, PERHAPS A PARTING POEM...
NNG... RRGH...

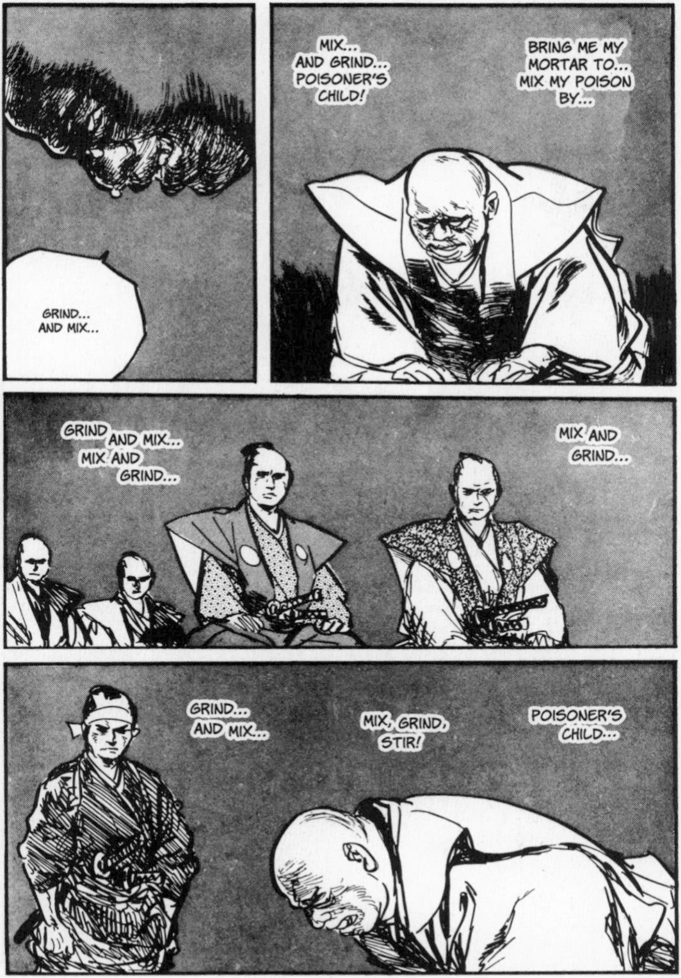
GRIND... AND MIX...
MIX... AND GRIND... POISONER'S CHILD!
BRING ME MY MORTAR TO... MIX MY POISON BY...
GRIND AND MIX... MIX AND GRIND...
MIX AND GRIND...
GRIND... AND MIX...
MIX, GRIND, STIR!
POISONER'S CHILD...

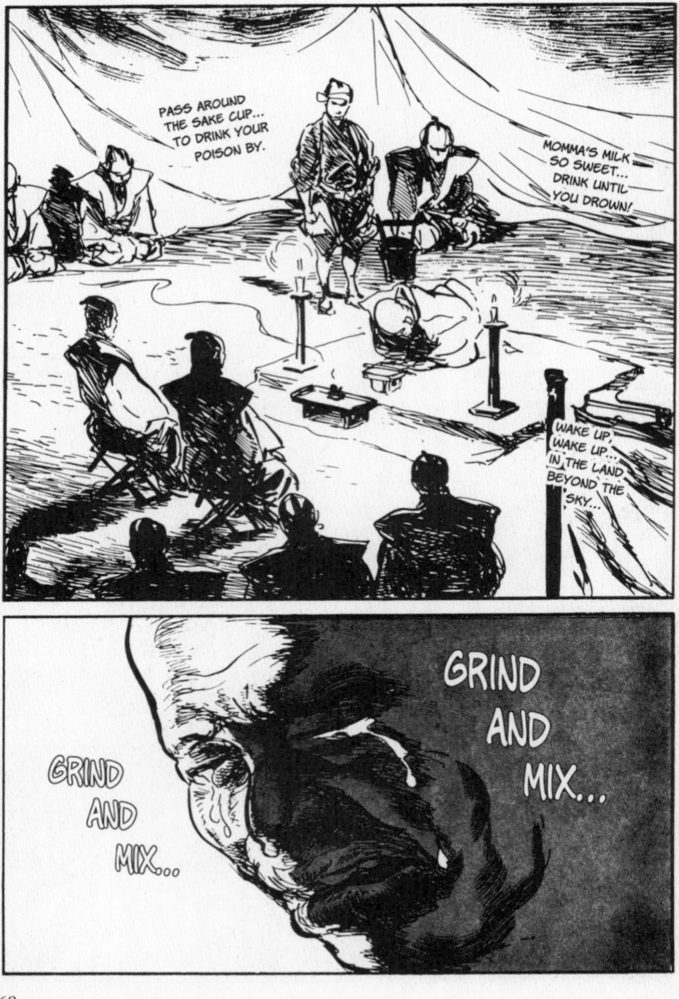
PASS AROUND THE SAKE CUP... TO DRINK YOUR POISON BY.
MOMMA'S MILK SO SWEET... DRINK UNTIL YOU DROWN!
WAKE UP, WAKE UP... IN THE LAND BEYOND THE SKY...
GRIND AND MIX...
GRIND AND MIX...

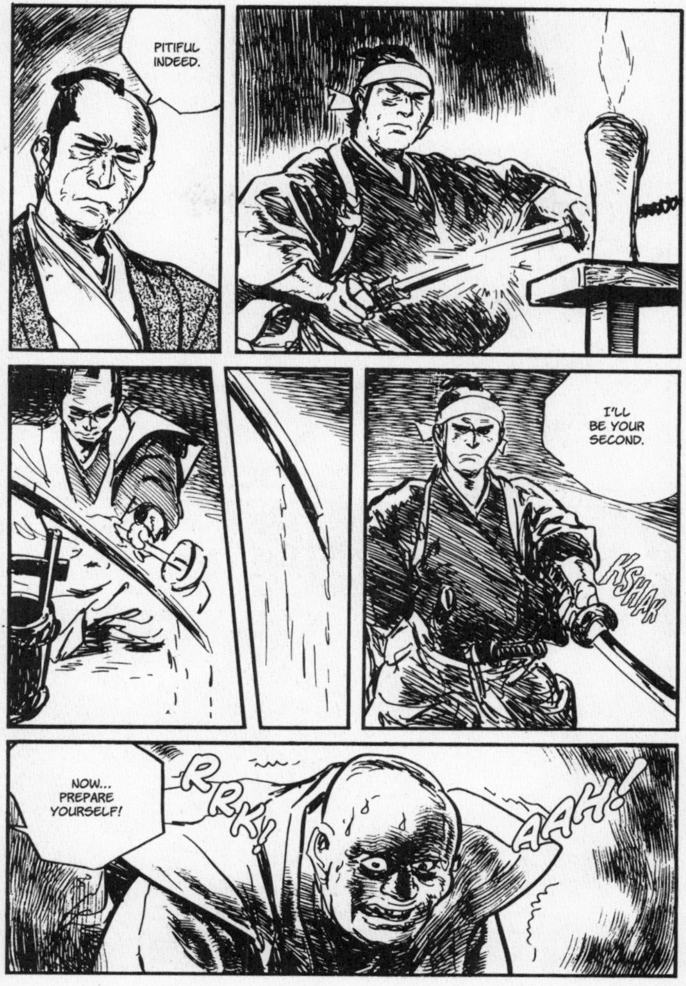
PITIFUL INDEED.
I'LL BE YOUR SECOND.
KSHAK
NOW... PREPARE YOURSELF!
RRK!
AAH!

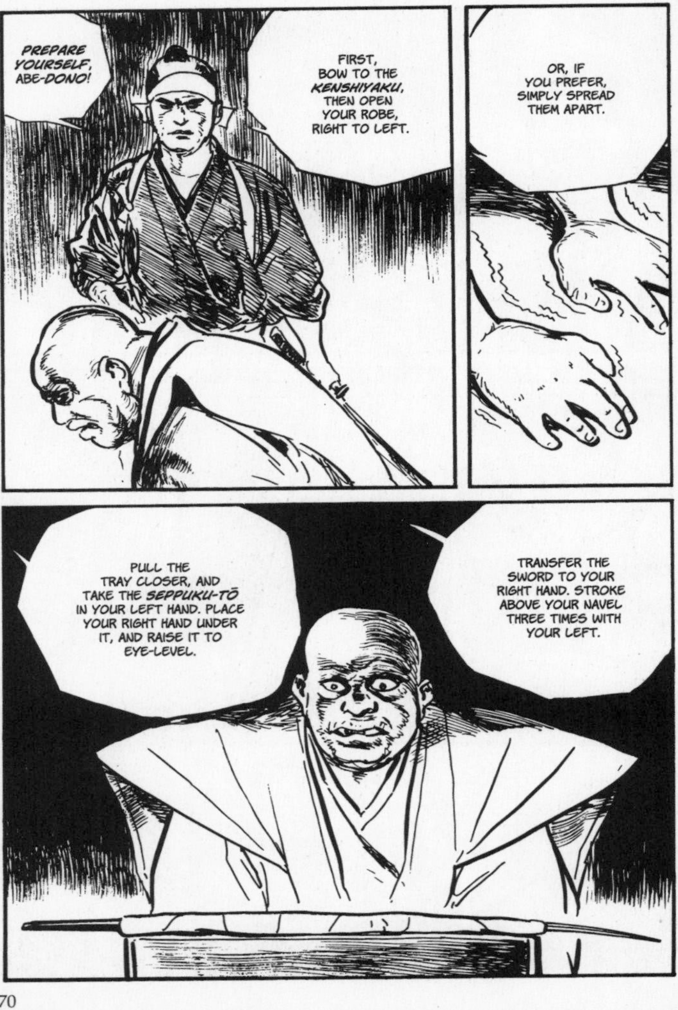
PREPARE YOURSELF, ABE-DONO!
FIRST, BOW TO THE *KENSHIYAKU*, THEN OPEN YOUR ROBE, RIGHT TO LEFT.
OR, IF YOU PREFER, SIMPLY SPREAD THEM APART.
PULL THE TRAY CLOSER, AND TAKE THE *SEPPUKU-TŌ* IN YOUR LEFT HAND. PLACE YOUR RIGHT HAND UNDER IT, AND RAISE IT TO EYE-LEVEL.
TRANSFER THE SWORD TO YOUR RIGHT HAND. STROKE ABOVE YOUR NAVEL THREE TIMES WITH YOUR LEFT.

CALM YOUR
SPIRIT... THEN
THRUST.

UNDERSTAND?

ABE-
DONO...?!

BEGIN!

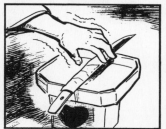

YOUR
OTHER
HAND.

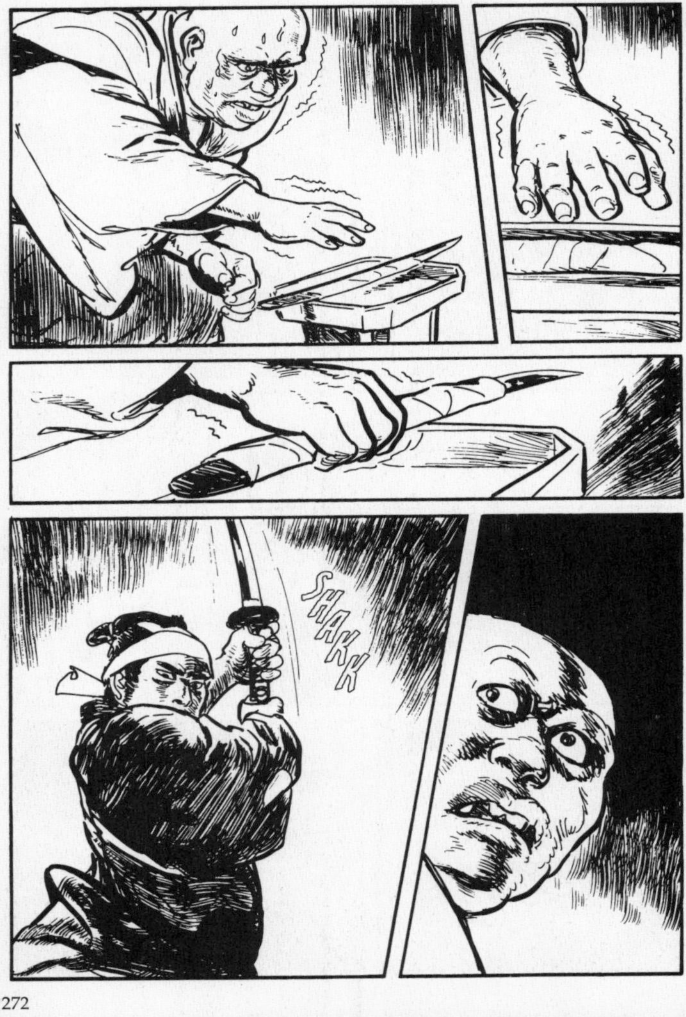
SHAKK

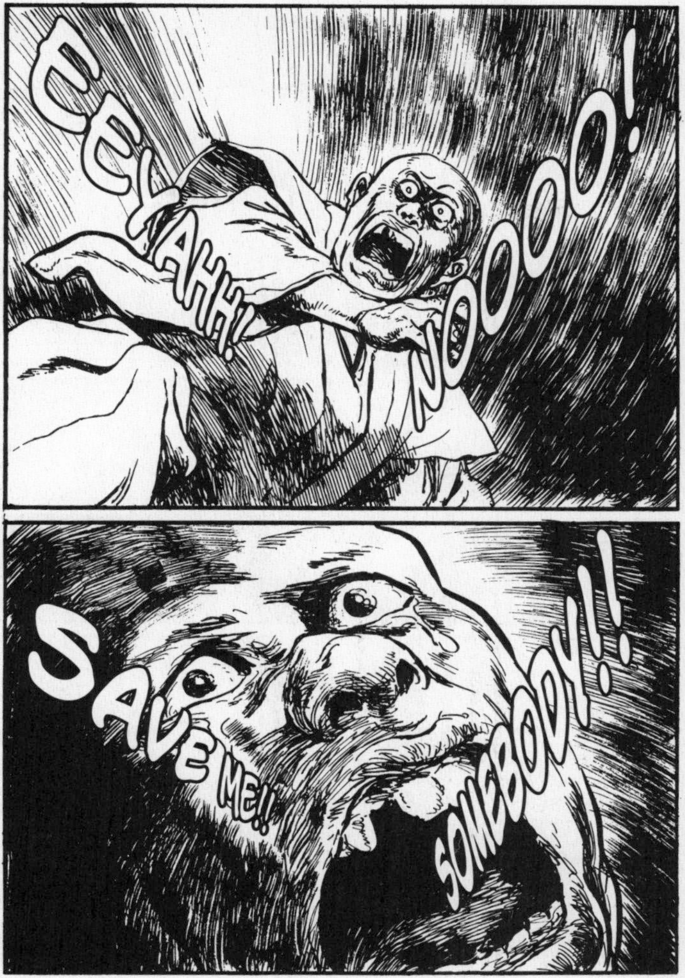
EEYAHH!
NOOOOOO!
SAVE ME!!
SOMEBODY!!!

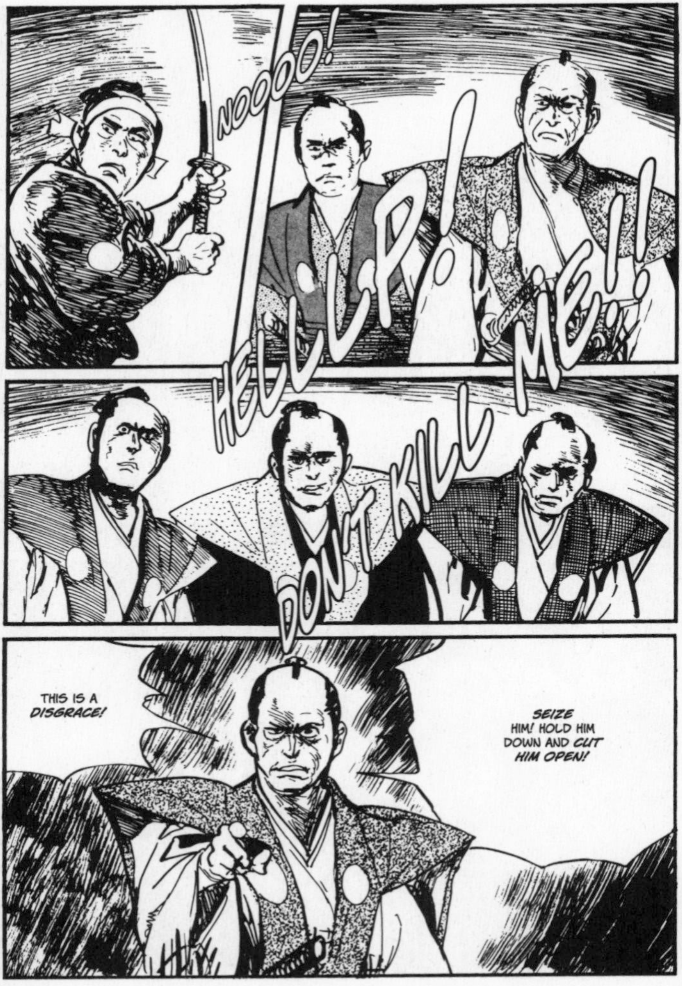
NOOOOO!
HELLLP!!
DON'T KILL ME!!
THIS IS A DISGRACE!
SEIZE HIM! HOLD HIM DOWN AND CUT HIM OPEN!

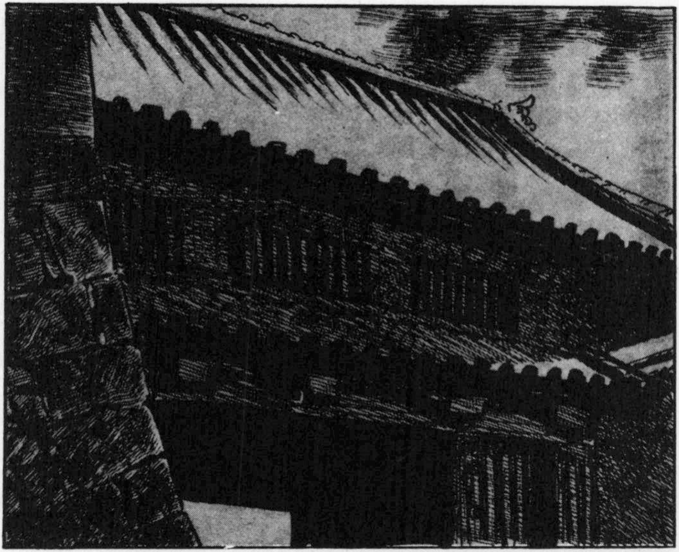
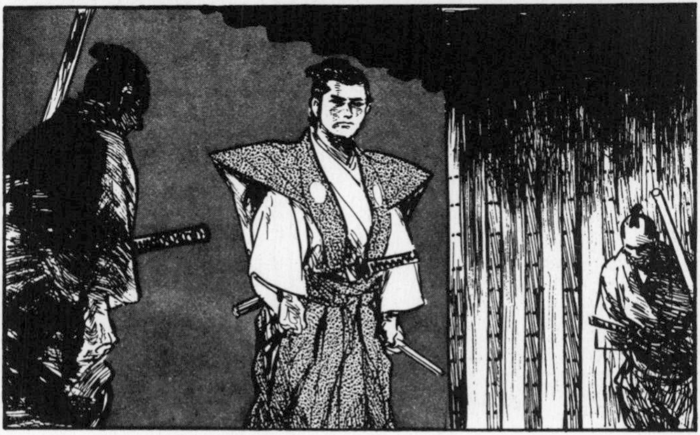

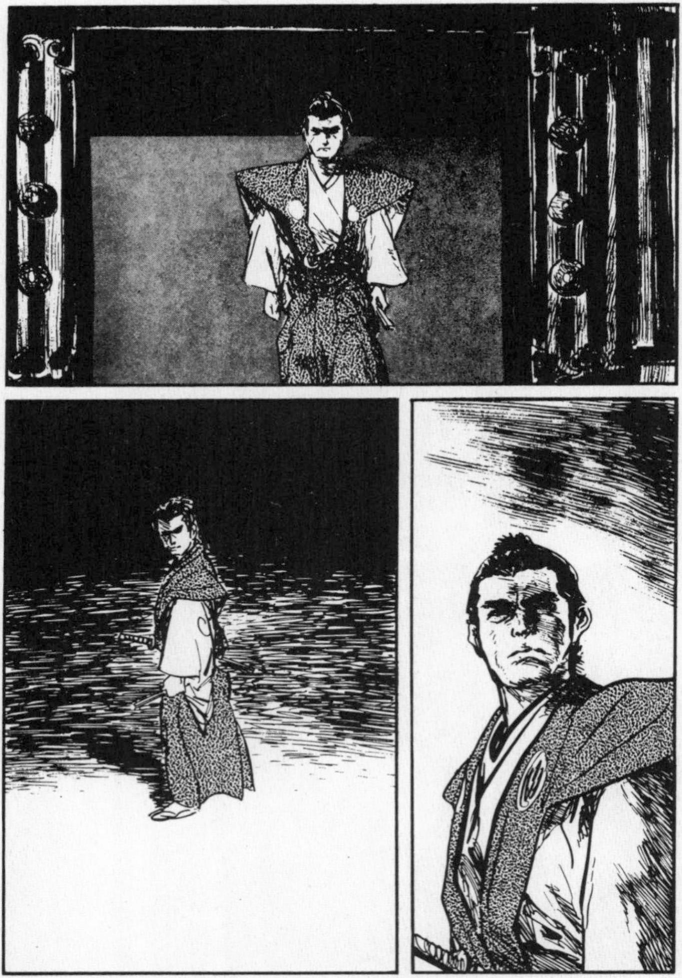

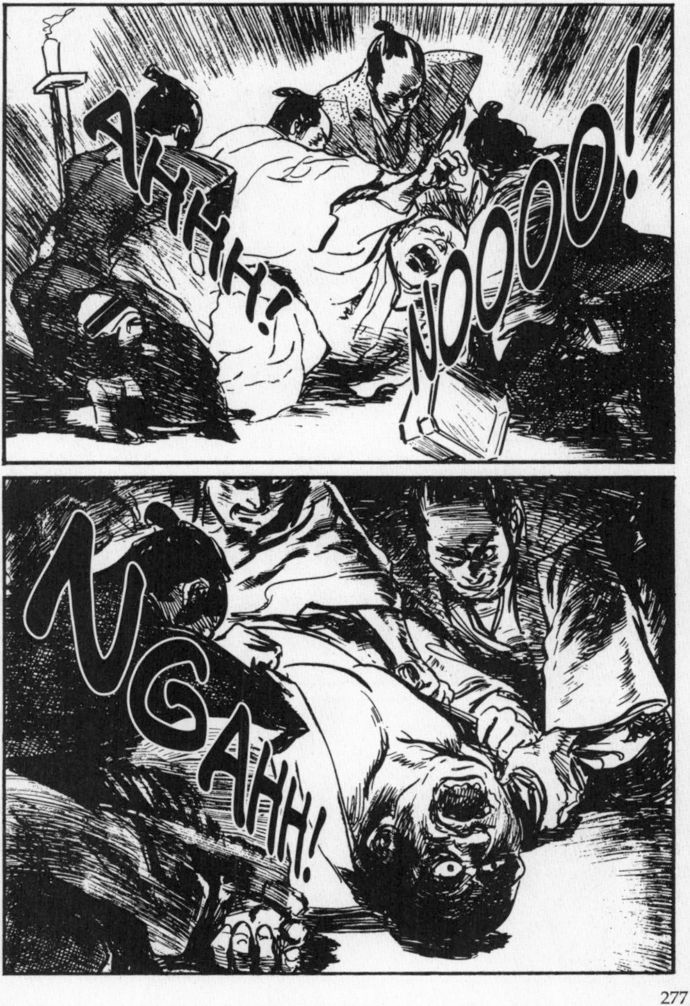
AHHHH!
NOOOOO!
NGAHH!

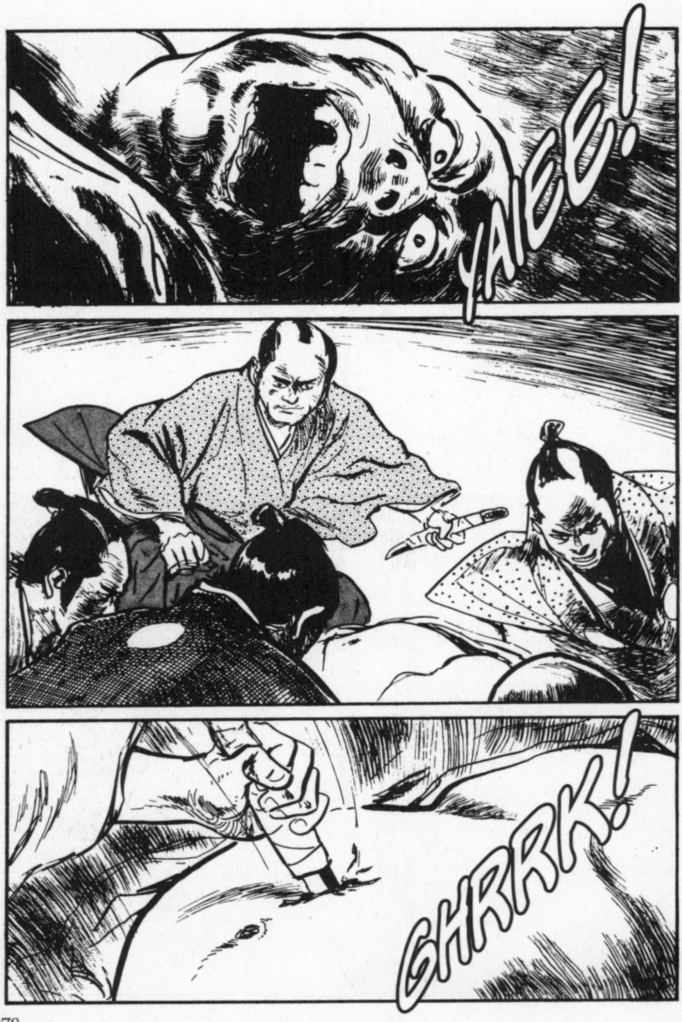
YAIEE!
SHRRK!

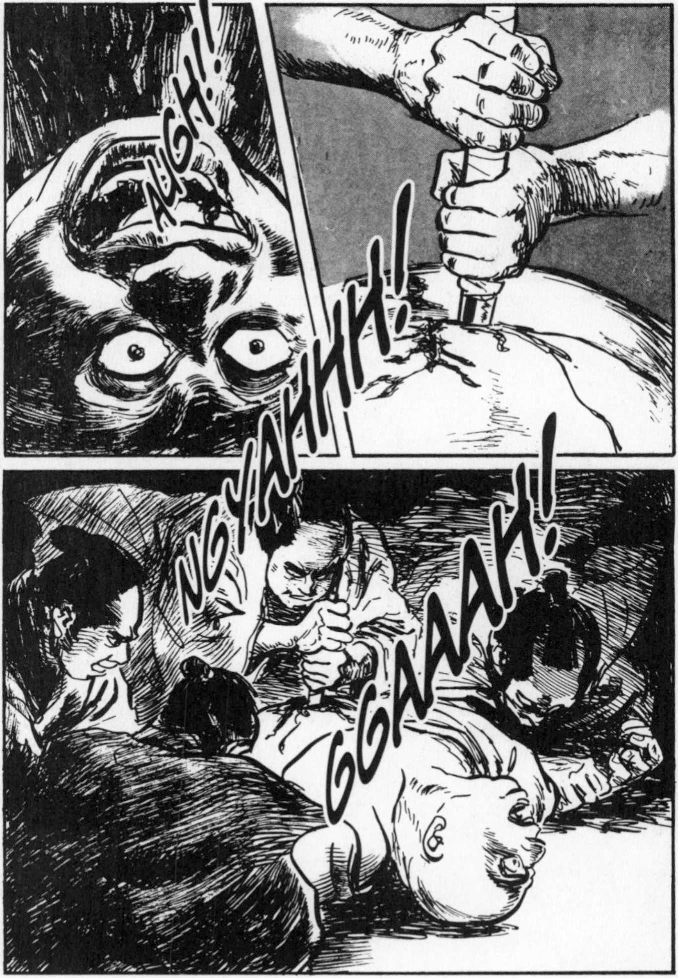
AUGH!!
NGYAHHH!
GGAAAH!

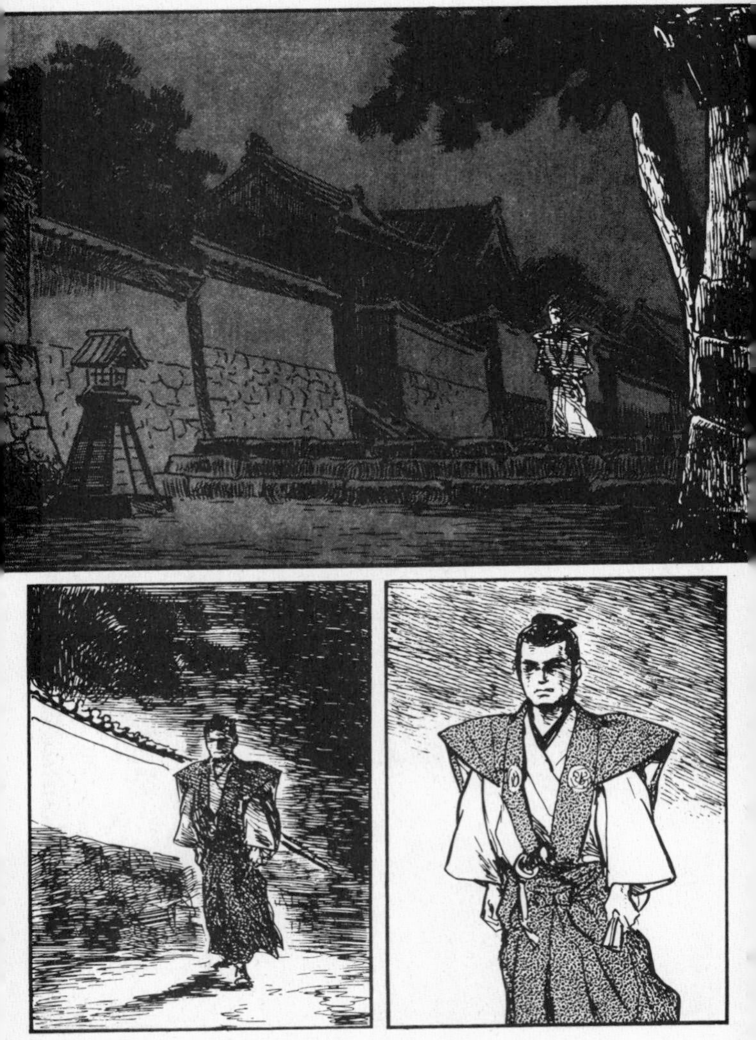

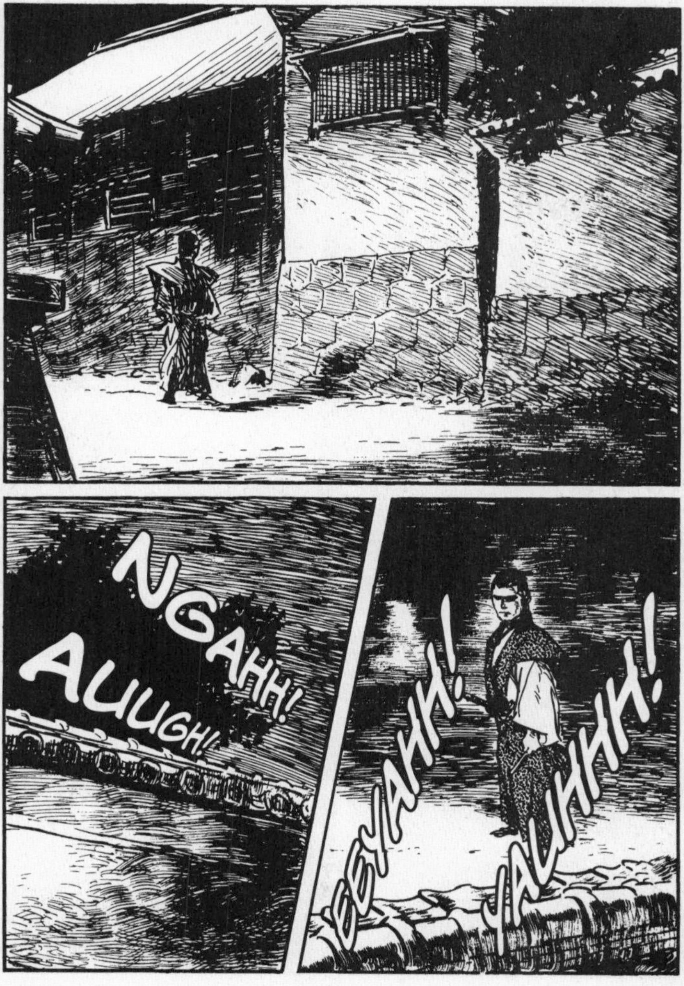
NGAHH!
AUUGH!
EEYAHH!
YAUHHH!

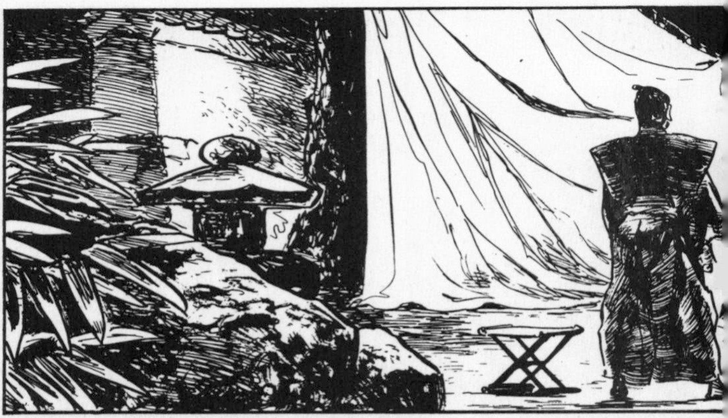

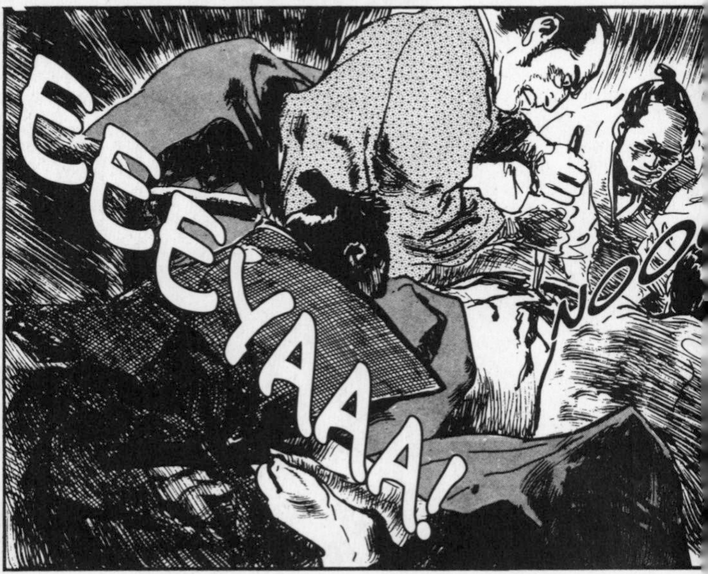
EEEYAAA!
NOO

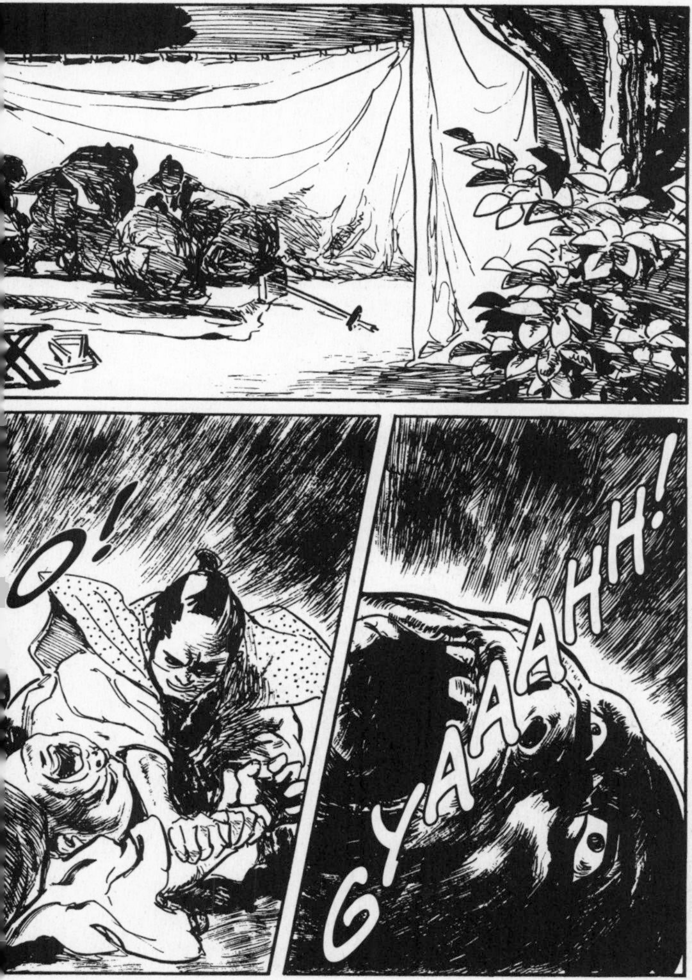
O!
GYAAAAHH!

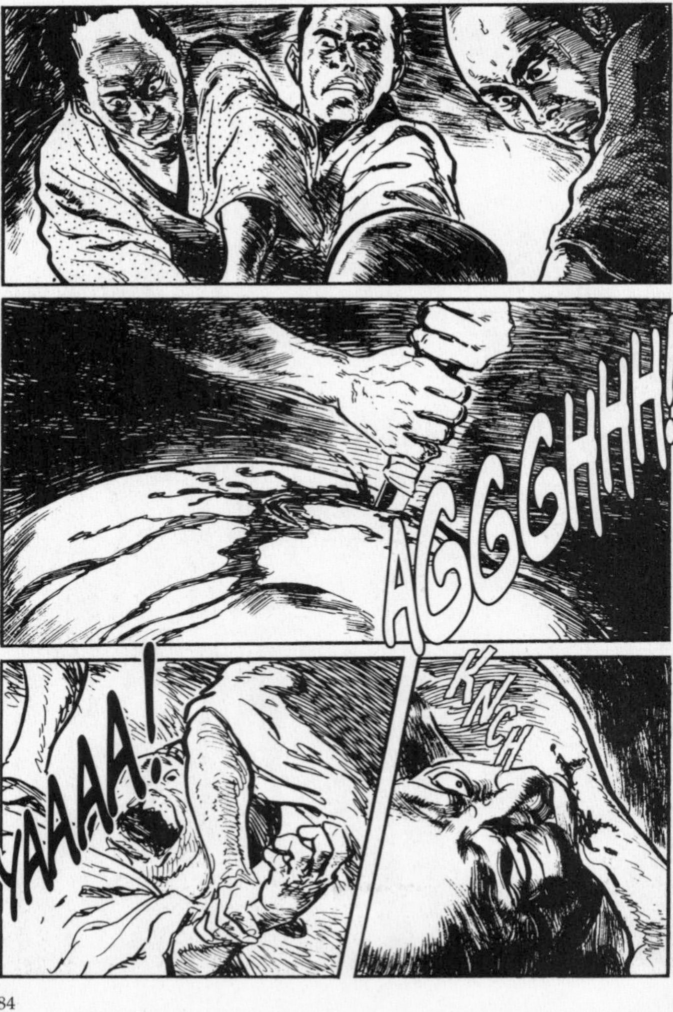
AGGGHHH!
YAAAA!
KNCH

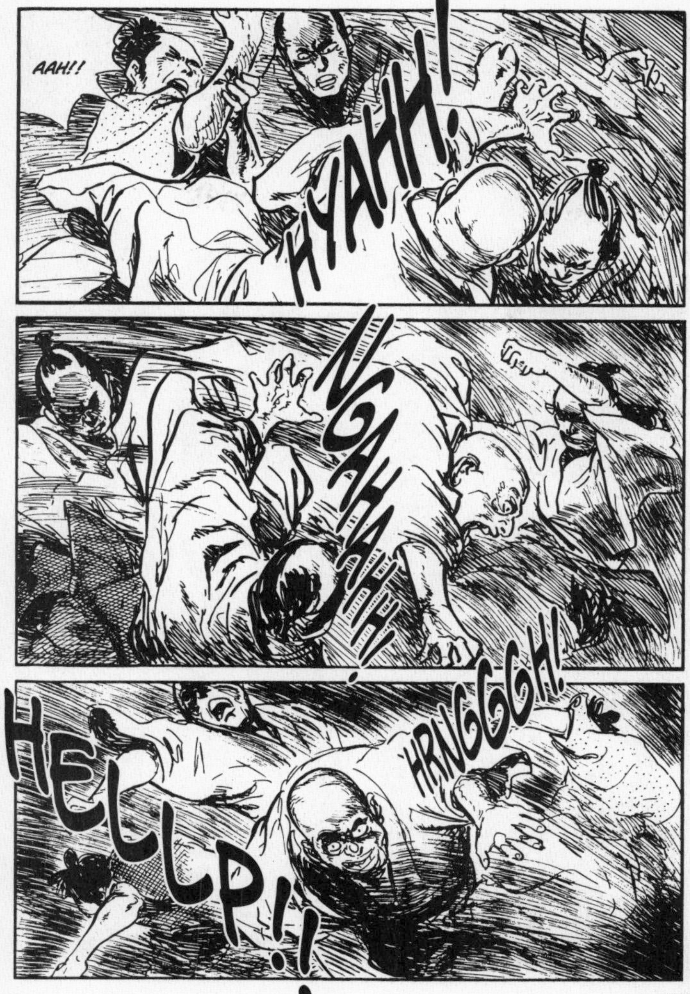
AAH!!
HYAAH!
NGAAAH!!
HELLLP!!
HRNGGGH!

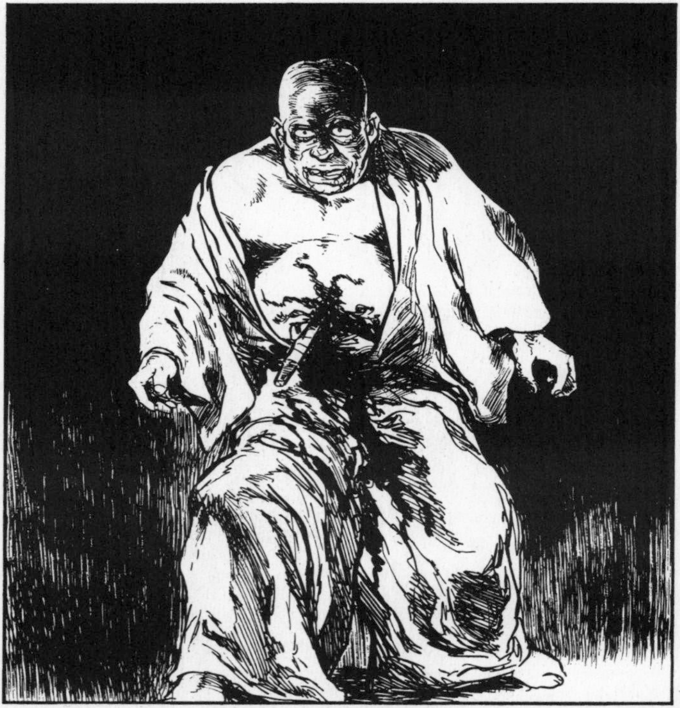

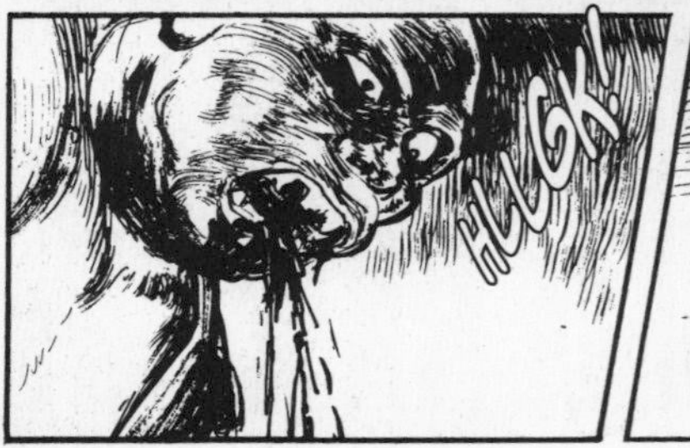
HLLGK!

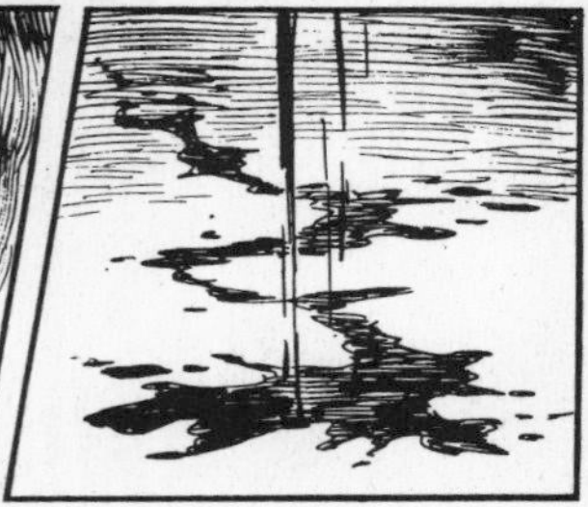

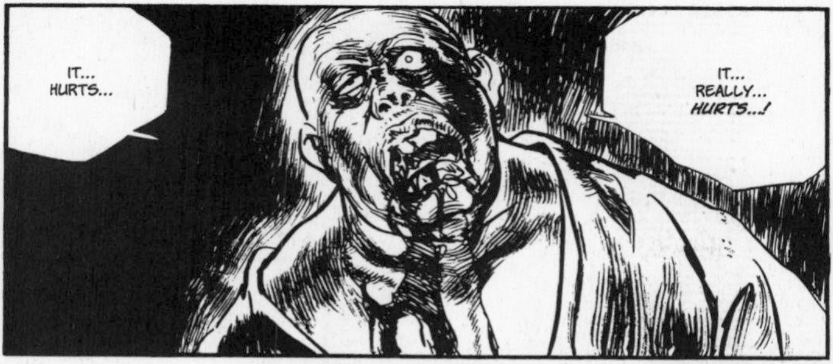
IT... HURTS...
IT... REALLY... *HURTS...!*

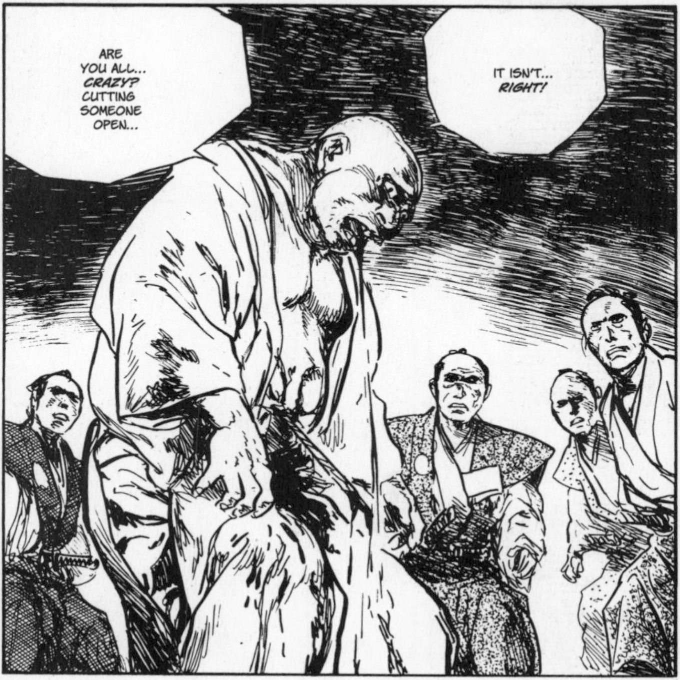
ARE YOU ALL... *CRAZY?* CUTTING SOMEONE OPEN...
IT ISN'T... *RIGHT!*

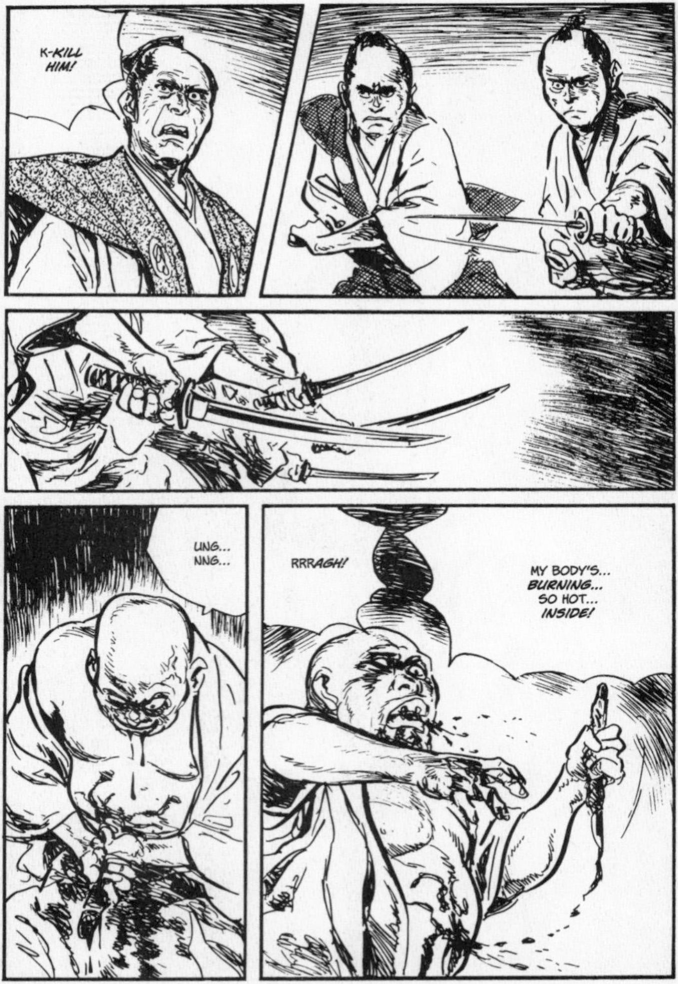
K-KILL HIM!
UNG... NNG...
RRRAGH!
MY BODY'S... BURNING... SO HOT... INSIDE!

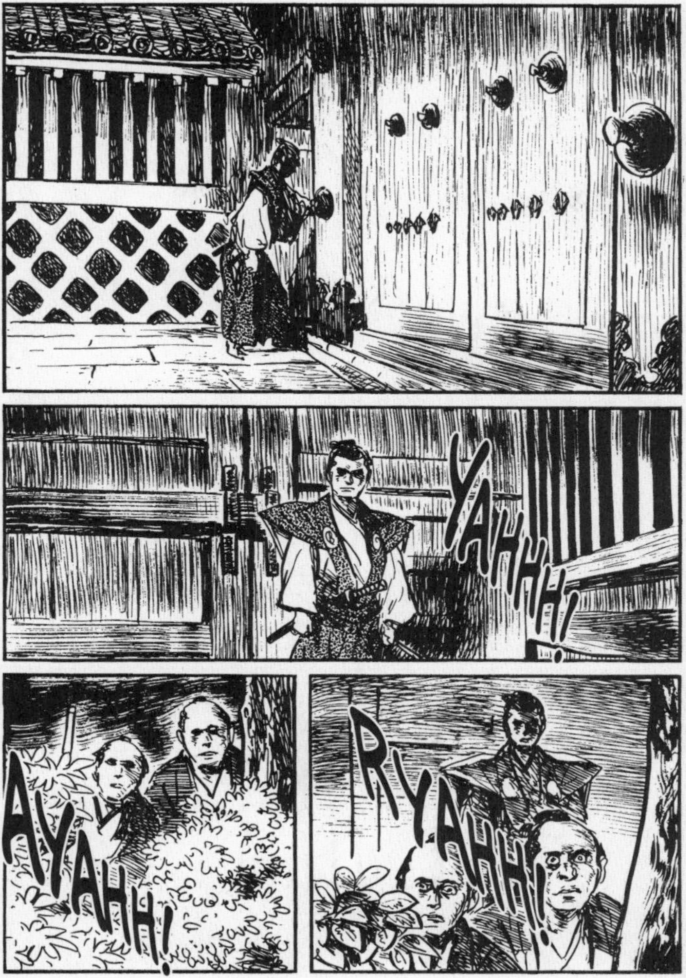
YAHHH!
AYAHH!
RIYAHH!

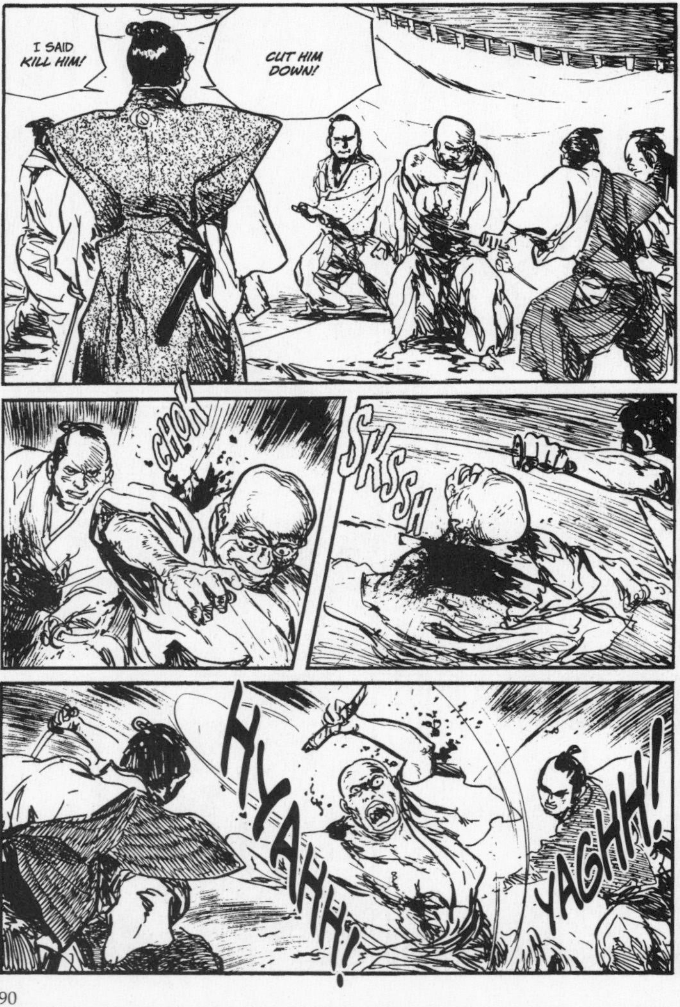
I SAID KILL HIM!
CUT HIM DOWN!
CHOK
SKSSH
HIYAHH!
YAGHH!

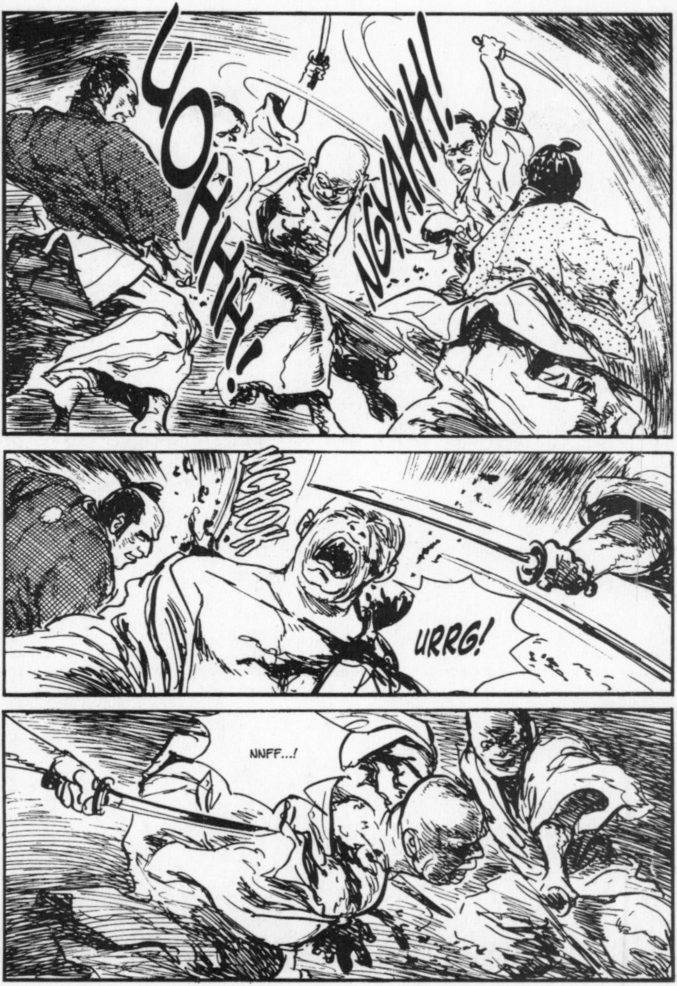
UOHHH!!
NGYAHH!
NCHO!
URRG!
NNFF...!

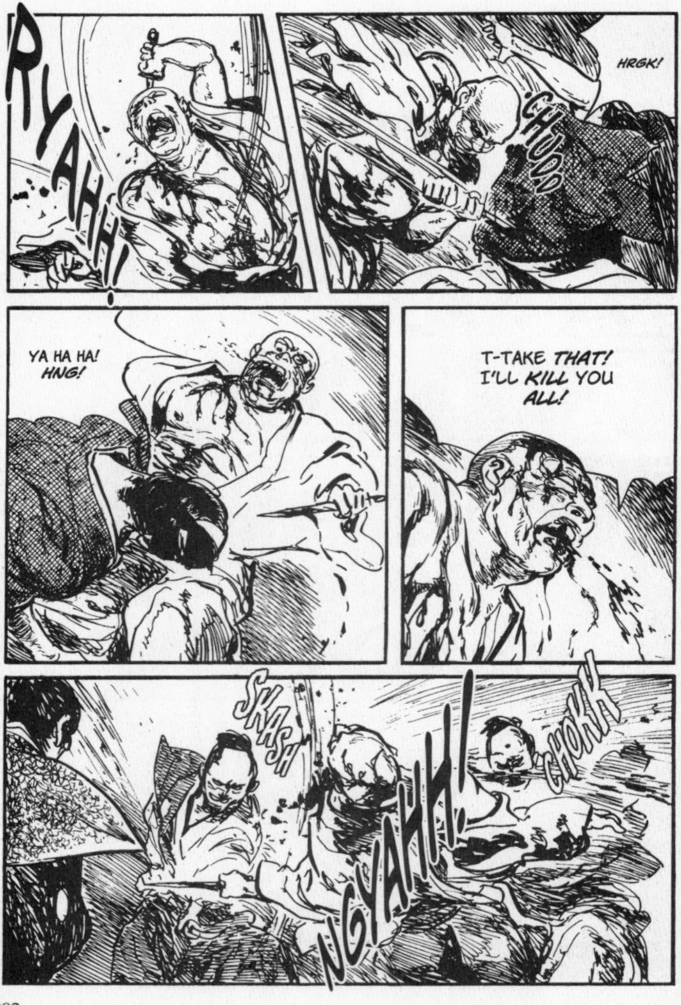
RYAHH!!
HRGK!
CHUNK
YA HA HA!
HNG!
T-TAKE THAT!
I'LL KILL YOU
ALL!
SKASH
NGYAHH!
CHOKK

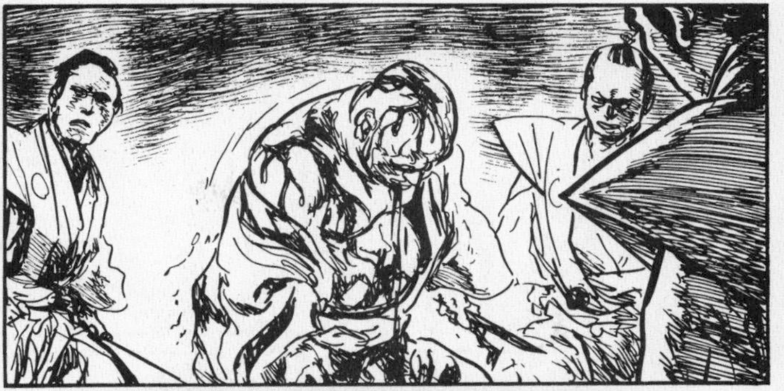

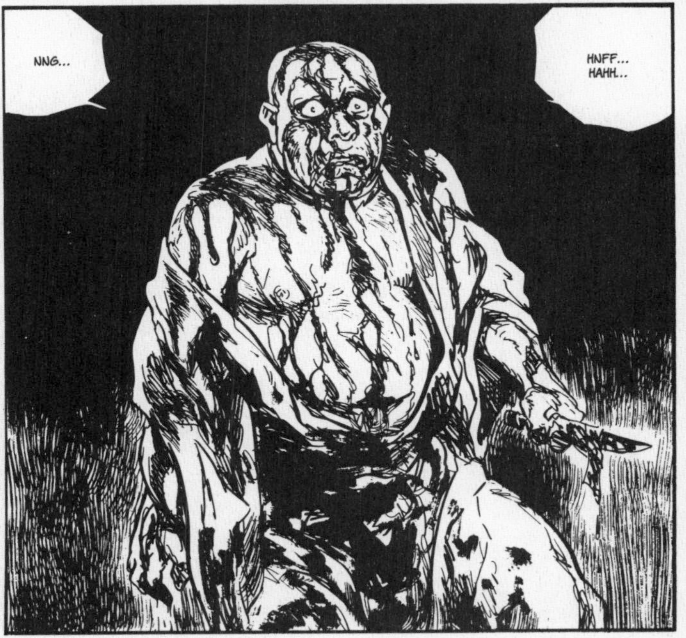
NNG...
HNFF...
HAHH...

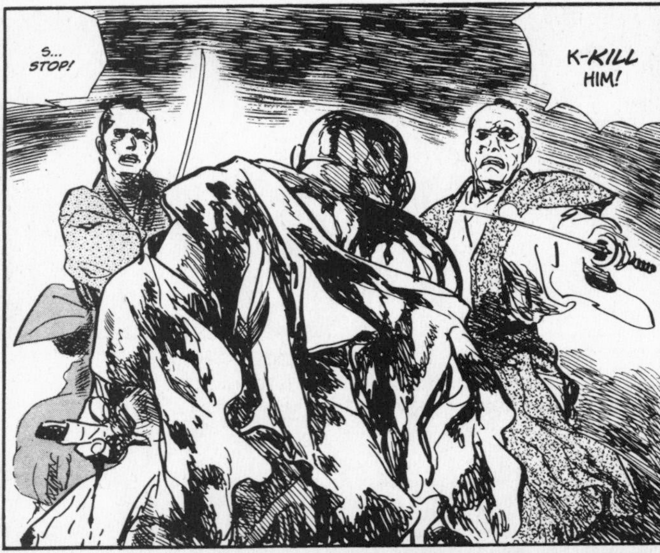
S... STOP!
K-KILL HIM!
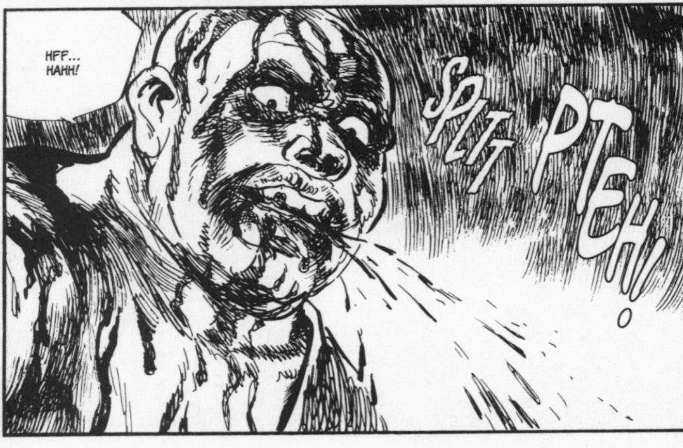
HFF... HAHH!
SPLIT
PTEH!!

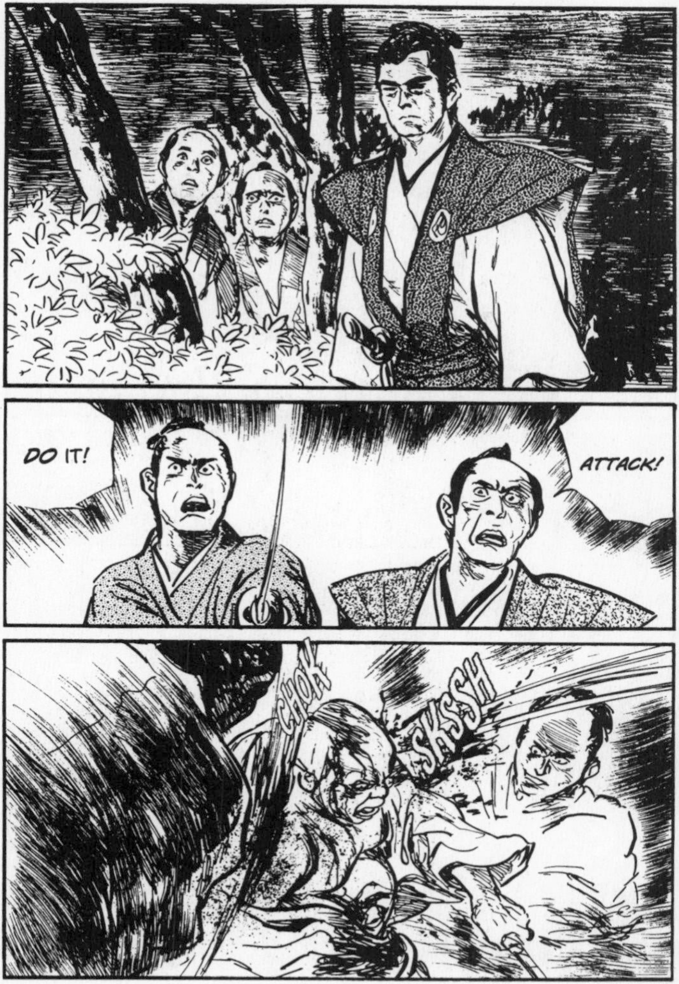
DO IT!
ATTACK!
CHOK
SKSSH

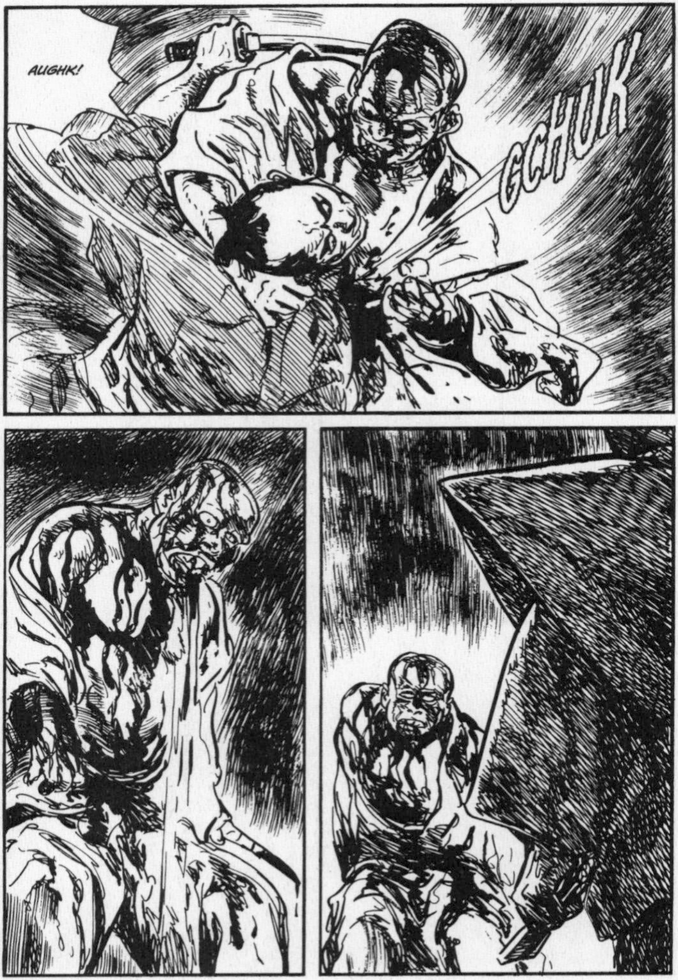
AUGHK!
GCHUK

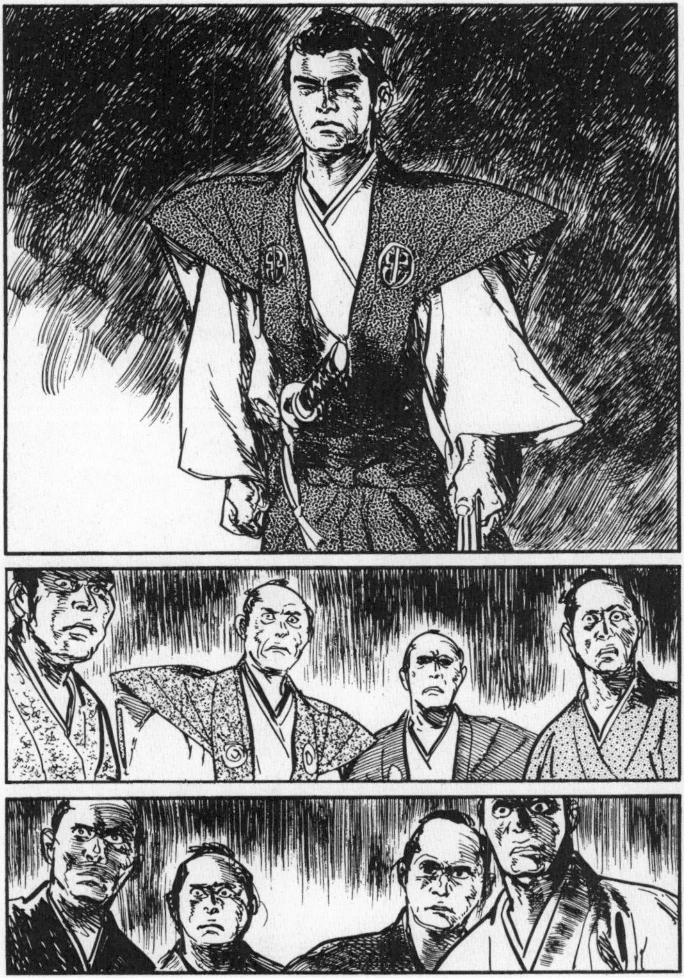

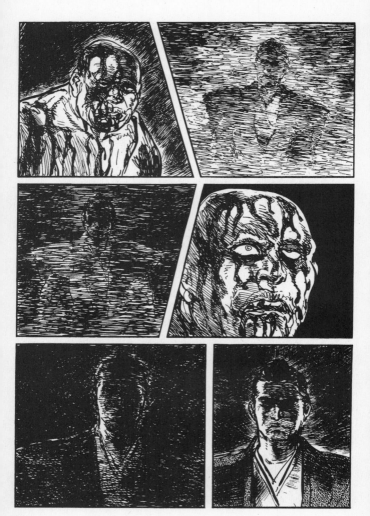

298

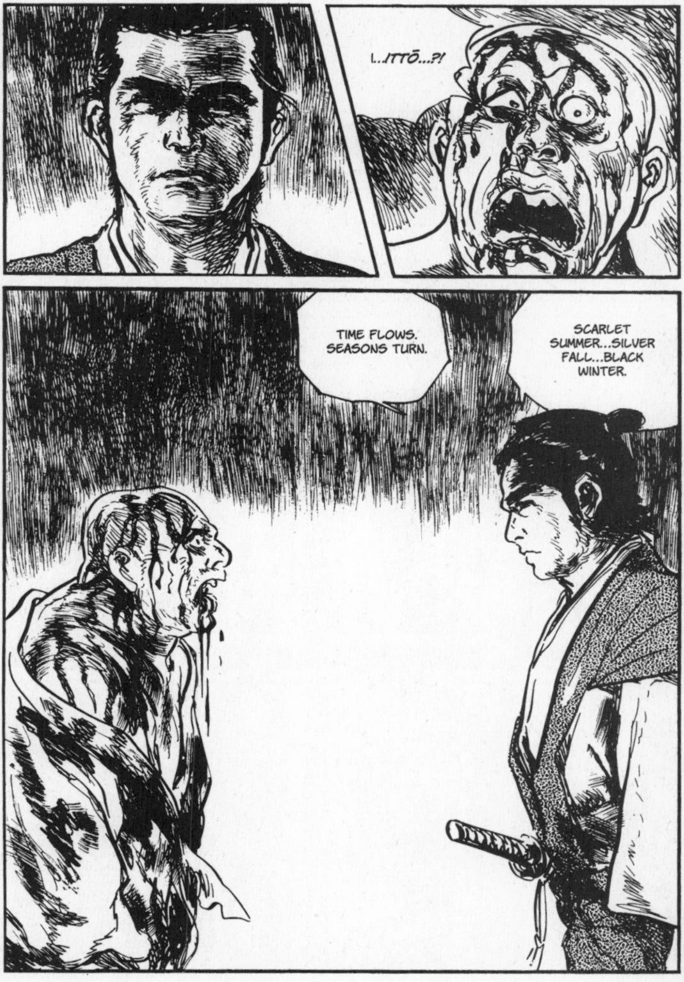
I...ITTŌ...?!
TIME FLOWS. SEASONS TURN.
SCARLET SUMMER...SILVER FALL...BLACK WINTER.

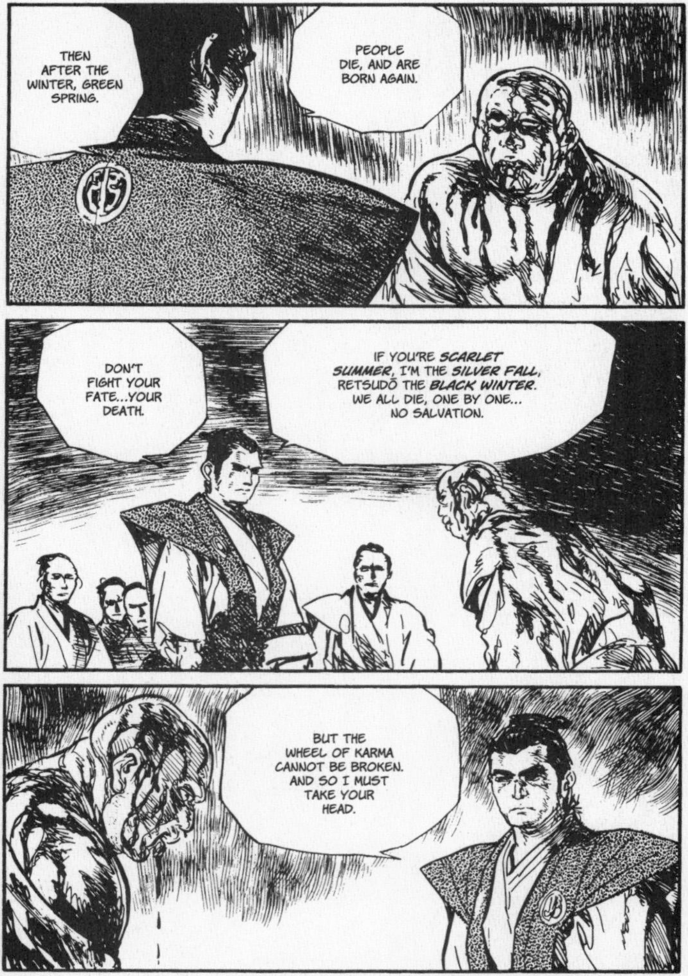
THEN AFTER THE WINTER, GREEN SPRING.
PEOPLE DIE, AND ARE BORN AGAIN.
DON'T FIGHT YOUR FATE...YOUR DEATH.
IF YOU'RE *SCARLET SUMMER*, I'M THE *SILVER FALL*, RETSUDŌ THE *BLACK WINTER*. WE ALL DIE, ONE BY ONE... NO SALVATION.
BUT THE WHEEL OF KARMA CANNOT BE BROKEN. AND SO I MUST TAKE YOUR HEAD.

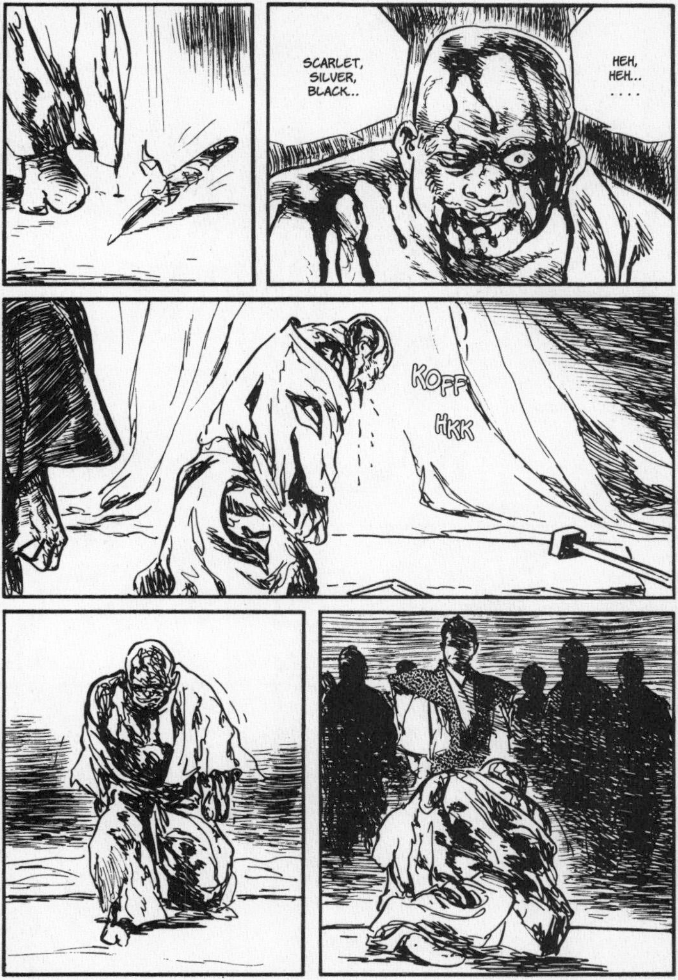
SCARLET, SILVER, BLACK...
HEH, HEH...
. . . .
KOFF
HKK

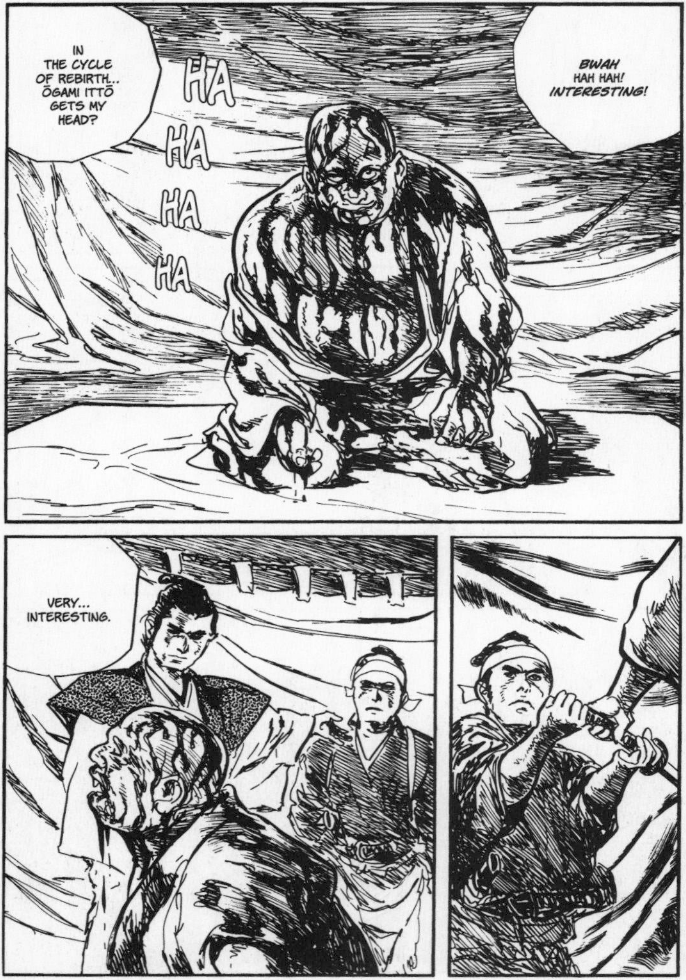

IN THE CYCLE OF REBIRTH... ŌGAMI ITTŌ GETS MY HEAD?
HA HA HA HA HA
BWAH HAH HAH! INTERESTING!
VERY... INTERESTING.

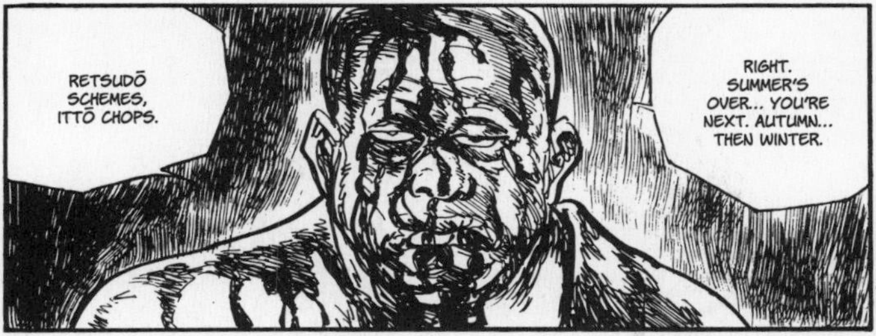
RETSUDŌ SCHEMES, ITTŌ CHOPS.
RIGHT. SUMMER'S OVER... YOU'RE NEXT. AUTUMN... THEN WINTER.

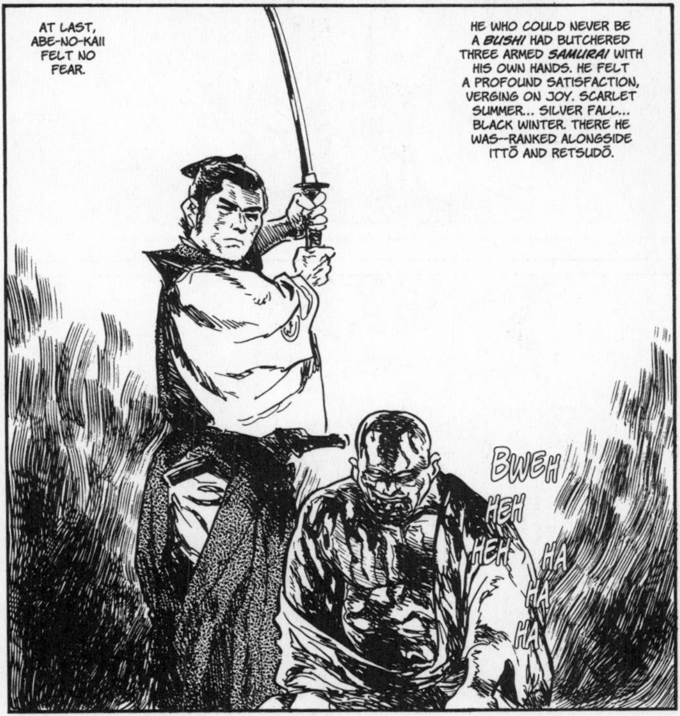
AT LAST, ABE-NO-KAII FELT NO FEAR.
HE WHO COULD NEVER BE A *BUSHI* HAD BUTCHERED THREE ARMED *SAMURAI* WITH HIS OWN HANDS. HE FELT A PROFOUND SATISFACTION, VERGING ON JOY. SCARLET SUMMER... SILVER FALL... BLACK WINTER. THERE HE WAS--RANKED ALONGSIDE ITTŌ AND RETSUDŌ.
BWEH
HEH
HEH
HA
HA
HA

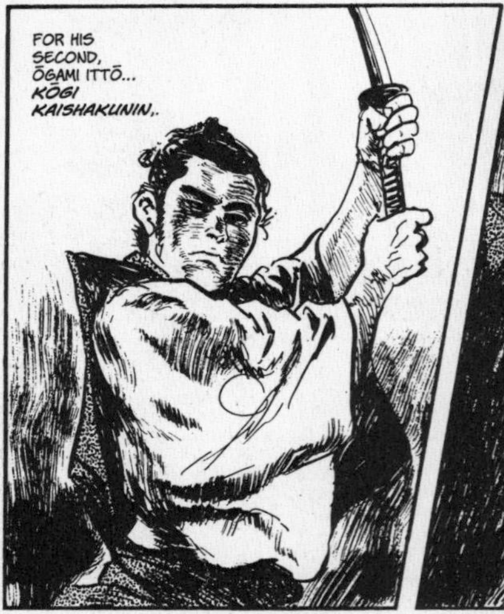
FOR HIS SECOND, ŌGAMI ITTŌ... *KŌGI KAISHAKUNIN*..

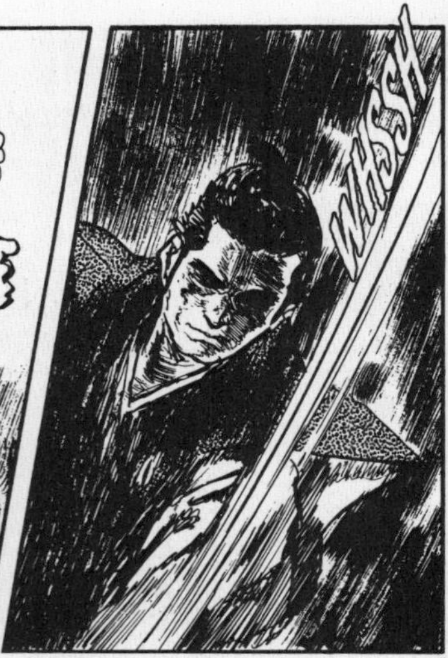
WHSSH

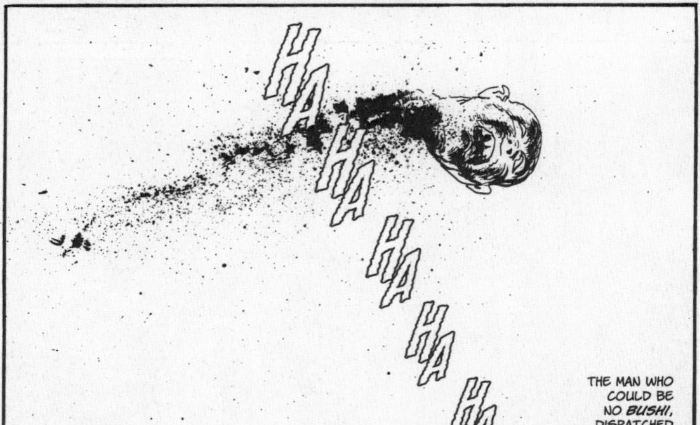
HA HA HA HA HA HA
THE MAN WHO COULD BE NO *BUSHI*, DISPATCHED BY THE LAST TRUE *BUSHI'S* BLADE.

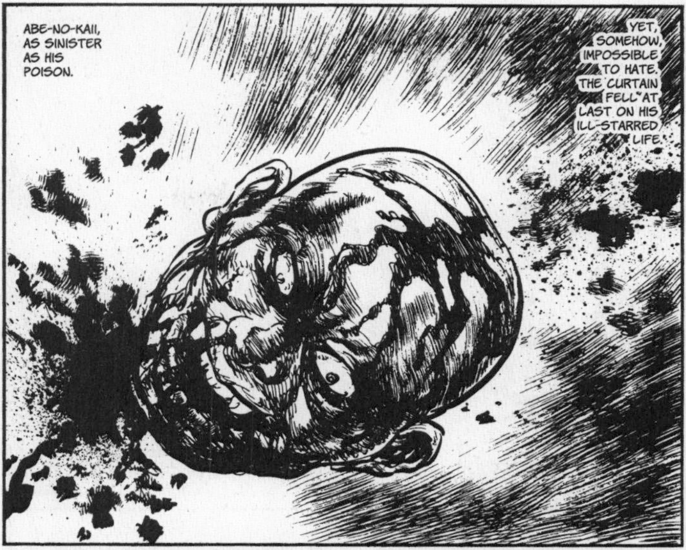
ABE-NO-KAII, AS SINISTER AS HIS POISON.
YET, SOMEHOW, IMPOSSIBLE TO HATE. THE CURTAIN FELL AT LAST ON HIS ILL-STARRED LIFE.
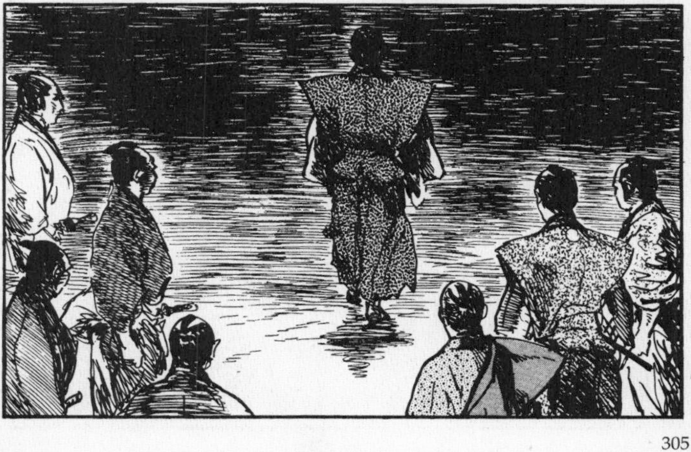

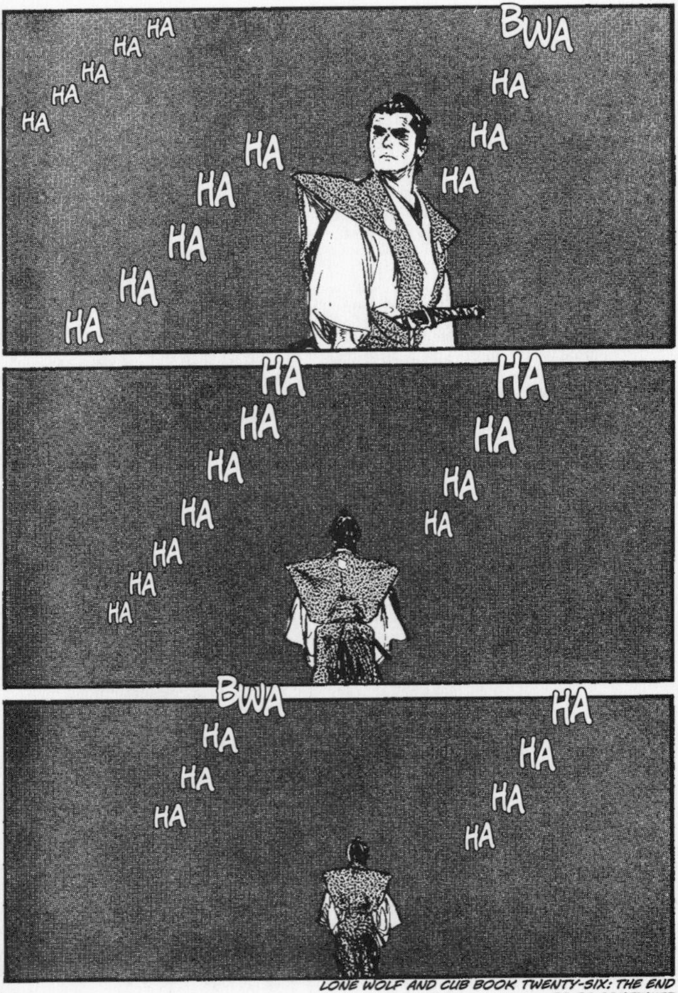
HA HA HA HA HA
BWA
HA
HA
HA HA
HA
HA
HA
HA
HA
HA
HA
HA
HA
HA
HA
HA HA HA
HA
HA
HA
BWA
HA
HA
HA
HA
HA
HA
HA
HA

LONE WOLF AND CUB BOOK TWENTY-SIX: THE END
TO BE CONTINUED

GLOSSARY

ashigara
A lightly armed foot soldier, one of the lowest ranks of the samurai caste.

bugyo
A position combining the post of mayor and chief of police for a town, in charge of administration, maintaining the peace, and enforcing the law. Rule was extended only to commoners.

buke
Samurai families.

bushi
A samurai. A member of the warrior class.

enishi
A fateful, chance connection between two people.

fudasashi
Merchant houses specializing in rice. They loaned gold to *han* governments, loans secured by the *han*'s projected rice revenues.

han
A feudal domain.

honmaru
The central keep in Edo Castle, the living quarters of the shōgun.

honorifics
Japan is a class and status society, and proper forms of address are critical. Common markers of respect are the prefixes *o* and *go*, and a wide range of suffixes. Some of the suffixes you will encounter in *Lone Wolf and Cub*:
dono – archaic; used for higher-ranked or highly respected figures.

san – the most common, used among equals or near-equals.
sama – used for superiors.
sensei – used for teachers, masters, respected entertainers, and politicians.

ihai
A Buddhist mortuary tablet. The death name of the deceased, given after they die, is written on the tablet, which is kept at the family temple.

karō
Elders, usually the senior advisor to the *daimyō*, the lord of a *han*. Since the *daimyō* was required to alternate each year between life in his castle in the han and his residence in Edo, there was usually an *Edo-karō* (Edo elder) and a *kuni-karō* (*han* elder), who would administer affairs in Edo or in the *han* when their lord was away.

kenshiyaku
Official who administers *seppuku* and executions.

kikatsugan/suikatsugan
Secretive pellets of sustenance created by and for ninja.

kōgi kaishakunin
The shōgun's own second, who performed executions ordered by the shōgun.

koku
A bale of rice. The traditional measure of a *han*'s wealth, a measure of its agricultural land and productivity.

kuchiyaku
Kuchiyaku were the tasters for the shōgun family. They were called *kuchiyaku*, or "official mouths," because they checked for poison with their own tongues.

kusa

Grass. In this case, the term refers to the secret ninja living normal lives and serving as spies in towns across Japan, thriving as grass in a field. They serve Yagyū Retsudō and send reports back to Edo.

machi-bugyō

The Edo city commissioner, combining the post of mayor and chief of police. A post held in monthly rotation by two senior Tokugawa vassals, in charge of administration, maintaining the peace, and enforcing the law in Edo. Their rule extended only to commoners; samurai in Edo were controlled by their own *daimyō* and his officers.

machi-doshiyori

The town consul. The *machi-doshiyori* presided over official proclamations to the local headmen and merchants of individual wards in castle towns and in commercial areas.

monshō

Family crest.

namu

From the Sanskrit *namas*: "take refuge in the Buddha." A common prayer for the dead.

noshime

A samurai's ceremonial robes.

rōjū

Inner circle of councilors directly advising the shōgun.

rōnin

A masterless samurai. Literally, "one adrift on the waves." Members of the samurai caste who have lost their masters through the dissolution of *han*, expulsion for misbehavior, or other reasons.

ryū

Often translated as "school." The many variations of swordsmanship and other martial arts were passed down from generation to generation to the offspring of the originator of the technique or set of techniques, and to any *deishi* students that sought to learn from the master. The largest schools had their own *dōjō* training centers and scores of students. An effective swordsman had to study the different techniques of the various schools to know how to block them in combat.

ryūei

The shōgun and his family.

seppuku

The right to kill oneself with honor to atone for failure, or to follow one's master into death. Only the samurai class was allowed this glorious but excruciating death. The abdomen was cut horizontally, followed by an upward cut to spill out the intestines. When possible, a *kaishakunin* performed a beheading after the cut was made to shorten the agony.

seppuku-tō

Short sword used for *seppuku*.

shihai

Master.

shinan

Chief instructor.

wakadoshiyori

Junior councilors. The Tokugawa shōgunate was a hybrid government, both a national government empowered by the emperor to govern the nation as a whole, and a *daimyō* government like that of any *han*, concerned with protecting the interests of the Tokugawa clan itself. The council of *wakadoshiyori* junior councilors was the highest advisory body to the shōgun on matters affecting the clan, rather than the nation as a whole.

KAZUO KOIKE

Though widely respected as a powerful writer of graphic fiction, Kazuo Koike has spent a lifetime reaching beyond the bounds of the comics medium. Aside from co-creating and writing the successful *Lone Wolf and Cub* and *Crying Freeman* manga, Koike has hosted television programs; founded a golf magazine; produced movies; written popular fiction, poetry, and screenplays; and mentored some of Japan's best manga talent.

Lone Wolf and Cub was first serialized in Japan in 1970 (under the title *Kozure Okami*) in *Manga Action* magazine and continued its hugely popular run for many years, being collected as the stories were published, and reprinted worldwide. Koike collected numerous awards for his work on the series throughout the next decade. Starting in 1972, Koike adapted the popular manga into a series of six films, the *Baby Cart Assassin* saga, garnering widespread commercial success and critical acclaim for his screenwriting.

This wasn't Koike's only foray into film and video. In 1996, *Crying Freeman*, the manga Koike created with artist Ryoichi Ikegami, was produced in Hollywood and released to commercial success in Europe and is currently awaiting release in America.

And to give something back to the medium that gave him so much, Koike started the *Gekiga Sonjuku*, a college course aimed at helping talented writers and artists — such as *Ranma 1/2* creator Rumiko Takahashi — break into the comics field.

The driving focus of Koike's narrative is character development, and his commitment to character is clear: "Comics are carried by characters. If a character is well created, the comic becomes a hit." Kazuo Koike's continued success in comics and literature has proven this philosophy true.

GOSEKI KOJIMA

Goseki Kojima was born on November 3, 1928, the very same day as the godfather of Japanese comics, Osamu Tezuka. While just out of junior high school, the self-taught Kojima began painting advertising posters for movie theaters to pay his bills.

In 1950, Kojima moved to Tokyo, where the postwar devastation had given rise to special manga forms for audiences too poor to buy the new manga magazines. Kojima created art for *kami-shibai*, or "paper-play" narrators, who would use manga story sheets to present narrated street plays. Kojima moved on to creating works for the *kashi-bon* market, bookstores that rented out books, magazines, and manga to mostly low-income readers. He soon became highly popular among *kashi-bon* readers.

In 1967, Kojima broke into the magazine market with his series *Dojinki*. As the manga magazine market grew and diversified, he turned out a steady stream of popular series.

In 1970, in collaboration with Kazuo Koike, Kojima began the work that would seal his reputation, *Kozure Okami* (*Lone Wolf and Cub*). Before long the story had become a gigantic hit, eventually spinning off a television series, six motion pictures, and even theme song records. Koike and Kojima were soon dubbed the "golden duo" and produced success after success on their way to the pinnacle of the manga world.

When *Manga Japan* magazine was launched in 1994, Kojima was asked to serve as consultant, and he helped train the next generation of manga artists.

In his final years, Kojima turned to creating original graphic novels based on the movies of his favorite director, Akira Kurosawa. Kojima passed away on January 5, 2000 at the age of 71.

THE RONIN REPORT

By Tim Ervin-Gore

Symbolism and meaning in *Lone Wolf and Cub*

A reader would have a hard time plowing through the 8300 or so pages of *Lone Wolf and Cub* without gathering some extra meaning and subtext from the story. For the American reader, it might not be so obvious. It's hard to cram the situation of the obsolete samurai seamlessly into a Western perspective. In the end, though skill is the basis for expressing *bushido*, it is the spirit that remains alive in society, while the steel blade and social structure drift away.

It becomes somewhat obvious, the effect Itto Ogami has on samurai society: he's cutting it down, destroying it, the very society he was once part of. In one way, it's saddening, and Ogami even sheds a few tears seeing that which he respects go down in so many pools and splatters of blood; but in another way of seeing things, it was one ultimate goal amongst samurai to be the very best at the way of the sword, some going so far as to challenge everyone with an unmatched reputation on a path that could be considered obsessive. Itto Ogami challenges the best swords in all of Japan for four years straight, and beats every one, all the way up to the top of the ladder. From the very first story, "Son for Hire, Sword for Hire," when Ogami assassinates a *han* lord using tactics unused for years in a post-war society; through the defeat of the *Bentenrai* brothers, who respected Ogami's sword work even in death; in every honorable samurai cut down in Ogami's path: Shino Sakon, Yagyū Gunbei, Yamada Asaemon, Ishine Ozuno of the Kurokuwa, the former Makabe Shōgen, and so forth, Ogami is testing modern *bushido*. In this way, he's filtering out the impurities. But it's not simply prowess with the sword that works as a filter.

Those characters who watch the ways of Itto and Daigoro, those who recognize true *bushido* often remark how rare it is, as if it's been decades since one has seen such honor and dignity. It happens throughout the series. In these cues one understands that the samurai society is no longer what it used to be. Of course, this becomes obvious as the series progresses. Back in Volume 3, when Torizō of the *bohachi* brothels tortures Ogami, who is protecting a young girl, she marvels that "there are so few of them left," referring to the samurai. The priest in "The Gateless Barrier" (Vol. 2) even notices Ogami's perfection in *bushido* when he's already been sliced in half! And of course, that's not the only priest who notices Ogami's form and honor. In this very volume we see a monk remark of the rarity of true samurai, asking "the scent of a *bushi*...when did I smell it last?" And the sentiment is echoed by just about every slice of life as we pull in to the end of this epic series.

In searching for subtext and deeper meaning in *Lone Wolf and Cub*, it's easy to draw a few simple lines in an attempt to understand the author's intentions. One could assume that Yagyū Retsudō is the face of modern business: ruthless, talented, and sly, but corrupt with power. But where does Ogami fit in the equation? Is he representative of bygone innocence? Given his experience in war, it's likely that innocence is not the subject. And then there's Daigoro's *shishogan* eyes, in which the innocence of a child is combined with the soul of someone who has seen more death than is imaginable. These elements suggest that maybe innocence is beside the point, that it's honor itself, and discipline that has withered on the vine, or been plucked and thrown away altogether. But how does this transfer to everyday society? How does the moral of this tale translate to the West? What elements do we see in people that remind us of a time forgotten, and ever more rare, which of these elements make us proud of our past? It's certainly not a simple warrior spirit that drives Ogami. Tactics and intelligence don't quite cover it, because confidence and culture seem to be just as important. It's possible that *Lone Wolf and Cub* is an emotional yet hearty push toward democracy, away from the archaic systems. Or maybe Koike and Kojima are trying to tell us that humanity has been in decline for quite some time. Despite our new age of international community and modern ways, one thing remains obvious when reading *Lone Wolf and Cub*, we've got a lot to learn from our past.